MUTATIONS II MOVING STILLS

EXHIBITION PRESENTED THANKS TO THE SIGNIFICANT PATRONAGE OF

Mr Bertrand Delanoë
Mayor of Paris

Mr Andrej Ďurkovský
Mayor of Bratislava

Mr Michael Häupl
Mayor and Governor of Vienna

Mr Yury Luzhkov
Mayor of Moscow

Paul Helminger
Mayor of the City of Luxembourg

Mr Gianni Alemanno
Mayor of Rome

Mr Klaus Wowereit
Governing Mayor of the City of Berlin

Alcatel-Lucent is honored to be the first partner of the European Month of Photography and of the exhibition "Mutations II / Moving stills".

The 2008 Alcatel-Lucent Prize for the European Month of Photography has been awarded to Tuomo Rainio.

Awarded every two years, the Alcatel-Lucent Prize for the European Month of Photography provides a unique showcase for distinctive European photographers and video artists selected thanks to the collaborative vision of the seven directors of the partner festivals. This year featured video art with a focus on link between video and photography.

As a company focused on innovation Alcatel-Lucent supports contemporary creation in photography and video art. Our longstanding support to photography reflects a corporate citizenship policy that includes a strong commitment to cultural diversity. By adding support to video art, Alcatel-Lucent is actively promoting the creation of quality content for people to share each day via modern communication networks.

Caroline Guillaumin, Vice President of corporate communications and sustainable development.

VENUES OF MUTATIONS II

02.11.2008 > 02.02.2009
Berlinische Galerie, Berlin

03.11.2008 > 07.12.2008
Bast'Art, Bratislava

05.11.2008 > 25.01.2009
Maison européenne de la photo, Paris

31.10.2008 > 31.01.2009
Museum auf Abruf, Vienna

18.02.2009 > 25.05.2009
Musée d'art moderne Grand-Duc Jean, Luxembourg

02.04.2009 > 26.05.2009
Palazzo delle Esposizioni, Rome

March > April 2009
Moscow House of Photography, Moscow

SUMMARY

JEAN-LUC SORET

with the collaboration of Gunda Achleitner, Berthold Ecker, Paul di Felice, Anna Gianesini, Kathrin Kohle, Ekaterina Kondranina, Zuzana Lapitkova, Emiliano Paoletti, Jean-Luc Monterosso, Pierre Stiwer, Olga Sviblova and Barbara Wolffer. (Translations from French by Martin Back.)

Mutations II. Moving Stills / images and distortions

In the context of the European Month of Photography first held in 2004 and which now includes festivals in Paris, Berlin, Bratislava, Luxembourg, Moscow, Rome and Vienna, it was both legitimate and necessary to look collectively at the profound changes afoot in the world, and in particular those taking place in the field of contemporary images. This was the motivation behind the 2006 exhibition entitled "Mutations I", an event focusing on technological and artistic change in the area of photography.

The second edition of the event, "Mutations II", aims to pursue this line of thought on the subject of video, this time exploring the productive relationships that have developed between fixed and moving images and providing a sense of where contemporary art stands in Europe today.

In a context where all means of communication and artistic media are affected by globalization and digital convergence, the era of "post-medium" we are entering is "a period characterized by the exploration of hybrid technology, in which artists combine and recombine video with a wide variety of other materials"[1] – i.e. photography, sound art, digital video, film, DVD, computer art, CD-Rom, graphics and animation.

1 RUSH (MICHAEL). 2007. L'ART VIDÉO. LONDRES. THAMES & HUDSON.

Each artform thus increasingly falls "within the bounds of its own material limits (...) pushing them further, to cover the entire spectrum of the community it forms along with other artforms"[2].

By abandoning its status as a medium for freezing recorded reality and by borrowing one of its essential features, namely the temporal dimension, from video art, photography is becoming emancipated via all kinds of artistic manipulations and technical hybridizations, both analogue and digital.

The people behind "Mutations II" have thus chosen to showcase European artists who have in common a taste for experimenting with new forms of expression. Like Nancy Spector in her essay "Art Photography after

2 BELLOUR (RAYMOND). 1999. L'ENTRE-IMAGES 2. P.O.L. PARIS.

Photography"[3], they have effectively questioned the specific criteria that used to make it possible to draw a distinction between a photographer and an artist working with photography.

A growing number of photographers are using video, and this is changing the specific criteria that define both crafts. Apart from the diversity of their aesthetic standpoints and of the visual techniques they use, the artists presented in "Mutations II" encourage us to step beyond the territorial considerations and academic definitions which tend to ring-fence artistic fields, and to explore the boundaries that separate them. In other words "Mutations II" invites us to discover new territory, investigating both fixed and moving images via the tensions that motivate them. These include an ontological tension between that which is momentary and that which takes place over time, an aesthetic tension arising from the hybridization of the traditional photographic image and the moving image, and a dialectical tension between the limited display possibilities open to photographs and "the infinity of perceptional combinations within which electronic images can be defined and articulated"[4], particularly video installation.

According to Gilles Deleuze and Felix Guattari, "there can be no territory without a vector for exiting that territory (...), without an effort to re-territorialize oneself elsewhere"[5]. If we restrict this philosophical question to the field of art, we might suggest that the specific dynamic of any artistic trend is a centrifugal force that tends to move it away from current conventions and norms, an "exit vector" whose very existence is predicated upon how new its worldview is.

Peter Aerschmann's original worldview involves odd little scenes that illustrate the challenge that is central to his work: seeking a means to photograph a given space while maintaining temporal depth, to produce a photograph that is not a record of an instant and which makes movement palpable instead of freezing it. Peter Aerschmann thus involves time in the representation of space, shifting the principle of the fixedness of the image and applying it to movement, which he freezes even as it is produced. In this way Aerschmann produces a "stammering" effect in

3 MOVING PICTURES, CONTEMPORARY PHOTOGRAPHY AND VIDEO FROM THE GUGGENHEIM MUSEUM COLLECTIONS. 2003. NEW YORK. GUGGENHEIM MUSEUM PUBLICATIONS, P. 31-39.

4 VAILLANT (ALEXIS), PARFAIT (FRANÇOISE), JANKOVIC (NIKOLA). 2001. LES NOUVELLES IMAGES. TOME 1. CHRONIQUES DE L'AFAA, PARIS.

5 DELEUZE (GILLES). 2004. L'ABÉCÉDAIRE DE GILLES DELEUZE. PARIS. MONTPARNASSE, DVD.

the idiom of video by showing human figures who seem to be prisoners of repetitive movements produced in endless loops.

The semantic and stylistic richness inherent in repetition has also inspired Gast Bouschet and Nadine Hilbert in the construction of Dreamsequence, a video work created in 2006/07. Going back to the location of Philipp Kaufman's film "Invasion of the Body Snatchers" made in 1978, the artists update and re-contextualize the idea of paranoia via the use of obsessively recurrent images. Deliberately sacrificing the conventional reflex of linear narrative, this poetic and political dreamsequence hangs on a network of relationships between fragments of photos, videos, sounds and texts which challenges our objectivity and hones our sharpest perceptions.

Although Christoph Brech also plays with our perceptive faculties, this is first and foremost to attract our attention. Apparently motionless but always moving, the objects, figures and landscapes he films lead the eye from one level of interpretation to the next; the eye oscillates between a desire to decipher the image and a desire for contemplation inspired by extremely pared-down videographic construction. Break, a hypnotic work made as a single sequence shot with no camera effects, perfectly illustrates this formal sobriety. We grasp the fact that the very essence of movement is transitivity, and at the same time we almost viscerally feel the tectonic force of time. Temporality is here engaged with what is shown to us: slow clouds of water vapour sweep across the immense expanse of a frozen river, responding to the almost imperceptible shifting of the ice. The icebreaker that passes through these hostile elements before disappearing – leaving behind it a wake that the ice attacks and immediately absorbs – provides an inspired allegory of the human condition.

Big Bang by Ori Gersht hinges on a political metaphor of humanity thrown into the chaos of war. It is precisely because conflict and its attendant violence constitute a breaking point that Gersht's aesthetic and plastic investigations explore the notion of transition with such intensity; the transitional process is transposed into the idea of a fixed image becoming a moving image. At first sight, Big Bang looks like a baroque still life. But the way Ori Gersht uses sound brings a temporal dimension to the fixed tableau and instils a dramatic tension which reaches its peak in an exploding flower arrangement filmed in slow motion – the deliberate recording of an object moving towards its own dislocation. This transition from the figurative to the purely abstract ends in optical stasis, recalling the image that the sirens and explosions of the Israel-Palestine conflict branded into the artist's mind as a child. This is an artistic process that, while exploring the relationships between photography, painting and video, involves both literally and figuratively "passing through" form in order to lead us to sacrifice it.

Like Gersht, the young Finnish artist Tuomo Rainio deals with time and change in his work, but his approach is totally different. Instead of starting from the aesthetic nature of the image, he proceeds from the nature of movement. Through a self-written image processing program, images captured with a simple camera show urban environments where the activity of the city-dwellers is only visible thanks to the ghostly traces they leave behind. The process is both political (in that it refers to a public space controlled by a network of CCTV cameras) and conceptual (in that it represents the tension of the "in-between": the permanence of presence and absence).

Jutta Strohmaier also uses the potential of digital technology, either to make the fixed image grow from within or to reconfigure it via lighting effects, cut outs or electronic sweeps that constantly modify it. In Journey or Im Dickicht (In the Thicket) the feeling of movement arises from the fact that the image never seems completely finished but always appears to be in a state of transition between what went before and what comes after; this means that the present never provides temporal unity but brings an explosion of temporalities that destructure the image. In Passenger, the compression of time obtained by shots taken once a minute over several days from inside an empty room offers a distanced approach to daily life seen through the accelerated rhythm of the cycles of day and night. In Silent Stories the photographs used are submitted to effects of superimposition, blurring and transparency which offer a fictional re-reading of reality. Though Jutta Strohmaier uses photography as a raw material in the composition of her scenarios, the perception of movement and processes of transformation and temporal deconstruction play a central role, allowing the image to liberate the many meanings it holds.

What prevails in the formal exploration behind Olga Chernysheva's Windows is an investigation of space and the image. Fascinated by the vestiges of vanished Communism, the artist observes the daily life of Russian people today and reconstitutes it in the form of an installation whose staging has left nothing to chance. Filmed at night with a hand-held camera, every window of a building becomes the frame for a scene where the inhabitants appear and disappear like characters in a play, vanishing into the intimacy of the dark backstage areas of their apartments. The theatrical nature of these slices of life is emphasized by the use of several screens, giving the image great presence within the exhibition space and producing an intimate "mise en abîme" which in turn provokes a dialogue between the work and the viewer.

What these European artists have in common is the way they submit photography and/or video to various forms of distortion. In this way they explore the lines of perspective that form at the boundaries of the two territories, setting up a new regime of image and perception; by the same token they push the photographic and videographic idiom to its limits, and it is these very limits that constitute the necessary condition for the emergence of originality and of "style" as defined by Deleuze.

These new experiments in pushing photography and video over the edge of their habitually assigned boundaries give us a unique opportunity to take a fresh look at the world and encourage us to re-invent our daily lives, seeing them "according to the artwork" to quote Merleau-Ponty[6].

6 MERLEAU-PONTY (MAURICE). 1960. L'ŒIL ET L'ESPRIT. PARIS. FOLIO. ESSAIS.

Cultivating the in-between

Photography and video have a proximity which is as great as what originally separates them in their relationship with time. Technical developments are now encouraging artists to bring the two closer together: it is possible to film with a photographic camera and take photos with a video camera. What is more, both go through digital stages, even including emulsion processes. Thanks to software, freezing the image is easy and the slideshow function can be launched with a single click. Thus it is possible to stop movement or introduce a temporal continuum: two gestures of great technical simplicity but whose disruptions are considerable. What is at issue is not so much the frontier between two media (video art has always existed in proximity to other artistic practices) but the artworks that this porosity generates. It is this intermediate territory that is explored in "Mutations II". The selected artists all use video in terms of the tension that links it to the photographic image and its components: the unity of the frame, the passage of time and the particular quality of the passing of the moment. Some of these artists develop their video research alongside photographic work, constantly switching between them. The result is a special relationship with the image that invites us to grasp it in terms of its instability but also in terms of the issues that it raises through these mutating practices.

MATHILDE ROMAN

Working with temporal depth

In his essay "The Reflecting Pool de Bill Viola", Jean-Paul Fargier analyses Viola's videotape, with its processes of masking, as the artist plunging into video art, because "the divided image can be seen as the essence of video."[1] Images created through masking, containing various temporalities and multiple and parallel stories, would therefore be strong characteristics of video art. In any case, this is what is apparent in a certain number of works that have a strong relationship with the photographic image and with suspended time and which, like Bill Viola in this famous videotape, operate in terms of disturbances, generating confusion in the perception of stillness and movement. For example, David Claerbout creates pieces in which appropriated photographs are brought into the domain of video by intervening in their temporal density in order to find the present time of the image. In Sans titre (Carl et Julia), 2000, the black and white image shows a man and his daughter having breakfast. When we enter the projection space, the girl turns her gaze on us, fixing us in turn by the power of video to give back life and to replay in the present that which was fixed in the past. In one of Claerbout's latest pieces, Dancing couple (after: Couples at square dance, McIntosh County, Oklahoma, 1939 or 1940), 2008, his intervention is even more radical: a young couple are photographed on a dance floor, surprised by the flash which has interrupted them and lifted them out of the present moment. Claerbout has salvaged this image and projected it, overlaying the action of the flash with the light from the projector. The temporality of the projection thus affirms its necessary presentness, contrasting the stillness of the photographic process with the movement of the projection. The artificiality of the construction is affirmed and this introduction of a moving temporality at the heart of the still image provokes a feeling of vertigo and discomfort. The "in between" is close to the void in that it is produced in the obscurity of carefully orchestrated installations and in mostly silent environments in which spatialized sound is used sparingly.

The animation process is currently quite prevalent, particularly as an extension of drawing. It allows a more radical temporality and the combination of different image supports, as in Hans op de Beeck's disturbing animation of drawings and photographs. The spaces thus represented are strange because they are close to reality while never becoming confused with it. Jutta Strohmaier, a young Austrian artist, also produces still images that are then slowly animated. As with Claerbout, we are endlessly confronted with a situation of indecision concerning the status of the image, its nature and its relation to time. The accumulation of photographs introduces an impression of movement but without being sufficiently momentous to break the

1 THE REFLECTING POOL DE BILL VIOLA, JEAN-PAUL FARGIER, ÉDITIONS YELLOW NOW CÔTÉ FILMS # 2, 2005, P.14.

stability provided by the still image. Light plays a fundamental role by marking the passage of time at the heart of the space photographed where mostly nothing much happens. In Passenger (2004) there is a change of lighting atmosphere with a fixed shot of a window filmed from inside an empty room. We go from one coloured state to another, white changing to blue, to pink and then to yellow in a jerky metamorphosis. Strohmaier's videos never seek to create the illusion of continuity, they introduce us to intermediate spaces (empty rooms, crowded undergrowth, urban traffic spaces) through a considerable effort involving distance and framing, from the point of view of an attentive but out-of-phase observer. The image is also subject to a number of artistic operations, including overprinting, outlining and a modification of colours that highlight the fabricated, constructed dimension of the gaze focused on the world.

The gap between photography and video thus provides a space for meditations on our perceptive experiences. Swiss artist Peter Aerschmann also explores temporal depth by deconstructing our relationship with space-time. His images are the result of keying different shots in which the elements are juxtaposed by resisting a unitary perception of the whole. Each character and each aspect of the decor is, of course, part of a global composition but without being linked by a shared atmosphere. As in Uccello's paintings, proportions are respected and visual arrangements are coherent but what is stated is great solitude. The camera glides laterally through these set-ups, gradually discovering the lonely characters, enclosed within the repetition of a gesture and in landscapes that lack unity. In Aerschmann's videos, space-time is fundamentally deregulated, but our gaze nevertheless continues to travel slowly with the camera. Between the austere stasis of the architectural elements and the movement of the characters in a loop, between photography, video and painting, Aerschmann's work lies at the heart of the issues addressed by "Mutations II".

Framing

Framing the image is a gesture of definition, of grasping but also of distancing the visible and implies taking a stance concerning the world. An essential approach in the history of art video was the turning of the camera on oneself. Vito Acconci, Peter Campus, Bruce Nauman, Joan Jonas (and many others) placed their own bodies in front of the mirror-video in various ways. But beyond the fascinating, voyeuristic immediacy of filming the self, the relationship with the reflection allows the exploration of the appearance and disappearance of one's own image. Thus, in the 1970s, Jean Otth, another Swiss artist, developed a video and mirror apparatus in which he played with his own image by defining and obscuring it and by questioning the emotions that are projected when faced with this manipulation of the image of oneself. Video allows him play with reflection by taking the time to disturb it, to endanger it and thus to show and make heard the relationship that we maintain with our own image. Miroir (2000) by Elina Brotherus, a Finnish artist who works both with photography and video, is also a staging of the self that distances reflection by conditioning its appearance in the passage of time. In the photographic series, Brotherus poses nude in front of a steamed-up bathroom mirror. At first reflection is therefore prevented, thus imposing the experience of dislocation between a body and its image. But the passage from one image to another allows the mirror to gradually reveal the reflection. The framing is almost the same in the video, thus echoing the photographic series at first sight. However, the movement of the image allows the reintroduction of the vitality of the process by giving an esssential place to the body in the changing surface of the mirror. Brotherus's respiration is a central element, it acts on the atmosphere and participates in the phenomenon of the appearance/disappearance of the image in the mirror, reintroducing the organic dimension into a situation in which the body is what essentially makes up the image.

In his introduction to his essay "L'entre-images", Raymond Bellour explains that "it seems that with video, and all that goes with it, we are entering into another image time"[2]. Even when the video is composed in a photographic manner, by fixing the frame, what happens in the time period gives rise to another relationship with time and space. The young Czech artist Jan Kuděj has made several videos that question the experience of time. For example, he puts together two projections that show two fixed shots, one of a group of four escalators and the other of a tree in a field. The escalators are a short video loop paced by their ascending and descending movements while the tree is a montage of still images in which the foliage develops in a jerky way. The association of mechanical fluidity and natural discontinuity distances the dynamic perception of reality. In contrast to a society in which movement is the rule, Kuděj creates disjunctions and cuts in the image, preventing us from enjoying the peaceful state of watching a tree trembling in the breeze (a motif that Claerbout also magnificently filmed for Boom, a fixed shot of a tree that resembles Kuděj's but which basks in the fascinating fluidity of movement). By investing video in its relationship with photography, its capacity to create the illusion of continuity is put in doubt. The artworks introduce disequilibrium and instability into our relationship with the world through the construction of situations of retention of flux.

Quest for the gaze

If video is thus put in doubt by photography, it is also a space for the development of ideas concerning the photographic gaze. This is precisely

2 RAYMOND BELLOUR, L'ENTRE-IMAGES, PHOTO, CINÉMA, VIDÉO, ÉDITIONS DE LA DIFFÉRENCE, 2002.

what French artist Laurent Goldring does by working in the tradition of the photographic portrait. He questions photographic representations of the body by frontally filming models in a photographic studio. The temporality of the video allows him to investigate the "becoming an image" aspect of the bodies of his models, who are all dancers (and most of them choreographers). As the stage is narrow and the camera is fixed, the dancers can hardly move so their movements are concentrated on posture. Once the pose is struck, the body gently slips from one appearance to another, guided by Laurent Goldring and accentuated by the lighting and the play of shadows and light. The images that emerge often have monstrous qualities, they catch the gaze and capture the imagination. The movement allows the passage from one state of the visible to another as well as engagement in a process of symbolic distortion, but finally the videos show themselves as a succession of still images. The gaze is captured by each shape. Laurent Goldring then develops photos from the video. He thus ends up with a still image via a creative space that allows things to become apparent at the heart of an extremely constructed mechanism. The instability of video distances the transubstantiation reflex that we are subject to when faced with a photograph: Laurent Goldring's images/bodies affirm their symbolic status, spreading their pixels when developed on paper. They exemplify the displacement of photographic research at the heart of the video medium.

The passage from one medium to another is thus what allows the distancing of a practice and the questioning of its qualities, as in the German photographer Oliver Möst. His work is derived from his personal relation to vision. His eyesight problems have effectively led him to construct a photographic vision dominated by blurring and its pictorial qualities. However, his use of video is not merely an extension of his experiments into the domain of motion. It corresponds to another necessity, that of staging his relation to the visible through films of himself. brown eyes, hide & seek and between are thus short scenes filmed in his studio by combining a video and a pinhole camera. In the first one, Möst plays with his eyes, marbles that he handles and puts in his mouth. In the second one, he counts out loud with his eyes covered with red blinkers until a flash dazzles him. In the third one he struggles against two wall partitions he closes and separates. He is always bare-chested, physically implicated in metaphorical situations concerning his relationship with the gaze: the ironical critique of the deficient organ of vision in brown eyes and the construction of a parallel between two states of visual impairment in hide & seek, one caused by the obturation of the moment of perception (blindfold), the other caused by an excess of light (flash). In between, Möst explores the right way of perceiving the world by diversifying the construction of the presentation space. Of course, all these situations also question photographic activity, its conditions and its bias. The framing of the last video, landescape, assumes the shape of an optical lens and was also obtained by combining a pinhole and a video camera. The sound comes from outside the visual field of the camera, thus contrasting the immobility of the imaginary landscape divided peacefully into two symmetrical shots and the sound of a stone launcher. Möst is not visible in the image but is present through his actions. This time, like him, we see nothing apart from the imagination that he provokes, the signs that are apparent on the frozen surface of water are largely the bearers of vision.

Sound images

Video art has benefitted enormously from its complicity with musical creation, since its emergence at the heart of Fluxus and Nam June Paik. Sound is often much more than a sound track accompanying the image, it is intrinsic to it, to such an extent that sometimes the image is treated in a sonorous way. Robert Cahen's videos thus place musical composition at the heart of the filming situation and if time has a particular importance it is because it emerges from the close relationship between sound and image, expressing the subjective perception of reality. Photographer and video artist Gast Bouschet and composer Nadine Hilbert work together from this perspective: in their videos image and sound are inextricably linked, one contaminates the other and impregnates its coming into being. The image is again most often composed of fixed frames in succession without transition, through accumulation. In Dreamsequence, the camera and the sound deliver bits of the universes crossed (such as misty forests, motorways and city centres) but without letting us settle or follow the gaze. We go from one point of view to another, as if faced with photographic series, from one sound situation to another, with repetitions but without the reassuring reference of continuity. The title places this operation in relation to a dream state in which distances are continually crossed, various time-spaces wandered through, the only constant being the subjective viewpoint of the dreamer, and in this case the viewer. Video art thus allows us to find a pace that echoes the experience of perception, as in Christoph Brech's Opus 110a (2001). In this video, the image is tightly focussed on a conductor's back during a concert. The sound is extremely present and with the image the musical rhythm becomes monochrome movement close to abstraction, while charged with the physical nature of the conductor's gestures. Brech harmonizes the movements of the back, he orchestrates the whole, slowing, accelerating, holding back or liberating time to create harmony between sound and image. The back becomes a projection space, each fold in the suit a landscape, an anchoring point for the deployment of the imagination.

Sound can also drive the image, guide it and fill it with meaning. It can also create a narrative, integrate language into image or create a dialogue between them, as in Gary Hill's work. A text that is spoken, read or proclaimed by a body is at the heart of his videos, questioning what creates an image in verbal terms. The practice of video is both inspired by the cinema and distanced from it due to ambiguous or contradictory constructs that explode narrative and question its codes. Alice Anderson's videos are thus aesthetically very close to cinema but are very different when it comes to narrative means. The gap is at its most pronounced in Journal, with very short cinematic sequences edited together through sound. The narrative thread is maintained, and while the title cards indicate a time period (a month, a day, a year) the intimate story stops there. The images can be seen as clues for entering in on a moment in a life but mostly leave any attempt at interpretation dangling. The length is also very short and this does not leave much time for rambling. Journal leaves the viewer in the grip of evasive music and images.

Installing the image

Video has presentation requirements that are more constraining than those of photography, needing to be installed in a space adapted to its technical nature. While exhibited photography is above all a dialogue with the exhibition space where the images are equally present to the gaze, video tends to require isolation and the negation of real space (as in the "black boxes" where the image is presented hidden away in darkness and with good sound conditions). Video thus imposes its own space-time, as in Bill Viola's installations. But some artists present videos that dialogue with what lies beyond the image. Claerbout's screen/walls exemplify this "in-between-ness" since the videos echo each other as in a photography exhibition, being visible through walls of pierced thin canvas, which also serve as supports for the projections. "In situ" installation is also important, where video takes possession of a space and inhabits it by echoing what emanates from it. Ulrich Gebert conceived Keine Dialoge (2004) for a specific space, a windowless concrete structure divided into narrow rooms, which accentuated the oppressive aspect of the piece. The conditions of the presentation were provided by the exhibition space, the Kunstbunker Tumulka in Munich, without needing to modify anything. Viewers were thus submerged in a cold military environment in which they attended a psychological test endured by a GSG 9 team (an élite anti-terrorist unit set up in the aftermath of the events at the 1972 Munich Olympics). Ulrich Gebert shows us these men submitted to flashes of stroboscopic light, prolonging the experience for the viewer confronted by a video made up of visually aggressive still images shown in jerky succession. The title draws attention to the regression inflicted on these men who are judged on their self-control. Movement is the locus of aggressivity because it is in removing the image from its fixity and creating a sensorial continuity through video that the stereoscopic action becomes meaningful and implicates the body of the viewer.

Video also has a sculptural dimension when, instead of effacing its materiality through projections disconnected from the time and space of exhibition, artists focus on its relation to its dependence on what it might arise from (and which it needs to express its intangible presence). The surface-screen can extend the image in volume, like the eyes in Tony Oursler's work, or the artist can create environments into which the image is integrated, as in Thomas Hirschhorn's installations. In this vein, Pirmin Blum builds cardboard sculptures with still images pinned on them and video monitors inserted into them. The video image does without the monumentality of projection and the effect of appearance and affirms its basis in reality. One installation by Blum combines photos with two videos of safety test procedures filmed in a car factory. Airbag is a slow-motion fixed shot of the activation of an airbag. The fabric inflates and deflates in a fascinating manner. We witness the slight deployment of a form in a state of permanent evolution. The second video, Spuk is a rapid montage from the viewpoint of two cameras during a windscreen test. Framed by the airy and poetic calm of Airbag, Spuk is visually and aurally violent. The combined pieces thus ironically bring together very different rhythms with a DIY approach that contrasts with the industrial sophistication of the place where the images were produced.

Alice Anderson selected a sequence from Journal to create the installation Insomnia (2006). The viewer is invited to lie on a violet velvet four-poster bed and watch the one-minute video extract (presented as a loop) on a screen suspended above. It is a setting which makes the viewer see these images as those of a half-consciousness between waking and sleep without really giving time to become fully immersed in it: almost as soon as the viewer lies down the video is back to the start, thus discouraging any lounging about. Art video is generally difficult to watch because the works are often too long and the trying viewing conditions are tiring. That is undoubtedly its biggest constraint and makes it less easy to exhibit and watch than photography. It is therefore perhaps necessary to cultivate the state of insomnia, of in-between-ness, which installs us in these practices that lie halfway between two media and make us circulate between different states of images.

Mathilde Roman has a PhD in art and art sciences from the Sorbonne. She is an expert in video art and the author of "Art vidéo et mise en scène de soi" ("Video art and the staging of the self") published by L'Harmattan in 2008. An art critic and member of the AICA, she contributes to several publications including www.lacritique.org, Art press and Mouvement. She teaches art history at the Pavillon Bosio college of art and scenography in Monaco.

Time divided and time regained (On Space and Duration in Photography and Video Art)

"In reality there is no one rhythm of duration; it is possible to imagine many different rhythms which, slower or faster, measure the degree of tension or relaxation of different kinds of consciousness and thereby fix their respective places in the scale of being."
Henri Bergson[1]

The caveat of an either/or, which is to say the static image or the time-based continuum of images, has dogged photography since the advent of cinematic film in the last decade of the nineteenth century. A fiction has been created around the dead moment of the excised photograph, a moment extracted from time, as if it were oppositional to the continuous frame narrative presented by film.[2] With the advent of magnetic videotape, and more recently digital pixelated technologies, we might have imagined that this dichotomy has come to an end. However, it does not end in "time" but in duration, the latter being without a fixed or certain definition. Today the linear supposition of a universal time is no longer the determinant of how the photographic image is experienced. Time as Bergson

---

1 HENRI BERGSON, "THE DELIMITING AND FIXING OF IMAGES", MATTER AND MEMORY, ENG. TRANS., N.M. PAUL AND W.S. PALMER, NEW YORK, ZONE BOOKS, 1991 (PP. 177-223) P. 207.

2 BOTH ROLAND BARTHES AND SUSAN SONTAG SPOKE OF EITHER FATALITY OR MELANCHOLY IN RELATION TO PHOTOGRAPHY, FORMING SOMETHING AKIN IN THE PROCESS TO A STRUCTURAL ROMANTICISM, AND AS A RESULT PHOTOGRAPHY SOMEHOW BECAME TRAPPED BETWEEN THE PUNCTUM, THE "POIGNANT MOMENT", AND THE STUDIUM (BARTHES), OR A "NARROWLY SELECTIVE TRANSPARENCY" (SONTAG). SEE, ROLAND BARTHES, CAMERA LUCIDA, ENG. TRANS., RICHARD HOWARD, LONDON (1982), 1984, PP. 26-27, AND SUSAN SONTAG "IN PLATO'S CAVE", ON PHOTOGRAPHY (1971), LONDON, HARMONDSWORTH, 1979, P. 6.

MARK GISBOURNE

contended, is experienced differently by different people in different places, and even experienced differently by the same person in the different stages of their life. The linear or diachronic past may be freely conceptualised, but is not the basis for how time is actually synchronically interiorised.

To call a photography and video exhibition "Mutations II", touches directly upon the ongoing processes of change. To mutate means to undergo or cause to undergo mutation which in turn defines itself by being an alteration or change, as in nature, form, or quality. And, mutation or becoming (the liminal) cannot be as simple linear time; by its literal definition, it is as an ongoing process of continual change. Therefore becoming exists as "time suspended" in an ongoing process that can only be understood as time that is continuous duration. It is, perhaps of this colliding impact that Eliot said: "Time present and time past are both always present in time future, and time future contained in time past."[3] In consequence "becoming" remains as "perpetual possibility". This was a durational bridge crossed long ago by Bruce Nauman and others, and reveals why new media dealing with performance and video create a greater elasticity in our understanding of what constitutes the basis of a static or time-based image. Deleuze makes that clear (drawing no doubt on Bergson) when he writes: "so that each time we find ourselves confronted with duration, or in a duration, we may conclude that there exists somewhere a whole which is changing, and which is open somewhere."[4] This does not deny causality but suggests that it is sometimes hidden and not immediately apparent. To clarify things, mutation draws upon this very principle, just as the most common forms of mutation are of amoebae seen in a laboratory petri dish.[5] The historical addiction to a dualistic schism between the static and the movement-image is what is now being systematically challenged by contemporary photography and video practitioners. The mechanism of alteration remains the response of human consciousness, but not consciousness as an end in itself, rather in the process of a continual "opening up" as a singular aim but with multiple outcomes.

In new digital photography, and even in modern developments in analogue technologies, practitioners have been able to re-align photography and video art outside the frame of the determinism of a fixed time linearity. The

---

3 T.S. ELIOT "BURNT NORTON", IN FOUR QUARTETS, LONDON, FABER AND FABER (1944), 1979, P. 13; THEY FORM THE FIRST FOUR LINES WHICH CONTINUES "...IF ALL TIME IS ETERNALLY PRESENT ALL TIME IS UNREDEEMABLE."

4 GILLES DELEUZE, CINEMA I, THE MOVEMENT IMAGE, LONDON, THE ATHLONE PRESS, 1992, PP. 9-10; DELEUZE ACTUALLY REFERENCES EXTENSIVELY BERGSON'S MATTER AND MEMORY (OP. CIT) AND CREATIVE EVOLUTION (1907). FOR HIS RELATIONSHIP TO BERGSON, SEE, GILLES DELEUZE, BERGSONISM, NEW YORK, ZONE BOOKS, 1988.

5 THE NAME AMIBE, DERIVED FROM THE GREEK AMOIBÈ, AND WHICH LITERALLY MEANING "CHANGE", WAS FIRST USED BY THE FRENCH NATURALIST JEAN-BAPTISTE BORY DE SAINT-VINCENT (1778-1846).

new photography has rid itself of the excised image that can be reduced to the moment of pressing a button, just as the notion of video or film editing has long ago lost its dependence on suppositions of continuity. In both cases the conditions have become increasingly manipulatable. With this in mind we must accept and encompass the increasing discontinuities that form the basis of our modern life, something Foucault pointed out long ago.[6] There is a useful analogy and corollary that comes from the word mutation itself when used in linguistics: it designates a change caused in a sound by its assimilation of another sound in its proximity. It may be hardly surprising therefore that mutation and mutuality have the same Latin stem. Their relationship is reciprocal and freely adaptive within a discontinuous working system. The non-biological use of the word mutation (relatively value free) has long stood in opposition to evolution (relatively value laden). The former describes change as simply a discontinuous or random state of adaptation, while the latter usually implies the purposive teleology of natural selection – things mutate into something, things evolve towards something.

Thus the increasing relevance to photography and video over the last thirty years or so is not only that of eliding old clichés as to the former boundaries between the static and moving image; it has also allowed a greater interplay within the processes of their shared media origins. It is the increased interiorisation of the integrated processes of photography and video that I have referred to in my subtitle as "on space and duration". A personal time-space characterisation or accompaniment is found, and incorporated like an individual defining shadow, within each artist's adaptation of the new technologies that he or she applies to his or her visual practices. Hence contemporary photography and video today are less about a pre-defined or given subject matter than about what the subject matter is being subjected to. But what it does respond to is a self-reflexive condition where time-contents are elastic and frequently fold back on and into themselves. Time is no longer the watch but the loop, and the loop (or ellipse) is the condition of an internal circularity or inflection measured by its own self-defining system.[7]

6 FOUCAULT SPEAKS OF AN INEVITABLE MULTIPLICATION OF DISCONTINUITIES, "HISTORY APPEARS THEN NOT AS A GREAT CONTINUITY UNDERNEATH AN APPARENT DISCONTINUITY, BUT A TANGLE OF SUPERIMPOSED DISCONTINUITIES," MICHEL FOUCAULT 'RETURN TO HISTORY', MICHEL FOUCAULT, ESSENTIAL WORKS OF FOUCAULT 1954-1984, VOL. 2, AESTHETICS, JAMES D. FAUBION (ED.), LONDON, HARMONDSWORTH (1998), 2000, (PP. 419-32) P.429.

7 GILLES DELEUZE, "WHAT IS AN EVENT?", THE FOLD: LEIBNITZ AND THE BAROQUE, ENG. TRANS., TOM CONLEY, LONDON, THE ATHLONE PRESS, 1993 "INSEPARABLE FROM THE PROCESS OF ACTUALIZATION OR REALIZATION INTO WHICH THEY ENTER, THEY GAIN PERMANENCE ONLY IN THE LIMITS OF THE FLUX THAT CREATES THEM, OR THE PREHENSIONS THAT ACTUALISE THEM (PP. 76-82) PP. 80-81.

With the advent of video art in the 1960s, and 70s, either in terms of its application as a critique of the increased commercialisation and consumerism brought about by television, or in what later became called art video, there was a possibility of questioning the nature of linear time unrealisable by earlier media.[8] While the frame by frame configuration of film offered the system of cut and paste editing, it had nothing like the immediacy of videotape with its ability of near instantaneous feedback, superimposition, and potential for inconclusive or abstract narratives.[9] But if video art started as a critique of the mass media of television and advertising, it soon began (unlike structuralist film, which worked from within the film system) to deconstruct the very principle of linear and narrative consistency.[10] It offered alternative approaches whereby time and space were brought together in a new way. Not only was it used in performance and in recording and questioning the very nature of the performative, as with for example Nauman and Acconci. But it developed numerous others. But it developed rapidly into questioning the nature of sites of representation, through what later became called installation video art.[11] The last, using the element of multiple channels, quite literally shuffled the use of differential temporality. A sense of immediacy is in essence the "always present", and videotape became by extension of immediate presence in many artist's studios, to be thought of no differently than any other appropriate tool that an artist might find in his/her atelier. Indeed the frequently espoused relationship between video and painting bears clear witness to the phenomenon. The ability of the video monitor to act as an object inclusive of image, and by extension as sculpture, and thereafter a complete environmental installation, meant that video became an interstitial reality or point of linkage between different media. It embraced relations with things made (traditional notions of the art work), interrogated their status as art works, the sites of reception, and questioned the historiography of the boundaries between different media. Like the space between the words in a Beckett play, it operated as the "becoming" space of an uncertain temporal duration.[12]

---

8 VIDEO FIRST EMERGED IN THE TERMS OF POLITICAL ACTIVIST DOCUMENTARY APPROACHES OF ARTISTS LIKE LES LEVINE AND FRANK GILLETTE, OR VIDEO AS ART WITH THE FLUXUS ARTIST NAM JUNE PAIK, SEE, MICHAEL RUSH, NEW MEDIA IN THE LATE TWENTIETH CENTURY, LONDON, THAMES & HUDSON, 1999, PP. 80-81 FOR AN EXTENDED ANALYSIS OF PAIK, SEE, THE WORLDS OF NAM JUNE PAIK, SOLOMON GUGGENHEIM MUSEUM, NEW YORK, 2000.

9 MICHAEL RUSH, VIDEO ART, LONDON THAMES & HUDSON, 2003, "WHAT WAS SO EXCITING ABOUT THIS NEW TECHNOLOGY WAS THAT IT CAPTURED REAL EVENTS INSTANTANEOUSLY. TIME IN A SENSE WAS BEING MANIPULATED BY HUMAN INTERVENTION." P. 15.

10 SEAN CUBITT, TIMESHIFT: ON VIDEO CULTURE, LONDON, ROULEDGE, 1991. SEE ALSO, DOUG HALL AND SALLY JO FIFER (EDS.), ILLUMINATING VIDEO: AN ESSENTIAL GUIDE TO VIDEO ART, NEW YORK, APERTURE, 1990, AND SUBSEQUENT EDITIONS.

11 MICHAEL RUSH, 'VIDEO INSTALLATION ART', IN NEW MEDIA....OP CIT, PP. 116-167.

12 IT IS HARDLY SURPRISING THAT MANY EARLY VIDEO ARTISTS LOOKED TO BECKETT FOR INSPIRATION, ITS WAS CERTAINLY THE CASE WITH NAUMAN, AND JOHN JESURUN'S ONGOING MEDIA THEATRE, AND EVEN TO SOME EXTENT THE EARLY WORKS OF BILL VIOLA. SEE, ALAN RICKMAN (ET AL), BECKETT ON FILM, DVD, 2005, AND GIJS VAN TIJL, "HUMAN CONDITION/HUMAN BODY: BRUCE NAUMAN AND SAMUEL BECKETT", BRUCE NAUMAN, EX. CAT., HAYWARD GALLERY, LONDON, 1998, PP. 60-75.

early claims), but that it posed a new and extended set of multi-temporal or pluralized subjectivities. Hence the elasticity of time re-entered photography, and the shift was discernable from concerns about reproduction (instantaneous outcomes) to production and process intervention.

In relation to video the practice of photography itself was compelled to rethink itself. And, this was the case long before the latest digital technologies entered the fray, not least because the still image extracted from video undercut notions of the decisive moment of the camera.[13] The first effect was to compel photography to re-engage with the time contents of image-making. If instantaneity had been the initial impulse that drove photography forward in the wake of modern developments in camera and lens technology, it was clear that the exposure time of whatever length framed (in two senses) the conditions of extraction. The decisive moment, like the existential period whence it came, was cast as a moment of pure subjectivity. Set against early video, which presented the immediacy of the "real", as distinct from the edited "reel" of film, photography might be said to have lost contact with the "objective reality" by which it was originally formulated.[14] In consequence, there was a return to pin-hole camera technologies and the camera obscura since the 1980s. What was at issue was not the fact that the reality of video was any more objective (though this might have been part of its

Following the advent of digitalisation in the 1990s, the role of video and VHS has begun to decline in part, and in recent times its use has gravitated back towards the cinematic. Many new virtual film technologies have usurped its former role, and its claim to be instantaneous and a presentation of the real is no longer tenable. At its extreme the mytho-poetic excesses of Matthew Barney reflect the increased tendency of video towards cinema.[15] As reproducibility is no longer of great concern, modern electronic media and computer technologies increasingly replace videotape's former function.[16] In terms of temporality video and photography exist side by side often in the virtual space of the computer, and in the manipulative possibilities that exist between the extracted image, its process of production, and subsequent presentation. What this implies is an increasing multiplicity of time contents, the precise nature of which are unfixed or not determinable. In short, both photography and video have shifted from the specific into the unspecific as regards time contents. The unspecific

---

13 HENRI CARTIER BRESSON, THE DECISIVE MOMENT, NEW YORK, SIMON AND SCHUSTER, 1952. THIS BOOK WAS ONCE CONSIDERED THE MOST IMPORTANT BOOK ON PHOTOGRAPHY IN THE TWENTIETH CENTURY.
14 FOR AN OVERVIEW OF THE CULTURAL SHIFTS IN PHOTOGRAPHY FROM ITS INCEPTION TO THE PRESENT DAY, SEE, MARY WARNER MARIEN, PHOTOGRAPHY: A CULTURAL HISTORY, LONDON, LAURENCE KING PUBLISHING, 2002.
15 NANCY SPECTOR, THYRZA GOODEVE, AND NEVILLE WAKEFIELD, MATTHEW BARNES: THE CREMASTER CYCLE, NEW YORK, GUGGENHEIM MUSEUM PUBLICATIONS, 2002; ALSO STEPHAN URBASCHEK AND BRANDON STOSUY, MATTHEW BARNEY, MUNICH, INGVILD GOETZ PUBLICATIONS, 2008.
16 TIMOTHY DRUCKREY (ED.), ARS ELECTRONICA: FACING THE FUTURE - A SURVEY OF TWO DECADES (ELECTRONIC CULTURE: HISTORY, THEORY AND PRACTICE), CAMBRIDGE MASS., MIT PRESS, 2001.

generality of time is duration. This duration, further, is of course always virtual, and therefore ungraspable, indeed the very definition of the word implies a "becoming" state of simulated possibility. The virtual, however, is not in opposition to the real because it still exists in essence or effects but not in fact. Which is to say it exists in the mind or the imagination. The virtual world is not an alternative world, that would be an epistemological impossibility, but it does offer an imagined or alternative engagement with what is understood by the term reality. A speculative reality generated and, perhaps, following Bergson's suggestion, that we are able to "imagine many different rhythms" at work in consciousness.

The photographers and video artists exhibiting in "Mutations II" are touched, either directly or indirectly, by all these shifts and trends over the last thirty years. Not surprisingly this makes for a great diversity of practice and procedural approach both in video and photography, the individual defining shadow to which I alluded earlier. Temporality and time-space are constituted not only in visual but also in aural terms. But while sound is usually linear, that is to say in the continuum from the first moment of hearing, it too has been placed at the service of fragmentation and temporal re-assembly. In a work like Christoph Brech's <u>Opus 110a</u>, while we hear the symphonic music what we see filling the video image frame is the back of the jacket (evening tails we might speculate) of what we imagine to be the conductor – though it could just as easily be the simulated equivalent of someone performing symphonic air guitar.[17] The effect brings a collision between the visual of what we see, and the aural of what we hear, as we become hypnotised by the rhythmic movements and configurations of the jacket's fabric and seams. In the process you lose the sound-image connectedness at one level but reconnect them at another. The experience is transitive, and is common to much of Brech's work, which means that it expresses an action from subject to object but requires a direct object to complete its meaning. The assumption being that the viewer is the direct object to which it is addressed. We are familiar enough with the longstanding relationship between music and video, but in the case of pop videos the effect is usually illustrative. What Brech does is afford a minimal degree of information (the video ends with an image of the sheet music) and leaves the viewer to complete the work for themselves. In fact the viewer and reception become a necessity to give meaning to the work.

This strategy is characteristic of many video artists working today, which is to say that it is anti-illustrative and frequently expressed in terms of the

---

17 IT IS CHRISTOPH POPPEN CONDUCTING THE MUNICH CHAMBER ORCHESTRA IN SHOSTOKOVITCH'S CHAMBER SYMPHONY, OPUS 110A, AND WHAT BRECH CALLS AN EXERCISE IN THE "VISUAL DYNAMICS OF MUSIC". IT IS IMPORTANT, HOWEVER, TO UNDERSTAND THAT THIS IS MERELY EXTRANEOUS INFORMATION, AND IS NOT IMPLICIT TO COMPREHENDING THE WORK, THOUGH THE COMPREHENSION MIGHT DIFFER IF YOU ARE ACTUALLY FAMILIAR WITH THE PIECE OF MUSIC.

post-narratological.[18] That is to say it does not analyse narrative or linear story-telling in a structural sense of determining the outcomes of perception a priori, but provokes and requires extended perceptions that contribute to completing the work. This brings the time and time contents of the viewer into play in response to the video work. The work of Olga Chernysheva operates inversely to Brech. In her video Windows, the viewer is cast into the role of unseen voyeur or peeping tom. In a series of small excised temporal views through windows at night we are introduced to what amounts to a lexicon of daily life. The windows are banal and commonplace, suggestive of modern mass housing, and the opaque and poorly lit interiors are ordinary and undistinguished. In her multiple screen video snapshots of the every day, a man watches television, three people dance in a circle, a man alone plays a guitar, a woman irons, a man is in his bathroom, and so on. Apart from the habitual behaviour which is deliberately invoked and implicit to the work, there is no direct connection between the windows, save that which is loosely typological. However, the a-temporality implies little in terms of suggesting a place or location to the events seen. Were they filmed at the same time, at different time periods, or in different urban spaces? What becomes important is that they are simply video images, and as time-based images they generate the viewer being cast into the context of the unseen voyeur or peeping tom. If they had been still images or photographs no such sense of viewer complicity would ensue.

The interstitial role of video, what a colleague in this catalogue has called "cultivating the in-between", remains prevalent in video production. In the works of the Israeli artist Ori Gersht called Big Bang and Pomegranate the appropriation is from still life and flower painting. In Big Bang a black screen appears and a high-pitched sound intensifies, then the flower still life in a glass vase gradually appears, derived from the tradition of the Dutch seventeenth century genre. The sound-image and high pitch intensifies and in slow motion a feeling of expectancy ensues until the flowers and vase eventually explode. The fragments shower downwards and the image gradually fades to black to begin again on a loop. Looked at closely in all of Gersht's work there is a deep sense of personal and political identity and biography, and it seems no coincidence that he chose a pomegranate for the other video. In Pomegranate we have a perspective picture frame and still life of a suspended cabbage and pomegranate, while a pumpkin and marrow rest on what in a painting would be the foreshortened lower

—

18 TRADITIONALLY STRUCTURAL "NARRATOLOGY" IS ASSOCIATED WITH A GROUP CALLED THE RUSSIAN FORMALISTS. TZVETAN TODOROV (BULGARIAN B. 1939) COINED THE WORD, AND REFERS TO THE EXAMPLE OF VLADIMIR PROPP (1895-1970). SEE, MORPHOLOGY OF A FOLKTALE (RUSSIAN 1928), AUSTIN, UNIVERSITY OF TEXAS PRESS, 1968, AND SUBSEQUENT EDITIONS.

frame. The video is silent until a bullet passes from the right shattering the pomegranate whose seeds cascade down in the same slow motion. In a personal sense not only do we have a particular and chosen biblical connotation as one of the seven fruits of Israel, but also that the Hebrew word for pomegranate is the same as that for a grenade.[19] In Gersht's work it is less the case of shuffling time, so much as altering time experience and generating the conditions of an unforeseen but violent expectancy. In other words, to "measure the degree of tension or relaxation of different kinds of consciousness."

If the references in these particular works by Gersht are to painting, the in-betweenness of the Finnish Tuomo Rainio seems to conjure up a sense of the relationship of drawing and video, which he has created through his own processing programme. In his works Staircase (Crosswise) and City, the former creates a ghostly uncanny effect: a spectral figure ascending a staircase, and the pictorial sense is blurred and indistinct. The tone is somewhat Gothic, the surface of the image is that of a ghosting effect with multiple exposures, and of course reminds us immediately of early Futurist sources and of Duchamp's "Nude Descending a Staircase".[20] While making such a reference might seem facile, it reminds us of how both video and photography have returned to question and investigate their origins over the last twenty years. Conversely, City is a visually still image but again intensified as a sound-image through its soundtrack, a black-grey urban view of a city rail or tram stop, where the evocation is shaped purely by the sound of eerie winds, unseen trains rattling by, and occasional footsteps. The still time-image acts as the referent to repetition and is looped, and the suggested repetition a potentially infinite duration. The sound-image work City operates at the interface of the still image and video, collating the space between the long-term exposés of someone like the photographer Michael Wesely into a highly personal and programmed system.[21]

---

19 THE SEVEN FRUITS (SHIVAT HAMINIM) OF ISRAEL ARE LISTED IN DEUTERONOMY 8:7-8, AND THE HEBREW WORD FOR BOTH A POMEGRANATE AND A BALLISTIC GRENADE IS RIMMÔN. "FOR THE LORD THY GOD BRINGETH THEE INTO A GOOD LAND, A LAND OF BROOKS OF WATER, OF FOUNTAINS AND DEPTHS, SPRINGING FORTH IN VALLEYS AND HILLS; A LAND OF WHEAT AND BARLEY, AND VINES AND FIG-TREES AND POMEGRANATES; A LAND OF OLIVE-TREES AND HONEY." THE WORD IN SPANISH, FRENCH AND ENGLISH DERIVES FROM THE SAME WORD GRENADE (LE GRENADE), AND THE LIQUEUR GRENADINE IS SIMILARLY MADE FROM POMEGRANATES.

20 BOTH THE FUTURISTS AND DUCHAMP WERE DEEPLY INDEBTED TO EADWEARD MUYBRIDGE (1830-1904) AND ETIENNE-JULES MAREY (1830-1904), BOTH CHRONO-PHOTOGRAPHERS DEEPLY INTERESTED IN TIME-SPACE LOCOMOTION AND THE SEQUENCING OF MOVEMENT. SEE, PHILLIP PRODGER, TIME STANDS STILL: MUYBRIDGE AND THE INSTANTANEOUS PHOTOGRAPHY MOVEMENT, LONDON, OXFORD UNIVERSITY PRESS, 2003, AND MARTA BRAUN, PICTURING TIME: WORK OF ETIENNE-JULES MAREY (1839-1904), CHICAGO AND LONDON, CHICAGO UNIVERSITY PRESS, 1994.

21 THE CONTINUOUS THREE AND FOUR YEAR LONG TERM PHOTOGRAPHY EXPOSES OF MICHAEL WESELY ARE WELL KNOWN, AND IN SOME RESPECTS WORKS FROM THE REVERSE SIDE OF VIDEO ALLOWING TIME ITSELF GENERATE THE GHOSTING CONTENTS OVER VERY LONG PERIODS. SEE, MICHAEL WESELY OPEN SHUTTER, EX. CAT., THE MUSEUM OF MODERN ART NEW YORK, 2004, WHICH COVERS CONTINUOUSLY THE PERIOD OF THE DEMOLITION AND REBUILDING OF MOMA, AND FOR THE BUILDING OF POTSDAMER PLATZ, MICHAEL WESELY: DIE ERFINDUNG DES UNSICHTBAREN, EX. CAT., GUARDINI GALERIE BERLIN/FOTOHOF SALZBURG, 2005.

The effect of a renewed enquiry touches directly upon the work of Oliver Möst whose use of pinhole video finds a direct echo in the pre-history and early development of photography. In a whole series of works called either Pinhole videos or Shortcuts, like landescape, hide and seek or kill your idols, he either segments and superimposes different time elements, and simultaneously returns to the basic premise of time, light and exposure. Whether simply counting in hide and seek or in the barely discernible variances of landescape, we are left with strange sense of infinity and numbness. If video began in the political and cultural sphere of contestation with the prevailing mass media, it has evolved in the intervening period into a highly personal medium. A work like Dreamsequence by Gast Bouschet and Nadine Hilbert, while it may make reference to cinematic history, is intentionally nonlinear, blending suggestions of personal politics and attitudes with disconnected fragments of text and sound from many locations. Like a jumble of sensory experiences recalled in a dream it presents a mixture of identification and memory revocation – in short a type of personal catharsis. Any connectedness is left to the perceptions of the viewer to assimilate. It remains culturally political if only to the extent that as an art video it does not seek generally to pacify the viewer, and while it might seek to entertain indirectly, its primary intention is to question the limits of representation and image comprehension. When put literally it challenges the viewer to ask what do these images mean? What does Ulrich Gebert mean if he places five figures in soldier's uniforms at ease in a row staring at a blank wall, and repeats the rat-ta-tat of light on light off? Apart from an indirect homage to forbears like Gary Hill, and the evocation of repetition, we are left to expand on the field of reception possibilities for ourselves.

The most telling development is that both video and photography have entered the computer and digital manipulation. Far from closing down possibilities, the virtual reality of the computer world has liberated photography from the static image, the frozen moment, and freed video from the self-delusion that it captured some sort of definitive reality. It has allowed an artist like Peter Aerschmann to become polyphonic in his ability to collage together many different elements from the social to the surreal. In works like Paternoster, and Union Square he reveals a diversity of approach that typifies many artists of today. In Paternoster a stage backdrop of open elevators appears where figures travel up and down in all their idiosyncratic variety. They represent little worlds of social self-concern, common human behaviours in displaced situations: a woman plays a violin, a male figure appears in overalls sweeping, a woman with a vase of flowers, a solitary pot plant, and so on. Aerschmann frequently focuses on archetypes, perhaps an inflection of his Swiss (possibly Jungian) background. In Union Square we find a surreal counterpoint of a white snow laden space and tree stumps, a flat matt red background with an airplane passing, and battalions of the Swiss Army standing four square in the snowscape, while the image scans from left to right passing from the barren tree stumps into a coniferous wood. Aerschmann directly contests the dialectic of the frozen and movement image, the work is all about space and undefined temporal passage. Thus in a certain sense the virtual when used with photography and video allows a greater state of temporal and image synthesis than was ever possible with earlier technologies. In photography it allows for the superimposition of multiple time moments as duration, while in video those temporalities are compressed, extended, or turned around and shuffled into new and seemingly endless possibilities.

Where does the greater meaning of time stand in all this? It remains, as Bergson suggested, in different kinds of consciousness. It should not be surprising that people's relationship to time is deeply personal. What the world imposes is not necessarily what the mind and imagination contends. As we immerse ourselves in the electronic age we should have less to do with fear than with possibility. "Mutations II" simply refers to those changes in the parameters of self-generated and realisable possibilities within today's uses of photography and video. How we utilise them, or to what purposes we apply them in the world, remains entirely our own.

But our nature, the office and function of our personality, remain enveloped in equal mystery. For these elementary unextended sensations which develop themselves in space, whence do they come, how are they born, what purpose do they serve? We must posit them as so many absolutes, of which we see neither the origin nor the end.[22]

Mark Gisbourne
Former Lecturer and Senior Lecturer in Post-Graduate Studies in Contemporary Art, Slade School of Fine Art, University of London and Sotheby's Institute (University of Manchester Master's Programme). Ex-President of AICA (Great Britain) and an International Vice President, AICA. He has published numerous books and catalogues, and has written for nearly all major English language art publications. His recent exhibitions include Paul Klee: Adult Memories of Childhood (Centro Atlántico de Arte Moderno, Las Palmas), and he is a resident curator for Rohkunstbau (see: www.rohkunstbau.de). He lives and works in Berlin.

---

22 HENRI BERGSON "OF THE SELECTION OF IMAGES", OP CIT, (PP. 17-76) P. 63.

Peter Aerschmann
Gast Bouschet & Nadine Hilbert
Christoph Brech
Olga Chernysheva
Ori Gersht
Tuomo Rainio
Jutta Strohmaier

5TH STREET, 2006

PATERNOSTER, 2006

PETER AERSCHMANN

Photographing space while preserving the depth of temporality, producing images that go beyond the instant and the fixed to render motion and life: the fundamental challenge that underlies Peter Aerschmann's work is how to represent time in space.

In "Eye and Mind" (1964), the philosopher and art theorist Maurice Merleau-Ponty held that vision and movement are intertwined: if we were not able to move in space we would be unable to see. Nonetheless, the movement of the body is not merely

the displacement of an object from A to B. Movement that is actually perceived is an autonomous whole, and must not be confused with the space that is covered when it occurs. This is where the paradox of movement lies: it takes place in space, yet appears to be a stranger to it.

In Peter Aerschmann's videos, that which is random occurs alongside that which is predetermined, offering the viewer only a fragmented vision of the reality of life. This is how he manages to make us lose our bearings. Is this where the impression of life comes from, even though the number of elements is predetermined and their movements follow predefined trajectories? Instead of showing an image, Peter Aerschmann captures the rhythm of things via the image, and the way they fit with passing time and repetition. He reconstitutes an environment that retains the formal characteristics of reality: the ability to change, permanence, duration and the presence of objects. It is no accident that the filmed mini-sequences are almost all fragments of movements whose repetitive presentation and predetermined progression give rise to a sort of melancholic humour.

By calling on archetypes of collective memory, Peter Aerschmann's works refer us to our own reality, becoming metaphors of a world stripped of its hierarchies in which we are all strangers to each other.

Peter Aerschmann
born in Fribourg/CH in 1969, lives and works in Bern
1994-1999 Berne University of Design and Fine Arts
www.aerschmann.ch

UNION SQUARE, 2007

DREAMSEQUENCE (THEY ARE US)
VIDEO INSTALLATION BY NADINE HILBERT AND GAST BOUSCHET
SOUNDTRACK: "THE BOMARR MONK AND TELEPHONE JIM JESUS"
© THE ARTISTS AND CENTRE D'ART NEI LIICHT
DUDELANGE, LUXEMBOURG.

GAST BOUSCHET & NADINE HILBERT

Nadine Hilbert and Gast Bouschet have shot – and exhibited – their photos and videos all over the world since the 1980s. They are particularly fascinated by the recorded image and its capacity to reflect and comment on the transformation of political and socio-economic systems and their symbolism, which is especially visible in the morphology of urban structures and border zones.

Their work has been shown in numerous exhibitions, most notably at the Center of Contemporary Arts (Glasgow), the Museum van Hedendaagse Kunst Muhka (Antwerp), the Casino, Forum d'Art Contemporain (Luxembourg), the Nei Liicht Gallery (Dudelange, Luxembourg), the Busan Biennale of Contemporary Arts (Busan, Korea), Camouflage, Centre of African Contemporary Art (Brussels and Johannesburg), the Domaine départemental in Chamarande (Paris) and within the framework of the Krinzinger Projekte (Vienna).

"I am always the other. If I say we, I designate the guilty me. Henceforth all is clear. Nobody is the same person any more. Aggression has

not changed anything, we are one with our enemies, we share the mindset of our opponents. There are no more limits or barriers, our identities are intertwined. But we are consumed by fear, anxiety remains with us. The threat is daily, it destroys us from inside. The world is no longer the same, the light is different. Nature is irreconcilable, it wants to get us. We are strangers in our country, we all speak an unknown language that frightens us.
Our worst nightmares are henceforth stripped of their delicious cold sweat. Our most beautiful dreams worry us with their deceptive comfort. Every day, our mind produces and reproduces its slow poison. We have been unable to go without it for quite some time.
We have an urgent need for this daily bread. We look off colour in the fields where we sow our own terror.
The sombre mirror of Nadine Hilbert and Gast Bouschet".
(François Olivieri)

Gast Bouschet & Nadine Hilbert
born in Dudelange/LUX in 1958 /
born in Luxembourg in 1961, live in Brussels and elsewhere
www.thetrustfiles.net

FROM
DREAMSEQUENCE
GAST BOUSCHET
AND NADINE
HILBERT

BREAK, CANADA, 2004

BREAK, CANADA, 2004 / VIDEO, 8:12 MIN. / © CHRISTOPH BRECH / COURTESY SAMMLUNG GOETZ, MUNICH

BREAK, CANADA, 2004 / VIDEO, 8:12 MIN. / © CHRISTOPH BRECH / COURTESY SAMMLUNG GOETZ, MUNICH

CHRISTOPH BRECH

"Christoph Brech's video works transform ordinary occurrences into moments of significance."

The work of Christoph Brech ranges from room installations to photography, video and art in public places.

Brech's videos are characterized by the severity and clarity of their conception, the linearity of their execution and the simplicity of the means employed. Natural phenomena, everyday objects and impressions and the static and quietly observing focus of the camera are

OPUS 110A, GERMANY, 2001 / VIDEO, 24:23 MIN. / © CHRISTOPH BRECH / COURTESY MUSEUM FÜR MODERNE KUNST, FRANKFURT AM MAIN

PASSAGE, CANADA, 2003 / VIDEO, 10:43 MIN. / © CHRISTOPH BRECH COURTESY KUNSTAGENTEN GALLERY, BERLIN

typical features of the work presented in this exhibition.

Brech uncovers situations which reveal their poetic dimension through the stretching of time and the quality of slowness that this creates – ordinary occurrences transformed into significant moments.

In the video Passage, he shows a glass of water on a table in the cabin of a container ship, subjected to the ebb and flow of vibrations and pitching on board. In Break, he presents a calm and initially silent observation of the mist-covered, frozen St. Lawrence River, contrasting the sluggish tempo of nature with the violence of a passing Canadian icebreaker. In Opus 110a, he films the back of the conductor Christoph Poppen so as to render the dynamism of the music of Dimitri Shostakovich visible in the play of the folds in his tailcoat jacket – Christoph Brech is able to capture an event's "own time" in images. The viewer is subjected to a slowed rhythm, creating almost meditative moods, as in the video Transito, made in Rome in 2007 in which a heavy curtain in the doorway of a church swings rhythmically in the wind, creating a dance of light and shade on the floor. Moments of time and transition like these are the essence of Christoph Brech's video work.

Christoph Brech
born in Schweinfurt/GER in 1964, lives and works in Munich
1989-1995 Art at the Academy of Fine Arts, Munich
www.christophbrech.com

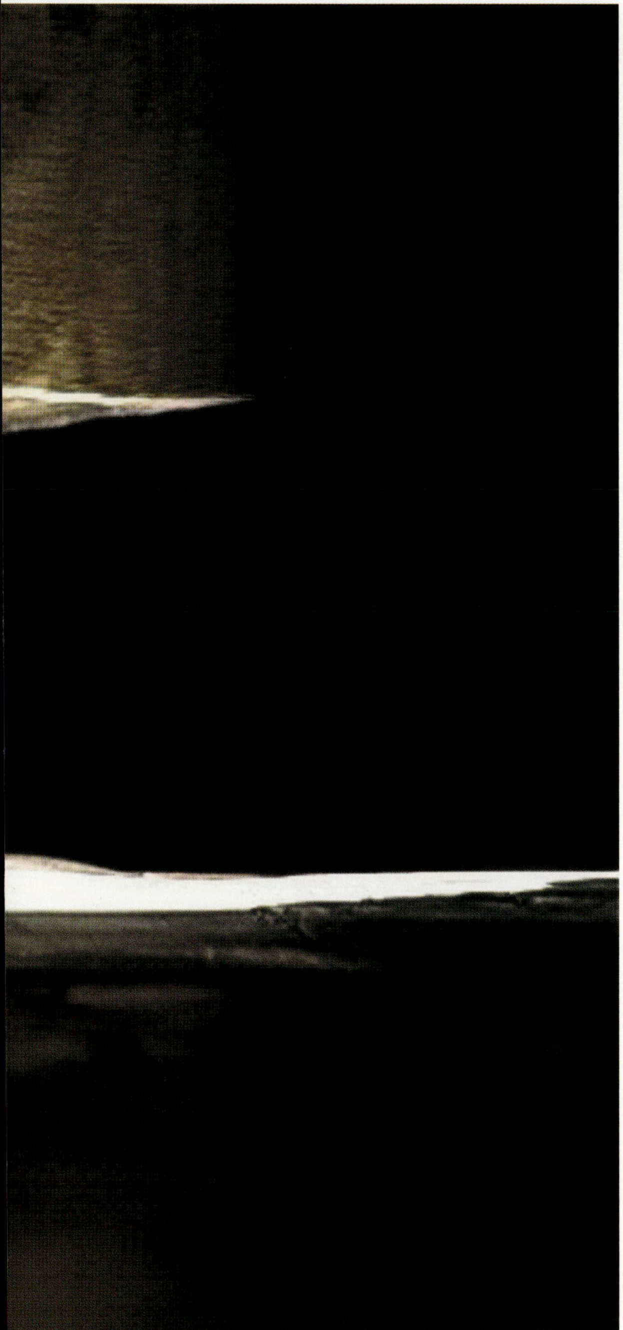

TRANSITO, ITALY, 2007 / VIDEO, 16:20 MIN. / © CHRISTOPH BRECH / COURTESY KUNSTAGENTEN GALLERY, BERLIN

WINDOWS, 2007 / VIDEO, 1 MIN., LOOP, MULTI-SCREEN INSTALLATION / © THE ARTIST.

OLGA CHERNYSHEVA

Olga Chernysheva has a degree in cinematography. Her sphere of interest includes photography, painting, experimental video and video installations. Her project Windows, created in 2007, takes the viewer back to daily life in the Soviet era: in the windows of the Moscow "Khrushchev" apartment blocks one can see clothing, crockery, underwear, a glass of tea, a naked male torso, an iron, a TV set, some tulle with a floral pattern, drying linen, a windowpane glued with paper… People come and go: a man drinks from a kettle, an old man stretches himself, young people enjoy themselves… Here the window itself becomes the border of a stage, a frame, creating lighted space

similar to that of a theatre, where the characters/inhabitants appear and then vanish into the dark backstage area of the apartments.

Chernysheva's windows disclose Russian everyday life, turning it inside out, allowing us to contemplate the common daily routine, slowly, but steadily, creating the feeling of what existence is. And all this is done without a tinge of voyeurism, peeping or curiosity – everything is very distanced, calm and concentrated.

Several video clips that run simultaneously in the black frame of the night and on TV create a model of ideal communal life (accompanied by Chopin's music), producing an effect of presence and giving rise to a warm feeling of nostalgia for that Soviet reality that has not yet completely departed.

Olga Chernysheva
born in Moscow in 1962, lives and works in Moscow
1986 graduation at the Moscow Cinema Academy
1995-1996 graduation at the Royal Academy of Fine Arts, Amsterdam
www.olgachernysheva.ru

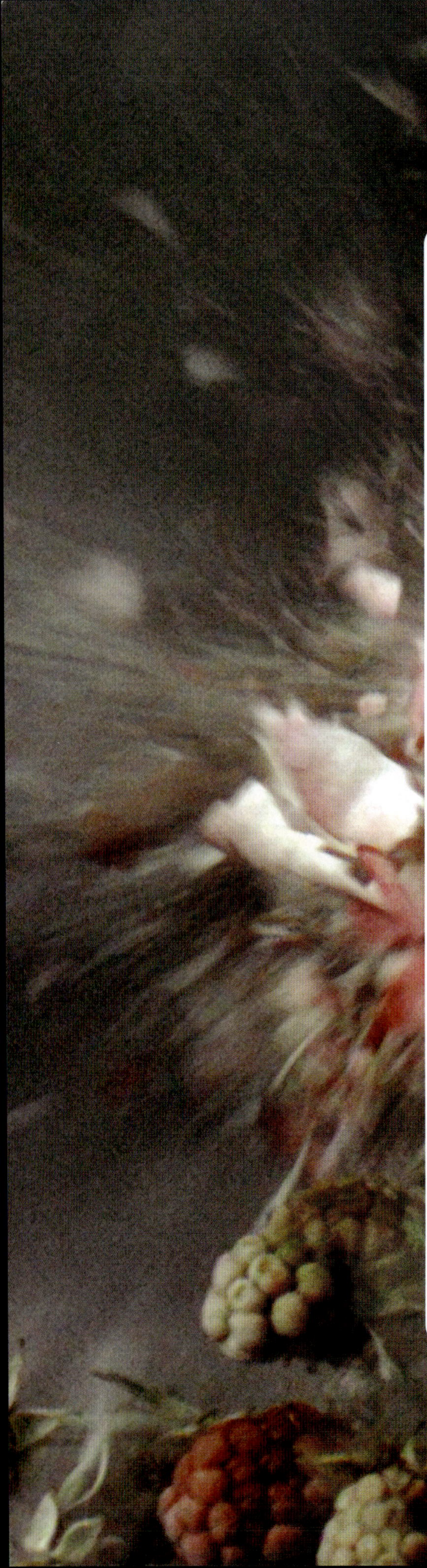

ORI GERSHT, BIG BANG, 2007 / HD DIGITAL FILM, 5:33 MIN / © THE ARTIST, COURTESY CRG GALLERY NEW YORK, MUMMERY + SCHNELLE GALLERY LONDON, NOGA GALLERY TEL AVIV, ANGELS GALLERY LOS ANGELES

ORI GERSHT

In his latest work Ori Gersht investigates the relationship between film, photography, technology and optical perception at a pivotal moment in the history of art where digital technology both threatens a crisis and promises a breakthrough. In his two recent films Pomegranate and Big Bang, Gersht has recreated still-life compositions in the style of Old Master paintings, tracing the evolution of artists' fascination with representing reality from the seventeenth century to the present day. Whereas in their original form such paintings attempted to preserve motionless moments frozen in time, Gersht's compositions are shattered by fast and violent interventions. In Pomegranate, a film that references both a Baroque still life painting by Juán Sanchez Cotán and Harold Edgerton's stroboscopic photography, a high velocity bullet flies across the frame in slow motion and

BIG BANG

obliterates a suspended pomegranate, bursting it open and wheeling it slowly into the air like a smashed, violated mouth spraying blood red seeds. A peaceful image is transformed into bloodshed, and a dialogue is established between stillness and motion, peace and violence. Such dichotomies are also present in Big Bang, a film that at first sight appears to be a Dutch still-life painting of flowers. The illusion shatters suddenly as the flowers and the vase explode to the intense sound of war sirens, which are slowly transformed into a high-pitched mechanical voice. The scene subsequently transforms into a silent, slow-moving cosmic downpour of colourful flower particles and dust. Both Pomegranate and Big Bang radiate the shockwaves of human history.

At a time when many film and video artists dealing with the political are producing work that has more in common with the medium of documentary, Gersht's work explores a genre where he is in the forefront – that of a provocative meditation.
(Andrew Mummery, Director Mummery + Schnelle Gallery, London)

Ori Gersht
born in Tel Aviv in 1967, lives and works in London
1989-1992 BA in Photography, Film and Video at the University of Westminster, London
1993-1995 MA in Photography at the Royal College of Art, London
www.mummeryschnelle.com

BIG BANG

BIG BANG

CITY

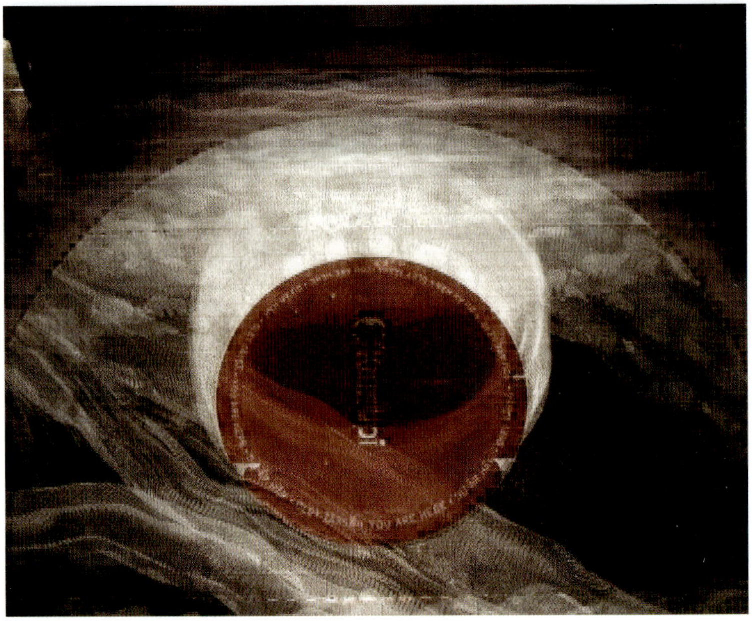

CIRCLE

TUOMO RAINIO

(Winner of the Alcatel-Lucent Prize for the European Month of Photography).

Presence of the Crowd

Change, movement and time are the central topics of photographs and videos by Finnish artist Tuomo Rainio. Visual thinking in his purist works is tuned between the aesthetics of b/w photographs and the tradition of post-conceptual video art. Perhaps a moving image without genre specificity is the best way to describe the field in which those interests intertwine. What do we actually see when we look at Rainio's works from the Tracescape series? Firstly a black image, like a blackboard, then melancholic anonymous cityscapes, street views and architectural structures gradually appear. In fact, the only thing that is certain is the line of movement. The works start like ghost-like animations and turn suddenly into familiar, or at least recognizable, surroundings. There is something eerie in the atmosphere – perhaps the presence of the crowd.

Social reality is present in the form of traces of passersby taking their daily routes. As Rainio points out, "Tracescape is a series of video works about the social structure in public space. In urban space each person"s behaviour is observed and controlled by the others and by themselves."

The works City (2005) and Crosswise (2006) present visible crossroads, pathways, and the cycle of city life, which turns out to the blind map of the city. They are like piles of x-ray images: you can imagine the living body, but still there is only structural support. The soundscapes of the videos bring the images back to the level of the daily experience of immersion. We can hear traffic lights, passing cars, trams and echoing footsteps. At the same time, different motion lines bunch up together, overlapping and brightening the image. Finally, it's not about the film and its light-sensitive membrane, but the computer-programmed algorithm that calculates the images frame by frame and makes the changes visible. As an analogy, videos witness the rapid change occurring in the digitalized picture industry. Technique and content are inseparable. The pixel grid has found another level of meaning at the top of Rainio's memorable moving images. It renders the matrix of our time visible. (Leevi Haapala, Curator and Researcher, Kiasma, Museum of Contemporary Art, Helsinki)

Tuomo Rainio
born in Espoo/FI in 1983, lives and works in Helsinki.
2003-2006 Bachelor of Arts at the University of Art and Design Helsinki
since 2006 MA Programme for Photography at the University of Art and Design Helsinki
2007-2008 Department of Imaging Arts and Photography at the Musashino Art University, Tokyo
www.rainio.pp.fi

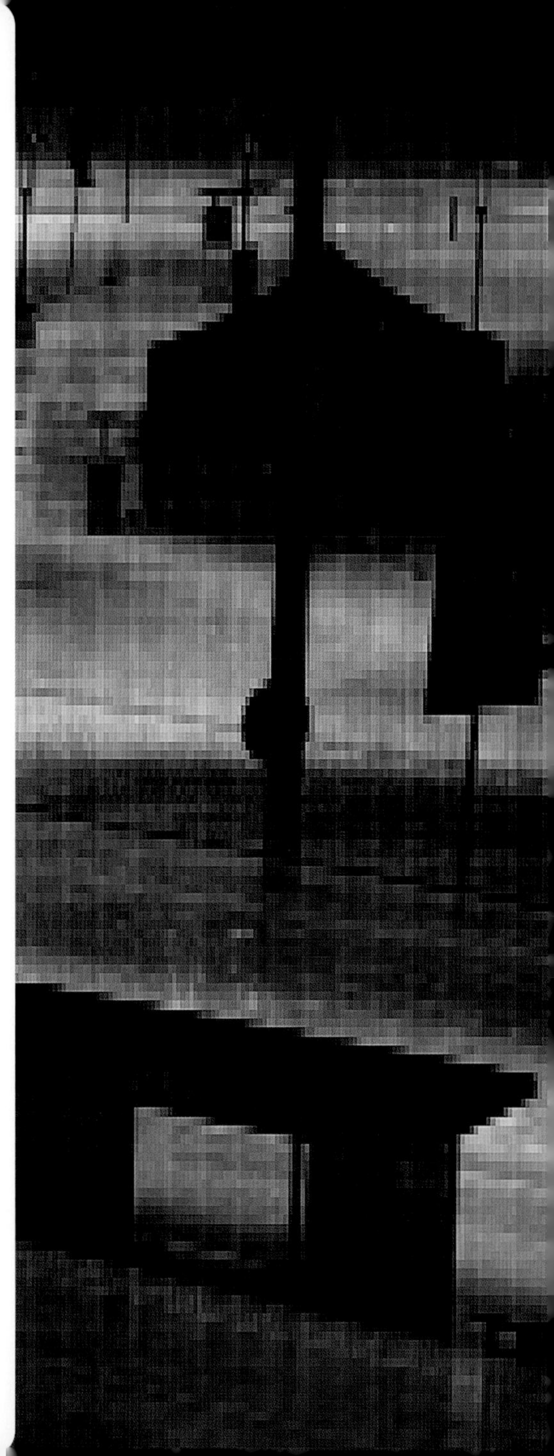

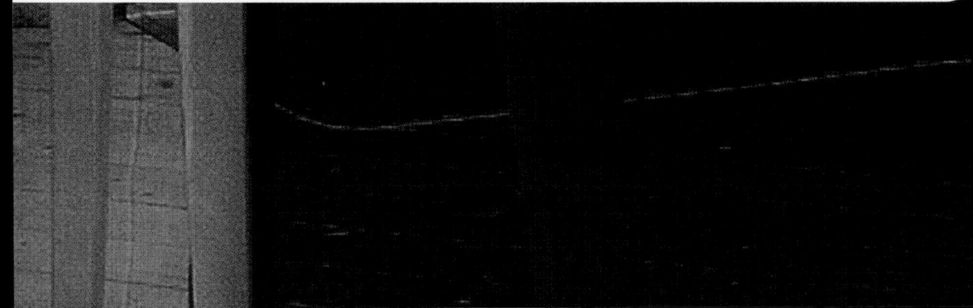

PASSENGER, 2004 / VIDEOPROJECTION, 13:31 MIN. / © THE ARTIST

JUTTA STROHMAIER

How do images and reality relate? What sort of reality can images create? These are the questions Jutta Strohmaier's videos, photographs, and installations pursue.

Passenger (2004) compresses images of an empty interior with two large windows captured each minute over the course of days into a video of just under 15 minutes. While, during the day, the windows render the room so bright that it is difficult or impossible to see anything beyond them, as dusk sets in the outside and the façade of a building across the street gradually come into view. The work plays with the perception of a room as it gradually shifts, examining the concept of space with respect to categories such as inclusion/exclusion, domestic/foreign, openness/closure (see also Sarah Kolb's

remarks on the exhibition "Jutta Strohmaier. diese Welt und andere," Galerie Hohenlohe, Vienna, 2004).

Strohmaier returns to the principle of ongoing photographic shots presented as animated video in works such as Im Dickicht (In the Thicket, 2005) and Silent Stories (2006). In the former, she releases the shutter with every step through the undergrowth of a wetland forest preserve. Strohmaier edits the "gaps" between the individual shots using Photoshop; the tangle of branches initially seems to be "eaten away" before growing back to greater density in a later sequence and ultimately dissolving into a blue sky.

The satellite photographs assembled to form the video loop Journey (2005) offer a view of earth from outer space – a vantage point we are all perfectly familiar with, thanks to television and the Internet, but one which very few people have been able to adopt for themselves. Strohmaier digs through her archive of surveillance satellite imagery that she has assembled over the course of years. Yet instead of presenting a linear sequence of the cities and natural landscapes, these images perforate and interpenetrate each other, are abraded layer by layer, straight through planet earth and back again.

Jutta Strohmaier
born in Tulln/A in 1966, lives in Vienna
1996-1999 Painting, focus Photography and New Media, with Eva Schlegel at the Academy of Fine Arts, Vienna
www.jutta-strohmaier.net

IM DICKICHT (IN THE THICKET), 2005 / ANIMATIONMOVIE, 2:09 MIN. / SOUND BY MARKUS MAYERHOFER / © THE ARTIST

Alice Anderson
Pirmin Blum
Elina Brotherus
Ulrich Gebert
Terézia Golasová
Laurent Goldring
Laurent Grasso
Jan Kuděj
Ange Leccia
Oliver Möst
Tim Parchikov
Matteo Peterlini
Peter Puklus
Wolfgang Thaler

3 EXTRACTS OF ALICE ANDERSON'S PERSONAL DIARY: UNTITLED, JOURNEY TO THE INVISIBLE CITIES, STAR CATCHER, 2006 / 2:00 MIN / © ALICE ANDERSON

ALICE ANDERSON

Putting together stories drawn from her memories and a world of imagination closely linked to her childhood, Anglo-French artist and filmmaker Alice Anderson returns to the tradition of folk tales and reinvents their meanings. Possessing as it does elements of both fiction and autobiographical citation, her work highlights the duality which she believes corresponds to the very essence of the folk tale, both superficial and profound, normative and subversive, plunging the viewer into an intense dreamlike world from which a form of darkness springs, creating an atmosphere that is at times violent and frightening. While

childhood and the notion of play take on great importance in her work, they are nonetheless underpinned by a sense of seriousness.

She builds her stories by emphasizing the symbolic and poetic power of the objects from the past that she uses. Far from linear logic, the narrative process she constructs is somewhat circular, evoking the winding paths of a maze, the fluctuating world of Lewis Carroll or the Freudian principles that determine the interpretation of the unconscious mind. We can detect in each of Alice Anderson's fantastic stories a quest for identity that invites us to go through the looking glass in search of our own experience, halfway between delight and terror.

Alice Anderson
born in London in 1976, lives and works in London
1998-2001 Ecole Nationale Supérieure des Beaux-Arts, Paris
2002-2004 M.A Goldsmiths College, London
www.alice-anderson.org

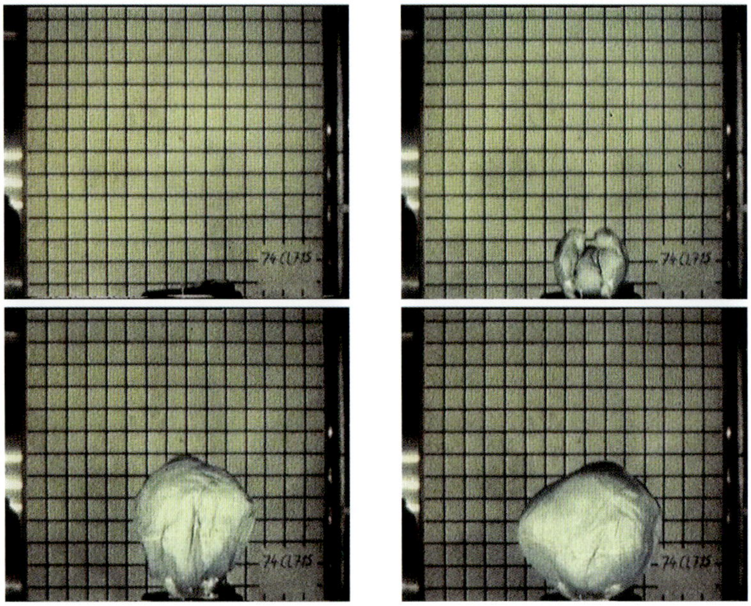

AIRBAG, 2000 / 1:00 MIN (LOOP) / © THE ARTIST

PIRMIN BLUM

For a number of years, the work of Swiss artist Pirmin Blum has focused on the Internet. He rummages through online auction sites, search engines, and chatrooms. His interest in the world wide web arises from the fact that anyone has access to it today; anyone can fill it with personal photographs, videos, texts, etc., and read personal material others have submitted. Consciously or unconsciously – in Blum's case, the former – we become "voyeurs" and consumers of the private lives of others. Besides such found footage, Blum also draws on film materials from industrial and commercial producers, such as footage of safety test procedures performed by various car manufacturers. An analytical selection of specific sequences from these videos and

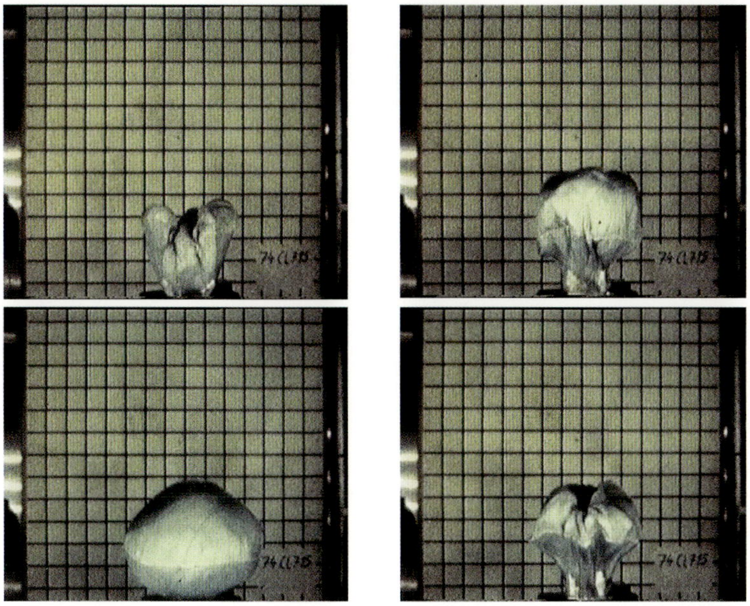

their montage elevates imagery that started out without any artistic value to a new level of meaning. For instance, fast cuts combined with loops stylize footage of an airbag as it explodes and collapses into a peculiar and seemingly organic bubble (Airbag, 2000). Blum adapts the moment of the airbag's impact to the rhythm of human breathing; after a few loops, the viewer "breathes" in synch with the video.

A similar effect is achieved in Spuk (2001) for which Blum selected a test video showing an armored security vehicle whose windshield is being fired at. The rapid sequence of two camera perspectives–shots of the windshield from outside the vehicle alternated with ones from inside–creates an uncanny tension, a sense that the viewer is in the middle of the action. The viewer alternates between being the perpetrator firing a shot and a victim seated in the car, watching the bullets approach. A decisive factor is the sound; low bass notes thud from Techno rave speakers at 130 beats per minute, the frequency used by DJs during raves to achieve optimum stimulation of the human heart.

Pirmin Blum
born in Pfaffnau/CH in 1969, lives in Vienna
1997-1999 Ecole supérieure des Beaux-Arts, Geneva
1999-2005 Digital Media with Peter Kogler at the Academy of Fine Arts, Vienna
www.pirminblum.com

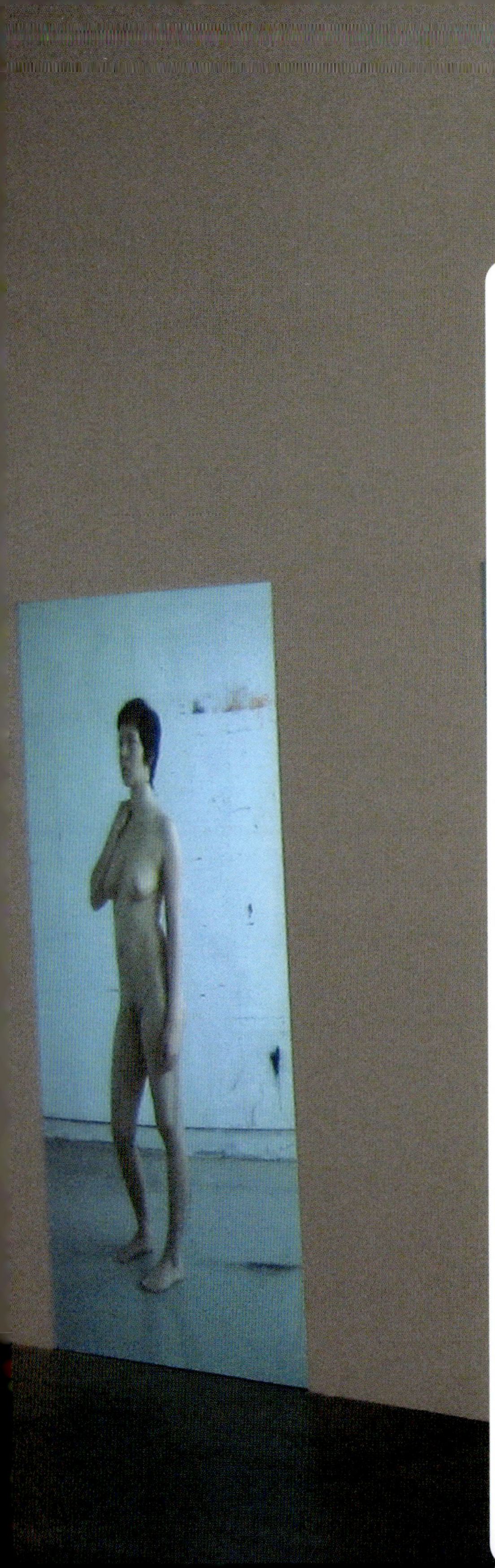

"The photographs Le miroir (2000) and the video Miroir (2001) are not about "the female identity" or anything like that, as some people have suggested. I simply wanted to see what this everyday physical phenomenon of disappearing vapour would look like when photographed. On second thoughts, the work can be seen as a little allegory of photography. At its beginnings, a photograph was a silver-coated copper plate – thus a mirror – from which a portrait emerged in the process of development. Here, too, we see the image gradually appearing from the mirror. It is curious to observe how different the two works are, even if the only difference between them really is that the photographs show separate instants whereas the video interpolates the gaps between the individual images into a continuous timeline.

Model Studies is not about personal stories or a documentary about someone's life. The images have been constructed for visual reasons. The artist is attached to light, colours, the rhythm of the masses, and to subject matter with classical notions. The figure often turns her back to the spectator.
This gesture invites peaceful contemplation rather than confrontation.[1]"

In her videos of the same title, Elina Brotherus has used professional models who pose as if in a

1 FROM "ELINA BROTHERUS IN CONVERSATION WITH BIRGIT EUSTERSCHULTE". EXHIBITION SELF-TIMER (SELBSTAUSLÖSER), KUNSTHALLE FRIDERICIANUM, KASSEL 2005.

LE MIROIR

MODEL STUDIES

life-drawing class. Instead of drawing, she looks at them with her camera. The question is about the special gaze of an artist watching a model: the distanced eye freed from voyeurism. "An artist who draws or paints doesn't pretend to know or understand the personality of the model; that's not the point. One looks attentively, that's all: where are the lights and the shadows, how do the lines go. I want to show the public this active but neutral gaze of an artist, to share it with them. It's a privilege to be able to look at a human figure in this way.[2]"

2 FROM THE PRESS RELEASE FOR ELINA BROTHERUS: MODEL STUDIES, EXHIBITION AT GB AGENCY,PARIS 2005.

Elina Brotherus
born in Helsinki in 1972, lives in Helsinki and Avallon/F
2000 graduation at the University of Art and Design, Helsinki
www.sag.se/foto/elinabrotherus/elina.html

ULRICH GEBERT

Ulrich Gebert's photography frequently moves around concepts that initially seem abstract and ungraspable, but nonetheless have a crucial impact on the way we act in social settings.

Gebert brings principles of order, systemic thinking, hierarchisation and mechanisms of power into sharp focus and renders them palpable in their artistic context. Depending on the context, he uses staged, filmic, documentary or portrait modes of representation, employing them in the process of creating his mostly photographic works in a way that reflects on the media themselves.

For his video work Keine Dialoge (no dialogues) in 2004, Ulrich Gebert used found film material on the training of elite border guards of the GSG 9, the anti-terrorism unit of the German federal police. From this material he assembled a minimalistic loop showing five uniformed officers standing in a row in a darkened and locked room undergoing a stress test with strobe light flashes. During the test the officers are given instructions which they later have to carry out. Through the rapid, lightning-flash sequence of static single images, which seem as they follow each other in rapid succession to create minimal movements by the

KEINE DIALOGE (NO DIALOGUES), 2004 / DVD, LOOP / © ULRICH GEBERT / COURTESY KLEMM'S, BERLIN

officers, the constant clicking of the flash confronts the viewer directly with the projection and the room surrounding her or him. She or he is, like the GSG 9 officers, exposed to visually violent flashes and standing in a similarly small, dark space in which the video is presented. The constricting and tense situation of the stress test in which the GSG 9 officers find themselves is thus opened to full sensory experience by the viewer, too.

Ulrich Gebert
born in Munich in 1976, lives and works in Leipzig/GER.
1998-2005 Photography at the Academy of Visual Arts, Leipzig
2006 MA graduation in Photography at the Royal College of Art, London
www.klemms-berlin.com

IN ONE BED

TERÉZIA GOLASOVÁ

Terézia Golasová, still a student of fine arts, fulfils to the word the criteria of a young emerging artist. Her work, created in a photography studio, deals exclusively with the issue of employing different means of photography and video to depict the concept of change. No action is developed in her videos. It is the movement and the flow of time that are the subjects. To stress the impact, she uses a fixed video camera.

In the video ...In One Bed..., a camera fixed to one spot turns 360 degrees. It creates the impression of a panoramic picture, a room

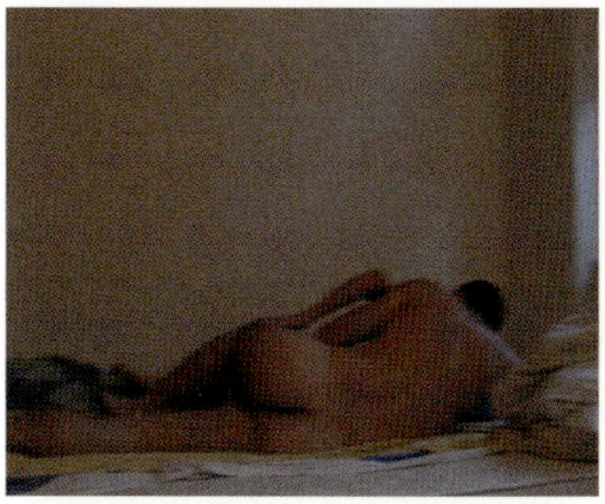

being entered by people in a direction opposite to the movement of the camera. This underlines the illusion of sequencing the action just as in stills.

" Quo vadis is a short document on the flow of time," says the author. A fixed video camera captures a passenger sitting in one place while moving - travelling from one stop to another on the underground. Through the window, we can see objects passing by quickly, suggesting the actual speed of the vehicle in striking contrast to the quasi-immobility of the passengers. Their occasional movements only enhance the impression that we are, in fact, looking at a still image taken inside the carriage. To visualize the flow of time, a clock below displays the current time, exact to the second.

The last work by Golasová, To Be at a Loss can be seen as a natural development of her research in change and media. Again, she uses a fixed video camera. This time, the illusion of a still image is strengthened by capturing a deliberately still person (the author herself) and her reflection in a mirror. The only element of change is steam slowly covering the mirror image and the sound of running water. The video ends when the mirror image has completely disappeared. The idea may not be that unique in a production on the border between video and photography, but it is definitely a logical step in the work of Golasová.

Terézia Golasová
born in Bratislava in 1980, lives in Bratislava.
2002-2007 Academy of Fine Arts, Bratislava, specialization on Photography and New Media
since 2004 Faculty of Philosophy of the Comenius University, Bratislava
www.golasova.marencin.sk

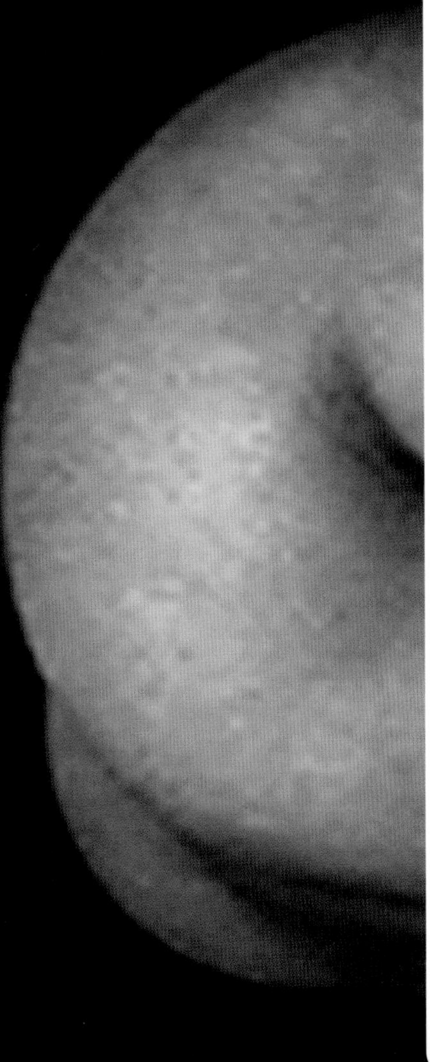

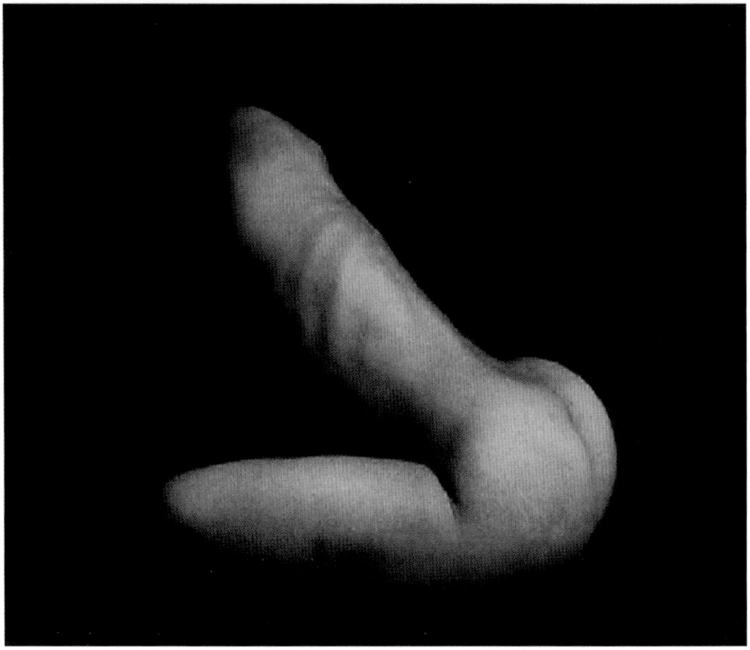

LAURENT GOLDRING

"The cinema knows the secret of the photo.

Photography was about resemblance and Arago pushed through the law that authenticated it as such. Now, the cinema, which was still chronophotography, knew straight away that this fiction was only based on its own incantatory postulate. That is why it never claimed to show twenty-four photos per second but twenty-four images per second.

The cinema takes series of photos at the same time. It just deals with

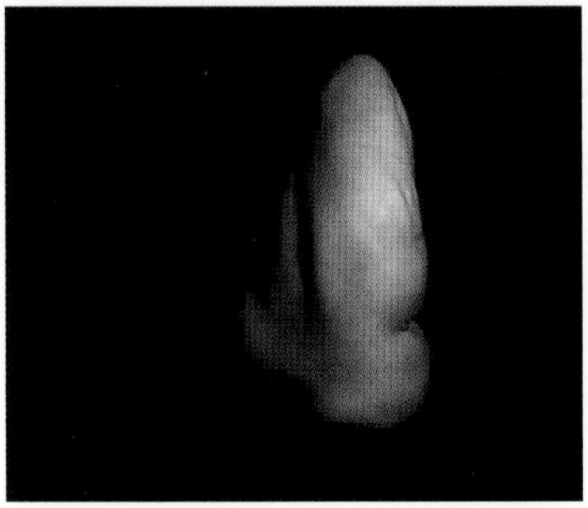

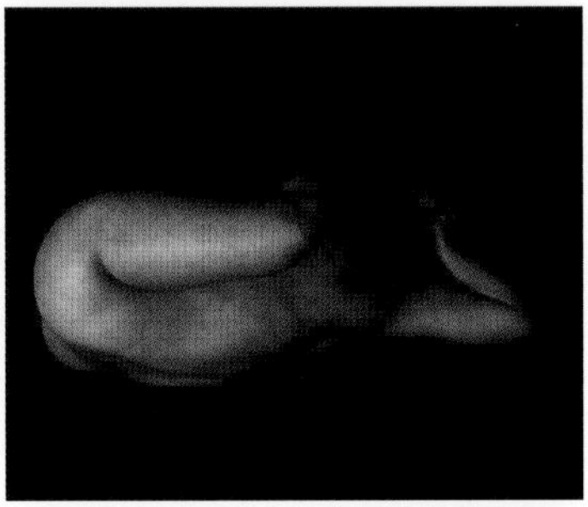

two very close shots that are different in a way that disqualifies the idea of resemblance. The cinema symmetrically explodes the idea of the resemblance between the world and itself. In the case of the portrait, it is the fiction of the individual that is exploded. In the case of landscape, the truth of perspective collapses. A fundamental difference takes root that photography had proclaimed non-existent.

The cinema saw, could have made see, refused to see, decreed that it had seen nothing, and frenetically forbade itself to see.

The cinema instantly became the massive and fully (un)conscious denial of the secret of the photo: that it was not a resemblance. It set itself up in the business of the unequivocal and of resemblance, and firstly the resemblance to oneself, the guarantor of all other businesses. Hollywood was the big publicity machine of this way of life in which objects and humans were invariably commanded to resemble themselves.

Everything in cinema is explained by this denying frenzy: casting, scenario, storyboard, shooting. Everything is destined to make us believe that an individual exists, with a face and a body, a personality, an aim and an idea… because we also understand why an industry that only exists to create a fiction can only conceive an image conceivable as fiction.

The work I do consists of trying to make a moving image outside of fiction, in other words, outside of resemblance."
(Laurent Goldring)

Laurent Goldring
born in Paris in 1957, lives, paints, sculpts, draws and makes videos in Paris
His work lead to important evolutions in the field of contemporary dance, and has been widely exhibited a bit everywhere

UNTITLED, 2003/2005, VIDEO, 3:00 MIN (LOOP), © THE ARTIST, COLLECTION OF THE ARTIST, COURTESY GALERIE CHEZ VALENTIN, PARIS

LAURENT GRASSO

Whether he is (re)working the more or less identifiable forms of our control-oriented society or subverting the cinematic techniques and conventions that shape our collective imagination, Laurent Grasso creates environments with a strong narrative potential, combining atavistic fears, scientific evidence and ominous contemporary mythologies. In his video Untitled, an enormous and threatening cloud is rolling through the streets of Paris, moving toward the viewer and swallowing cars and buildings in its way. Facing this moving screen of dust, this fictional trace of an invented catastrophe, we are urged to enter a process of narration, to project our

fears or to invent our own scenario. According to our individual sensibilities and cultural-historic references, it conjures up images of the collapse of the Twin Towers, scenes of urban violence or perhaps spectacular moments from special-effect action films.

His works could in some way revive a taste for the paranoid retro-futuristic prophecies pronounced by Charles Fourier two centuries ago. In fact, light, sound, natural, paranormal and meteorological phenomena are regularly incorporated in his works to create totally new sensory experiences that become vehicles for partially finished products of the imagination to be completed by the viewer.

By generating a tension between the works on show, their environment and the sometimes dramatic interpretations they give rise to, Laurent Grasso creates nagging mental images that tend to obscure our view of what we commonly call "reality."

Laurent Grasso
born in Mulhouse/F in 1972, lives and works in Paris.
Cooper Union School, New York; Central Saint Martins School of Art, London;
Ecole Nationale Supérieure des Beaux-Arts, Paris.
www.galeriechezvalentin.com/fr/artistes/laurent_grasso/works/

Jan Kuděj systematically explores the question of time in his work. "An absolute record of the continuity of time is not possible", he says. He has produced several "Projections" which combine two techniques: that of photographic still images and that of video moving pictures. All deal with the fact that a video camera is able to capture 25 images per second. This is a constraint that inevitably leads to movement and time being fragmented, although the human eye perceives them as continuous.

In his projection of escalators, he follows the cyclic motion of the machines. With a video camera fixed to one spot, he recorded a whole cycle. In a loop projection the escalator therefore appears to run continuously.

With an opposite intention, he animated the picture of a tree, whereby the movements of its crown are sequentially interrupted in the act of recording itself.

JAN KUDĚJ

The projection with waves rippling against the shore we selected for this exhibition derives from the same principle as the escalators: the perception of the continuity of time passing.

"However, from a certain point of view, all projections are enclosed, fixing an action in the form of a still image. Time is a mere illusion." (...)

"For me, my approach consists of a continuous recording by a video camera and an intentionally interrupted recording of shots. We recognize two perceptions of time – a time of instant and a time of duration. This sensation helps us experience the simultaneous contradictions of reality as it unfolds. The concept one has of oneself (of the world) is not continuous. It changes character with each new thinking process. This process itself is just a continuously repeating interruption. We perceive time as unfolding in instants." (from Kuděj's dissertation, 2005)

Jan Kuděj
born in Prague in 1978, lives in Prague.
1997-1999 Ethnology at the Faculty of Philosophy and Arts, Charles University, Prague
1999-2005 Architecture and Design at the Academy of Arts, Prague
2002-2003 Berlin University of Arts (scholarship)

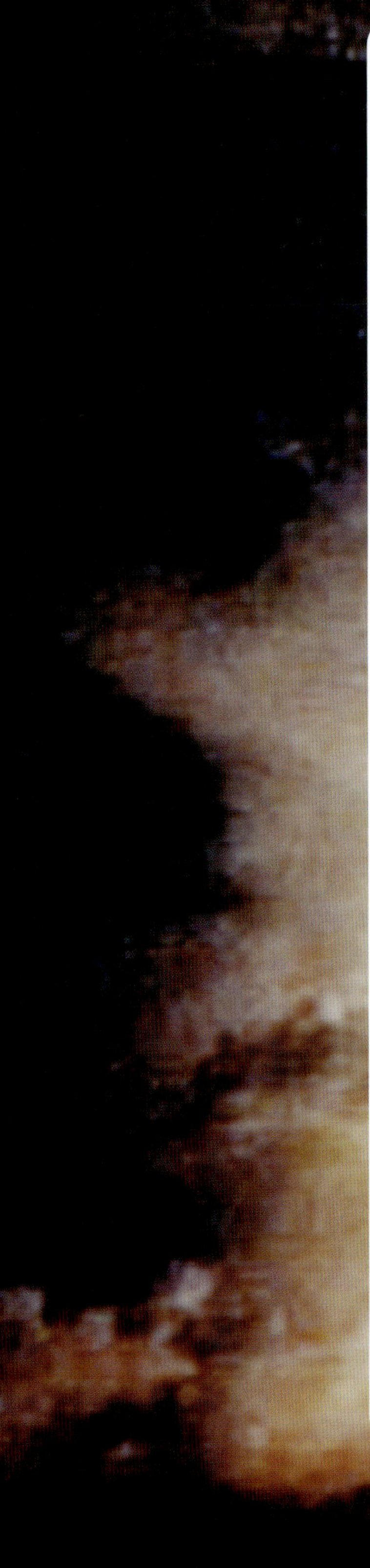

ANGE LECCIA

The video installation Orage is a metaphysical and contemplative piece that invites us on an introspective journey, and is highly characteristic of the dreamlike power of Ange Leccia's work as a whole. Leccia has been fascinated since childhood by the cinema and animated images, and his entire work is suffused by a poetics of energy and nourished by an investigation into image and film; this brings him as close as possible to the inexpressible, as well as imparting a strong emotional density to his pieces.

Set in a space plunged into darkness, this diptych in the form of a looped projection on two perpendicular screens transports us into a

ORAGE (STORM) 1999, VIDEO ARRANGEMENT: DOUBLE PROJECTION IN RIGHT ANGLE, 2 DVDs, 30:00 MIN (LOOP),
© ANGE LECCIA, COURTESY GALERIE ALMINE RECH, BRUXELLES-PARIS

roiling night sky in which lightning strikes in seemingly suspended temporality. Filmed as a static shot, this flow of violent energy fills both the image and the soundtrack, putting us face to face with the palpable and all-powerful presence of the elements and symbolizing the fact that Nature always surpasses us in spite of our efforts to gain mastery over it. Situated somewhere between visual stasis and the stretching of time, its repetitive rhythm and apparent permanence shift it towards pure abstraction, while opening the way to the transcendental and the sublime. The use of repetition and looping that characterizes Ange Leccia's images brings with it a feeling of permanent regeneration that must be interpreted, according to art critic Pascal Beausse, "with respect to an organic dimension of the image, inviting us into an eternal present." This stretching of time, associated with the sensorial immersion made possible by the way the images are presented, means that we can call upon the most subterranean forces of our own imagination.

Ange Leccia
born in Minerviu, Corsica/F in 1952, lives and works in Paris
Cinema and Philosophy, Université Paris-Sorbonne, Paris
www.galeriealminerech.com

BROWN EYES, 2007 / PINHOLE VIDEO, 0:56 MIN / © OLIVER MÖST / COURTESY K4 GALLERY, SAARBRÜCKEN

"Pictures that are sharply in focus have overcome lack of focus. They ignore the things that can be experienced in lack of focus and definition."[1]

Oliver Möst's video work, produced in 2007, is a continuation of his photographic work. At first glance it is characterised by a conspicuous lack of definition, which is the artist's guiding aesthetic principle both in his photographs and in his video work. The principle of sharp-

1 BASTIAN BRETTHAUER, „SO EINE WELT OHNE ECKEN UND KANTEN" IN K4 GALERIE, EDS., OLIVER MÖST, CLACKASTIGMAT 6.0 / K4 GALERIE (BERLIN, DORN, 2005).

OLIVER MÖST

HIDE & SEEK, 2007
PINHOLE VIDEO, 1:40 MIN.
© OLIVER MÖST
COURTESY K4 GALERIE, SAARBRÜCKEN

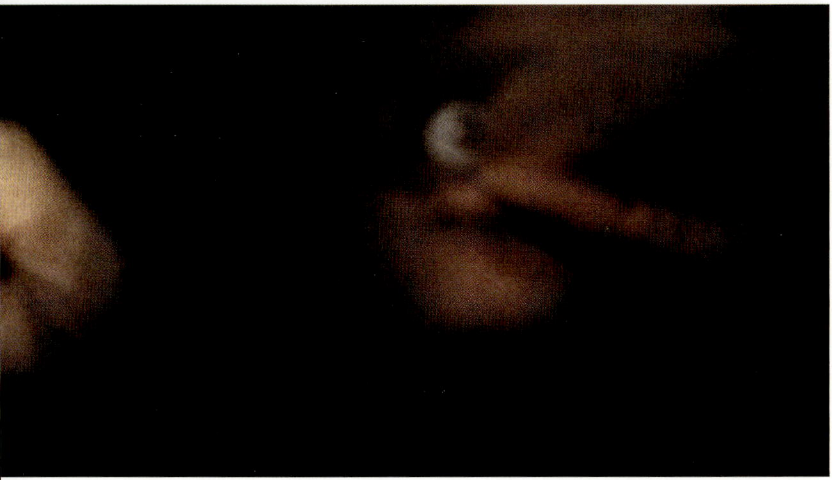

ness make us aware of the core of the artist's perceptional awareness.

Oliver Möst's own process of perception is the theme of all his work. He suffers from poor sight, so that his glasses have to compensate for 2.0 dioptres in the left eye and 6.0 in the right. His photographic and film work allow us to experience the photographer's subjective eye in the form of "that's-what-he-saw-and-perceived-there-in-this-way" and to see moreover his idiosyncratic perception and the way he experiences the space around him (between, hide & seek, brown eyes).

Another prominent theme in Möst's video work is reflection on photography and its media-immanent qualities by way of a confrontation of film and photography. The idea of combining two photographic techniques led him to use a pinhole camera (without a lens), a camera obscura, the basic camera form. He combined this technique with digital video technology by filming and recording with a video camera the image cast on the plate of the pinhole camera. In this confrontation between "old" pinhole camera technology on the one hand and modern digital video technology on the other Möst creates "pinhole videos", as he calls his work.

They reflect the technical development of photography from the simple pinhole camera to the digital and technically highly developed video camera, and thus also the underlying qualities of the medium of photography as they have been constantly expanded over the years.

Oliver Möst
born in Füssen/Allgäu/GER in 1968, lives and works in Berlin
Freelance photographer and video artist. First video project in 1999 in collaboration with a dance choreographer
www.olivermoest.de

GONE TO SEA, 2007 / VIDEO, 1:48 MIN. / © THE ARTIST

TIM PARCHIKOV

Tim Parchikov, poet and photographer, is a Muscovite in his twenties. For this generation, the world truly became too small and, in terms of geography, sometimes even too visible and accessible. Fortunately, Tim Parchikov perceives life as an authentic poet and reconstructs for the viewer his own model of the world, a model charged with so much energy and the fresh feeling of youth that one can forget about the problems of being predictable or obvious. This work is full of ozone. The feeling of universal grief, often characteristic of young people, and a profound knowledge of Russian and world photography do not in any way reduce that electric feeling of freshness his works emanate.

The creative individuality of the young artist and the scope of his personality clearly indicate a true, mature and independent talent in several classical arts. A subtle sense of colour, a strong feeling for the

golden section and bold metaphorical thinking allow Tim Parchikov to express himself in a daring and original way. His is a new voice worth listening to.

The video Gone to Sea is a miniature devoted to the possibility of disappearing for no particular reason at sea, that is: nowhere. Gone to Sea brings to mind Michelangelo Antonioni's "L'Avventura," where the heroine suddenly disappears for no apparent reason. But what each of us is particularly interested in is not just the problem of disappearance, but whether it will remain unnoticed...

Tim Parchikov
born in Moscow in 1983, lives and works in Moscow
2006 graduation at the Cameraman Department of the Russian Institute of Cinematography, Moscow

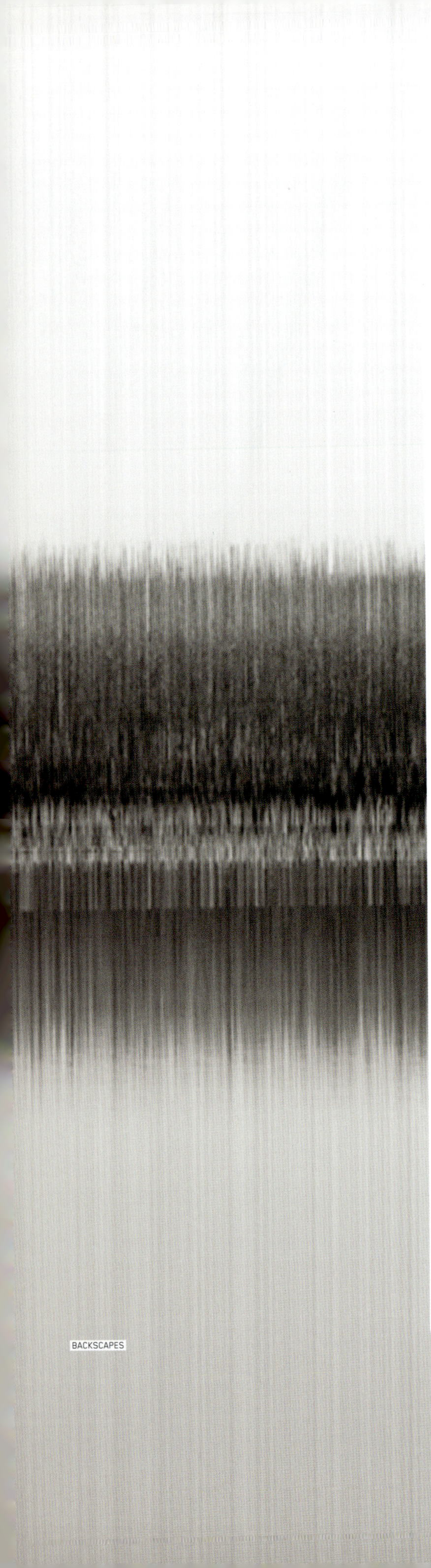

BACKSCAPES

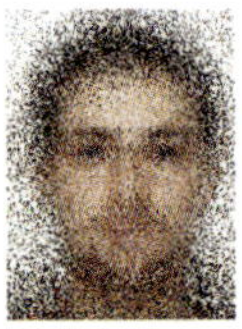

MEYOUOTHER

MATTEO PETERLINI

Using pixels as a measuring unit: in photographic works by Matteo Peterlini this is a very real conceptual element, a programmatic choice.

Disjointed and recomposed in this manner, the images in his photographic series are the result of a calculating process tending to the infinite, in which the system used for combining the fragments is entrusted to chance and applied with an algebraic function.

Peterlini even dares envisaging original sin and focuses closely on the very mechanisms of perception in specially created specific types of software. How are images generated in our minds? Chosen by imitation, learning and sharing, the mechanisms we usually use for understanding the world lose their effectiveness when faced with the associative flow generated by the

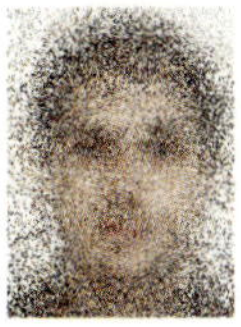

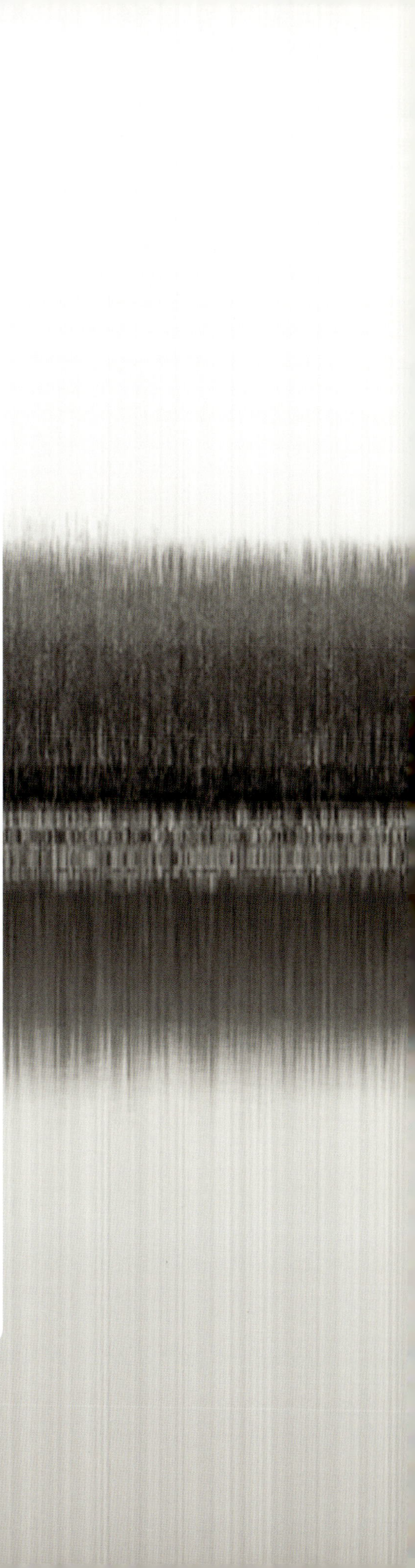

electronic process. Hence, it does not seem to be a contradiction that these are traditional pictorial genres: portraits, nudes, landscapes. In fact, thanks to the frontal aspect of the faces (those required for a standard passport photograph in Meyouother), the silhouettes of the bodies (those outlined in the six poses asked of the models in V6), the fixedness of landscapes that are almost abstract (Backscapes), it is possible to acknowledge the unconscious tendency to recognize what is "already known" (Gestalt, stereotypes) that usually allows us to address the diversity of phenomena.

Furthermore, it is precisely the hoax provided by a technique that is only apparently "craftsman-like", used by Peterlini to give life to his photographic series, that reveals the analytic nature of his work. In fact, if one observes these images closely (actually the result of a continuously creative flow) they work like a collage, while,by the contrast, the process involved in recognizing the overall image is suspended within a virtual coexistence of all possible combinations.
(Cristina Natalicchio)

Matteo Peterlini
born in Rovereto/I in 1970, lives and works in Rovereto.
Degree in Informatics, course of Graphic Design and Advertising in 1992
He started exhibiting his works in 1997 and has since been present in Trento, Venice, Turin, at the Istanbul Contemporary Art Museum
www.matteopeterlini.it

Peter Puklus & Melinda Sipos both work individually; both have their own, unique artistic approach. However, they produced the two projects Imported Lights and Garden together as a group called DEUX. The titles of the works don't have any further meaning than the raw data. DEUX_ 00 Imported Lights is the group's "nil project", as they call it. The idea is rather conceptual: to capture the reflection of the light coming through a window and project it into a blind room. From the point of view of "Mutations II", we get a still image projected as a video.

A similar logic is applied to DEUX_ 01 Garden, the first common project undertaken by Peter Puklus and Melinda Sipos, as the title clearly states. It is a detailed recording of a garden over the course of a long period. They took a picture each day, out of the same window and for a whole year. The result is a portfolio of tiny changes in space; moved chairs,

PETER PUKLUS

seasons following one another... As a slide show, it creates the impression that the changes happen in the actual time of the projection.

Both works are based on simple but well applied ideas. The technical aspects, such as the choice of media, photography and video, and the conversion of one into the other, are rather of secondary importance and driven by their artistic conception, unlike in other authors in this selection whose creations were inspired by the technical possibilities. For Puklus and Sipos, the approach of overstepping from photography to video was a logical solution for the realisation of their artistic intention.

Peter Puklus
born in Koloszvár/H in 1980, lives in Budapest
2005 graduation in Photography at the Moholy-Nagy University of Art and Design, Budapest
http://photolumen.hu/puklus
www.deuxprojects.blogspot.com

Melinda Sipos
born in Budapest/H in 1979, lives in Budapest
2005 graduation in glass design at the Moholy-Nagy University of Art and Design, Budapest
http://siposmelinda.blogspot.com
www.deuxprojects.blogspot.com

MATTER OF SELECTION. # 1 (BOOKS), 2007 / 58:00 MIN /
© THE ARTIST

WOLFGANG THALER

Wolfgang Thaler's work encompasses architecture photography (series on Vienna's Südbahnhof railway station or on traffic circles) and documentary photography (on the Viennese traditional coffeeshop chain Aida, etc.), manifesting his – in most cases highly analytical – interest in space.

The series Matter of Selection (2007) permits us to peer into a collector's apartment. Using high-resolution black-and-white stock, Thaler first photographs his furniture (a dresser, a bookshelf); then, like a detective, he scans every single detail of the resulting photographs on a computer screen. This produces a transmutation on a number of levels: a photographic capture of a single moment is expanded into an endless tracking shot; reality is dis-

MATTER OF SELECTION. # 2 (WARDROBE), 2007 / 32:00 MIN / © THE ARTIST

MEP'YUK. DIE ZENTRALE (MEP'YUK. THE HEADQUARTER), 1999 / 15:00 MIN / © THE ARTIST

placed as the photograph of an object is filmed instead of the object itself; and of that photograph, we only ever see details, never getting a full view.

Welcome to Mep'Yuk – this is the way Thaler welcomes the visitors of his imaginary deserted city Mep'Yuk. Die Zentrale (Mep'Yuk. The Head-quarter, 1999) that consists exclusively of interior spaces. The artist takes photographs of prosaic corporate entrance halls, lobbies, office spaces and waiting rooms in various cities all over the world; despite the different cultural backgrounds and settings, these places have one thing in common: they are (semi-) public spaces whose dominant function is administrative, structural, or organizational. He places the resulting photographs in series and scans them, step by step, in slow horizontal tracking shots. Once again, Thaler denies the viewer a totalizing perspective, offering only details of the interiors. The impression soon arises that we are observing these sites through surveillance cameras, and with it the question: what is there to observe if no human beings man this "command center"?

Wolfgang Thaler
born in Salzburg/A in 1969, lives in Vienna
1989-1991 Bavarian State Institute of Photography, Munich (now: Munich University of Applied Sciences)
www.wolfgangthaler.at

EUROPEAN MONTH OF PHOTOGRAPHY
In partnership with Alcatel-Lucent and the support of Culturesfrance – Mairie de Paris

BERLIN
Kulturprojekte Berlin GmbH:
Thomas Friedrich
Curator European Month of Photography, Berlin
Oliver Bätz
Project Manager
Kathrin Kohle
Curator "Mutations II"
Antonia Kausch
Project Assistant

BRATISLAVA
Central European House of Photography Bratislava:
Vaclav Macek
Chairman of FOTOFO, Director of Month of Photography
Zuzana Lapitková Curator SEDF (Central European House of Photography)

LUXEMBOURG
Café-Crème asbl:
Paul di Felice & Pierre Stiwer
Curators, Directors of European Month of Photography
Sneja Dobrovsavljevic
Communication Manager
in association with the Musée d'Art moderne Grand-Duc Jean:
Marie-Claude Beaud
Director
Clément Minighetti & Christophe Gallois
Curators

partners:
Marguy Conzemius
Representative of the Department of Photography CNA

Danielle Igniti
Director of Cultural Services of the City of Dudelange, Director of Centre d'Art Nei Liicht

MOSCOW

Moscow House of Photography:
Olga Sviblova
Director
Ekaterina Kondranina
Curator
Mikhail Krasnov
Project Manager

PARIS

Maison Européenne de la Photographie:
Jean-Luc Monterosso
Director
Jean-Luc Soret
Curator
Barbara Wolffer
Project Manager
City of Paris:
Carole Prat
Department of Cultural Affairs

ROME

Zone Attive:
Emiliano Paoletti
Chief Executive
Anna Gianesini
Project Manager

VIENNA

Department for Cultural Affairs of the City of Vienna:
Berthold Ecker, Gunda Achleitner
Curators
Roland Fink, Johannes Karel
Assistant Project Managers
Vladimir und Estragon:
Thomas Licek
Project Manager
Agnes Reinthaler
Assistant Project Manager

ACKNOWLEDGEMENTS

ALCATEL-LUCENT
Alcatel - Lucent Corporate Communications
Caroline Guillaumin
Vice President of Corporate Communications and CSR
Véronique de Fournoux
Corporate Image Director

VOCATIF
Alcatel-Lucent advisor

CULTURESFRANCE
Olivier Poivre d'Arvor
Director
Alain Reinaudo
Visual arts and architecture advisor
Sophie Robnard
In charge of photography
Vanessa Sily
Manager - Territorial Communities Unit

SAISON CULTURELLE EUROPEENNE
Laurent Burin Des Roziers
Curator
Carole Scipion
Deputy Curator

LUXEMBOURG
Guy Dockendorf
Director of Cultural Affairs, Ministery of Culture
Lydie Polfer
Head of Department for Cultural Affairs City of Luxembourg
Christiane Sietzen
Chief executive of Cultural Affairs City of Luxembourg

CITY OF BERLIN
André Schmitz
State Secretary for Cultural Affairs
Volker Heller
Head of Department for Cultural Affairs

CITY OF MOSCOW
Liudmila Shvetsova
Vice - Mayor of Moscow in charge of Culture
Serguei Khudiakov
President of the Committee of Culture of Moscow

CITY OF PARIS
The exhibition "Mutations II" would never have been possible in Paris without the enthusiastic support of Mr Christophe Girard, Deputy Mayor for Culture, and of Mr Pierre Schapira, Deputy Mayor in charge of International Relations, European Affairs and French language and culture abroad.
Departement of Cultural Affairs
Laurence Engel
Director
Catherine Hubault
Assistant Director of the Patrimony and History
General Delegation for International Relations
Bernard Pignerol
General Delegate
Juliette Salzmann
Head of Cultural Affairs

CITY OF VIENNA
Andreas Mailath-Pokorny
Executive City Councillor for Cultural Affairs and Science
Bernhard Denscher
Head of the Department for Cultural Affairs of the City of Vienna

LENDERS
Angles Gallery, L.A.
Centre d'Art Nei Liicht, Dudelange
CRG Gallery, New York
Galerie Almine Rech, Paris
Galerie Anne de Villepoix, Paris
Galerie Chez Valentin, Paris
Galerie Yvon Lambert, Paris
Mummery + Schnelle Gallery, London
Noga Gallery, Tel Aviv

www.europeanmonthofphotography.eu

Catalogue Project Manager
Pierre Stiwer, Café Crème asbl

Catalogue design
a|part, Luxembourg

Publisher: Café-Crème asbl
2 rue Alphonse Munchen
L-2172 Luxembourg

First edition 2008
ISBN 978-287978074-0

Mutations II – Moving Stills / Bilder und Verzerrungen

Im Zusammenhang mit dem Europäischen Monat der Fotografie, der zuerst 2004 veranstaltet wurde und mittlerweile Festivals in Paris, Berlin, Bratislava, Luxemburg, Moskau, Rom und Wien verbindet, war es nur angemessen und zugleich nötig, einen umfassenden Blick auf die tiefgreifenden Veränderungen, die weltweit im Gange sind, zu werfen; und insbesondere auf diejenigen, die sich im Bereich der zeitgenössischen Bilder abspielen. Diese Überlegung gab 2006 den Anstoß zur Ausstellung „Mutations I", die sich Fragen des technologischen und künstlerischen Wandels im Bereich der Fotografie zuwandte.

Die zweite Auflage dieser Veranstaltung, „Mutations II", möchte diese Fragestellung in Bezug auf das Medium Video verfolgen und dazu die produktiven Verhältnisse erkunden, die sich zwischen starren und bewegten Bildern entwickelt haben, und einen Eindruck davon vermitteln, wo zeitgenössische Kunst in Europa heute steht.

In einer Situation, in der alle Mittel der Kommunikation und künstlerischen Medien von Globalisierung und digitaler Konvergenz betroffen sind, ist die Epoche des „Post-Mediums", die nunmehr anbricht, „eine Phase, für die die Erkundung hybrider Technologie charakteristisch ist, in der Künstler Video mit einer breiten Palette anderer Materialien kombinieren und rekombinieren"[1] – also Fotografie, Klangkunst, digitalem Video, Film, DVD, Computerkunst, CD-Rom, Grafik und Animation. Jede einzelne Kunstform neigt so mehr denn je dazu, „innerhalb der Grenzen, die ihr durch ihre materiellen Schranken gezogen sind, aber auch durch ein Anstreben gegen diese Schranken das gesamte Spektrum abzudecken, das ihr die Gemeinschaft mit anderen Kunstformen eröffnet"[2].

Indem Fotografie ihren Status als Medium für die Fixierung aufgezeichneter Wirklichkeit aufgibt und sich von der Videokunst eines von deren zentralen Merkmalen, nämlich die zeitliche Dimension, ausborgt, emanzipiert sie sich mittels vielschichtiger künstlerischer Manipulationen und technischer Hybridisierungen, amaloger ebenso wie digitaler.

Die Organisatoren von „Mutations II" haben sich daher entschieden, europäische Künstler in den Vordergrund zu stellen, denen die Lust am Experimentieren mit neuen Ausdrucksformen gemeinsam ist. Wie Nancy Spector in ihrem Aufsatz „Art Photography after Photography"[3] stellen sie letztlich die spezifischen Kriterien in Frage, anhand derer man einmal zwischen einem Fotografen und einem Künstler, der mit Fotografie arbeitet, unterscheiden konnte.

Eine wachsende Zahl von Fotografen verwendet Video, woraus sich Veränderungen der Bestimmungsmerkmale beider Techniken ergeben. Von der Vielfalt ihrer ästhetischen Standpunkte und der verwendeten visuellen Techniken einmal abgesehen, derer sie sich bedienen, ermuntern uns die in der Ausstellung präsentierten Künstler dazu, uns über die Gebietsabgrenzungen und akademischen Definitionen, die so oft künstlerische Felder einzäunen, hinwegzusetzen und die dazwischen liegenden Grenzgebiete zu erforschen. Mit anderen Worten, „Mutations II" lädt uns ein, Neuland zu entdecken, sowohl das starre als auch das bewegte Bild aus der Perspektive der Spannungen, die beide motivieren, ins Auge zu fassen. Dazu gehören eine ontologische Spannung zwischen dem Augenblickhaften und dem, was sich im Lauf der Zeit abspielt; eine ästhetische Spannung, die aus der hybriden Verbindung des traditionellen fotografischen Bildes und des bewegten Bildes erwächst; und eine dialektische Spannung zwischen den beschränkten Präsentationsformen, die für Fotografien zur Verfügung stehen, und „der unendlichen Vielfalt von

1 RUSH (MICHAEL). 2007. L'ART VIDÉO. LONDON, THAMES & HUDSON.
2 BELLOUR (RAYMOND). 1999. L'ENTRE-IMAGES 2. P.O.L. PARIS.
3 MOVING PICTURES, CONTEMPORARY PHOTOGRAPHY AND VIDEO FROM THE GUGGENHEIM MUSEUM COLLECTIONS. 2003. NEW YORK. GUGGENHEIM MUSEUM PUBLICATIONS. S. 31-39.

GERMAN
(Übersetzungen: Gerrit Jackson)

Wahrnehmungskombinationen, innerhalb derer elektronische Bilder definiert und artikuliert werden können"[4], insbesondere Videoinstallationen.

Gilles Deleuze und Félix Guattari zufolge „kann es kein Territorium geben ohne einen Vektor, dieses Territorium zu verlassen [...], ohne ein Bestreben, sich anderswo neu zu verorten"[5]. Beschränken wir diese philosophische Frage einmal auf das Gebiet der Kunst, so liegt der Gedanke nahe, die spezifische Dynamik einer jeden Tendenz in der Kunst sei eine Fliehkraft, die danach strebt, diese Kunst von den jeweils geltenden Konventionen und Normen wegzubewegen, ein „Exit-Vektor", dessen Existenz sich geradezu darauf gründet, wie neu seine Weltanschauung ist.

Peter Aerschmanns originelle Weltanschauung besteht aus merkwürdigen kleinen Szenen, die die für seine Arbeit zentrale Herausforderung illustrieren: Er sucht nach Mitteln, einen gegebenen Raum zu fotografieren, ohne an zeitlicher Tiefe zu verlieren, eine Fotografie zu erzeugen, die nicht eine Momentaufnahme darstellt, die Bewegung spürbar werden lässt, anstatt sie einzufrieren. Daher bezieht Peter Aerschmann Zeit in die Darstellung von Raum mit ein, indem er das Prinzip der Unbeweglichkeit des Bildes verschiebt und auf Bewegung anwendet, die er in genau dem Moment einfriert, da sie entsteht. So stellt Aerschmann einen „Stammeleffekt" im Idiom des Mediums Video her, indem er menschliche Gestalten zeigt, die in endlosen Schleifen wiederholter Bewegungen gefangen zu sein scheinen.

Der semantische und stilistische Reichtum, der der Wiederholung innewohnt, diente auch Gast Bouschet und Nadine Hilbert bei der Konstruktion von Dreamsequence, einer Videoarbeit aus dem Jahr 2006/07, als Inspirationsquelle. Das Künstlerpaar kehrte an den Drehort von Philip Kaufmans „Invasion of the Body Snatchers" von 1978 zurück, von wo es sie die Idee des Verfolgungswahns durch die Verwendung obsessiv wiederkehrender Bilder aktualisiert und neu kontextualisiert. Unter bewusster Aufopferung der konventionellen Widerspiegelung linearer Erzählweisen ist diese poetische und politische Traumsequenz an einem Netzwerk von Beziehungen zwischen Fotos, Videos, Klängen und Texten aufgehängt, das unsere Objektivität in Frage stellt und unsere geschärfte Wahrnehmungsfähigkeit aufs äußerste spannt.

Auch wenn Christoph Brech ebenfalls mit unseren Wahrnehmungsvermögen spielt, dient das zuallererst dazu, unsere Aufmerksamkeit zu gewinnen. Scheinbar bewegungslos und doch stets in Bewegung, leiten die Gegenstände, Figuren und Landschaften, die er filmt, das Auge von einer Interpretationsebene zur nächsten; es schwankt zwischen dem Begehren, das Bild zu entziffern, und dem durch die extrem reduzierte videografische Konstruktion erweckten Wunsch nach Kontemplation. Break, eine hypnotische Arbeit, die aus einer einzigen Einstellung besteht und ohne Kameraeffekte auskommt, ist das perfekte Beispiel für diese formale Nüchternheit. Wir werden der Tatsache gewahr, dass Vergänglichkeit geradezu das Wesen von Bewegung ist, und spüren zugleich mit beinahe körperlicher Intensität die tektonische Kraft der Zeit. Zeitlichkeit wird hier über das, was uns gezeigt wird, thematisiert: Wasserdampfwolken streichen langsam über die Weiten eines zugefrorenen Flusses und antworten auf das beinahe unmerkliche Schieben des Eises. Der Eisbrecher, der diese feindlichen Elemente durchquert und daraufhin verschwindet – hinter sich eine Spur ziehend, die das Eis sogleich angreift und verschluckt – erscheint als geglückte Allegorie auf die conditio humana.

Big Bang von Ori Gersht dreht sich um eine politische Metapher für eine in die Wirren des Krieges geworfene Menschheit. Eben weil Konflikte und die mit ihnen verbundene Gewalt eine Bruchstelle markieren, erkunden Gershts ästhetische und plastische Recherchen die Vorstellung des Übergangs mit solcher Intensität; dessen Prozess wird auf die Idee eines starren Bildes, das zum bewegten Bild wird, verschoben. Auf den ersten Blick sieht Big Bang wie ein barockes Stillleben aus. Doch die Art, wie Ori Gersht Ton einsetzt, verleiht diesem starren Tableau eine zeitliche Dimension, flößt ihm dramatische Spannung ein, die ihren Gipfelpunkt in einem in Zeitlupe aufgenommenen explodierenden Blumenstrauß erreicht – die genau erwogene Aufnahme eines Gegenstandes auf dem Weg zu seiner eigenen Entortung. Dieser Übergang von der darstellenden zur rein abstrakten Kunst mündet schließlich in den visuellen Stillstand, eine Erinnerung an das Bild, das die Sirenen und Explosionen des Konflikts zwischen Israelis und Palästinensern dem Künstler in seiner Kindheit ins Gedächtnis eingebrannt haben. Hier handelt es sich um einen künstlerischen Prozess, der im Zuge seiner Erkundung der Beziehungen zwischen Fotografie, Malerei und Bild sowohl im wörtlichen als auch im übertragenen Sinne „durch die Form hindurchgeht", um uns dahin zu bringen, sie aufzugeben.

Wie Gersht beschäftigt sich der junge finnische Künstler Tuomo Rainio in seinen Arbeiten mit Zeit und Veränderung, wobei seine Herangehensweise eine ganz und gar andere ist. Statt an der ästhetischen Natur des Bildes anzusetzen, geht er von der Natur der Bewegung aus. Durch ein selbstgeschriebenes Bildbearbeitungsprogramm zeigen mit einer einfachen Kamera aufgenommene Bilder urbane Umgebungen, in denen die Handlungen ihrer Bewohner nur in Form geisterhafter Spuren, die sie hinterlassen, sichtbar sind. Dieser Prozess ist zugleich politisch (da er sich auf einen öffentlichen Raum bezieht, der durch ein Netzwerk von Überwachungskameras kontrolliert wird) und konzeptuell (da er die Spannung des „Dazwischen" darstellt: die Dauer von An- und Abwesenheit).

Jutta Strohmaier bedient sich ebenfalls der Möglichkeiten digitaler Technologie,

4 VAILLANT (ALEXIS), PARFAIT (FRANÇOISE), JANKOVIC (NIKOLA). 2001. LES NOUVELLES IMAGES. TOME 1. CHRONIQUES DE L'AFAA. PARIS.
5 DELEUZE (GILLES). 2004. L'ABÉCÉDAIRE DE GILLES DELEUZE. PARIS. MONTPARNASSE (DVD).

teils um das starre Bild von innen her wachsen zu lassen, teils um es durch Beleuchtungseffekte, cut outs oder elektronische Wogen, die es fortlaufend verändern, zu rekonfigurieren. In Journey oder Im Dickicht (In the Thicket) erwächst der Eindruck von Bewegung aus der Tatsache, dass das Bild niemals ganz fertig, sondern stets in einem Übergangszustand zwischen dem Vorangegangenen und dem Folgenden begriffen scheint; Gegenwart bringt also niemals zeitliche Einheit mit sich, sondern eine Explosion von Zeitlichkeiten, die die Struktur des Bildes zersetzen. In Passenger ermöglicht die Verdichtung von Zeit, die sich aus über mehrere Tage minütlich aufgenommenen Bilder eines leeren Zimmers ergibt, einen distanzierten Zugang zum Alltagsleben, das hier durch den beschleunigten Rhythmus der Tag-Nacht-Zyklen wahrgenommen wird. In Silent Stories werden die verwendeten Fotos Effekten von Überlagerung, Verwischung und Durchsichtigkeit unterworfen, die eine fiktive Neuinterpretation der Wirklichkeit anbieten. Obwohl Jutta Strohmaier in der Herstellung ihrer Szenarien Fotografien als Rohmaterial verwendet, spielen die Wahrnehmung von Bewegung und Prozesse der Verwandlung und zeitlichen Dekonstruktion eine zentrale Rolle und erlauben so dem Bild, die vielfältigen in ihm enthaltenen Bedeutungen freizusetzen.

Vorherrschend in der formalen Erkundung, die Olga Chernyshevas Windows motiviert, ist eine Untersuchung von Raum und Bild. Die Künstlerin, fasziniert von den Überresten des verschwundenen kommunistischen Systems, beobachtet das heutige Alltagsleben in Russland und konstruiert es in Form einer Installation nach, deren Inszenierung nichts dem Zufall überlässt. Jedes Fenster eines Hauses, nachts mit einer Handkamera aufgenommen, wird zum Rahmen einer Bühne, auf der die Bewohner auf- und abtreten wie Figuren in einem Theaterstück und von der sie nach hinten in die Intimität des dunklen Backstagebereiches ihrer privaten Wohnungen verschwinden. Der theatralische Charakter dieser Ausschnitte aus dem Leben wird durch die Verwendung mehrerer Bildschirme betont, die der Installation eine große Präsenz im Ausstellungsraum verleihen und eine intime mise en abyme hervorrufen, die wiederum einen Dialog zwischen Werk und Betrachter anregt.

Gemeinsam ist diesen europäischen Künstlern, dass sie Fotografie und/oder Video verschiedenen Formen der Verzerrung unterwerfen. So erkunden sie die Fluchtlinien der Perspektiven, die sich an den Grenzen zwischen den beiden Medien ergeben, und ein neues Bild- und Wahrnehmungsregime errichten; zugleich treiben sie das fotografische und videografische Idiom an seine Grenzen – an eben jene Grenzen, welche die nötigen Voraussetzungen für das Entstehen von Originalität und „Stil" im Sinne Deleuzes ausmachen.

Diese neuen Experimente, die Fotografie und Video über ihre gewohnten Grenzen hinaustreiben, geben uns eine einzigartige Gelegenheit, die Welt neu zu sehen, und laden uns ein, unser Alltagsleben neu zu erfinden, es „mit den Augen des Kunstwerks" zu sehen, um Merleau-Ponty zu zitieren.[6]

Jean-Luc Soret

in Zusammenarbeit mit Gunda Achleitner, Berthold Ecker, Paul Di Felice, Anna Gianesini, Kathrin Kohle, Ekaterina Kondranina, Zuzana Lapitkova, Emiliano Paoletti, Jean-Luc Monterosso, Pierre Stiwer, Olga Sviblova und Barbara Wolffer.

6 MERLEAU-PONTY (MAURICE). 1960. L'ŒIL ET L'ESPRIT. PARIS. FOLIO. ESSAIS.

Mutations II - Moving Stills

Das Dazwischen pflegen

Zwischen Fotografie und Video besteht eine Nähe, die ebenso stark ist wie das, was sie in ihrem Verhältnis zur Zeit ursprünglich trennt. Technische Entwicklungen ermuntern Künstler heute dazu, die zwei einander anzunähern: Es ist möglich geworden, mit einer Fotokamera zu filmen oder mit einer Videokamera zu fotografieren. Darüberhinaus operieren beide mit digitalen Verfahrensschritten, einschließlich sogar des Emulsionsverfahrens. Mit digitaler Hilfe ist es leicht, das Bild einzufrieren; die Diashow ist mit einem einzigen Mausklick gestartet. So kann man Bewegung anhalten oder eine zeitliche Dimension einführen: zwei Gesten, die technisch höchst einfach, aber von erheblicher Störkraft sind. Zur Rede steht dabei nicht so sehr die Grenzlinie zwischen zwei Medien (Videokunst stand schon immer anderen künstlerischen Praktiken nahe), sondern die Kunstwerke, die diese Durchlässigkeit hervorbringt. Diesen Übergangsbereich erkundet „Mutations II". Alle für diese Ausstellung ausgewählten Künstler verwenden Video so, dass sie mit der Spannung umgehen, die dieses Medium an das fotografische Bild und seine Komponenten bindet: die Einheit des Bildrahmens, das Verstreichen der Zeit und die besonderen Qualitäten des vorübereilenden Augenblicks. Manche dieser Künstler entwickeln ihre Untersuchungen zum Video parallel zu ihrer fotografischen Arbeit und wechseln fortlaufend zwischen beiden Medien. Daraus ergibt sich ein besonders Verhältnis zum Bild, das uns auffordert, es mit Blick auf seine Instabilität zu begreifen, aber mit Blick auch auf die Fragen, die es in Folge dieser sich wandelnden Praktiken aufwirft.

Mit zeitlicher Tiefe arbeiten

In seinem Aufsatz „The Reflecting Pool de Bill Viola" analysiert Jean-Paul Fargier Violas Video mit seinen Einblendungsprozessen als einen gewagten Sprung des Künstlers in die Videokunst, da man „das geteilte Bild als das Wesen des Mediums Video betrachten"[1] könne. Durch Einblendungen erzeugte Bilder, die verschiedene Modi von Zeitlichkeit und eine Vielzahl paralleler Geschichten enthalten, wären demnach ein wichtiges Charakteristikum von Videokunst. So jedenfalls möchte es in einer Reihe von Arbeiten scheinen, die zum fotografischen Bild und zur aufgehobenen Zeit eine enge Beziehung unterhalten und die, wie Bill Violas berühmtes Video, auf der Grundlage von Störungen verfahren und so Verwirrung in Bezug auf die Wahrnehmung von Bewegungslosigkeit und Bewegung stiften. So stellt David Claerbout Arbeiten her, in denen angeeignete Fotos in den Bereich des Mediums Video einbebracht werden, indem der Künstler in ihre zeitliche Dichte eingreift, um die Gegenwart des Bildes zu finden. In Sans titre (Carl et Julia) (2000) zeigt das Schwarzweißbild einen Mann und seine Tochter beim Frühstück. Beim Betreten des Projektionsraumes finden wir die Augen des Mädchens auf uns gerichtet; sie bannen uns durch die Macht des Mediums Video, Leben wiederzugeben und in der Gegenwart das in der Vergangenheit Gebannte abzuspielen. In einer von Claer-bouts jüngsten Arbeiten, Dancing couple (after: Couples at square dance, McIntosh County, Oklahoma, 1939 or 1940), 2008, ist sein Eingriff noch radikaler: Ein Foto zeigt ein junges Paar beim Tanz, überrascht von dem Blitz, der die beiden unterbrochen und aus der Gegenwart herausgehoben hat.
Claerbout hat dieses Bild gerettet und projiziert und dabei den Akt des Blitzes mit dem Licht des Projektors überlagert. So bekräftigt die Zeitlichkeit der Projektion ihre notwendige Gegenwärtigkeit in einer Gegenüberstellung der Bewegungslosigkeit des fotografischen Prozesses und der Bewegtheit der Projektion. Bekräftigt wird die Künstlichkeit der Konstruktion; diese Einführung einer bewegten Zeitlichkeit im Kern des Standbilds ruft Schwindelgefühle und Unwohlsein hervor. Das „Dazwischen" kommt dem Nichts darin nahe, dass es im Dunkel sorgfältig arrangierter Installationen erwächst und in weitgehend stillen Umgebungen, in denen verräumlichter Ton sparsam verwendet wird.

Das Animationsverfahren ist derzeit recht weit verbreitet, insbesondere als Verlängerung der Zeichnung. Es erlaubt eine radikalere Verzeitlichung und die Verknüpfung verschiedener Bildträger, wie etwa in Hans op de Beecks verstörenden Animationen von Zeichnungen und Fotografien. Die so dargestellten Räume sind eigenartig, weil sie der Wirklichkeit so nahestehen, ohne dass doch die Grenze zwischen jenen und dieser verwischt würde. Jutta Strohmaier, eine junge österreichische Künstlerin, stellt ebenfalls Standbilder her, die sie dann langsam animiert. Wie bei Claerbout sind wir unablässig mit einer Situation konfrontiert, in der der Status des Bildes, sein Wesen und sein Verhältnis zur Zeit unentschieden bleiben. Die Ansammlung von Fotografien führt eine Anmutung von Bewegung ein, die jedoch nicht genügend Schwungkraft gewinnt, um die Stabilität, die das Standbild bietet, zu durchbrechen. Licht spielt eine grundlegende Rolle, indem es das Verstreichen von Zeit im Innersten des fotografierten Raumes bezeichnet, wo zumeist kaum viel geschieht. Passenger (2004) besteht aus einem Wechsel der Lichtatmosphäre in Verbindung mit einer Aufnahme eines Fensters aus fester Perspektive in einem leeren Zimmer. Wir gehen von einem Zustand der Einfärbung in den nächsten über, auf Weiß folgt in einer ruckartigen Metamorphose Blau, dann Rosa und Gelb. Strohmaiers Videos streben niemals danach, eine Illusion von Stetigkeit zu erzeugen; sie verwenden beträchtliche Distanzierungs- und Rahmungstechniken aus der Perspektive eines aufmerksamen, aber phasenverschobenen Beobachters darauf, uns in Übergangsbereiche (leere Zimmer, dichtes Unterholz, städtische Verkehrsflächen) zu führen. Darüberhinaus ist das Bild einer Vielzahl von künstlerischen Verfahren wie Doppeldruck, Konturierung und Farbmanipulation unterworfen, die die Hergestelltheit, die Konstruiertheit des auf die Welt konzentrierten Blicks betonen.

1 THE REFLECTING POOL DE BILL VIOLA, JEAN-PAUL FARGIER, ÉDITIONS YELLOW NOW CÔTÉ FILMS # 2, 2005, S. 14.

Im Abstand zwischen Fotografie und Video öffnet sich so ein Spielraum für ein Nachdenken über unsere Wahrnehmungserfahrungen. Auch der Schweizer Künstler Peter Aerschmann erkundet zeitliche Tiefe, indem er unser Verhältnis zur Raumzeit dekon-stru-iert. Seine Bilder sind Ergebnisse einer Verknüpfung von verschiedenen Einstellungen, in der die verschiedenen Elemente so nebeneinandergesetzt werden, dass sie sich einer einsinnigen Wahrnehmung des Ganzen widersetzen. Natürlich ist jede Figur und jeder Aspekt der Dekoration Teil einer umfassenden Komposition, jedoch ohne dass eine gemeinsame Atmosphäre sie verbände. Wie in Uccellos Gemälden sind die Proportionen gewährleistet und die visuellen Anordnungen in sich stimmig, doch die Aussage gilt einer großen Einsamkeit. Die Kamera gleitet seitwärts durch diese Aufbauten, entdeckt nach und nach die einsamen, in die Wiederholung einer Geste und in einheitslose Landschaften eingeschlossenen Figuren. In Aerschmanns Videos ist die Raumzeit zutiefst regellos geworden, doch unser Blick folgt weiterhin der Kamera auf ihrer langsamen Reise. Seine Arbeiten sind zwischen der herben Statik der Architekturelemente und der Bewegung von Figuren in einer Schleife angesiedelt, zwischen Fotografie, Video und Malerei: im Kern der Fragen, denen sich „Mutations II" zuwendet.

Rahmungen

Dem Bild einen Rahmen zu geben ist eine Geste der Abgrenzung und des Ergreifens, aber auch der Distanzierung des Sichtbaren und bedeutet implizit eine Stellungnahme der Welt gegenüber. Eine für die Geschichte der Videokunst wesentliche Herangehensweise war es, die Kamera auf sich selbst zu richten. Vito Acconci, Peter Campus, Bruce Nauman, Joan Jonas (und viele andere) zeigten ihre eigenen Körper in verschiedener Weise im Spiegel der Videoaufzeichnung. Doch jenseits der faszinierenden und voyeuristischen Unmittelbarkeit einer filmischen Darstellung des Selbst ermöglicht das Verhältnis zum eigenen Spiegelbild eine Erkundung des Erscheinens und Verschwindens des eigenen Abbilds.
So entwickelte Jean Otth, ebenfalls ein Schweizer Künstler, in den 1970er Jahren eine Video-Spiegel-Apparatur, in der er mit seinem eigenen Bild spielte, es bestimmte und verschleierte, und die Gefühle hinterfragte, die wir erkennbar werden lassen, wenn wir uns einer solchen Manipulation des Bildes unserer selbst gegenübersehen. Das Video ermöglicht ihm das Spiel mit dem eigenen Spiegelbild, indem er sich die Zeit nahm, es zu stören, es in Gefahr zu bringen und so die Beziehung sichtbar und hörbar zu machen, die wir zu unserem eigenen Abbild unterhalten. Miroir (2000) von Elina Brotherus, einer finnischen Künstlerin, die sowohl fotografisch als auch mit Video arbeitet, ist gleichfalls eine Inszenierung des Selbst, die das Spiegelbild distanziert, indem sie sein Erscheinen dem Verstreichen der Zeit unterwirft. In der Fotoserie posiert Brotherus nackt vor einem beschlagenen Badezimmerspiegel. Zunächst wird das Spiegelbild also unterdrückt, um zwischen dem Körper und seinem Abbild die Erfahrung einer Verschiebung einzuziehen. Doch der Übergang von einem Foto zum nächsten enthüllt nach und nach das Spiegelbild. Die Rahmung im Video ist beinahe die gleiche, sodass dieses auf den ersten Blick die Fotoserie wiederholt. Doch ermöglicht die Bewegtheit des Bildes nun, die Lebendigkeit des Prozesses wieder einzuführen, indem dem Körper ein zentraler Ort in der sich verändernden Oberfläche des Spiegels eingeräumt wird. Hier ist Brotherus' Atem ein Hauptelement: Durch seine Wirkung auf die Atmosphäre wird er ein Teil des Phänomens des erscheinenden und verschwindenden Spiegelbildes und führt so erneut die Dimension des Organischen in eine Situation ein, in der der Körper Hauptbestandteil des Bildes ist.

In der Einleitung seines Aufsatzes L'entre-images erklärt Raymond Bellour, es scheine, „als träten wir mit dem Video und allem, was dazugehört, in eine andere Bildzeit ein"[2]. Selbst wenn das Video auf fotografische Weise komponiert ist, durch Sistierung des Rahmens, ruft das im Verlauf der Zeit Geschehende eine neue Beziehung zu Zeit und Raum hervor. Der junge tschechische Künstler Jan Kuděj hat mehrere Videos produziert, die die Erfahrung der Zeit hinterfragen. Zum Beispiel kombiniert er zwei Projektionen, die zwei feste Einstellungen zeigen, einerseits eine Reihe von vier Rolltreppen, andererseits einen Baum auf einem Feld. Die Rolltreppen erscheinen in einer kurzen Videoschleife, der ihre auf- und absteigenden Bewegungen das Tempo vorgeben, während der Baum in einer Montage von Standbildern dargestellt wird, sodass das Laub sich ruckartig entfaltet. Die Verknüpfung mechanischen Flusses und natürlicher Unstetigkeit setzt eine Distanz zur dynamischen Wahrnehmung der Wirklichkeit. Im Widerspiel zu einer Gesellschaft, in der Bewegung die Regel ist, fügt Kuděj Zerlegungen und Schnitte ins Bild ein und entzieht uns so den friedvollen Anblick eines im Wind sanft zitternden Baumes (ein Motiv, das Claerbout ebenfalls auf großartige Weise in Boom gefilmt hat: eine feste Einstellung auf einen Baum, der Kudějs Baum ähnlich ist; diese Aufnahme jedoch schwelgt in der faszinierenden Flüssigkeit der Bewegung). Indem das Video in sein Verhältnis zur Fotografie gesetzt wird, wird seine Fähigkeit, die Illusion von Stetigkeit hervorzubringen, in Zweifel gezogen. Die Arbeiten führen ein Ungleichgewicht, eine Instabilität in unsere Beziehung zur Welt ein, indem sie Situationen konstruieren, deren Fluss gestaut wird.

Auf der Suche nach dem Blick

Weckt die Fotografie so Zweifel am Video, so ist dieses auch ein Spielraum, indem sich Ideen bezüglich des fotografischen Blicks entwickeln lassen. Genau das unternimmt der französische Künstler Laurent Goldring mit seinen Arbeiten in der Tradition des fotografischen Porträts. Er hinterfragt fotografische Darstellungen des Körpers, indem er Modelle in einem Fotostudio frontal abfilmt. Die Zeitlichkeit des Videos erlaubt es ihm, das „Bildwerden" der Körper

2 RAYMOND BELLOUR, L'ENTRE-IMAGES, PHOTO, CINÉMA, VIDÉO, ÉDITIONS DE LA DIFFÉRENCE, 2002.

seiner Modelle zu untersuchen, die allesamt Tänzer sind (die meisten sind auch Choreografen). Da der Bühnenraum eng und die Videokamera fest montiert ist, können sich die Tänzer kaum bewegen, wodurch ihre Bewegungen sich auf die Einnahme von Posituren konzentrieren. Sobald eine Pose eingenommen wird, gleitet der Körper unter Laurent Goldrings Anleitung sanft von einem Erscheinungsbild in das nächste hinüber, hervorgehoben noch durch die Ausleuchtung und das Spiel von Licht und Schatten. Die Bilder, die so entstehen, haben oft etwas Monströses; sie fangen den Blick ein und fesseln die Einbildungskraft. Die Bewegung ermöglicht den Übergang von einem Zustand von Sichtbarkeit in einen anderen wie auch den Eintritt in einen Prozess symbolischer Verfremdung, zuletzt erweisen sich die Videos jedoch als Folge von Standbildern. Jede Form nimmt den Blick gefangen. Daraufhin entwickelt Laurent Goldring aus dem Video Fotografien. So gelangt er über einen schöpferischen Spielraum, der die Dinge im Zentrum eines extrem konstruierten Mechanismus erscheinen lässt, am Ende zu einem Standbild. Die Instabilität des Mediums Video entfernt die reflexive Neigung zur Transsubstantiation, die wir beim Anblick eines Fotos verspüren: Laurent Goldrings Bilder/Körper bekräftigen ihren Symbolstatus, breiten bei der Entwicklung auf Papier ihre Pixel aus. Sie stehen beispielhaft für die Verschiebung fotografischer Untersuchungen, die im Kern des Mediums Video stattfindet.

So ermöglicht der Übergang von einem Medium ins andere die Distanzierung einer Praxis und die Hinterfragung ihrer Qualitäten, wie im Fall des deutschen Fotografen Oliver Möst. Seine Arbeiten beruhen auf seinem persönlichen Verhältnis zum Gesichtssinn. Seine eingeschränkte Sehkraft hat ihn letztlich dazu veranlasst, eine Sicht auf die Welt zu konstruieren, in der Unschärfen und ihre bildnerischen Qualitäten vorherrschen. Allerdings ist sein Einsatz des Mediums Video nicht lediglich eine Fortsetzung seiner Experimente im Bereich der Bewegung. Dieser entspricht vielmehr einer anderen Notwendigkeit, nämlich der, sein Verhältnis zur sichtbaren Welt durch Filme von sich selbst zu inszenieren: So zeigen brown eyes, hide & seek und between kurze in seinem Atelier aufgenommene Szenen. In der erstgenannten Arbeit spielen Mösts Hände mit seinen Augen, Murmeln, die er sich anschließend in den Mund steckt. Die zweite zeigt ihn mit einer roten Augenbinde; er zählt laut, bis ein Blitzlicht ihn blendet. In der dritten kämpft er mit zwei Trennwänden, die er öffnet und schließt. Stets ist er ohne Oberbekleidung zu sehen, unmittelbar körperlich in Situationen verwickelt, die metaphorisch für sein Verhältnis zum Blick stehen: die ironische Kritik des unzulänglichen Sehorgans in brown eyes, die Konstruktion eines Parallelismus zwischen zwei Formen der Beeinträchtigung des Sehsinns in hide & seek, deren eine durch Blockade des Wahrnehmungsmoments (die Augenbinde), die andere durch ein Übermaß an Licht (das Blitzlicht) verursacht wird. In between erkundet Möst die richtige Art, die Welt wahrzunehmen, indem er die Konstruktion des Präsentationsraums variiert. Natürlich hinterfragen diese Situationen sämtlich auch den Akt des Fotografierens an sich, seine Bedingungen und Gegebenheiten. Die Rahmung des letzten Videos, landescape, nimmt die Form einer optischen Linse an; sie ist ebenfalls das Ergebnis der Kombination einer Lochblende und einer Videokamera. Die Tonquelle liegt außerhalb des Sichtfelds der Kamera, wodurch ein Kontrast entsteht zwischen der Unbeweglichkeit der friedlich in zwei symmetrische Aufnahmen geteilten imaginären Landschaft und dem Geräusch eines in regelmäßigen Abständen geworfenen und aufprallenden Steines. Möst ist im Bild nicht zu sehen, aber durch sein Handeln anwesend. Diesmal sehen wir, wie er selbst, nichts außer der von ihm hervorgerufenen Einbildung; die auf der zugefrorenen Oberfläche des Wassers erscheinenden Zeichen sind im Wesentlichen die Träger des Sehsinns.

Tonbilder

Seit ihrer Entstehung im Kern des Fluxus und seit Nam June Paik hat Videokunst außerordentlich von ihren Verbindungen zur Kreativität im Bereich der Musik profitiert. Ton ist oftmals weit mehr als eine das Bild begleitende Tonspur, ist vielmehr diesem innerlich; und dies so sehr, dass das Bild manchmal auf klanghafte Weise behandelt wird. So siedeln Robert Cahens Videos musikalische Kompositionen im Zentrum der Filmaufnahmesituation an, und wenn der Zeit besondere Bedeutung zukommt, dann deshalb, weil sie der engen Beziehung zwischen Ton und Bild entspringt, dem Ausdruck subjektiver Wahrnehmung der Wirklichkeit. Der Fotograf und Videokünstler Gast Bouschet und die Komponistin Nadine Hilbert arbeiten aus dieser Perspektive zusammen: In ihren Videos sind Bild und Ton unauflöslich verbunden, jedes infiziert das andere und prägt seiner Entstehung seinen Stempel auf. Das Bild ist wiederum zumeist aus Festeinstellungen zusammengesetzt, die einander in übergangsloser Reihung folgen. In Dreamsequence tragen uns Kamera und Tonspur Bruchstücke durchquerter Universen (wie nebliger Wälder, Autobahnen und Stadtzentren) zu, aber ohne dass wir uns eingewöhnen oder dem Blick folgen dürften. Wir gehen von einem Blickpunkt zum nächsten über – als stünden wir vor einer Fotoserie –, von einer Klangsituation zur nächsten; Wiederholungen gibt es, aber keinen beruhigenden Verweis auf Kontinuität. Der Titel setzt diese Operation in Beziehung zu einem Traumzustand, in dem Entfernung fortlaufend durchquert, verschiedene Raumzeiten durchwandert werden; durchgehalten ist dabei einzig die subjektive Perspektive des Träumenden und in diesem Falle des Betrachters. Damit erlaubt die Videokunst, ein Tempo zu finden, bei dem die Erfahrung der Wahrnehmung widerhallt; so in Christoph Brechs Opus 110a (2001). In diesem Video ist das Bild ganz auf den Rücken eines Dirigenten während eines Konzerts konzentriert. Die Klangkomponente ist eine starke Präsenz; im Bild wird der Rhythmus zu einer monochromen, beinahe abstrakten Bewegung und ist zugleich mit der körperlichen Wirklichkeit der Gesten des Dirigenten aufgeladen. Brech stimmt die Bewegungen des Rückens ab, instrumentiert das Ganze, verlangsamt, beschleunigt, hält die Zeit zurück oder lässt sie laufen, um eine

Harmonie von Ton und Bild zu erreichen. Der Rücken wird zur Projektionsfläche, jede Falte im Anzug des Dirigenten eine Landschaft, ein Ankerplatz, an dem die Einbildungskraft einsetzen kann.

Ton kann das Bild auch vorantreiben, leiten und mit Bedeutung füllen. Er kann eine Erzählung entspinnen, Sprache in das Bild einführen oder zwischen beiden einen Dialog entfalten, wie in Gary Hills Arbeiten. Von einem Körper gesprochener, vorgelesener oder vorgetragener Text steht im Zentrum seiner Videos und hinterfragt so auf der verbalen Ebene, was ein Bild ausmacht. Die Praxis der Videokunst lässt sich vom Kino inspirieren, distanziert sich aber auch von ihm durch mehrdeutige oder widersprüchliche Konstruktionen, die die Erzählform sprengen und ihre Codes in Frage stellen. So kommen Alice Andersons Videos in ihrer Ästhetik dem Kino sehr nahe, unterscheiden sich von ihm aber deutlich in ihren Erzählmitteln. Dieser Abstand erscheint am deutlichsten in Journal, wo sehr kurze filmische Sequenzen durch den Tonschnitt zusammengefügt werden. Der Erzählfaden zieht sich hindurch, und während Zwischentitel einen Zeitraum anzeigen (einen Monat, einen Tag, ein Jahr), ist der zutiefst persönlichen Geschichte hier eine Grenze gesetzt. Die Bilder bieten Anhaltspunkte, Einblicke in einen biographischen Augenblick, lassen aber zumeist jeden Versuch einer Deutung unbefriedigt. Auch sind die Einstellungen äußerst kurz, sodass uns nicht viel Zeit bleibt, sich in ihnen umzusehen. Journal hält den Betrachter im Banne der Musik und Bilder, die jedoch eine Erklärung schuldig bleiben.

Das Bild installieren

Videokunst unterliegt stärkeren Anforderungen an die Präsentation als Fotografie, da sie in einem Raum installiert werden muss, der ihren technischen Eigenschaften gerecht wird. Während Fotografie vor allem einen Dialog mit dem Ausstellungsraum darstellt, in dem sich die Bilder gleichrangig dem Blick darbieten, neigt Video dazu, Isolation und Negation des Realraums erforderlich zu machen (wie in den „Black Boxes", wo das Bild in Dunkelheit geborgen und unter günstigen klanglichen Bedingungen gezeigt wird). So setzt Video, wie in Bill Violas Installationen, seine eigene Raumzeit durch. Einige Künstler jedoch zeigen Videos, die mit dem, was jenseits des Bildes liegt, in Dialog treten. Claerbouts Bildschirm-Wände stehen beispielhaft für dieses „Dazwischen", da die Videos – sie sind durch Wände aus durchlöcherter dünner Leinwand sichtbar, die auch als Projektionsflächen dienen – wie in einer Fotoausstellung aufeinander antworten. Auch „in situ"-Installation ist hier von Bedeutung, wo Video von einem Raum Besitz ergreift, ihn bewohnt, indem es auf das, was er ausstrahlt, antwortet. Ulrich Gebert entwarf Keine Dialoge (2004) für einen bestimmen Raum – einen fensterlosen und in schmale Zimmer unterteilten Betonbau, was die Beklemmung der Arbeit noch unterstrich. Die Darstellungsbedingungen waren mit dem Ausstellungsraum, dem Kunstbunker Tumulka in München, gegeben, ohne das noch etwas hätte geändert werden müssen. So tauchten die Betrachter in eine militärisch-kalte Umgebung ein, wo sie einem psychologischen Test beiwohnten, den eine Mannschaft der GSG 9 (einer Elite-Antiterroreinheit, die nach den Ereignissen während der Olympischen Spiele in München im Jahr 1972 geschaffen wurde) zu ertragen hatte. Ulrich Gebert zeigt uns, wie diese Männer blitzendem Stroboskoplicht ausgesetzt werden, und verlängert die Erfahrung für den Betrachter, der sich einem aus optisch aggressiven Standbildern in ruckhafter Folge zusammengesetzten Video gegenübersieht. Der Titel lenkt die Aufmerksamkeit auf die den Männern zugefügte Regression, deren Selbstbeherrschung hier auf der Probe steht. Bewegung ist der Ort von Aggressivität, denn indem das Video das Bild seiner Fixierung entreißt und eine sensorielle Stetigkeit erzeugt, wird der stereoskopische Akt bedeutungstragend und bezieht den Körper des Betrachters ein.

Darüberhinaus wächst dem Medium Video eine skulpturale Dimension zu, sobald Künstler, statt seine Materialität durch von Zeit und Raum der Ausstellung abgekoppelte Projektionen durchzustreichen, sich seinem Abhängigkeitsverhältnis von dem zuwenden, was ihm als Quelle dienen mag (und das es zur Artikulation seiner ungreifbaren Gegenwart benötigt). Die Schirmoberfläche kann den Rauminhalt des Bildes ausdehnen – so die Augen in Tony Ourslers Arbeiten – oder der Künstler kann Umgebungen schaffen, in die das Bild integriert ist – so in Thomas Hirschhorns Installationen. In diesem Sinne errichtet Pirmin Blum Kartonskulpturen mit daran aufgehängten Standbildern und integrierten Videoschirmen. Das Videobild kommt ohne die Monumentalität der Projektion und die Wirkung seines Erscheinens aus und bekräftigt seine realen Grundlagen. Eine von Blums Installationen verbindet Fotos mit zwei in einer Autofabrik aufgenommenen Videos von Sicherheitstestverfahren. Airbag ist eine Zeitlupenaufnahme aus fester Perspektive, die die Aktivierung eines Airbags zeigt. Es ist faszinierend zu sehen, wie der Stoffsack sich aufbläst und zusammenfällt. Wir werden Zeugen des geringfügigen Einsatzes einer Form in einem Zustand fortwährender Entwicklung. Das zweite Video, Spuk, besteht aus rasant montierten Aufnahmen aus der Perspektive zweier Kameras während eines Windschutzscheibentests. Im durch die luftige und poetische Ruhe von Airbag vorgegebenen Rahmen ist Spuk von optisch wie akustisch gewaltsamer Wirkung. Zusammengenommen vereinigen die beiden Arbeiten so auf ironische Weise sehr verschiedene Rhythmen, und das auf der Grundlage einer Heimwerker-Ästhetik, die gegen den industriell hochentwickelten Ort absticht, an dem die Bilder hergestellt wurden.

Alice Anderson wählte eine Sequenz aus Journal aus, um daraus ihre Installation Insomnia (2006) herzustellen. Der Besucher ist eingeladen, sich auf einem violetten Himmelbett niederzulassen und die (als Loop gezeigte) einminütige Videoauswahl auf einem über dem Bett aufgehängten Bildschirm zu betrachten. Dieser Rezeptionsrahmen lässt den Betrachter die Bilder als die eines halbbewussten Zustands zwischen Wachen und Schlafen wahrnehmen, ohne ihm doch wirklich die Zeit zu lassen, sich ganz in sie zu vertiefen: kaum hat sich der Betrachter hingelegt, fängt das Video schon wieder von vorne an, was der Versuchung, es sich bequem zu machen, entgegenwirkt. Es fällt uns meistens schwer, uns Videokunst anzusehen, weil die Arbeiten oft zu lang sind und die anstrengenden Bedingungen, unter denen wir sie betrachten, schnell ermüdend wirken. Gegenüber der Fotografie ist dies sicher ihre größte Einschränkung, die erschwert, sie auszustellen und zu bestrachten. Vielleicht muss man daher die Schlaflosigkeit pflegen, das Dazwischen, das uns in die Praktiken versetzt, die auf halbem Weg zwischen den zwei Medien liegen, und uns zwischen verschiedenen Zuständen des Bildes kreisen lässt.

Mathilde Roman

Als promovierte Kunstwissenschaftlerin der Universität Paris-Sorbonne, hat sich Mathilde Roman auf die Videokunst spezialisiert. Sie ist Autorin der Publikation „Art vidéo et mise en scène de soi" (erschienen im Verlag L'Harmattan, 2008). Als Mitglied des Verbandes AICA (Association Internationale des Critiques d'art) schreibt Roman für verschiedene Magazine wie www.lacritique.org (online-Magazin für zeitgenössische Kunst), Art press und Mouvement. Sie unterrichtet Kunstgeschichte am „Pavillon Bosio", einer Hochschule für Kunst und Szenographie in Monaco, Frankreich.

Geteilte und wiedergewonnene Zeit (Zu Raum und Dauer in Foto- und Videokunst)

„In Wirklichkeit gibt es keinen durchgehenden Rhythmus der Dauer; man kann sich verschiedene Rhythmen vorstellen, langsamere oder schnellere, welche jeweils dem Grad der Spannung oder Entspannung der Bewußtseine entsprechen und ihnen dadurch ihren Platz in der Reihe der Wesen anweisen."
Henri Bergson[1]

Die Mahnung zur Vorsicht einem Entweder-Oder gegenüber – nämlich entweder das statische Bild oder das verzeitlichte Kontinuum der Bilder – verfolgt die Fotografie seit der Ankunft des Kinofilms im letzten Jahrzehnt des 19. Jahrhunderts. Eine Vorstellung ohne Wirklichkeitsbezug hat sich herausgebildet, die sich um den toten Moment der herausgeschnittenen Fotografie rankt, einen der Zeit entnommenen Moment, als wäre er der Gegensatz zur laufenden Rahmenerzählung, die der Film zeigt.[2] Mit der Einführung des Magnetvideobands und, in jüngerer Vergangenheit, digitaler, pixel-basierter Technologien mögen wir uns vorgestellt haben, diese Dichotomie sei zu Ende gegangen. Doch endet sie nicht in der „Zeit", sondern in der Dauer; letztere ist ohne festgeschriebene oder gesicherte Definition. Heute ist die Annahme einer linearen und universellen Zeit als Grundlage nicht mehr bestimmend für die Wahrnehmung des fotografischen Bildes. Zeit wird, wie Bergson behauptete, von verschiedenen Menschen an verschiedenen Orten und sogar von der selben Person in verschiedenen Lebensphasen verschieden erfahren. Die lineare oder diachrone Vergangenheit lässt sich beliebig begrifflich erfassen, aber darin liegt nicht die Grundlage der wirklichen synchronen Verinnerlichung von Zeit.

Eine Foto- und Videoausstellung „Mutations II" zu betiteln, bedeutet, sich direkt den fortlaufenden Prozessen der Veränderung zuzuwenden. „To mutate" bedeutet, eine Verwandlung zu erfahren oder zu verursachen; letztere wiederum ist als ein Anderswerden, eine Veränderung des Wesens, der Form, der Eigenschaften von etwas definiert. Und „mutation" oder Werden (das, was auf der Schwelle ist) kann nicht als einfache lineare Zeit existieren; seiner wörtlichen Definition nach existiert es als fortlaufender Prozess unausgesetzter Veränderung. Das Werden besteht demnach als in einem fortlaufenden Prozess „aufgehobene Zeit"; dieser Prozess kann nur als Zeit, die unausgesetzte Dauer ist, verstanden werden. Womöglich meinte Eliot diesen Zusammenstoß, diesen Aufprall, als er von davon sprach, dass „Gegenwart und Vergangenheit / [...] stets beide in der Zukunft gegenwärtig [sind] / Und die Zukunft in der Vergangenheit."[3] Daher bleibt das „Werden" bestehen als „ewige Möglichkeit". Die Brücke dieser Dauer haben vor langer Zeit Bruce Nauman und andere beschritten; das erhellt, warum neue Medien, die sich mit Performance und Video auseinandersetzen, uns zu einem flexibleren Verständnis dessen verhelfen, worin die Grundlage eines statischen oder verzeitlichten Bildes besteht. Deleuze macht das (zweifellos im Bezug auf Bergson) deutlich, wenn er schreibt: „Sodass man, wann immer man sich vor einer Dauer oder in einer Dauer finden wird, auf die Existenz eines sich wandelnden und irgendwo offenen Ganzen wird schließen können."[4] Das bedeutet nicht, Kausalität zu leugnen; es legt jedoch nahe, dass diese manchmal verborgen ist

1 HENRI BERGSON, MATERIE UND GEDÄCHTNIS. EINE ABHANDLUNG ÜBER DIE BEZIEHUNG ZWISCHEN KÖRPER UND GEIST, HAMBURG: MEINER, 1991, S. 205F.

2 SOWOHL ROLAND BARTHES ALS AUCH SUSAN SONTAG SPRACHEN MIT BLICK AUF DIE FOTOGRAFIE ENTWEDER VON SCHICKSAL ODER VON MELANCHOLIE, WORAUS SICH SO ETWAS WIE EINE STRUKTURALISTISCHE ROMANTIK ERGAB, UND DADURCH BLIEB DIE FOTOGRAFIE IRGENDWIE ZWISCHEN DEM PUNCTUM ODER „ERFÜLLTEN AUGENBLICK" UND DEM STUDIUM (BARTHES) ODER „ENGBEGRENZTEN SPIEGELBILD" STECKEN. SIEHE ROLAND BARTHES, DIE HELLE KAMMER. BEMERKUNGEN ZUR PHOTOGRAPHIE, FRANKFURT A. M.: SUHRKAMP, 1989, UND SUSAN SONTAG, „IN PLATOS HÖHLE", IN ÜBER PHOTOGRAPHIE, (1971), MÜNCHEN UND WIEN, CARL HANSER, 1989.

3 T.S. ELIOT, „BURNT NORTON", IN FOUR QUARTETS, LONDON, FABER AND FABER (1944), 1979, S. 13; DIE ZWEI NÄCHSTEN ZEILEN LAUTEN: „IST ALLE ZEIT EWIG GEGENWÄRTIG,/ SO IST ALLE ZEIT UNERLÖSBAR."

4 GILLES DELEUZE, CINÉMA. I. L'IMAGE-MOUVEMENT, PARIS: LES ÉDITIONS DE MINUIT, 1983, S. 20. DELEUZE BEZIEHT SICH AUSFÜHRLICH AUF MATERIE UND GEDÄCHTNIS UND DIE SCHÖPFERISCHE ENTWICKLUNG (1907, DT. 1921). ZU SEINEM VERHÄLTNIS ZU BERGSON SIEHE GILLES DELEUZE, BERGSON ZUR EINFÜHRUNG (1966), HAMBURG, 1989.

und nicht unmittelbar erkennbar. Um es deutlich zu sagen: Auf eben dieses Prinzip gründet sich „mutation" oder Verwandlung, wie eben die weitestverbreitete Form von Verwandlung die von Amöben ist, die man in einer Petrischale beobachten kann.[5] Zeitgenössische Foto- und Videokünstler bestreiten heute systematisch das dualistische Schisma zwischen dem statischen und dem Bewegungsbild, von dem das Denken der Vergangenheit abhängig war. Mechanismus dieses Anderswerdens ist nach wie vor das menschliche Bewusstsein, doch dieses nicht als Zweck an sich, sondern als Bewusstsein im Prozess eines unablässigen „Offenwerdens": einer einheitlichen Zielvorstellung, der eine Vielfalt von Ergebnissen entspricht.

In der jüngeren Digitalfotografie und sogar in zeitgenössischen Entwicklungen in den analogen Techniken ist es Künstlern gelungen, Foto- und Videokunst jenseits des deterministischen Rahmens einer festen linearen Zeit neu zu orientieren. Die neue Fotografie hat sich vom herausgeschnittenen Bild befreit, das auf den Augenblick, da ein Knopf gedrückt wird, reduzierbar ist; wie umgekehrt die Vorstellung dessen, was Video- und Filmschnitt sind, sich längst schon von Kontinuitätsannahmen unabhängig gemacht hat. In beiden Fällen sind die Verhältnisse zunehmend für Manipulationen offen. Bedenken wir das, so müssen wir die zunehmenden Diskontinuitäten akzeptieren und zu umfassen suchen, die die Grundlage unseres modernen Lebens darstellen, worauf Foucault schon vor langer Zeit hingewiesen hat.[6] Eine nützliche Analogie und flankierende Beobachtung betrifft hier das Wort „Mutation" selbst in seinem linguistischen Sinn: Ein Laut verändert sich, indem er an einen anderen Laut in der Nähe assimiliert wird. Kaum überraschend dürfte insofern sein, dass „Mutation" und „mutuality" (Gegenseitigkeit) vom selben lateinischen Stamm abgeleitet sind. Ihr Verhältnis zueinander ist von wechselseitiger freier Anpassung aneinander in einem diskontinuierlich wirkenden System geprägt. Der nichtbiologische Gebrauch des Words „Mutation" (relativ wertfrei) stand lange im Gegensatz zu „Evolution" (relativ wertbeladen). Jenes beschreibt Wandel einfach als diskontinuierlichen oder zufälligen Zustand der Anpassung, während dieses normalerweise die zweckgerichtete Teleologie natürlicher Selektion impliziert – etwas mutiert zu etwas anderem, aber es entwickelt sich evolutionär in Richtung auf etwas.

Die zunehmende Bedeutung für Fotografie und Video in den letzten etwa dreißig Jahren hat so nicht nur mit der Aufhebung alter stereotyper Vorstellungen bezüglich der ehemaligen Grenzen zwischen dem statischen und dem bewegten Bild zu tun; sie hat auch ein ausgeprägteres Wechselspiel innerhalb der Prozesse ihrer gemeinsamen medialen Wurzeln ermöglicht. Auf diese zunehmende Verinnerlichung der integrierten Prozesse von Fotografie und Video bezog ich mich mit meinem Untertitel „zu Raum und Dauer". In der Weise, wie sich jeder einzelne Künstler die neuen Technologien, die er auf seine bildnerische Praxis anwendet, nutzbar macht, findet er eine persönliche Charakterisierung oder Begleitfigur von Raum und Zeit, prägt er sie ihr wie einen individuellen und unverwechselbaren Schatten ein. Daher geht es in zeitgenössischer Foto- und Videokunst weniger um ein vornweg definiertes oder gegebenes thematisches Material als darum, welcher Behandlung dieses Material unterworfen wird. Worauf sie jedoch Antwort gibt, ist eine reflexive Situation, in der die Zeitinhalte elastisch sind und oftmals auf sich zurück und in sich selbst hinein gefaltet sind. Zeit ist nicht länger die Uhr, sondern nun die Schleife; und die Schleife (oder Ellipse) ist der Stand einer inneren Kreisförmigkeit oder Beugung, die durch ihr eigenes sich selbst definierendes System ermessen wird.[7]

Seit den Anfängen der Videokunst in den 1960er und 70er Jahren, einerseits in Anwendung als Kritik der zunehmenden Kommerzialisierung und der Konsumkultur, die das Fernsehen bewirkte, andererseits als das, was später Kunstvideo genannt wurde, bot sie ein Potential, das Wesen der linearen Zeit zu hinterfragen, das in den früheren Medien nicht bestanden hatte.[8] Der Aufbau von Filmen aus Einzelbildern ermöglichte zwar das System des Schneidens und Kopierens in der Filmbearbeitung, blieb aber weit hinter dem zurück, was die Unmittelbarkeit des Videobands brachte und die damit verbundenen Möglichkeiten beinahe sofortiger Rückkopplungen und Überlagerungen und die Fähigkeit, unabgeschlossene oder abstrakte Erzählstränge auf den Schirm zu bringen.[9] Doch begann Videokunst auch als Kritik der Massenmedien Fernsehen und Werbung, ging sie bald dazu über (anders als der strukturalistische Film, der innerhalb des Systems ansetzte), noch das Prinzip linearen und erzählerischen Zusammenhangs selbst zu dekonstruieren.[10] Sie ermöglichte neue Herangehensweisen, durch die Zeit und Raum auf neue Weise zusammengebracht wurden. Sie wurde nicht nur im Performancebereich eingesetzt,

5 DAS WORT AMIBE, VOM GRIECHISCHEN AMOIBÊ („WANDLUNG" ODER „UMTAUSCH") ABGELEITET, WURDE ZUERST VON DEM FRANZÖSISCHEN NATURFORSCHER JEAN-BAPTISTE BORY DE SAINT-VINCENT (1778-1846) VERWENDET.

6 FOUCAULT SPRICHT VON DER UNAUSWEICHLICHEN VERVIELFÄLTIGUNG DER DISKONTINUITÄTEN: „GESCHICHTE ERSCHEINT DANN NICHT ALS GROSSE KONTINUITÄT HINTER EINER DISKONTINUIERLICHEN ERSCHEINUNG, SONDERN ALS GEWIRR EINANDER ÜBERLAGENDER DISKONTINUITÄTEN". MICHEL FOUCAULT, "RETURN TO HISTORY", MICHEL FOUCAULT, ESSENTIAL WORKS OF FOUCAULT 1954-1984, BD. 2, AESTHETICS, HG. VON JAMES D. FAUBION, LONDON, HARMONDSWORTH (1998), 2000, S. 429.

7 GILLES DELEUZE, « QU'EST-CE QU'UN ÉVÉNEMENT? », IN LE PLI. LEIBNIZ ET LE BAROQUE, PARIS: LES ÉDITIONS DE MINUIT, 1988, S. 108: « INSÉPARABLES DE PROCESSUS D'ACTUALISATION OU DE RÉALISATION DANS LESQUELS ILS ENTRENT, ILS N'ONT DE PERMANENCE QUE DANS LES LIMITES DES FLUX QUI LES RÉALISENT, OU DES PRÉHENSIONS QUI LES ACTUALISENT. »

8 VIDEO ERSCHIEN AUF DER BÜHNE ZUERST IM SINNE DER POLITISCH-AKTIVISTISCH DOKUMENTARISCHEN HERANGEHENSWEISEN VON KÜNSTLERN WIE LES LEVINE UND FRANK GILLETTE ODER ALS VIDEO-ALS-KUNST BEI DEM FLUXUS-KÜNSTLER NAM JUNE PAIK. SIEHE MICHAEL RUSH, NEW MEDIA IN THE LATE TWENTIETH CENTURY, LONDON, THAMES & HUDSON, 1999, S. 80-81. SIEHE AUCH DIE AUSFÜHRLICHE ANALYSE VON PAIKS WERK IN THE WORLDS OF NAM JUNE PAIK, SOLOMON GUGGENHEIM MUSEUM, NEW YORK, 2000.

9 MICHAEL RUSH, VIDEO ART, LONDON THAMES & HUDSON, 2003, S. 15: „WAS AN DIESER NEUEN TECHNOLOGIE SO AUFREGEND WAR, WAR IHRE FÄHIGKEIT, EREIGNISSE IN ECHTZEIT SOFORT AUFZUZEICHNEN. IN GEWISSER WEISE WURDE DIE ZEIT SELBST DURCH EINEN EINGRIFF DES MENSCHEN MANIPULIERT."

10 SEAN CUBITT, TIMESHIFT: ON VIDEO CULTURE, LONDON, ROULEDGE, 1991. SIEHE AUCH DOUG HALL UND SALLY JO FIFER (HG.), ILLUMINATING VIDEO: AN ESSENTIAL GUIDE TO VIDEO ART, NEW YORK, APERTURE, 1990 UND NEUAUSGABEN.

um das Wesen des Performativen selbst aufzuzeichnen und in Frage zu stellen, wie etwa bei Nauman und Acconci. Sie entwickelte sich rasch in Richtung einer Hinterfragung der Natur von Orten der Repräsentation, eine Richtung, die später installative Videokunst genannt wurde.[11] Diese mischte durch Verwendung einer Vielzahl von Kanälen ganz wörtlich den Einsatz differentieller Zeitformen auf. Ein Eindruck von Unmittelbarkeit ist der Kern der „ewigen Gegenwart", und Video wurde zur Verlängerung unmittelbarer Gegenwart in den Ateliers vieler Künstler, darin durchaus nicht von jedem anderen angemessenen Werkzeug zu unterscheiden, das ein Künstler dort finden mochte. In der Tat legt das oftmals befürwortete Verhältnis zwischen Video und Malerei von diesem Phänomen deutliches Zeugnis ab. Dass der Videobildschirm als ein Bild einschließendes Objekt, im weiteren dann als Skulptur und schließlich als vollständige Umgebungsinstallation eintreten konnte, bedeutete, dass Video zur Übergangswirklichkeit oder zur Schnittstelle zwischen verschiedenen Medien wurde. Es öffnete sich für Beziehungen zum Gemachten (traditionelle Begriffe des Kunstwerks), hinterfragte ihren Status als Kunstwerke, die Orte ihrer Rezeption, und stellte die Geschichtsschreibung der Grenzen zwischen verschiedenen Medien in Frage. Wie der Zwischenraum zwischen den Worten in einem Stück von Beckett wirkte es als der Raum des „Werdens" einer ungesicherten zeitlichen Dauer.[12]

Fotokünstler sahen sich veranlasst, ihre Praxis im Verhältnis zum Video zu überdenken; und zwar schon lange bevor die neusten digitalen Technologien auf den Plan traten, nicht zuletzt, weil das aus dem Video entnommene Standbild Vorstellungen vom entscheidenden Moment der Kamera untergrub.[13] Die erste Wirkung war, dass die Fotografie gezwungen war, sich aufs neue mit dem Zeitinhalt des Bildermachens auseinanderzusetzen. War die Unmittelbarkeit des Augenblicks das zündende Moment gewesen, das die Fotografie im Gefolge moderner Entwicklungen in der Kamera- und Linsentechnik antrieb, so war deutlich, dass die Belichtungszeit in einem doppelten Sinn die Rahmenbedingung solcher Entnahme darstellte. Der entscheidende Augenblick, wie auch der existenzielle Zeitraum, von dem er abstammt, wurde als Augenblick reiner Subjektivität aufgefasst. Im Spannungsverhältnis mit dem frühen Video, das die Unmittelbarkeit des „Wirklichen" („real") im Gegensatz zum geschnittenen „Streifen" („reel") des Films vorstellte, verlor die Fotografie, so könnte man sagen, die Fühlung mit der „objektiven Wirklichkeit", auf deren Grundlage sie ursprünglich definiert worden war.[14] Daher gab es seit den 1980ern eine Rückkehr zu Lochkamera-Techniken und zur Camera obscura. Dabei ging es nicht darum, dass die Wirklichkeit von Video irgend objektiver gewesen wäre (auch wenn das zunächst für es in Anspruch genommen wurde), sondern darum, dass Video eine neue und erweiterte Vielfalt zeitlich verstreuter oder pluralisierter Subjektivitäten in Stellung brachte. So drang die Elastizität der Zeit erneut in die Fotografie ein, und eine merkliche Verschiebung des Interesses von Fragen der Reproduktion (unmittelbar vorliegender Ergebnisse) zu solchen der Produktion und der Intervention in Prozesse setzte ein.

Mit dem Aufkommen der Digitalisierung in den 1990ern ging die Bedeutung von Video und VHS teils zurück; in jüngster Zeit neigt ihre Verwendung wieder mehr zu kinohaften Formaten. Viele neue technologische Entwicklungen im Bereich virtueller Film haben sie aus ihrer früheren Rolle verdrängt; ihr Anspruch darauf, Wirklichkeit sofort und unvermittelt darzustellen, ist nicht länger haltbar. Die mythopoetischen Ausschweifungen Matthew Barneys bezeichnen als Extrembeispiele die zunehmende Neigung des Mediums Video hin zum Kino.[15] Da Reproduzierbarkeit kein großes Problem mehr darstellt, nehmen moderne elektronische Medien und Computertechnologie zunehmend die Funktion ein, die das Video einmal erfüllte.[16] Was die Frage der Zeitlichkeit angeht, so existieren Video und Fotografie oftmals nebeneinander im virtuellen Raum des Computers und in den Möglichkeiten von Manipulation, die zwischen dem entnommenen Bild, dem Prozess seiner Produktion und seiner späteren Präsentation bestehen. Daraus ergibt sich implizit eine zunehmende Vielfalt der Zeitinhalte, deren Wesen instabil ist oder nicht letztlich zu bestimmen. Kurzum, die Fotografie ebenso wie das Video haben sich, was ihre Zeitinhalte angeht, in Richtung auf geringere Bestimmtheit verschoben. Die unbestimmte Allgemeinheit der Zeit ist die Dauer. Diese Dauer ist darüber hinaus natürlich stets virtuell und insofern ungreifbar; ja aus der Definition des Wortes selbst ergibt sich ein „werdender" Zustand simulierter Möglichkeit. Doch steht das Virtuelle nicht im Gegensatz zum Wirklichen, weil es nach wie vor seiner Natur oder seinen Wirkungen, jedoch nicht den Tatsachen nach existiert; das heißt, es existiert in Gedanken oder in der Einbildungskraft. Die virtuelle Welt ist nicht eine andere Welt als diese – das wäre eine epistemologische Unmöglichkeit –, sondern ermöglicht vielmehr ein vorgestelltes oder alternatives Verhältnis zu dem, was unter dem Begriff der Wirklichkeit verstanden wird. Eine spekulative Wirklichkeit, hervorgebracht und womöglich, wie Bergson nahelegt, dass wir uns viele „verschiedene

11 MICHAEL RUSH, "VIDEO INSTALLATION ART", IN NEW MEDIA...OP CIT, S. 116-167.
12 ES KANN KAUM ÜBERRASCHEN, DASS SO VIELE FRÜHE VIDEOKÜNSTLER SICH VON BECKETT INSPIRIEREN LIESSEN; SO JEDENFALLS NAUMAN, DAS FORTLAUFENDE MEDIENTHEATER JOHN JESURUNS UND SOGAR BIS ZU EINEM GEWISSEN GRAD DIE FRÜHEN ARBEITEN BILL VIOLAS. SIEHE ALAN RICKMAN U.A., BECKETT ON FILM, DVD, 2005, UND GIJS VAN TIJL, „HUMAN CONDITION/HUMAN BODY: BRUCE NAUMAN AND SAMUEL BECKETT", BRUCE NAUMAN, AUSSTELLUNGSKATALOG HAYWARD GALLERY, LONDON, 1998, S. 60-75.
13 HENRI CARTIER-BRESSON, THE DECISIVE MOMENT, NEW YORK, SIMON AND SCHUSTER, 1952. DIESES BUCH GALT EINMAL ALS DAS WICHTIGSTE BUCH ÜBER FOTOGRAFIE IM ZWANZIGSTEN JAHRHUNDERT.
14 SIEHE DEN ÜBERBLICK ÜBER DIE KULTURELLEN VERSCHIEBUNGEN INNERHALB DER FOTOGRAFIE VON DEN ANFÄNGEN BIS HEUTE BEI MARY WARNER MARIEN, PHOTOGRAPHY: A CULTURAL HISTORY, LONDON, LAURENCE KING PUBLISHING, 2002.
15 NANCY SPECTOR, THYRZA GOODEVE UND NEVILLE WAKEFIELD, MATTHEW BARNEY: THE CREMASTER CYCLE, NEW YORK, GUGGENHEIM MUSEUM PUBLICATIONS, 2002; AUSSERDEM STEPHAN URBASCHEK UND BRANDON STOSUY, MATTHEW BARNEY, MÜNCHEN: INGVILD GOETZ, 2008.
16 TIMOTHY DRUCKREY (HG.), ARS ELECTRONICA: FACING THE FUTURE - A SURVEY OF TWO DECADES (ELECTRONIC CULTURE: HISTORY, THEORY AND PRACTICE), CAMBRIDGE MASS., MIT PRESS, 2001.

Rhythmen vorstellen" können, die in den Bewusstsein am Werk sind.

Die in „Mutations II" ausgestellten Werke von Foto- und Videokünstlern zeigen Spuren des mal direkten, mal indirekten Einflusses all dieser Verschiebungen und Tendenzen der letzten dreißig Jahre. Es kann kaum überraschen, dass dies zu einer großen Vielfalt in den Praktiken, Verfahren und Herangehensweisen in beiden Bereichen, Video und Fotografie, führt, der Ausprägung jener individuellen und unverwechselbaren Schatten, auf die ich oben angespielt habe. Zeitlichkeit und Zeit-Raum werden nicht nur visuell, sondern auch akustisch hergestellt. Doch wenngleich die Tonspur normalerweise linear ist, also ein Kontinuum ab dem ersten Moment des Hörens darstellt, wurde auch sie dem Zweck der Fragmentierung und zeitlichen Remontage dienstbar gemacht. In einer Arbeit wie Christoph Brechs Opus 110a hören wir symphonische Musik, doch was vor unseren Augen das Videobild füllt, ist der Rücken einer Oberbekleidung (eines Fracks, wie wir versuchsweise annehmen mögen), in der wohl der Dirigent steckt – obwohl es sich ebenso gut um die simulierte Entsprechung eines Mannes handeln könnte, der symphonische Luftgitarre spielt.[17] Die Wirkung ist die eines akuten Widerspruchs zwischen der visuellen Ebene dessen, was wir sehen, und der akustischen dessen, was wir hören, während uns die rhythmischen Bewegungen und Konfigurationen des Stoffs und der Nähte des Jacketts hypnotisieren. Im Verlauf dieser Wahrnehmung geht einem der Zusammenhang von Ton und Bild auf einer Ebene verloren; zugleich verbindet man sie auf einer anderen Ebene neu. Diese Erfahrung ist transitiv – sie ist in Brechs Werk weit verbreitet –; das heißt, sie drückt eine Handlung des Subjekts auf das Objekt aus, erfordert aber ein direktes Objekt, um ihre volle Bedeutung hervorzubringen.

17 ES HANDELT SICH UM CHRISTOPH POPPEN, DER DAS MÜNCHENER KAMMERORCHESTER DIRIGIERT; GESPIELT WIRD SCHOSTAKOWITSCHS KAMMERSYMPHONIE OPUS 110A. BRECH NENNT DIE ARBEIT EINE „STUDIE ZUR VISUELLEN DYNAMIK DER MUSIK". ZU BETONEN IST ALLERDINGS, DASS DIES REIN ÄUSSERLICHE ANGABEN SIND, DIE ZU EINEM VERSTÄNDNIS DER ARBEIT NICHT ERFORDERLICH SIND; OBWOHL DIESES VERSTÄNDNIS NATÜRLICH EIN ANDERES SEIN MAG, WENN DER BETRACHTER MIT DEM MUSIKSTÜCK VERTRAUT IST.

Dahinter steht die Annahme, dass der Betrachter das direkte Objekt ist, an das sie sich wendet. Das seit langem bestehende Verhältnis zwischen Musik und Video ist uns wohlbekannt, doch im Fall von Popmusikvideos ist die Wirkung normalerweise die einer bildlichen Verdeutlichung. Brech dagegen stellt uns ein Mindestmaß an Information zur Verfügung (das Video endet mit einer Einstellung auf die Partitur) und überlässt es dem Betrachter, die Arbeit zu vervollständigen; ja der Betrachter und die Rezeption durch ihn sind nun erforderlich, soll die Arbeit Bedeutung erlangen.

Diese Strategie ist für viele heute tätige Videokünstler bezeichnend; das heißt, sie ist anti-illustrativ und wird oftmals in Begriffen der Post-Narrative ausgedrückt.[18] Das heißt, sie analysiert nicht eine Narration oder die lineare Erzählung einer Geschichte im strukturellen Sinn einer Feststellung der Endergebnisse von Wahrnehmung a priori, sondern reizt zu und erfordert erweiterte Wahrnehmungen, die zur Vervollständigung der Arbeit beitragen. Dadurch kommen Zeit und Zeitinhalt des Betrachters in Antwort auf die Videoarbeit ins Spiel. Olga Chernyshevas Arbeit von funktioniert genau umgekehrt wie die von Brech. In ihrer Arbeit Windows sieht sich der Betrachter in die Rolle des unsichtbaren Voyeurs oder Spanners versetzt. In einer Reihe kurzer ausgeschnittener zeitlicher Einblicke durch nächtliche Fenster wird uns letztlich ein Lexikon des Alltagslebens präsentiert. Die Fenster sind banal und gewöhnlich, lassen an modernen Massenwohnungsbau denken, und die undurchsichtigen und unzulänglich beleuchteten Innenräume sind ordinär und in nichts auffällig. In Chernyshevas Videomomentaufnahmen aus dem Alltagsleben, die auf den Bildschirmen laufen, sieht ein Mann fern, tanzen drei Menschen im Kreis, spielt ein Mann allein Gitarre, bügelt eine Frau, ist ein Mann im Badezimmer und so weiter. Abgesehen von den Gewohnheitshandlungen, die hier ganz bewusst aufgerufen werden und in der Arbeit implizit enthalten sind, besteht keine direkte Verbindung zwischen den Fenstern außer einer vage typologischen. Die Zeitlosigkeit der Arbeit jedoch zeigt wenig an, das auf einen Ort oder Drehort deuten würde, an dem sich die gesehenen Ereignisse abspielen. Wurden sie gleichzeitig aufgenommen, zu verschiedenen Zeiten, in verschiedenen städtischen Räumen? Was wichtig wird, ist die einfache Tatsache, dass es Videobilder sind, und als verzeitlichte Bilder bringen sie den Betrachter als einen in den Kontext des unsichtbaren Voyeurs oder Spanners versetzten hervor. Wären es Standbilder oder Fotografien, so ergäbe sich kein solcher Eindruck einer Verstrickung des Betrachters.

18 DIE STRUKTURALE „NARRATOLOGIE" WIRD TRADITIONELL MIT EINER GRUPPE IN VERBINDUNG GEBRACHT, DIE ALS RUSSISCHE FORMALISTEN BEZEICHNET WERDEN. TZVETAN TODOROV (GEB. 1939 IN BULGARIEN) PRÄGTE DEN AUSDRUCK UND VERWEIST AUF DAS VORBILD WLADIMIR PROPPS (1895-1970). SIEHE DESSEN MORPHOLOGIE DES MÄRCHENS (1928), MÜNCHEN: HANSER, 1972.

Die Mittler-Rolle des Mediums Video – was einer meiner Mitautoren in diesem Katalog ein „Pflegen des Dazwischen" nannte – bestimmt nach wie vor die Videoproduktion. In den Arbeiten des israelischen Künstlers Ori Gersht mit den Titeln Big Bang und Pomegranate bedient sich die Aneignung des Stilllebens und der Blumenmalerei. In Big Bang ist der Bildschirm zunächst schwarz, ein pfeifendes Geräusch wird lauter, dann erscheint nach und nach ein Blumenstillleben in einer Glasvase, die sich an die Tradition niederländischer Genremalerei im siebzehnten Jahrhundert anlehnt. Das Ton-Bild und die Tonhöhe werden intensiver und ein Gefühl spannungsvoller Erwartung baut sich auf, bis die Blumen und die Vase schließlich explodieren. Die Bruchstücke gehen in einem Regen nieder und das Bild wird langsam dunkler, bis es ganz schwarz ist und die Videoschleife von vorne beginnt. Bei genauer Betrachtung ist überall in Gershts Werk ein eindringliches Gefühl persönlicher und politischer Identität und Biographie wahrnehmbar, und es dürfte kaum Zufall sein, dass er für das andere Video einen Granatapfel gewählt hat. In Pomegranate sehen wir einen perspektivischen Bilderrahmen und ein Stillleben bestehend aus einem aufgehängten Kohlkopf und einem Granatapfel, während zwei Kürbisse auf dem ruhen, was in einem Gemälde der in Verkürzung dargestellte untere Rahmen wäre. Das Video ist stumm, bis eine Kugel von rechts eintritt und den Granatapfel durchschlägt, dessen Kerne – das Video ist weiterhin eine Zeitlupenaufnahme – niederregnen. In persönlicher Hinsicht haben wir nicht nur die besondere und gewählte Konnotation einer der sieben Früchte Israels, sondern auch die Tatsache, dass das selbe hebräische Wort „Granatapfel" und „Granate" bedeuten kann.[19] In Gershts Arbeit geht es nicht so sehr um eine Neumischung der Zeit als um eine Veränderung der Erfahrung von Zeit und eine Herstellung der Bedingungen einer unvorhergesehenen, aber gewaltsamen Erwartungshaltung; mit anderen Worten darum, den „Grad der Spannung oder Entspannung der Bewußtseine" zu ermessen.

Beziehen sich die Verweise in diesen spezifischen Arbeiten Gershts auf die Malerei, so scheint das „Dazwischen" des Finnen Tuomo Rainio einen Eindruck des Verhältnisses zwischen Zeichnung und Video heraufzubeschwören; seine Werke sind Produkte eines von ihm verfassten Bearbeitungsprogramms. In den Arbeiten Staircase (Crosswise) und City ruft jene ein den gespenstisch-unheimlichen Effekt einer geisterhaften Figur hervor, die eine Treppe hinaufsteigt; der Bildsinn ist verschwommen und undeutlich. Der Farbton ist ein wenig spukhaft, die Bildoberfläche ist die von Schablonierungen und Mehrfachbelichtungen und erinnert uns natürlich sofort an frühe futuristische Quellen und an Duchamps „Nu descendant un escalier."[20] Ein solcher Verweis mag oberflächlich scheinen, doch er erinnert uns daran, wie sowohl das Medium Video als auch die Fotografie in den letzten zwanzig Jahren sich auf ihre eigenen Ursprünge zurückgewendet und sie hinterfragt haben. City andererseits ist ein visuell unbewegtes Bild, das wiederum durch die Tonspur als Ton-Bild intensiviert wird: eine schwarz-graue Ansicht einer städtischen Eisenbahn- oder Straßenbahnhaltestelle, deren evokative Kraft gänzlich durch die Geräusche schauriger Winde, ungesehen vorüberratternder Züge und gelegentlicher Schritte geformt wird. Das unbewegte Zeitbild tritt als Verweis auf Wiederholung ein, wird in einer Schleife gezeigt, und die angedeutete Wiederholung der Zeit ist von potentiell unendlicher Dauer. Die Tonbildarbeit City operiert an der Schnittstelle zwischen Standbild und Video, indem es den Raum zwischen den Langzeitbelichtungen eines Künstlers wie des Fotografen Michael Wesely in ein höchst persönliches und programmiertes System sortiert.[21]

Die Auswirkungen einer erneuten Befragung haben unmittelbare Spuren hinterlassen im Werk Oliver Mösts, in dessen Verwendung von Lochkameravideo die Vorgeschichte und frühe Entwicklung der Fotografie unmittelbar nachklingt. In einer ganzen Serie von Arbeiten, die entweder Pinhole Videos oder Shortcuts heißen, wie landescape, hide and seek oder kill your idols, werden verschiedene Zeitelemente entweder segmentiert und übereinandergelegt; zugleich kehrt Möst auf die Grundlagen von Zeit, Licht und Belichtung zurück. Ob in einfacher Abzählung in hide and seek oder in den kaum wahrnehmbaren Abweichungen in landescape, bei uns bleibt ein seltsamer Eindruck von Unendlichkeit und Betäubung zurück. Liegen die Anfänge von Video in der politischen und kulturellen Sphäre einer streitbaren Auseinandersetzung mit den vorherrschenden Massenmedien, so hat es sich in der Zwischenzeit zu einem höchst persönlichen Medium entwickelt. Eine Arbeit wie Dreamsequence von Gast Bouschet und Nadine Hilbert ist, wenngleich sie auf die Geschichte des Kinos verweist, vorsätzlich nichtlinear, indem sie Andeutungen persönlicher Politiken und Einstellungen mit unverbundenen Text- und Tonfragmenten, die von einer Vielzahl von Orten stammen, vermengt. Wie ein im Traum erinnertes Durcheinander sinnlicher Erfahrungen präsentiert sie eine Mischung von Identifikation und Widerruf von Erinnerungen – kurz, eine Art persönliche Katharsis. Jegliche Verbundenheit bleibt der Aufnahmefähigkeit der Wahrnehmungen des Betrachters überlassen. Die Arbeit bleibt kulturell politisch, und sei es auch nur, insofern sie, als Videokunst, im allgemeinen nicht eine Beschwichtigung des Betrachters anstrebt; und mag sie auch indirekt zu unterhalten suchen, so bleibt ihre vorherrschende Absicht, die Grenzen der Repräsentation und des Verstehens von Bildern zu hinterfragen. Wörtlich genommen fordert sie den Betrachter heraus, zu fragen, was diese Bilder bedeuten. Was meint Ulrich Gebert, wenn er fünf Figuren in Soldatenuniformen in gelöster Haltung in eine Reihe stellt, sie eine leere Wand anstarren lässt und das Knattern von „Licht an" und „Licht aus" wiederholt? Von einer indirekten Hommage an Vorläufer wie Gary Hill und der Evokation von Wiederholung einmal abgesehen bleibt es uns überlassen, uns im Feld der Rezeptionsmöglichkeiten zu ergehen.

Die bezeichnendste Entwicklung ist, dass sowohl Video als auch Fotografie in den

19 DIE SIEBEN FRÜCHTE (SHIVAT HAMINIM) ISRAELS SIND IM 5. BUCH MOSE 8:7-8 GENANNT; DAS HEBRÄISCHE WORT FÜR „GRANATBAUM", RIMMÔN, BEDEUTET AUCH „HANDGRANATE": „DENN DER HERR, DEIN GOTT, BRINGT DICH IN EIN GUTES LAND, EIN LAND VON WASSERBÄCHEN, QUELLEN UND GEWÄSSERN, DIE IN DER EBENE UND IM GEBIRGE ENTSPRINGEN; EIN LAND DES WEIZENS UND DER GERSTE, DER WEINSTÖCKE, FEIGENBÄUME UND GRANATBÄUME; EIN LAND MIT ÖLREICHEN OLIVENBÄUMEN UND HONIG [...]". DAS WORT „GRANATE" IN DEN MODERNEN SPRACHEN LEITET SICH EBENSO VOM GRANATAPFEL HER WIE DER NAME „GRENADINE" FÜR FRUCHTSIRUP.

20 SOWOHL DIE FUTURISTEN ALS AUCH DUCHAMP VERDANKEN VIELES EADWEARD MUYBRIDGE (1830-1904) UND ÉTIENNE-JULES MAREY (1830-1904), CHRONOFOTOGRAFEN MIT GROSSEM INTERESSE AN BEWEGUNGEN IN ZEIT UND RAUM UND DER SEQUENZIERUNG VON BEWEGUNG. SIEHE PHILLIP PRODGER, TIME STANDS STILL: MUYBRIDGE AND THE INSTANTANEOUS PHOTOGRAPHY MOVEMENT, LONDON, OXFORD UNIVERSITY PRESS, 2003 UND MARTA BRAUN, PICTURING TIME: WORK OF ETIENNE-JULES MAREY (1839-1904), CHICAGO UND LONDON, CHICAGO UNIVERSITY PRESS, 1994.

21 MICHAEL WESELYS DREI UND VIER JAHRE DAUERNDEN LANGZEITBELICHTUNGEN, ALLGEMEIN BEKANNTE ARBEITEN, GEHEN IN GEWISSER WEISE AUS DER DEM VIDEO ENTGEGENGESETZTEN RICHTUNG VOR UND ERLAUBEN ES DER ZEIT SELBST, DIE GEISTERHAFT SCHABLONIERTEN BILDINHALTE ÜBER EXTREM LANGE ZEITRÄUME HERVORZUBRINGEN. SIEHE MICHAEL WESELY: OPEN SHUTTER, AUSSTELLUNGSKATALOG, THE MUSEUM OF MODERN ART NEW YORK, 2004, DAS DEN ZEITRAUM DES ABRISSES UND NEUBAUS DES MOMA KONTINUIERLICH ABDECKT; SOWIE ZUR NEUGESTALTUNG DES POTSDAMER PLATZES MICHAEL WESELY: DIE ERFINDUNG DES UNSICHTBAREN, AUSSTELLUNGSKATALOG, GUARDINI GALERIE BERLIN/ FOTOHOF SALZBURG, 2005.

Computer und die digitale Manipulation eingetreten sind. Weit davon entfernt, Möglichkeiten zu verschließen, hat die virtuelle Realität der Computerwelt die Fotografie vom statischen Bild, vom eingefrorenen Augenblick und das Video von der Selbsttäuschung befreit, es fange eine irgend endgültige Fassung von Wirklichkeit ein. Sie hat es einem Künstler wie Peter Aerschmann ermöglicht, die polyphone Fähigkeit zu erwerben, eine Vielzahl von Elementen, vom Gesellschaftlichen bis zum Surrealen, zusammenzucollagieren. In Arbeiten wie Paternoster und Union Square lässt er eine Vielfalt der Herangehensweisen erkennen, die für viele heutige Künstler typisch ist. In Paternoster erscheint ein Bühnenhintergrund aus offenen Aufzügen, in denen Gestalten in ihrer ganzen eigenwilligen Mannigfaltigkeit auf- und abfahren. Sie stellen kleine Welten gesellschaftlicher Selbstsorge vor, allgemeinmenschliche Verhaltensweisen in verschobenen Situationen: eine Frau spielt Geige, die Gestalt eines fegenden Mannes in einem Overall erscheint, eine Frau mit einer Blumenvase, eine einsame Topfpflanze und so weiter. Aerschmann konzentriert sich oftmals auf Archetypen; das ist vielleicht eine indirekte Konsequenz seiner schweizerischen (jungschen) Wurzeln. In Union Square stoßen wir auf einen surrealen Kontrapunkt aus einem weißen schneebeladenen Raum, Baumstümpfen, einem flachen und glanzlosen roten Hintergrund, vor dem ein Flugzeug kreuzt und Korps der Schweizer Armee, die wacker in der Schneelandschaft stehen, während die Einstellung von links nach rechts schwenkt, von den öden Baumstümpfen auf einen Tannenwald. Aerschmann bestreitet ganz unmittelbar die Dialektik des eingefrorenen und des Bewegungsbilds, die Arbeit dreht sich ganz zentral um den Raum und das unbestimmte Vergehen der Zeit. So erlaubt das Virtuelle, wenn es mit Fotografie und Video verwendet wird, in gewissem Sinne ein höheres Maß an zeitlicher und bildnerischer Synthese, als das mit älteren Technologien je möglich war. In der Fotografie ermöglicht es die Überlagerung mehrerer Momente in der Zeit als Dauer, während diese Zeitlichkeiten im Medium Video komprimiert, ausgedehnt, oder umgewendet und in neue und scheinbar unendliche Möglichkeiten umgemischt werden.

Wo steht in all dem die umfassendere Bedeutung der Zeit? Sie bleibt, wie Bergson nahegelegt, in verschiedenen Bewusstseinsformen. Es sollte nicht überraschen, dass das Verhältnis der Menschen zur Zeit ein zutiefst persönliches ist. Das von der Welt aufgezwungene nicht notwendig das von Geist und Einbildungskraft verfochtene. Da wir uns tief ins elektronische Zeitalter begeben, sollten wir weniger mit Angst als mit Möglichkeiten zu tun haben. „Mutations II" verweist einfach auf diese Veränderungen in den Parametern selbstgenerierter und verwirklichbarer Möglichkeiten innerhalb der heutigen Verwendungsweisen von Fotografie und Video. Wie wir sie anwenden, zu welchen Zwecken wir sie in der Welt zum Tragen bringen, bleibt ganz uns überlassen.

Aber dann bleibt auch unser eigenes Wesen, bleibt Aufgabe und Bestimmung unserer Person in ein mystisches Dunkel gehüllt. Denn woher kommen, wie entstehen und wozu dienen jene unausgedehnten elementaren Empfindungen, die im Raum zur Entwicklung kommen? Man muß sie als lauter Absoluta setzen, deren Ursprung und Endzweck unerkennbar ist.[22]

Mark Gisbourne

Mark Gisbourne war Lehrbeauftragter und Professor im Doktorandenprogramm Zeitgenössische Kunst an der Slade School of Fine Art (University of London) und am Sotheby's Institute (Master's-Programm der University of Manchester), Präsident der britischen Sektion von AICA und Vize-Präsident der internationalen AICA. Er hat zahlreiche Bücher und Kataloge veröffentlicht und für nahezu alle wichtigen englischsprachigen Kunstpublikationen geschrieben. Zu seinen Ausstellungen in jüngster Zeit gehört Paul Klee: Adult Memories of Childhood (Centro Atlántico de Arte Moderno, Las Palmas); er ist Kurator am Rohkunstbau (siehe www.rohkunstbau.de), lebt und arbeitet in Berlin.

22 BERGSON, MATERIE UND GEDÄCHTNIS, S. 51. (WIR HABEN „UNERKENNBAR" FÜR „UNVERKENNBAR" KORRIGIERT.)

Peter Aerschmann

1969 geboren in Freiburg/CH, lebt und arbeitet in Bern
1994-1999 Hochschule für Gestaltung und Kunst Bern
www.aerschmann.ch

Raum zu fotografieren und zugleich die Tiefe der Zeit zu bewahren, Bilder zu machen, die den Moment und das einmal Fixierte überschreiten, um Bewegung und Leben wiederzugeben: die grundlegende Herausforderung, der sich Peter Aerschmanns Arbeiten stellen, ist die Darstellung der Zeit im Raum.

In „Das Auge und der Geist" (1964) stellte der Philosoph und Kunsttheoretiker Maurice Merleau-Ponty fest, dass Gesichtswahrnehmung und Bewegung ineinander verflochten sind: könnten wir uns nicht im Raum bewegen, so wären wir auch nicht in der Lage zu sehen. Doch ist die Bewegung des Körpers nicht lediglich die Versetzung eines Gegenstandes von A nach B. Bewegung, wie sie tatsächlich wahrgenommen wird, ist ein eigenständiges Ganzes und darf nicht mit dem in ihrem Verlauf durchmessenen Raum verwechselt werden. Darin liegt die Paradoxie der Bewegung: Sie findet im Raum statt und scheint doch diesem fremd zu sein.

In Peter Aerschmanns Videos geschieht das Zufällige neben dem Vorbestimmten her, sodass der Zuschauer nur eine gebrochene Sicht auf die Wirklichkeit des Lebens gewinnt. So gelingt es ihm, uns unserer Orientierung zu berauben. Liegt darin die Quelle des Eindrucks von Lebendigkeit, der sich einstellt, obwohl die Zahl der Elemente vorher festgelegt ist, diese vorbestimmten Bewegungskurven folgen? Statt uns ein Abbild zu zeigen, fängt Peter Aerschmann mittels des Bildes den Rhythmus der Dinge ein, die Art, wie sie sich dem Verlauf der Zeit und der Wiederholung einfügen. Aus Bruchstücken setzt er eine Umgebung zusammen, der noch die formalen Merkmale der Wirklichkeit anhaften: die Fähigkeit zur Veränderung, Dauerhaftigkeit und Dauer, die Anwesenheit von Gegenständen. Es ist kein Zufall, dass beinahe alle der gefilmten Mini-Sequenzen Bruchstücke von Bewegungen sind, deren wiederholungsreiche Vorführung und vorherbestimmtes Fortschreiten eine Art melancholischen Humor evozieren.

Indem sie Archetypen des kollektiven Gedächtnisses aufrufen, verweisen Peter Aerschmanns Arbeiten uns auf unsere eigene Wirklichkeit, werden sie zu Metaphern einer ihrer Hierarchien entkleideten Welt, in der wir alle einander fremd sind.

Alice Anderson

1976 geboren in London, lebt und arbeitet in London
1998-2001 Ecole Nationale Supérieure des Beaux-Arts, Paris
2002-2004 MA am Goldsmiths College, London
www.alice-anderson.org

Die englisch-französische Künstlerin und Filmemacherin Alice Anderson verbindet Geschichten aus ihren Erinnerungen und eine Vorstellungswelt, die eng mit ihrer eigenen Kindheit zusammenhängt, um auf überlieferte Volkserzählungen zurückzukommen und ihre Bedeutung neu zu erfinden.
In der Verknüpfung von fiktiven Elementen und autobiographischen Zitaten streichen ihre Arbeiten eine Doppelheit heraus, die, so Anderson, den innersten Kern des Volksmärchens ausmacht: oberflächlich und tiefgründig, normativ und subversiv zugleich, versetzt es den Betrachter mit einem Mal in eine spannungsreiche und traumartige Welt, der eine Art Dunkelheit entspringt, die um sich her zuweilen eine beängstigende Atmosphäre der Gewalt verbreitet. Sind die Kindheit und der Begriff des Spiels für ihr Werk von erheblicher Bedeutung, so liegt ihnen doch ein großer Ernst zugrunde.

Andersons Geschichten bauen sich um eine Betonung der symbolischen und poetischen Kräfte der von ihr verwendeten Gegenstände aus der Vergangenheit auf. Der erzählerische Prozess, den sie entwirft, ist von einer linearen Logik weit entfernt und eher kreisförmig; er lässt an die gewundenen Pfade eines Irrgartens denken, an die schwankende Welt Lewis Carrolls oder an die Prinzipien, die nach Freud die Deutung des Unbewussten bestimmen. In jeder der fantastischen Geschichten Alice Andersons können wir das Ringen um eine Identität erspüren; wir sind eingeladen, durch den Spiegel zu treten auf der Suche nach unserer eigenen Erfahrung, auf halbem Wege zwischen Entzückung und Schrecken.

Gast Bouschet & Nadine Hilbert

1958 geboren in Dudelange/LUX / 1961 geboren in Luxemburg, leben u.a. in Brüssel
www.thetrustfiles.net

Seit den 1980er Jahren haben Nadine Hilbert und Gast Bouschet überall auf der Welt ihre Fotos und Videos aufgenommen (und ausgestellt). Besondere Faszinationskraft übt das aufgezeichnete Bild auf sie durch seine Fähigkeit aus, kommentierend auf die Umwandlung politischer und sozioökonomischer Systeme und ihre Symbolik zu reflektieren, eine Umwandlung, die in der Formensprache städtischer Strukturen und Randbereiche besonders deutlich sichtbar ist.

Ihr Arbeiten sind in zahlreichen Ausstellungen zu sehen gewesen, insbesondere im Center of Contemporary Arts (Glasgow), dem Museum van Hedendaagse Kunst Muhka (Antwerpen), dem Casino, Forum d'Art Contemporain (Luxemburg), der Galerie Nei Liicht (Dudelange, Luxemburg), der Busan Biennale für zeitgenössische Künste (Busan, Korea), dem Camouflage Zentrum für zeitgenössische Kunst aus Afrika (Brüssel und Johannesburg), dem Domaine départemental in Chamarande (Paris) und als Teil der Krinzinger Projekte (Wien).

„Ich bin immer der andere. Wenn ich „wir" sage, bezeichne ich das schuldige Ich. Von nun an ist alles klar. Niemand ist länger die selbe Person. Aggression hat nichts verändert, wir sind eins mit unseren Feinden, unsere Denkweisen sind die unserer Gegner. Es gibt keine Grenzen oder Schranken mehr, unsere Identitäten sind ineinander verflochten. Doch wir verzehren uns in Furcht, die Angst bleibt unsere Begleiterin. Die Bedrohung ist alltäglich und zerstört uns von innen. Die Welt ist nicht mehr, was sie war, das Licht ist anders. Die Natur ist unversöhnlich, hat es auf uns abgesehen. Wir sind Fremde im eigenen Land; wir alle sprechen eine unbekannte Sprache, die uns ängstigt. Von nun an sind unsere bösesten Alpträume ihres köstlichen kalten Schweißes bar. Unsere schönsten Träume machen uns Sorgen mit ihren trügerischen Tröstungen. Unser Geist mischt Tag für Tag und stets neu sein schleichendes Gift. Schon seit einiger Zeit können wir nicht mehr ohne es. Dieses täglichen Brotes bedürfen wir dringend. In den Feldern, wo wir unsere eigenen Schrecken sähen, wirken wir fehlfarben. Der düstere Spiegel von Nadine Hilbert und Gast Bouschet." (François Olivieri)

Pirmin Blum

1969 geboren in Pfaffnau/CH, lebt in Wien.
1997-1999 Ecole supérieure des Beaux-Arts, Genf
1999-2005 Digitale Medien an der Akademie der Bildenden Künste Wien (Peter Kogler)
www.pirminblum.com

Der Schweizer Künstler Pirmin Blum arbeitet seit Jahren konsequent mit dem Internet, durchforstet Online-Auktionshäuser, Suchmaschinen und Chatrooms. Sein Interesse dafür beruht auf der Tatsache, dass heute jede/r jederzeit auf das world wide web zugreifen, es mit persönlichen Fotos, Videoaufnahmen, Texten usw. befüllen sowie persönliche Einträge lesen kann. Bewusst oder unbewusst – im Falle Blums ersteres – sind wir „VoyeurInnen" und KonsumentInnen des Privatlebens anderer. Neben diesem Found Footage verarbeitet Blum auch Filmmaterial aus Industrie und Wirtschaft, z.B. von Sicherheitstestverfahren diverser Autoproduzenten. Die analytische Auswahl bestimmter Sequenzen aus diesen Videos und ihre Zusammenfügung hebt die ursprünglich künstlerisch wertlosen Bilder auf eine neue Bedeutungsebene. Das schnelle Tempo des Schnitts, ergänzt durch loops, stilisiert so z.B. Aufnahmen eines aufgehenden und wieder zusammenfallenden Airbags zu einer eigentümlichen, organisch wirkenden Blase (Airbag, 2000). Den Moment des Aufpralls des Airbags passt Blum an den menschlichen Atemrhythmus an, sodass der Betrachter/die Betrachterin nach einigen loops im Gleichklang mit dem Video „atmet".

Ähnlich verhält es sich mit Spuk (2001), bei dem Blum ein Testvideo eines gepanzerten Security-Fahrzeuges auswählt, dessen Windschutzscheibe beschossen wird. Die rasante Aufeinanderfolge der zwei Kameraperspektiven – abwechselnd Außenansicht auf und Innenansicht vom Fahrzeug hinaus – erzeugt eine unheimliche Spannung und das Gefühl, mittendrin zu sein. Einmal ist man TäterIn, der/die den Schuss abfeuert, gleich darauf ein Opfer, das im Auto sitzt und die Kugeln auf sich zukommen sieht. Entscheidend hierbei der Sound, dessen tiefe Basstöne in 130 Beats pro Minute aus Techno-Rave-Lautsprechern dröhnen. Sie entsprechen der Frequenz, die DJs auf Raves spielen, um das menschliche Herz optimal zu stimulieren.

Christoph Brech

1964 geboren in Schweinfurt/GER, lebt und arbeitet in München
1989-1995 Studium der Freien Kunst an der Akademie der Bildenden Künste, München
www.christophbrech.com

„Christoph Brech's video works transform ordinary occurrences into moments of significance."
Die Arbeiten des Künstlers Christoph Brech reichen von Rauminstallationen über Fotografie- und Videoarbeiten bis zur Kunst im Öffentlichen Raum.

Brechs Videos zeichnen sich durch ihre strengen und klaren Konzepte, die gradlinige Umsetzung sowie durch die Einfachheit der eingesetzten Mittel aus. Phänomene der Natur, alltägliche Gegenstände und Impressionen sowie die statische und ruhig beobachtende Einstellung der Kamera sind charakteristisch für die Arbeiten, die in dieser Ausstellung vorgestellt werden.

Brech gelingt es, Situationen aufzuspüren, die durch die Dehnung der Zeit und die dadurch erzeugte Langsamkeit ihre poetische Dimension entfalten – alltägliche Erscheinungen, die sich in bedeutungsvolle Augenblicke verwandeln.

Ob er in dem Video Passage ein Wasserglas auf dem Tisch der Kabine eines Fischkutters filmt, das dem zu- und abnehmenden Vibrieren und Schwanken an Bord unterworfen ist, ob er in der Videoarbeit Break in der ruhigen und zunächst lautlosen Betrachtung des nebelverhangenen und zugefrorenen St.-Lorenz-Stroms dem trägen Zeitmaß der Natur die Gewaltigkeit eines vorüberziehenden kanadischen Eisbrechers gegenüberstellt, oder ob er in Opus 110a den Rücken des Dirigenten Christoph Poppen filmt, um im Spiel der Falten seines Fracks die Dynamik der Musik Dimitri Schostakowitschs zu visualisieren – es gelingt Christoph Brech, die „Eigenzeit" eines Ereignisses im Bild zu bewahren. Der Betrachter ist einem ent-schleunigten Rhythmus unterworfen, nahezu meditative Stimmungen werden erzeugt. So auch in der Videoarbeit Transito, die 2007 in Rom entstanden ist. Im Eingangsbereich einer Kirche schwingt ein schwerer Vorhang rhythmisch im Wind, ein tänzerisches Licht- und Schattenspiel auf dem Fußboden erzeugend. Es sind Momente der Zeit und des Übergangs, die Christoph Brech in seinen Videoarbeiten einfängt.

Elina Brotherus

1972 geboren in Helsinki, lebt in Helsinki und Avallon/F
2000 Diplom an der Universität für Kunst und Gestaltung, Helsinki
www.sag.se/foto/elinabrotherus/elina.html

„In der Fotoserie Le miroir (2000) und dem Video Miroir (2001) geht es in keiner Weise, wie behauptet wurde, um „die weibliche Identität". Ich wollte einfach herausfinden, wie das physikalische Alltagsphänomen verfliegenden Dampfes aussehen würde, wenn man es fotografiert. Bei näherem Nachdenken kann man in dieser Arbeit eine kleine Allegorie auf die Fotografie erkennen. In ihren Anfängen war eine Fotografie eine silberbeschichtete Kupferplatte – also ein Spiegel – auf der sich im Verlauf der Entwicklung ein Porträt abzeichnete. Auch hier sehen wir das Bild nach und nach im Spiegel erscheinen. Es ist interessant, zu beobachten, wie groß die Unterschiede zwischen den zwei Arbeiten sind, selbst wenn sie sich letztlich nur darin unterscheiden, dass die Fotos getrennte Augenblicke zeigen, während das Video die Lücken zwischen den Einzelbildern zu einer durchgehenden Zeitlinie auffüllt.

Model Studies hat nichts mit persönlichen Geschichten oder mit der Dokumentation einer Lebensgeschichte zu tun. Die Bilder wurden mit Blick auf visuelle Kriterien konstruiert. Das Interesse der Künstlerin gilt dem Licht, den Farben, dem Rhythmus der Massen und Themen mit klassischen Anklängen. Die Figur wendet dem Beobachter oftmals ihren Rücken zu. Diese Geste lädt zu friedlicher Betrachtung statt zur Konfrontation ein.[1]"

In ihren Videos mit dem selben Titel hat sich Elina Brotherus professioneller Modelle bedient, die wie für einen Kurs im Aktzeichnen posieren. Statt zu zeichnen, beobachtet sie sie mit der Kamera. Es geht dabei um den besonderen Blick der Künstlerin auf ihr Modell: das distanzierte und von Voyeurismus freie Auge. „Eine Künstlerin, die zeichnet oder malt, erhebt keinen Anspruch darauf, die Persönlichkeit des Modells zu kennen oder zu verstehen; das ist nicht der Sinn der Sache. Man betrachtet aufmerksam, und sonst nichts: wo sind helle und dunkle Partien, wie verlaufen die Linien. Ich möchte dem Publikum diesen aktiven und doch neutralen Blick der Künstlerin zeigen, ihn mit dem Betrachter teilen. Es ist ein besonderes Glück, einen menschlichen Körper auf diese Weise betrachten zu können.[2]"

Olga Chernysheva

1962 geboren in Moskau, lebt und arbeitet in Moskau
1986 Diplom an der Filmakademie Moskau
1995-1996 Diplom an der Royal Academy of Fine Arts, Amsterdam
www.olgachernysheva.ru

Olga Chernysheva ist ausgebildete Filmemacherin. Zu ihren Interessen gehören Fotografie, Malerei, experimentelle Videoarbeiten und Videoinstallationen. Ihr Projekt Windows aus dem Jahr 2007 nimmt den Betrachter mit auf eine Reise zurück ins Alltagsleben der Sowjetzeit: In den Fenstern der Wohnanlage „Chruschtschow" in Moskau sind Kleidungsstücke zu sehen, Geschirr, Unterwäsche, ein Glas Tee, ein nackter Männertorso, ein Bügeleisen, ein Fernseher, etwas Tüll mit Blumenmuster, zum Trocknen aufgehängtes Leinen, eine mit Papier abgeklebte Fensterscheibe ... Menschen kommen und gehen: ein Mann trinkt aus einem Wasserkessel, ein alter Mann streckt sich, junge Leute lassen es sich gut gehen ... Das Fenster wird hier selbst zur Rampe einer Bühne, zu einem Rahmen, der einen erleuchteten Raum wie in einem Theater abgrenzt, in dem die Figuren oder Bewohner erscheinen und wieder in die dunkle Tiefe der Wohnungen abtreten.

Chernyshevas Fenster enthüllen das Alltagsleben in Russland, wenden es nach außen, ermöglichen es uns, den üblichen Tagesablauf, die Routine zu beobachten, und baut so langsam aber sicher ein Gefühl dafür auf, was es heißt, zu existieren. Und all dies ohne einen Anflug von Voyeurismus, von Ausspähung oder Neugier – alles ist sehr distanziert, ruhig und konzentriert.

Eine Anzahl von Videoclips, die gleichzeitig im schwarzen Rahmen der Nacht und im Fernseher laufen, erzeugen das Modell eines idealen Gemeinschaftslebens (begleitet von Musik von Chopin) und rufen so einen Effekt von Anwesenheit hervor, ein warmes Gefühl der Nostalgie nach jener Sowjetwirklichkeit, die noch nicht ganz verschwunden ist.

Ulrich Gebert

1976 geboren in München, lebt und arbeitet in Leipzig/GER
1998-2005 Fotografie an der Hochschule für Grafik und Buchkunst, Leipzig
2006 MA der Fotografie am Royal College of Art, London
www.klemms-berlin.com

Ulrich Geberts fotografische Arbeiten kreisen häufig um Begriffe, die zunächst abstrakt und ungreifbar erscheinen, unser gesellschaftliches Handeln aber maßgeblich bestimmen: Ordnungsprinzipien, Systemdenken, Hierarchisierung und Machtmechanismen werden von Gebert in ihrem künstlerischen Zusammenhang zugespitzt formuliert und begreifbar gemacht. Je nach Zusammenhang bedient er sich inszenatorischer, filmischer, dokumentarischer oder porträthafter Darstellungsweisen und nutzt sie für die medienreflexive Vorgehensweise seiner zumeist fotografischen Arbeiten.

Für seine Videoarbeit Keine Dialoge aus dem Jahr 2004 nutzte Ulrich Gebert vorgefundenes Filmmaterial über die Ausbildung von Elite-Grenzschützern der GSG 9, der Antiterrorismuseinheit der deutschen Bundespolizei. Er montierte aus diesem Material einen minimalistisch anmutenden Loop, der fünf uniformierte und in einer Reihe stehende Beamte zeigt, die sich in einem abgedunkelten und verschlossenen Raum einem Stressbelastungstests mit Stroboskopblitzen unterziehen müssen. Während des Tests werden den Beamten Instruktionen erteilt, die sie später ausführen müssen. Durch das schnelle, blitzartige Aufeinanderfolgen der statischen Einzelbilder, die in der Abfolge minimale Bewegungen der Beamten zu erzeugen scheinen, sowie dem konstanten Klicken des auslösenden Blitzes wird der Betrachter direkt mit der Projektion und dem ihm umgebenden Raum konfrontiert. Er ist, wie auch die GSG 9-Beamten, visuell gewalttätigen Blitzen ausgesetzt und befindet sich in einem ähnlich beengten, abgedunkelten Raum, in dem das Video präsentiert wird. Die beklemmende und angespannte Situation des Stressbelastungstests, in der sich die GSG 9-Beamten befinden, wird somit für den Betrachter mit allen Sinnen erfahrbar.

Ori Gersht

Geboren 1967 in Tel Aviv, lebt und arbeitet in London
1989-92 BA in Fotografie, Film und Video an der Universität von Westminster,London
1993-95 MA in Fotografie, Royal College of Art, London
www.mummeryschnelle.com

1 „ELINA BROTHERUS IN CONVERSATION WITH BIRGIT EUSTERSCHULTE". AUSSTELLUNG SELBSTAUSLÖSER, KUNSTHALLE FRIDERICIANUM, KASSEL 2005.
2 AUSZUG PRESSEMAPPE ELINA BROTHERUS: MODEL STUDIES, AUSSTELLUNG GB AGENCY,PARIS 2005.

In seinen jüngsten Arbeiten untersucht Ori Gersht das Verhältnis zwischen Film, Fotografie, Technologie und visueller Wahrnehmung in einem entscheidenden Moment der Kunstgeschichte, da digitale Technologie einerseits eine Krise auszulösen droht und andererseits einen Durchbruch verheißt. Für seine zwei zuletzt entstandenen Filme Pomegranate und Big Bang hat Gersht stilllebenartige Kompositionen im Stil von Gemälden der Alten Meister nachgestellt und zeichnet so die Entwicklung der Faszination, die die Darstellung der Wirklichkeit auf Künstler ausübt, vom siebzehnten Jahrhundert bis in die Gegenwart nach. Während solche Gemälde in ihrer ursprünglichen Form Versuche darstellten, leblose Augenblicke in ewiger Erstarrung zu bewahren, werden Gershts Kompositionen durch schnelle und gewaltsame Eingriffe erschüttert. In Pomegranate, einem Film, der sowohl auf ein barockes Stillleben von Juán Sanchez Cotán als auch auf Harold Edgertons Stroboskopfotografie verweist, fliegt ein Hochgeschwindigkeitsprojektil in Zeitlupe quer durch das Bild, um einen aufgehängten Granatapfel zu zertrümmern; die Frucht wird aufgerissen und langsam in die Luft gewirbelt wie ein gewaltsam zerschmetterter Mund, der blutrote Samen spuckt. Ein friedliches Bild verwandelt sich in Blutvergießen; es entspinnt sich ein Dialog zwischen Bewegungslosigkeit und Bewegung, zwischen Frieden und Gewalt. Solche Dichotomien sind auch in Big Bang erkennbar, einem Film, der auf den ersten Blick ein niederländisches Blumenstillleben darstellt. Diese Illusion wird plötzlich zerstört, da die Blumen und die Vase explodieren, während zugleich Kriegssirenen erdröhnen, die dann langsam in eine hohe und mechanische Stimme übergehen. Daraufhin wandelt sich das Bild: lautlos und langsam geht ein dichter kosmischer Regen aus bunten Blumenfetzen und Staub nieder. Von Pomegranate wie von Big Bang gehen die Schockwellen menschlicher Geschichte aus.

In einer Zeit, da viele Film- und Videokünstler, die sich mit dem Politischen auseinandersetzen, Arbeiten produzieren, die mehr mit dem Medium der Dokumentation gemein haben, erkunden Gershts Arbeiten eine Gattung, als deren Pionier er gelten kann – die der provokanten Meditation. (Andrew Mummery, Director Mummery + Schnelle Gallery, London)

Terézia Golasová

1980 geboren in Bratislava, lebt in Bratislava.
2002-2007 Akademie für Bildende Künste, Bratislava, Spezialisierung auf Fotografie und Neue Medien
seit 2004 Studium an der Fakultät für Philosophie der Comenius Universität, Bratislava
www.golasova.marencin.sk

Terézia Golasová ist noch Kunststudentin und entspricht in jeder Hinsicht der Vorstellung, die man sich von einer Nachwuchskünstlerin macht. Ihre Arbeiten, die sie in einem Fotoatelier herstellt, konzentrieren sich ganz auf eine Auseinandersetzung mit dem Einsatz verschiedener fotografischer und videotechnischer Mittel, um den Begriff der Veränderung bildlich darzustellen. In ihren Videos entwickelt sich keine Handlung: ihr Gegenstand sind Bewegung und Fluss der Zeit selbst. Um ihre Wirkung zu steigern, verwendet sie eine fest montierte Videokamera.

In der Videoarbeit ...In One Bed... rotiert eine fest aufgehängte Kamera um 360 Grad. Es entsteht der Eindruck einer Panoramaaufnahme eines Raums, in den Menschen in einer der Bewegung der Kamera entgegengesetzten Richtung eintreten. Das unterstreicht die Illusion einer ähnlich wie in Standbildern in eine Sequenz aufgelösten Handlung.

„Quo vadis" ist, so die Künstlerin, „eine kurze Dokumentation über den Fluss der Zeit". Eine fest angebrachte Videokamera nimmt einen Reisenden in Bewegung auf, während einer U-Bahn-Fahrt von einer Haltestelle zur nächsten. Durch das Fenster können wir Gegenstände vorbeisausen sehen, was die wirkliche Geschwindigkeit des Fahrzeugs anzeigt und den Gegensatz zur weitgehenden Unbeweglichkeit der Reisenden hervorhebt. Ihre gelegentlichen Bewegungen verstärken nur den Eindruck, dass wir ein im Wagen aufgenommenes Standbild vor uns sehen. Um den Verlauf der Zeit sichtbar zu machen, zeigt darunter eine Uhr die aktuelle Zeit sekundengenau an.

Golasovás letzte Arbeit, To Be at a Loss, lässt sich als natürliche Fortsetzung ihrer Erforschung von Veränderung und Medien begreifen. Erneut verwendet sie eine fest angebrachte Videokamera. Diesmal wird die Illusion, es handle sich um ein Standbild, dadurch gesteigert, dass das Bild eine absichtlich reglose Person (die Künstlerin selbst) und ihr Spiegelbild zeigt. Elemente von Veränderung sind einzig der Dampf, durch den sich der Spiegel langsam beschlägt, und das Geräusch fließenden Wassers. Das Video endet in dem Moment, da das Spiegelbild vollständig verschwunden ist. Die Idee dahinter mag in einer Arbeit an der Grenze zwischen Video und Fotografie nicht allzu ungewöhnlich sein, stellt aber sicherlich einen logischen nächsten Schritt in Golasovás Werk dar.

Laurent Goldring

1957 geboren in Paris, lebt als Maler, Zeichner, Bildhauer und Videokünstler in Paris
Seine Arbeit beschreitet wichtige Entwicklungen im Bereich des zeitgenössischen Tanzes und wurde bereits zahlreich international präsentiert

„Das Kino kennt das Geheimnis der Fotografie.In der Fotografie ging es um die Ähnlichkeit, und Arago setzte das Gesetz durch, das sie als solche amtlich bestätigte. Nun war dem Kino, das damals noch Chronofotografie war, sofort klar, dass diese Fiktion auf nichts als sein eigenes, mantrahaft vorgetragenes Postulat gegründet war. Deshalb behauptete es stets, nicht vierundzwanzig Fotos pro Sekunde, sondern vierundzwanzig Bilder pro Sekunde zu zeigen.

Das Kino nimmt zur gleichen Zeit Serien von Fotos auf. Es hat es nur mit zwei sehr nahe beieinanderliegenden Aufnahmen zu tun, die sich so unterscheiden, dass die Vorstellung von Ähnlichkeit sich verbietet. Das Kino versetzt so auf symmetrische Weise der Vorstellung einer Ähnlichkeitsbeziehung zwischen der Welt und sich selbst den Todesstoß. Im Falle der Porträtaufnahme ist es die Fiktion des Individuums, der der Todesstoß versetzt wird. Im Falle der Landschaftsaufnahme bricht die Wahrheit der Perspektive zusammen. Eine grundlegende Differenz schlägt Wurzeln, von der die Fotografie erklärt hatte, es gebe sie nicht.

Das Kino sah, hätte sehen lassen können, weigerte sich zu sehen, erklärte verbindlich, nichts gesehen zu haben, und verbat sich selbst fieberhaft zu sehen.

Das Kino wurde sofort die massive und vollständig (un)bewusste Verleugnung des Geheimnisses der Fotografie: dass sie nicht ähnlich war. Es machte das Eindeutige und Ähnliche zu seinem Geschäft; und zuallererst die Ähnlichkeit der Dinge zu sich selbst, die Geschäftsgrundlage aller Geschäftemacherei. Hollywood war die große Werbetrommel dieses Lebensmodells, in dem den Dingen und den Menschen unablässig anbefohlen war, sich selbst ähnlich zu sein.

Alles am Kino lässt sich durch diesen Verleugnungsrausch erklären: Casting, Drehbuch, Storyboard, Dreharbeiten. Alles ist darauf angelegt, uns glauben zu machen, dass ein Individuum existiert, mit einem Gesicht und einem Körper, einer Persönlichkeit, einem Ziel und einer Idee, denn wir verstehen auch, warum eine Industrie, deren einziger Daseinszweck ist, eine Fiktion zu erschaffen, außerstande ist, sich ein Bild vorzustellen, das nicht als Fiktion vorstellbar ist."

„Meine Arbeit besteht in dem Versuch, ein moving image jenseits der Fiktion zu produzieren: mit anderen Worten, jenseits der Ähnlichkeit." (Laurent Goldring)

Laurent Grasso

1972 geboren in Mulhouse/F, lebt und arbeitet in Paris
Cooper Union School, New York; Central Saint Martins School of Art, London;
Ecole Nationale Supérieure des Beaux-Arts, Paris
www.galeriechezvalentin.com/fr/artistes/laurent_grasso/works/

Mal arbeitet er mit den (und gegen die) mehr oder minder identifizierbaren Formen unserer kontrollwütigen Gesellschaft, mal untergräbt er die kinematographischen Techniken und Konventionen, die unsere kollektive Einbildungskraft prägen: stets aber schafft Laurent Grasso Umwelten von starker Erzählkraft, in der sich Urängste, wissenschaftliches Beweismaterial und unheilverkündende Mythen der Gegenwart verbinden. In seinem Video Untitled rollt eine riesige und bedrohliche Wolke durch Paris auf den Betrachter zu, die Autos und Gebäude auf ihrem Weg verschlingend. Vor diese herannahende Wand aus Staub gestellt, diese fiktive Spur einer erfundenen Katastrophe, sehen wir uns gedrängt, einen Erzählprozess anzustrengen, unsere Ängste auf das Gesehene zu projizieren oder unser eigenes Drehbuch zu entwerfen. Je nachdem, wo unsere individuellen Empfindlichkeiten und unsere kulturhistorischen Referenzen angesiedelt sind, beschwört das Video Bilder vom Einsturz der Türme des World Trade Center herauf oder Szenen urbaner Gewalt oder vielleicht spektakuläre Augenblicke aus spezialeffektlastigen Actionfilmen.

Grassos Arbeiten mögen auf eine Wiedererweckung des Geschmacks an paranoiden rückwärtsgewandt-futuristischen Prophezeiungen hinauslaufen, wie sie Charles Fourier vor zweihundert Jahren vortrug. Tatsächlich verbinden seine Arbeiten regelmäßig Licht, Ton, natürliche und paranormale Phänomene und Himmelsereignisse zu gänzlich neuen Sinneserfahrungen, die der Übermittlung halbfertiger und vom Betrachter zu vervollständigender Hervorbringungen der Einbildungskraft dienen.

Indem er die ausgestellten Arbeiten in ein spannungsreiches Verhältnis zu ihrer Umgebung und zu den manchmal dramatischen Deutungen setzt, die sie wachrufen, schafft Laurent Grasso Bilder, die sich hartnäckig vor unser inneres Auge schieben und so den Blick auf das, was wir gemeinhin „Wirklichkeit" nennen, verstellen.

Tuomo Rainio

1983 geboren in Espoo/FI, lebt und arbeitet in Helsinki
2003-2006 Bachelor of Arts an der Universität für Kunst und Design, Helsinki
seit 2006 MA Programm für Fotografie an der Universität für Kunst und Design, Helsinki
2007-2008 Institut für Imaging Arts and Photography an der Musashino Art University, Tokyo
www.rainio.pp.fi

Die Anwesenheit der Menge.
Veränderung, Bewegung und Zeit sind die Themen, die im Zentrum der Fotografien und Videos des finnischen Künstlers Tuomo Rainio stehen. Das visuelle Denken ist in seinen puristischen Arbeiten in einer Abstimmung zwischen der Ästhetik der Schwarzweißfotografie und der Tradition postkonzeptueller Videokunst gelagert. Das Feld, in dem sich diese Interessen verschränken, ist vielleicht am ehesten als bewegtes Bild ohne gattungsmäßige Bestimmtheit zu beschreiben. Was genau sehen wir, wenn wir die Arbeiten Rainios aus der Serie Tracescape betrachten? Zunächst ein schwarzes Bild, wie eine Schultafel, dann zeichnen sich langsam melancholische und anonyme Stadtlandschaften, Straßenansichten und Gebäudestrukturen ab. Sicher ist dabei einzig die Linie der Bewegung. Die Arbeiten beginnen wie geisterhafte Animationen und verwandeln sich plötzlich in ein bekanntes oder zumindest wiedererkennbares Umfeld. Es liegt etwas schauerliches in der Luft – vielleicht die Anwesenheit der Menge.

Die gesellschaftliche Wirklichkeit ist anwesend in Form der Spuren von Passanten, die ihren täglichen Gängen nachgehen. Wie Rainio betont: „Tracescape ist eine Serie von Videoarbeiten über die gesellschaftliche Struktur im öffentlichen Raum. Im Stadtraum wird das Verhalten jeder Person von den anderen und von dieser Person selbst beobachtet und kontrolliert."

Die Arbeiten City (2005) und Crosswise (2006) stellen sichtbare Kreuzungen und Pfade dar und den Kreislauf des Lebens in einer Stadt, der sich als die blinde Karte dieser Stadt herausstellt. Sie sind wie Stapel von Röntgenbildern: Man kann sich den lebenden Körper dazu vorstellen, und dennoch zeigen sie nur die tragende Struktur. Die Geräuschkulissen zu den Videos bringen die Bilder zurück auf die Ebene alltäglicher Erfahrung, des Eingetauchtseins. Wir können Ampeln hören, vorüberfahrende Autos, Straßenbahnen und den Widerhall von Schritten. Zugleich bündeln sich verschiedene Bewegungslinien, überschneiden sich und hellen das Bild auf. Am Ende geht es nicht um den Film und seine lichtempfindliche Membran, sondern um den auf einem Computer programmierten Algorithmus, der das Video Bild für Bild berechnet und die Veränderungen sichtbar macht. Um eine Analogie zu nennen: Videos sind Zeugen des rapiden Wandels, der sich in der Digitalbildindustrie vollzieht. Technik und Inhalt sind voneinander nicht zu trennen. Das Pixelraster hat auf Rainios einprägsamen Bewegungsbildern eine weitere Bedeutungsebene gewonnen: Es macht die Matrix unserer Zeit sichtbar. (Leevi Haapala, Kuratorin und Wissenschaftlerin, Kiasma, Museum of Contemporary Art, Helsinki)

Jan Kuděj

1978 geboren in Prag, lebt in Prag
1997-1999 Ethnologiestudium an der Fakultät für Philosophie und Künste, Karls-Universität, Prag
1999-2005 Architektur und Design an der Akademie der Künste, Prag
2002-2003 Universität der Künste, Berlin

Jan Kuděj erforscht in seinen Arbeiten systematisch die Frage der Zeit. „Eine absolute Aufzeichnung der Stetigkeit der Zeit ist unmöglich", sagt er. Er hat eine Reihe von „Projektionen" hergestellt, die zwei Techniken verbinden – die des fotografischen Standbilds und die des bewegten Videobilds – und sich mit der Tatsache auseinandersetzen, dass eine Videokamera 25 Bilder pro Sekunde aufzeichnen kann, einer Beschränkung, in deren Folge Bewegung und Zeit unausweichlich zerstückelt werden, auch wenn das Auge sie als stetig wahrnimmt.

In seiner Projektion von Rolltreppen verfolgt er die kreisförmige Bewegung der Maschinen. Mit einer fest auf eine Stelle gerichteten Videokamera hat er einen vollen Zyklus aufgenommen. In der geloopten Projektion scheint die Rolltreppe daher fortwährend zu laufen. In entgegengesetzter Absicht animierte er das Bild eines Baumes so, dass die Bewegungen von dessen Krone im Aufnahmevorgang selbst seriell unterbrochen werden. Die für diese Ausstellung gewählte Projektion von Wellen, die gegen einen Strand auslaufen, leitet sich von dem selben Prinzip her wie die Rolltreppen: der Wahrnehmung der Stetigkeit ablaufender Zeit.

„Aus einer bestimmten Perspektive allerdings sind alle Projektionen abgeschlossen, fixieren sie einen Vorgang in Form eines Standbildes. Zeit ist bloße Illusion."

„Mein Zugang besteht für mich in einer fortlaufenden Aufnahme mit der Videokamera und einer absichtsvoll unterbrochenen Aufnahme von Einzelbildern. Wir erkennen zwei Wahrnehmungen von Zeit – einer Zeit des Augenblicks und einer Zeit der Dauer. Dieser Sinneseindruck hilft uns dabei, die gleichzeitig bestehenden Widersprüche der Zeit in ihrer Entfaltung zu erfahren. Der Begriff, den man von sich selbst (von der Welt) hat, ist nicht stetig. Er wandelt mit jedem neuen Denkvorgang seinen Charakter. Dieser Vorgang selbst ist nichts als eine sich fortwährend wiederholende Unterbrechung. Wir nehmen die Zeit als eine Entfaltung in Augenblicken wahr." (aus Kudějs Dissertation, 2005)

Ange Leccia

1952 geboren in Minerviu, Korsika/F, lebt und arbeitet in Paris
Film und Philosophie, Université Paris-Sorbonne, www.galeriealminerech.com

Die Videoinstallation Orage ist eine metaphysische und nachdenkliche Arbeit, die uns auf eine Reise nach innen einlädt, und darin für die träumerische Gewalt von Ange Leccias Werk insgesamt bezeichnend. Seit seiner Kindheit ist Leccia vom Kino und von bewegten Bildern fasziniert, und sein gesamtes Oeuvre ist getragen von einer Poetik der Energie und lebt von einer Erforschung von Bild und Film; das lässt ihn dem Unausdrückbaren so nahe kommen als nur möglich und verleiht zugleich seinen Arbeiten große emotionale Dichte.

Das in einem abgedunkeltem Raum installierte Diptychon in Form einer sich wiederholenden Projektion auf zwei zueinander gekehrten senkrechten Bildschirmen versetzt uns in einen aufgewühlten Nachthimmel, den Blitze durchzucken; die Zeit scheint zum Stillstand gekommen. Dieser statisch aufgenommene Fluss gewaltiger Energie füllt das Bild wie auch die Tonspur und konfrontiert uns so mit der spürbaren und allgewaltigen Gegenwart der Elemente, einem Symbol für die Tatsache, dass die Natur uns noch stets überlegen ist trotz unserer Bemühungen, uns ihrer zu bemächtigen. Der wiederkehrende Rhythmus der Installation, scheinbar unaufhörlich und irgendwo zwischen visuellem Stillstand und einer Ausdehnung der Zeit angesiedelt, nähert sie der reinen Abstraktion an und eröffnet zugleich einen Weg hin zum Transzendentalen und Erhabenen. Die Verwendung von Wiederholung und Loops in Ange Leccias Bildern erweckt ein Gefühl fortlaufender Erneuerung, das, so der Kunstkritiker Pascal Beausse, „mit Blick auf eine organische Dimension des Bildes, die uns in eine ewige Gegenwart einlädt", gedeutet werden muss. Diese Ausdehnung der Zeit in Verbindung mit der durch die Präsentation der Bilder ermöglichten Versenkung der Sinne bedeutet, dass wir die unterirdischsten Kräfte unserer Vorstellungskraft anrufen können.

Oliver Möst

1968 geboren in Füssen/Allgäu/GER, lebt und arbeitet in Berlin als freier Fotograf und Videokünstler. 1999 erstes Videoprojekt in Zusammenarbeit mit einer Choreographin für zeitgenössischen Tanz
www.olivermoest.de

„Bilder, die scharf sind, haben die Unschärfe überwunden. Sie ignorieren die Erfahrungen, die in der Unschärfe möglich sind." [3]

3 BRETTHAUER, BASTIAN, „SO EINE WELT OHNE ECKEN UND KANTEN" IN K4 GALERIE, EDS., OLIVER MÖST, CLACKASTIGMAT 6.0 / K4 GALERIE (BERLIN, DORN, 2005).

Oliver Mösts 2007 entstandene Videoarbeiten stellen die Fortsetzung seiner fotografischen Arbeiten dar. Sie zeichnen sich auf den ersten Blick durch eine auffallende Unschärfe aus, die sowohl in den Fotografien als auch in den Videos das leitende ästhetische Prinzip des Künstlers darstellen. Unschärfe-Techniken führen uns den Kern des Wahrnehmungsprozesses vor Augen.

Oliver Mösts eigener Wahrnehmungsprozess ist durchgehendes Thema seiner Arbeiten: Er leidet an einem „Sehfehler", seine Brille muss links 2,0 und rechts 6,0 Dioptrien ausgleichen. Seine fotografischen und filmischen Arbeiten machen den subjektiven Blick des Fotografen in Form eines „Das-hat-er-dort-auf-diese-Weise-gesehen-und-wahrgenommen" erfahrbar und verdeutlichen darüber hinaus seine Eigenwahrnehmung sowie die Erfahrung des ihn umgebenden Raumes (between, hide & seek, brown eyes).

Ein weiteres Thema, durch das sich Mösts Videoarbeiten besonders auszeichnen, ist die Reflexion der Fotografie und ihrer medienimmanenten Eigenschaften in der filmisch-fotografischen Auseinandersetzung. Entstanden aus der Idee, zwei fotografische Techniken miteinander zu verbinden, bedient er sich zum einen einer linsenfreien Lochkamera, einer camera obscura, der Grundform aller fotografischen Kameras. Diese Technik kombiniert er mit digitaler Videotechnik, indem er mit einer Videokamera das sich auf der Mattscheibe der Lochkamera abzeichnende Bild abfilmt und aufzeichnet. Durch die Auseinandersetzung mit der „alten" Lochkameratechnik einerseits und modernster digitaler Videotechnik andererseits entstehen „Lochvideos" (pinhole videos), wie Möst seine Arbeiten nennt. Sie spiegeln die technische Entwicklung der Fotografie von einer einfachen Lochkamera zur digitalen, technisch ausgereiften Videokamera wider und reflektieren somit auch die grundlegenden, über die Jahre erweiterten Eigenschaften des Mediums Fotografie.

Tim Parchikov

1983 geboren in Moskau, lebt und arbeitet in Moskau
2006 Diplom als Kameramann am Russischen Institut für Kinematographie, Moskau

Tim Parchikov ist ein Moskauer Dichter und Fotograf Mitte zwanzig. Für seine Generation ist die Welt wirklich zu klein und aus geografischer Sicht zuweilen allzu sichtbar und zugänglich geworden. Glücklicherweise nimmt Tim Parchikov das Leben wie ein echter Poet wahr und stellt für den Betrachter seine eigene Weltsicht dar, eine Weltsicht so voller Energie, so geladen mit dem frischen Gefühl der Jugend, dass sich alle Bedenken, seine Arbeit könne vorhersagbar oder offensichtlich sein, von selbst erledigen. Diese Arbeiten sind voller Ozon. Das Gefühl allumfassender Traurigkeit, wie es für junge Menschen oft typisch ist, und seine profunde Kenntnis russischer und internationaler Fotografie mindern um nichts jene elektrisierende Frische, die seine Werke ausstrahlen.

Die schöpferische Individualität dieses jungen Künstlers und die Weite seiner Persönlichkeit lassen deutlich ein echtes, reifes und unabhängiges Talent in mehreren klassischen Künsten erkennen. Ein feiner Sinn für Farbe, ein starkes Gefühl für den Goldenen Schnitt und ein Denken in kühnen Metaphern erlauben Tim Parchikov einen wagemutigen und originellen Ausdruck. Hier ist eine neue Stimme, die Gehör verdient.

Das Video Gone to Sea ist eine Miniatur, die sich der Vorstellung zuwendet, ohne besonderen Grund zur See – und das heißt: im Nirgendwo – zu verschwinden. Gone to Sea erinnert an Michelangelo Antonionis „L'Avventura", in dem die Heldin plötzlich und ohne erkennbaren Grund verschwindet. Doch was jeden einzelnen von uns besonders interessiert, ist nicht lediglich das Problem des Verschwindens, sondern ob es unbemerkt bleiben wird ...

Matteo Peterlini

1970 geboren in Rovereto/I, lebt und arbeitet in Rovereto
Abschluß in Informatik, gefolgt von einem Kurs für Grafisches Design und Werbung 1992
Erste Ausstellungen 1997, seitdem in Trient, Venedig, Turin, Istanbul Contemporary Art Museum
www.matteopeterlini.it

Den Pixel als Maßeinheit zu verwenden, ist in Matteo Peterlinis fotografischen Arbeiten ein durchaus ernstgemeintes konzeptionelles Element, eine programmatische Wahl.

Solcherart zerlegt und wieder zusammengesetzt sind die Bilder in seiner Fotoserie Ergebnisse eines Rechenprozesses, der nach dem Unendlichen strebt und in dem das System, das die Bruchstücke kombiniert, dem Zufall anvertraut und nach einer algebraischen Funktion angewandt wird.

Peterlini wagt es gar, die Ursünde ins Auge zu fassen und sich ganz auf die grundlegenden Mechanismen der Wahrnehmung zu konzentrieren, in eigens angefertigter Software einer bestimmten Art. Wie werden in unserem Geist Bilder hervorgebracht? Die durch Nachahmung, Lernvorgänge und Mitteilung ausgewählten Mechanismen, mittels derer wir normalerweise die Welt verstehen, verlieren ihre Wirkung, wenn wir uns dem assoziativen Fluss, wie ihn der elektronische Prozess erzeugt, gegenübersehen. Es scheint daher kein Widerspruch, dass es sich um traditionelle Gattungen der Malerei handelt: Porträts, Akte, Landschaften. Tatsächlich kann man dank der Frontalansicht der Gesichter (wie sie für ein normales Passfoto Pflicht sind, in Meyouother), der Silhouetten der Körper (die sich in den sechs von den Modellen verlangten Posen in V6 abzeichnen) und der Unbewegtheit der beinahe abstrakten Landschaften (in Backscapes) die unbewusste Tendenz anerkennen, das „bereits Bekannte" wahrzunehmen (Gestalt, Stereotypen), eine Tendenz, die es uns normalerweise ermöglicht, der Vielfalt der Phänomene gerecht zu werden.

Darüberhinaus enthüllt genau der von einer nur scheinbar „handwerklichen" Technik ermöglichte scherzhafte Betrug, den Peterlini einsetzt, um seinen Fotoserien Leben zu verleihen, den analytischen Charakter seiner Arbeiten. In der Tat: Betrachtet man die Bilder (genau genommen Ergebnisse eines fortlaufenden schöpferischen Flusses) aus der Nähe, funktionieren sie wie Collagen, während andererseits der Prozess, der der Wahrnehmung des Bildes als Ganzen dient, in der virtuellen Koexistenz aller möglichen Kombinationen aufgehoben ist. (Cristina Natalicchio)

Peter Puklus & Melinda Sipos

Peter Puklus
1980 geboren in Koloszvár/H, lebt in Budapest.
2005 Diplom für Fotografie an der Moholy-Nagy Universität für Kunst und Design, Budapest
http://photolumen.hu/puklus
www.deuxprojects.blogspot.com

Melinda Sipos
1979 geboren in Budapest/H, lebt in Budapest.
2005 Diplom für Glasdesign an der Moholy-Nagy Universität für Kunst und Design, Budapest
http://siposmelinda.blogspot.com
www.deuxprojects.blogspot.com

Peter Puklus & Melinda Sipos arbeiten beide eigenständig und haben je ihre eigene und unverwechselbare künstlerische Herangehensweise. Die zwei Projekte Imported Lights und Garden allerdings verwirklichten sie als Gruppe unter dem Namen DEUX. Die Titel der zwei Arbeiten beschränken sich auf einfache sachliche Angaben. DEUX_ 00 Imported Lights ist das „Nullprojekt" der Gruppe, wie sie es nennen. Die recht konzeptuelle Idee ist, das indirekte Licht, das durch ein Fenster eindringt, einzufangen und in einen fensterlosen Raum zu projizieren. Aus der Perspektive von „Mutations II" haben wir hier ein als Video projiziertes Standbild vor uns.

Eine ähnliche Logik findet in DEUX_ 01 Garden Anwendung, dem ersten von Peter Puklus und Melinda Sipos gemeinsam unternommenen Projekt, wie der Titel deutlich anzeigt. Es handelt sich um eine detaillierte Aufzeichnung eines Gartens über einen langen Zeitraum. Das Künstlerpaar machte ein Jahr lang jeden Tag aus dem selben Fenster ein Foto. Das Ergebnis ist eine Bestandsaufnahme kleinster Veränderungen im Raum: bewegte Stühle, der Verlauf der Jahreszeiten ... Als Diashow ruft es den Eindruck hervor, dass sich diese Veränderungen in der Realzeit der Projektion abspielen.

Beiden Arbeiten liegen einfache, aber sorgfältig zur Anwendung gebrachte Ideen zugrunde. Die technischen Aspekte, wie etwa die Wahl der Medien Fotografie und Video und die Konversion vom einen ins andere, sind von nachgeordneter Bedeutung und durch die künstlerische Konzeption motiviert, im Unterschied zu den Arbeiten anderer Künstler in dieser Auswahl, die sich von technischen Möglichkeiten inspirieren ließen. Für Puklus und Sipos war die Herangehensweise, die Fotografie auf das Video hin zu überschreiten, eine einleuchtende Lösung für die Verwirklichung ihrer künstlerischen Intention.

Jutta Strohmaier

1966 geboren in Tulln/A, lebt in Wien.
1996-1999 Malerei, Schwerpunkt Fotografie und Neue Medien, an der Akademie der Bildenden Künste Wien (Eva Schlegel)
www.jutta-strohmaier.net

Wie stehen Bilder und Wirklichkeit zueinander? Welche Wirklichkeit können Bilder erschaffen? Diesen Fragen geht Jutta Strohmaier in ihren Videos, Fotografien und Installationen auf den Grund.

In Passenger (2004) wird eine mehrere Tage dauernde, minütlich erfolgende Digitalaufnahme eines leeren Innenraumes mit zwei großen Fenstern auf eine knappe Viertelstunde komprimiert. Verhindern oder erschweren die Fenster bei Tag aufgrund der hellen Lichtverhältnisse den Blick nach außen, so treten ab Einbruch der Dämmerung der Außenraum und die gegenüberliegende Hausfassade zusehends in den Vordergrund. Es ist ein Spiel mit der Wahrnehmung eines Raumes, die sich laufend verschiebt und den Raumbegriff in Bezug auf Kategorien wie Zugehörigkeit/Ausgeschlossensein, Eigenes/Fremdes, Offenheit/Geschlossenheit untersucht (vgl. Sarah Kolb zur Ausstellung „Jutta Strohmaier. diese Welt und andere", Galerie Hohenlohe, Wien 2004).

Das Prinzip der kontinuierlichen fotografischen Aufnahme und Montierung zum Animationsvideo behält Strohmaier auch in Arbeiten wie Im Dickicht (2005) oder Silent Stories (2006) bei. Bei Ersterer ist jeder Schritt durchs Dickicht eines verwachsenen Auwaldes ein Abdrücken der Kamera. Die „Zwischenräume" zwischen den einzelnen Bildern werden am Computer mit Photoshop bearbeitet, sodass das Geäst zunächst regelrecht „zerfressen", in einer späteren Sequenz dann wieder verdichtet und zuletzt ins Blau des Himmels aufgelöst wird.

Die zum Videoloop montierten Satellitenfotos in Journey (2005) bieten den Blick vom Weltall auf die Erde – eine Perspektive, die uns allen dank Fernsehen und Internet wohl vertraut ist, die aber kaum jemand bis jetzt selbst einnehmen konnte. Strohmaier gräbt sich durch ihr über Jahre hinweg angelegtes Fotoarchiv von Beobachtungssatelliten. Statt einer linearen Aneinanderreihung der aufgenommenen Städte und Naturlandschaften perforieren und durchdringen sich diese jedoch gegenseitig, werden schichtweise abgetragen, quer durch die Erde und wieder retour.

Wolfgang Thaler

1969 geboren in Salzburg/A, lebt in Wien.
1989-1991 Bayerische Staatslehranstalt für Photographie, München (heute FH München)
www.wolfgangthaler.at

Wolfgang Thalers Arbeiten fallen in die Sparte der Architektur- (Serien über den Wiener Südbahnhof oder Kreisverkehre) und Dokumentarfotografie (u.a. über die Wiener Traditionscafehauskette Aida) und bekunden sein, zumeist sehr analytisches, Interesse am Raum.

Die Serie Matter of Selection (2007) gibt den Blick auf die Wohnung eines Sammlers preis. Mit einem hochauflösenden Schwarz-Weiß-Film fotografiert Thaler zunächst dessen Mobiliar (Kleiderschrank, Bücherregal) und tastet darauf in detektivischer Manier jedes Detail des entstandenen Fotos am Computer ab. Die Mutation erfolgt auf mehreren Ebenen: Die Ausdehnung einer fotografischen Momentaufnahme zu einer endlosen Kamerafahrt; die Verschiebung der Realität, indem nicht das Objekt, sondern ein Foto dessen abgefilmt wird; und hiervon wiederum werden ausschließlich Details, nie aber die komplette Ansicht preisgegeben.

Welcome to Mep'Yuk – so heißt Thaler die BesucherInnen seiner imaginären, menschenleeren, lediglich aus Innenräumen bestehenden Stadt mit dem Phantasienamen Mep'Yuk. Die Zentrale (1999) willkommen. In mehreren Städten weltweit fotografiert der Künstler nüchterne Firmeneingangshallen, Lobbys, Büros oder Warteräume, die trotz ihrer unterschiedlichen kulturellen Backgrounds und Ausstattungen eines gemeinsam haben – sie sind (halb-)öffentliche Räume mit vorwiegender Verwaltungs-, Strukturierungs- und Organisationsfunktion. Die entstandenen Fotografien werden aneinandergereiht und in langsamen, horizontalen Kameraschwenken Schritt für Schritt abgetastet. Thaler verweigert auch hier dem Betrachter/der Betrachterin die Gesamtansicht und erlaubt nur das ausschnittsweise Erfassen der Interieurs. Das auftretende Gefühl, man beobachte mittels einer Überwachungskamera diese Plätze, führt bald zur Frage – was gilt es zu beobachten, wenn keine Menschen in dieser „Zentrale" agieren?

Mutations II – Moving Stills / L'aventure d'une image sous tension

Dans le cadre du Mois Européen de la Photographie, initié en 2004 et regroupant aujourd'hui les festivals de Paris, Berlin, Bratislava, Luxembourg, Moscou, Rome et Vienne, il était légitime et nécessaire de s'interroger collectivement sur les mutations de notre monde et notamment sur celles de l'image contemporaine. C'est le parti pris qui a conduit à la mise en œuvre en 2006 d'une première exposition intitulée « Mutations I » ; événement centré sur les mutations technologiques et artistiques de la photographie.

La seconde édition de cette manifestation « Mutations II », se propose de prolonger la réflexion autour du médium vidéo, en poursuivant l'exploration des rapports féconds qu'entretiennent l'image fixe et l'image en mouvement et en esquissant un état des lieux de la création contemporaine en Europe.

Dans un contexte marqué par la globalisation et la convergence numérique de tous nos supports de communication et de création, l'ère du « post-medium » dans laquelle nous entrons est une « époque marquée par l'exploration de l'hybridation des technologies, où les artistes combinent et recombinent la vidéo avec un large éventail de matériaux »[1] – photographie, art sonore, vidéo numérique, cinéma, DVD, art informatique, CD-Rom, graphisme et animation. Chaque art devient donc plus que jamais susceptible de « couvrir en lui-même, à l'intérieur de ses limites matérielles, mais aussi en forçant sur elles, le spectre entier de la communauté qu'il forme avec les autres arts »[2].

En abandonnant son statut de matériau à fixer la réalité enregistrée et en empruntant à l'art vidéo l'une de ses données essentielles, la dimension temporelle, la photographie s'émancipe par toutes sortes de manipulations artistiques et d'hybridations techniques aussi bien analogiques que numériques.

Les auteurs de « Mutations II » ont donc choisi de mettre en lumière des artistes européens que rassemble le goût de l'expérimentation de nouvelles formes d'expression ; ils se sont interrogés, à l'instar de Nancy Spector dans son essai intitulé « Art Photography after Photography »[3], sur les critères spécifiques qui étaient à même de déterminer la distinction entre un photographe et un artiste travaillant avec la photographie.

Un nombre croissant de photographes utilise aujourd'hui la vidéo, faisant évoluer les spécificités qui définissent chacune de ces deux pratiques. Au-delà de la diversité des partis pris esthétiques et des techniques visuelles utilisées, les créateurs présentés dans le cadre de « Mutations II » nous invitent à dépasser les logiques territoriales et les définitions académiques qui enclavent chacun de ces champs artistiques afin d'explorer les frontières qui les séparent. Autrement dit « Mutations II » nous invite à la découverte des nouveaux territoires de l'image fixe et l'image en mouvement à travers les tensions qui les animent. Tension ontologique entre l'instantané et la durée, tension esthétique consécutive à l'hybridation de l'image argentique et d'une image-flux, tension dialectique entre les modalités limitées d'accrochage de l'image photographique et « l'infini des combinaisons perceptives dans lesquelles peuvent se définir et s'articuler les images électroniques »[4] et notamment l'installation vidéo.

Pour Gilles Deleuze et Felix Guattari, « il n'y a pas de territoire sans vecteur de sortie du territoire (...) sans effort pour se re-territorialiser ailleurs »[5]. En limitant ce questionnement philosophique au strict domaine artistique, on peut avancer que la dynamique propre à tout courant artistique est une force centrifuge qui tend à s'éloigner des conventions et des normes en vigueur, un

1 RUSH (MICHAEL). 2007. L'ART VIDÉO. LONDRES, THAMES & HUDSON.
2 BELLOUR (RAYMOND). 1999. L'ENTRE-IMAGES 2. P.O.L. PARIS.

3 MOVING PICTURES, CONTEMPORARY PHOTOGRAPHY AND VIDEO FROM THE GUGGENHEIM MUSEUM COLLECTIONS. 2003. NEW YORK. GUGGENHEIM MUSEUM PUBLICATIONS, P 31-19.
4 VAILLANT (ALEXIS), PARFAIT (FRANÇOISE), JANKOVIC (NIKOLA). 2001. LES NOUVELLES IMAGES. TOME 1. CHRONIQUES DE L'AFAA, PARIS.
5 DELEUZE (GILLES). 2004. L'ABÉCÉDAIRE DE GILLES DELEUZE. PARIS. MONTPARNASSE, DVD.

FRENCH
(Traductions françaises :
texte de Marc Gisbourne : Sarah Vermande
autres textes : Martyn Back)

« vecteur de sortie » qui pose comme condition nécessaire à son existence la nouveauté de son regard sur le monde.

Regard qui dans les travaux de Peter Aerschmann convoque l'étrangeté de saynètes illustrant l'enjeu fondamental de ses travaux : chercher le moyen de photographier un espace tout en conservant la profondeur temporelle, de produire une photographie qui ne serait pas un instantané et qui, loin de figer le mouvement, le donnerait à voir. Peter Aerschmann inclut ainsi le temps dans la figuration de l'espace. Il déplace le principe de la fixité de l'image pour l'appliquer au mouvement qu'il fige dans l'unité de sa réalisation. Aerschmann fait ainsi « bégayer » le langage vidéographique en montrant des personnages qui semblent prisonniers des actions répétitives qu'ils accomplissent en boucle.

Cette richesse sémantique et stylistique inhérente à la répétition inspire également Gast Bouschet et Nadine Hilbert dans la construction de Dreamsequence, œuvre vidéographique créée en 2006/07. En retournant sur les lieux du tournage du film de Philipp Kauffman « Invasion of the bodysnatchers » réalisé dans les années 1978, les auteurs réactualisent et re-contextualisent l'idée de paranoïa par l'usage d'images récurrentes et obsessionnelles. Sacrifiant à dessein le réflexe conventionnel d'une narration linéaire, cette séquence onirique à la fois poétique et politique, repose sur un réseau relationnel entre fragments de photo, vidéo, sons et textes qui interroge notre objectivité et mobilise toute l'acuité de notre perception.

Si Christoph Brech joue lui aussi avec nos facultés perceptives, c'est tout d'abord pour aimanter notre attention. Apparemment immobiles mais toujours en mouvement les objets, personnages ou paysages qu'il filme font cheminer le regard d'un niveau de lecture à un autre ; regard oscillant entre la volonté de décrypter l'image et la contemplation qu'inspire d'emblée une écriture vidéographique d'une extrême sobriété. Break, œuvre hypnotique réalisée en un seul plan-séquence, sans effet de caméra, illustre cette épure formelle. Nous saisissons l'essence même du mouvement : la transitivité, tout en ressentant de façon presque viscérale la force tectonique du temps. Temporalité mise en correspondance avec ce qui est donné à voir : l'immense étendue d'un fleuve gelé lentement balayée par des nuées de vapeur d'eau qui répondent à la presque imperceptible dérive des glaces. Le brise-glace qui traverse alors ces éléments hostiles avant de disparaître - ne laissant derrière lui qu'un sillage que la glace contrarie et absorbe aussitôt - offre une allégorie inspirée de la condition humaine.

Avec Big Bang d'Ori Gersht c'est la métaphore politique de l'humanité jetée dans le chaos de la guerre qui est en jeu. Et c'est précisément parce qu'un conflit et la violence qui s'y manifeste constituent un point de rupture que les questionnements esthétiques et les recherches plastiques de cet auteur explorent avec autant d'intensité la notion de transition ; démarche ici transposée au passage de l'image fixe à l'image en mouvement. A première vue, Big Bang ressemble à une nature morte baroque. Mais l'usage du son que fait intervenir Ori Gersht donne une dimension temporelle à la fixité du tableau et insuffle une tension dramatique qui atteint son apogée avec l'explosion d'une composition florale tournée au ralenti ; saisie appuyée du passage d'un objet à sa dislocation. Cette transition allant de la figuration à l'abstraction pure aboutit à une stase optique et renvoie à l'image mentale que les sirènes et les explosions du conflit israélo-palestinien ont laissées dans la mémoire d'enfant de l'artiste. Démarche artistique qui tout en explorant les relations entre photographie, peinture et vidéo consiste au sens propre comme au figuré à « traverser » la forme pour nous conduire à la sacrifier.

Si l'œuvre du jeune artiste finlandais Tuomo Rainio interroge le temps et la mutation tout comme le travail d'Ori Gersht, son approche est totalement différente. Au lieu de prendre comme point de départ la nature esthétique de l'image, sa démarche s'articule autour de la nature du mouvement. Grâce à un programme informatique de traitement de l'image qu'il a lui-même conçu, les images captées au moyen d'un simple appareil photo nous donnent à voir des environnements urbains où l'activité des citadins n'est visible que sous la forme des traces fantomatiques laissées par leurs passages. Ce processus correspond à une approche qui est à la fois politique et conceptuelle ; politique en ce qu'elle renvoie à un espace public quadrillé par les réseaux de caméras de télésurveillance, conceptuelle en ce qu'elle représente la tension de l'entre-deux, la permanence de la présence et de l'absence.

Jutta Strohmaier utilise elle aussi les potentialités qu'offrent les technologies numériques soit pour faire croitre l'image fixe par le milieu soit pour la reconfigurer avec des effets de lumière, cut outs ou de balayages électroniques qui la modifient en permanence. Dans Journey ou Im Dickicht la sensation de mouvement émane du fait que l'image n'apparaît jamais complètement achevée mais toujours en transition entre ce qui la précède et ce qui lui succède ; ainsi, le présent n'offre jamais une unité temporelle mais un éclatement de temporalités qui déstructure l'image. Avec Passenger, la compression du temps obtenue par des prises de vues effectuées chaque minute pendant plusieurs jours depuis l'intérieur d'une pièce vide offre une approche distanciée du quotidien perçu à travers le rythme accéléré des cycles diurnes et nocturnes. Pour Silent Stories les photographies mises en scène sont soumises à des effets de superposition, de fondu et de transparence qui nous proposent une relecture fictionnelle de la réalité. Même si Jutta Strohmaier utilise la photographie comme matière première dans la composition de ses scénarios, la perception du mouvement, les processus de transformation et la déconstruction du temps y occupent une place centrale, permettant ainsi à l'image de libérer la multiplicité des sens dont elle est chargée.

Pour Olga Chernysheva, c'est une réflexion sur l'espace de l'image qui prévaut dans la recherche formelle à l'origine de l'installation Windows. Fascinée par les vestiges de l'unité communiste disparue, l'artiste observe le quotidien des Russes d'aujourd'hui et le restitue sous la forme d'une installation dont la mise en scène n'a rien de fortuit. Filmée de nuit, caméra à l'épaule, chacune des fenêtres d'un immeuble devient le cadre d'une scène où les habitants apparaissent et disparaissent, comme des personnages de théâtre, dans l'intimité des coulisses sombres de leurs appartements. La nature scénique de ces instants de vie est soulignée par le dispositif multi-écrans qui, tout en spatialisant l'image dans l'espace d'exposition permet une mise en abîme de l'intime qui ouvre le discours entre l'œuvre et le spectateur.

Ces artistes européens ont donc en commun de faire subir à la photographie ou/et à la vidéo, chacun selon ses nécessités, un traitement déformateur. Ils explorent ainsi les lignes de fuites qui se forment à la frontière de ces territoires et instaurent un nouveau régime de l'image et de la perception ; par là même, ils poussent le langage photographique et vidéographique vers leurs limites propres, limites qui constituent la condition d'émergence de l'inédit, de l'originalité et du style selon Deleuze.

Gageons que ces nouvelles expérimentations qui poussent la photographie et la vidéo en marge ou en dehors du champs qui semblait devoir leur être assigné nous donnent une occasion inédite de renouveler notre regard sur le monde et nous engagent à réinventer notre quotidien, à le « voir selon l'œuvre » pour reprendre la formule de Merleau-Ponty[6].

Jean-Luc Soret

avec la collaboration de Gunda Achleitner, Berthold Ecker, Paul Di Felice, Anna Gianesini, Kathrin Kohle, Ekaterina Kondranina, Zuzana Lapitkova, Emiliano Paoletti, Jean-Luc Monterosso, Pierre Stiwer, Olga Sviblova, and Barbara Wolffer.

6 MERLEAU-PONTY (MAURICE). 1960. L'ŒIL ET L'ESPRIT. PARIS. FOLIO. ESSAIS.

Mutations II – Moving Stills

Cultiver l'entre-deux

La photographie et la vidéo ont une proximité tout aussi grande que ce qui les sépare, originellement, dans leur rapport au temps. Et les évolutions techniques incitent aujourd'hui les artistes à les rapprocher : on peut filmer avec un appareil photographique, et prendre des photographies avec des caméras vidéo. On passe en outre pour l'un comme pour l'autre par le stade numérique, même dans des procédés argentiques, et sur informatique l'arrêt sur image est aisé, et le diaporama lancé en un seul clic. Arrêter le mouvement d'un côté, introduire un continuum temporel de l'autre. Deux gestes d'une grande simplicité technique, dont les bouleversements sont pourtant très importants. La question n'est pas dans la fragilisation de la frontière entre deux médiums (l'art vidéo s'est toujours constitué dans la proximité avec d'autres pratiques artistiques), mais dans les oeuvres que cette porosité génère. C'est ce territoire de l'entre-deux que « Mutations II » explore. Les artistes sélectionnés ont en commun d'utiliser la vidéo dans la tension qui la relie à l'image fixe et à ses composantes : l'unité du cadre, la temporalité en fuite, la qualification particulière de l'écoulement de l'instant. Certains élaborent leurs recherches vidéo dans la proximité d'un travail photographique, dans un va-et-vient permanent. De là découle un rapport particulier à l'image, qui nous invite à la saisir dans son instabilité, mais aussi dans les enjeux qu'elle révèle à travers ces pratiques mutantes.

Travailler l'épaisseur temporelle

Dans son essai « The Reflecting Pool de Bill Viola », Jean-Paul Fargier analyse cette bande et ses procédés d'incrustation comme le basculement de l'artiste dans l'art vidéo. Car « l'image divisée peut être considérée comme l'apanage de la vidéo »[1]. Les images travaillées par l'incrustation, peuplées de différentes temporalités, de récits multiples et concomitants, seraient ainsi une caractéristique forte de l'art vidéo. C'est ce qui s'affirme en tous cas chez un certain nombre de travaux qui dialoguent fortement avec l'image photographique, avec la suspension temporelle, et qui comme Bill Viola dans cette bande célèbre, opèrent des basculements, génèrent un trouble dans la perception de l'arrêt et du mouvement. David Claerbout a ainsi élaboré une oeuvre où il se réapproprie des photographies et les amène sur le territoire de la vidéo en intervenant sur leur densité temporelle pour retrouver le présent de l'image. Dans Sans titre (Carl et Julia), 2000, l'image en noir et blanc nous montre un homme et sa fille photographiés en train de prendre le petit déjeuner. Mais lorsque l'on entre dans l'espace de projection, la fille tourne son regard vers nous, nous figeant à notre tour face au pouvoir de la vidéo à redonner vie, à rejouer au présent ce qui s'était figé dans le passé. Avec une de ses dernières pièces, Dancing couple (after : Couples at square dance, McIntosh County, Oklahoma, 1939 or 1940), 2008, son intervention gagne encore en radicalité : un jeune couple est photographié sur une piste de danse, surpris par le flash qui les a interrompus et prélevés du moment présent. D. Claerbout récupère cette image et la projette, redoublant l'action du flash par la lumière du projecteur. La temporalité de la projection affirme ainsi sa nécessaire prise dans le présent, et oppose à la fixité du tirage photographique le mouvement constitutif de la projection. L'artificialité de la construction est affirmée, et cette introduction d'une temporalité mouvante au sein de l'image fixe provoque une sensation de vertige et de malaise. L'entre-deux est proche du vide, d'autant qu'il se produit dans l'obscurité d'installations toujours finement orchestrées, et dans des atmosphères globalement silencieuses, où le son spatialisé est utilisé avec parcimonie.

Le procédé d'animation est aujourd'hui très présent dans la création, en particulier comme extension du dessin. Il permet d'explorer plus radicalement la temporalité, et d'associer différents supports d'images, comme le fait Hans op de Beeck en animant de manière troublante dessin et photographie. Les espaces ainsi représentés sont étranges car ils sont proches de la réalité sans pour autant se confondre avec elle. Jutta Strohmaier, jeune artiste autrichienne, réalise également des images fixes qu'elle anime lentement. Comme chez D. Claerbout, on est sans cesse confronté à une situation d'indécision quand au statut de l'image, sur sa nature, et sur son rapport au temps. L'accumulation de photographies introduit une impression de mouvement, mais sans qu'elles soient suffisamment nombreuses pour rompre la stabilité amenée par l'image fixe. La lumière a un rôle fondamental en marquant l'écoulement du temps au sein de l'espace photographié, où il ne se passe souvent pas grand chose. Dans Passenger (2004) on assiste ainsi à un changement d'atmosphère lumineuse à travers un plan fixe sur une fenêtre, filmée de l'intérieur d'une pièce vide. On passe d'un état coloré à un autre, le blanc vire au bleu, au rose puis encore au jaune, dans une métamorphose saccadée. Les vidéos de J. Strohmaier ne cherchent jamais à créer l'illusion de la continuité, elles nous mettent face à des lieux d'entre-deux (pièce vide, sous-bois encombré, espace urbain de circulation) avec un grand travail sur la distance et le cadrage, en observateur attentif mais décalé. L'image est aussi le lieu d'interventions plastiques par surimpression, par détourage, par une modification des couleurs qui met en avant la dimension fabriquée, construite du regard posé sur le monde.

L'écart entre la photographie et la vidéo est ainsi creusé pour inviter à des méditations sur nos expériences perceptives. Peter Aerschmann, artiste suisse, explore aussi l'épaisseur temporelle en déconstruisant notre rapport à l'espace-temps. Ses images sont le résultat d'incrustations de différents plans où les éléments se juxtaposent en résistant à une perception unitaire de l'ensemble. Chaque personnage, chaque aspect du décor est certes constitutif d'une composition globale mais sans qu'une atmosphère partagée vienne faire le lien entre eux.

1 THE REFLECTING POOL DE BILL VIOLA, JEAN-PAUL FARGIER, ÉDITIONS YELLOW NOW CÔTÉ FILMS # 2, 2005, P.14.

Comme dans les peintures d'Uccello, les proportions sont respectées, les agencements visuellement cohérents, mais ce qui s'affirme c'est une grande solitude. La caméra glisse sur ces mises en scène dans un mouvement de travelling latéral, découvrant au fur à mesure des personnages esseulés, enfermés dans la répétition d'un geste, dans des paysages où il manque une unité. Dans les vidéos d'Aerschmann, l'espace-temps est fondamentalement déréglé, mais notre regard continue néanmoins de circuler lentement avec la caméra. Entre fixité austère des éléments architecturaux et mouvement en boucle des personnages, entre photographie, vidéo et peinture, le travail d' Aerschmann est au coeur des enjeux dans lesquels s'est engagé « Mutations II ».

Mettre sous cadre

Le cadrage de l'image, geste de définition, de saisie, mais aussi de mise à l'écart du visible, est une prise de position face au monde. Une démarche essentielle dans l'histoire de l'art vidéo a été le retour sur soi de la caméra, l'affirmation d'une quête identitaire, d'une exploration de l'image de soi. Vito Acconci, Peter Campus, Bruce Nauman, Joan Jonas et bien d'autres, dans des démarches variées, ont mis leur propre corps face au miroir-vidéo. Mais au-delà de l'immédiateté fascinante, voire narcissique, de l'autofilmage, le rapport au reflet permet d'explorer l'intrigue de l'apparition et de la disparition de l'image de soi. Jean Otth, artiste suisse, a ainsi dans les années 70 développé un dispositif vidéo et miroir où il joue avec sa propre image en la cernant, en l'obscurcissant, en interrogeant les affects que l'on projette face à cette manipulation de l'image de soi. La vidéo lui permet de jouer avec le reflet en prenant le temps de l'inquiéter, de le mettre en danger, et de donner ainsi à voir et à entendre les relations que l'on entretient avec sa propre image. Miroir (2000) d'Elina Brotherus (artiste finlandaise), double travail en photographie et vidéo, est aussi une mise en scène de soi qui met à distance le reflet en conditionnant son apparition au passage du temps. Dans la série photographique, E. Brotherus pose nue devant un miroir de salle de bain embué. Au début, le reflet est donc empêché, imposant l'expérience de la non-coïncidence entre un corps et son image. Mais le passage d'une image à une autre permet au miroir de révéler progressivement, au fil du temps, le reflet. Dans la vidéo, le cadrage est quasiment le même, redoublant ainsi à première vue la série photographique. Mais le mouvement de l'image permet de réintroduire la vitalité du processus en donnant une place essentielle au corps dans l'évolution de la surface du miroir. La respiration d'E. Brotherus est en effet centrale, elle agit sur l'atmosphère et participe au phénomène d'apparition/ disparition de l'image dans le miroir, réintroduisant la dimension organique dans une situation où le corps fait avant tout image.

Dans son introduction à son essai L'entre-images, Raymond Bellour explique qu' « il s'est avéré qu'on était entré, avec la vidéo et tout ce qu'elle entraîne, dans un autre temps de l'image »[2]. Même lorsque la vidéo est composée d'une manière photographique, en fixant le cadre, ce qu'il se passe dans la durée fait advenir un autre rapport à l'espace et au temps. Jan Kuděj, jeune artiste tchèque a réalisé plusieurs vidéos qui interrogent l'expérience temporelle. Il associe par exemple deux projections qui présentent deux plans fixes, l'un sur un ensemble de quatre escalators et l'autre sur un arbre dans un champ. Les escalators sont une courte boucle vidéo rythmée par leurs mouvements ascendants et descendants tandis que l'arbre est un montage d'images fixes où le feuillage verdoyant évolue de manière saccadée. L'association des deux, fluidité mécanique d'un côté et discontinuité naturelle de l'autre, met à distance la perception dynamique du réel. A rebours d'une société où le mouvement fait loi, J. Kuděj opère des disjonctions, des coupes dans l'image et nous plonge dans l'incapacité à retrouver le paisible état du spectacle d'un arbre vibrant dans le vent (que Claerbout a par ailleurs filmé avec magnificence dans Boom, plan fixe sur un arbre proche de celui de J. Kuděj mais baigné dans la fluidité fascinante du mouvement). En investissant la vidéo dans sa relation avec la photographie, c'est sa capacité à créer l'illusion de la continuité qui est mise en doute. Par la construction de situations de rétention du flux, les oeuvres introduisent du déséquilibre, de l'instabilté dans notre relation au monde.

Quête du regard

Si la vidéo est ainsi travaillée et inquiétée par la photographie, elle est aussi le lieu où s'élabore une réflexion sur le regard photographique. C'est ce que fait Laurent Goldring, artiste français, en installant dans la tradition photographique du portrait, une relation frontale au modèle dans un studio de prise de vue, d'où il interroge les représentations photographiques du corps. La temporalité de la vidéo est ce qui lui permet de mettre en place avec le corps de ses modèles, tous danseurs et la plupart chorégraphes, une recherche de leur devenir-image. Comme la scène est étroite et la caméra fixe, le danseur ne peut guère se déplacer et ses mouvements se concentrent alors sur une posture. La pose prise, le corps glisse doucement d'une apparition à une autre, guidé par Laurent Goldring et accentué par l'éclairage, par les jeux d'ombre et de lumière. Les images qui en émergent ont souvent les qualités de la monstruosité, elles arrêtent le regard, elles captent l'imaginaire. Le mouvement est ce qui permet de passer d'un état du visible à un autre, ce qui enclenche un travail de distorsion symbolique, mais finalement les vidéos se donnent à voir comme une succession d'images fixes. Le regard s'arrête sur chaque forme avant de se laisser captiver par la suivante. Laurent Goldring fait ensuite des tirages photographiques issus de captations de la vidéo. Il revient ainsi à l'image fixe en dernière instance, après un détour par un espace de création permettant le « laisser apparaître » au sein d'un dispositif extrêmement construit. L'instabilité de la vidéo met à distance le réflexe de transsubstantiation que l'on a face à une photographie : les images-corps de Laurent Goldring affirment leur statut symbolique, étalent leurs pixels lorsqu'elles sont tirées

2 RAYMOND BELLOUR, L'ENTRE-IMAGES, PHOTO, CINÉMA, VIDÉO, ÉDITIONS DE LA DIFFÉRENCE, 2002.

sur papier. Elles font état du déplacement de la recherche photographique au sein du médium vidéo.

Le passage d'un médium à un autre est ainsi ce qui permet de mettre à distance une pratique, d'interroger ses qualités, comme le fait Oliver Möst, photographe allemand. Son travail dérive de son rapport personnel à la vision. Ses problèmes de vue l'ont en effet amené à construire un regard photographique dominé par le flou et par ses qualités picturales. Son utilisation de la vidéo n'est pas un simple prolongement de ses recherches transférées dans le régime de l'image en mouvement. Elle correspond à une autre nécessité, celle de mettre en scène son rapport au visible à travers des autofilmages. brown eyes, hide &seek et between sont ainsi de courtes saynètes tournées dans son atelier. Dans la première, Oliver Möst joue avec ses yeux, des billes qu'il manipule et met en bouche, dans la seconde il compte à voix haute les yeux recouverts d'un cache rouge jusqu'à ce qu'un flash l'éblouisse, dans la troisième il se débat contre deux parois de murs qu'il referme et écarte. Il est toujours torse nu, physiquement impliqué dans des situations métaphoriques de son rapport au regard : mise à mal de l'organe de vision déficient dans brown eyes et construction d'un parallèle entre deux états de mal-voir dans hide & seek, l'un pour cause d'obturation de l'instance percevante (bandeau), l'autre pour cause d'un trop plein de lumière (flash). Dans between, Oliver Möst exprime une quête du bon angle de perception du monde par la variation de la construction de l'espace de représentation. Toutes ces situations sont bien évidemment tout autant des interrogations de l'activité photographique, de ses conditions et de ses partis-pris. Le cadrage de la dernière vidéo, landescape, a la forme d'une lentille optique obtenue également par l'association d'un sténopé et d'une caméra vidéo. Le son ouvre sur du hors-champ en opposant à l'immobilité du paysage imaginaire divisé paisiblement en deux plans symétriques le bruit d'un lancer de pierre. Oliver Möst est invisible à l'image mais son action reste présente. Cette fois, comme lui, on ne voit rien, mais l'imaginaire qu'il parvient à éveiller, les signes que l'on devine sur la surface de la glace sont largement porteurs de vision.

Des images sonores

L'art vidéo s'est énormément nourri de sa complicité avec la création musicale, de son émergence au sein de Fluxus, de la figure de Nam June Paik. Le son est souvent bien plus qu'une bande sonore accompagnant l'image, il lui est intrinsèque, au point que parfois l'image est traitée de manière sonore. Les vidéos de Robert Cahen mettent ainsi la composition musicale au coeur du dispositif filmique, et si le temps y a une importance particulière, c'est parce qu'il émerge de ce rapport étroit entre le son et l'image, exprimant la perception subjective du réel. Gast Bouschet, photographe et vidéaste, et Nadine Hilbert, compositeur, se sont associés dans cette perspective : dans leurs vidéos, l'image et le son sont inextricables, l'un contamine l'autre et imprègne son devenir. L'image est ici encore le plus souvent composée de cadres fixes, se succédant sans transition, par accumulation. Dans Dreamsequence, la caméra et le son nous livrent des bribes des univers traversés, forêt brumeuse, autoroute, centre ville, mais sans nous laisser nous y installer, sans nous permettre de suivre du regard. Comme face à une série photographique, on passe d'un point de vue à un autre, d'un état sonore à un autre, avec des répétitions mais sans le repère rassurant de la continuité. Le titre met ce fonctionnement en relation avec l'état du rêve, où l'on ne cesse de franchir des distances, de déambuler dans des espaces-temps différents, sans autre constante que celle de notre subjectivité de rêveur, et ici de spectateur. L'art vidéo permet ainsi de trouver un rythme qui fasse écho à l'expérience perceptive, ce qu'a aussi produit Christoph Brech avec Opus 110a (2001). Dans cette bande, l'image est un cadrage serré sur le dos d'un chef d'orchestre pendant un concert. Le son est extrêmement présent et avec l'image le rythme musical devient mouvement monochrome, proche de l'abstraction bien que chargé de la physicalité de la gestuelle du chef d'orchestre. Brech harmonise, lui, les mouvements du dos, il orchestre l'ensemble, ralentissant, accélérant, retenant ou libérant le temps de façon à créer l'harmonie entre le son et l'image. Le dos devient un espace de projection, chaque pli du costume un paysage, un point d'ancrage pour le déploiement de l'imaginaire.

Le son peut ainsi conduire l'image, la guider, la charger de significations. Il peut aussi créer une narration, intégrer le langage à l'image, les faire dialoguer, comme dans l'oeuvre de Gary Hill. Le texte dit, lu, énoncé par un corps est au coeur de ses vidéos, dans une interrogation de ce qui fait image dans le dire. La pratique de la vidéo s'est aussi nourrie du cinéma, mais elle s'en éloigne tout autant en préférant des constructions ambigües, voire contradictoires, qui éclatent la narration, qui interrogent ses codes. Les vidéos d'Alice Anderson sont ainsi esthétiquement très proches du cinéma tout en étant très différentes dans le mode du récit. L'écart est à son paroxysme dans le Journal, très brèves séquences filmiques montées ensemble grâce au son. Le fil narratif est ténu, et si les intertitres nous indiquent une période de temps (un mois, un jour, une année) le récit intime s'arrête là. Les images peuvent être regardées comme des indices pour pénétrer un moment de vie, mais laissent le plus souvent en suspens toute tentative interprétative. La durée est aussi très courte, et ne laisse guère le temps de la divagation. Le Journal laisse le spectateur aux prises avec la musique et des images évasives.

Installer l'image

La vidéo a des impératifs scénographiques bien plus contraignants que la photographie, elle demande à être installée dans un espace adapté à sa technicité. Si la photographie exposée est avant tout un dialogue avec l'espace de l'accrochage, où les images sont coprésentes au regard, la vidéo demande plutôt l'isolement, la négation de l'espace réel comme cela se fait dans les « black box », où l'image est présentée en retrait, dans l'obscurité et dans de bonnes conditions sonores. La vidéo impose alors son propre espace-temps, comme dans les installations de Bill Viola. Mais certains artistes font des propositions qui dialoguent au contraire avec l'extérieur, avec le dehors de l'image. Les parois-écrans de Claerbout sont exemplaires de cet entre-deux puisque les vidéos se font écho comme dans une exposition de photographie, elles se répercutent dans les regards à travers des cimaises de toile fine et trouée qui servent aussi de supports aux projections. L'installation in situ est aussi importante, où la vidéo vient prendre possession d'un lieu et l'habiter en faisant écho à ce qui en émane. Ulrich Gebert a ainsi conçu Keine Dialoge (2004) pour un espace spécifique, une architecture de béton sans fenêtres et divisée en pièces étroites, qui accentuait la dimension oppressante de cette oeuvre. Les conditions scénographiques découlaient du lieu d'exposition, le Kunstbunker Tumulka à Munich, sans qu'il soit nécessaire de modifier quoi que ce soit. Le spectateur était ainsi immergé dans un environnement froid et militaire dans lequel il assistait à un test psychologique enduré par une équipe de GSG 9, élite antiterroriste formée après les attentats des Jeux Olympiques de Munich en 1972. Ulrich Gebert nous montre ces hommes soumis à des flashs de lumière stroboscopique, prolongeant l'expérience pour le spectateur confronté à une vidéo constituée d'images fixes enchaînées dans un rythme saccadé et visuellement agressif. Le titre attire l'attention sur la régression infligée à ces hommes jugés sur leur maîtrise nerveuse. Le mouvement est le lieu de l'agressivité puisque c'est en sortant l'image de sa fixité, en créant un continuum sensoriel par la vidéo que l'action stéréoscopique prend sens et investit le corps du spectateur.

La vidéo a aussi une dimension sculpturale, lorsqu'au lieu d'effacer sa matérialité par des projections déconnectées du temps et de l'espace d'exposition, les artistes insistent sur sa relation de dépendance avec ce sur quoi elle peut surgir, ce dont elle a besoin pour exprimer sa présence immatérielle. La surface-écran peut prolonger l'image en volume, comme avec les yeux de Tony Oursler, ou l'artiste peut concevoir des environnements où l'image s'intègre, comme dans les installations de Thomas Hirschhorn. Dans cette veine, Pirmin Blum construit des sculptures de carton où sont punaisées des images fixes et insérées des vidéos sur moniteurs. L'image vidéo se passe de la monumentalité de la projection, de l'effet d'apparition et affirme sa prise dans le réel. Une des installations de Blum réunit des photographies et deux vidéos de tests de sécurité réalisés dans une usine automobile. Airbag est un plan fixe ralenti sur le jaillissement d'un airbag. Le tissu se gonfle puis se dégonfle dans un mouvement fascinant. On assiste au déploiement léger d'une forme en évolution permanente. La deuxième vidéo, Spuk, est un montage rapide des points de vue de deux caméras lors d'un test d'impact sur des pare-brises. Encadré par le calme aérien et poétique d'Airbag, Spuk est d'une grande violence visuelle et sonore. L'ensemble associe ainsi avec ironie des rythmes très différents, dans une mise en forme bricolée qui contraste avec la sophistication industrielle où ont été produites les images.

Alice Anderson a également isolé une partie du Journal pour concevoir une installation, Insomnia (2006). Le spectateur est invité à s'étendre sur un lit à baldaquin de velours violet et à regarder l'extrait vidéo (1') présenté en boucle sur un écran au-dessus de lui. Une mise en scène qui incite à voir ces images comme étant issues d'une demi conscience, entre veille et sommeil, sans que le spectateur ait lui vraiment le temps de s'y immerger : à peine allongé, la vidéo reprend sa boucle, le décourageant à se prélasser plus longuement. L'art vidéo est généralement difficile à regarder : parce que les oeuvres sont souvent trop longues, et le spectateur trop fatigué des conditions de réception éprouvantes. C'est sans doute sa plus grande contrainte, ce qui le rend moins facile à exposer et à regarder que la photographie. Il faut alors peut-être cultiver l'état d'insomnie, d'entre-deux, qui nous installe dans ces pratiques à mi-chemin entre deux médiums, et nous fait circuler entre différents états d'images.

Mathilde Roman

Docteur en arts et sciences de l'art de l'université de Paris-Sorbonne, Mathilde Roman est spécialiste de l'art vidéo, auteur de l'essai « Art vidéo et mise en scène de soi », éd. L'Harmattan, 2008. Critique d'art membre de l'AICA elle collabore à plusieurs revues comme www.lacritique.org, Art press, Mouvement et elle enseigne l'histoire de l'art au Pavillon Bosio, école supérieure d'art et de scénographie de Monaco.

Temps séparé et temps retrouvé
(De l'espace et de la durée dans l'art photographique et vidéo)

« En réalité, il n'y a pas un rythme unique de la durée ; on peut imaginer bien des rythmes différents, qui, plus lents ou plus rapides, mesureraient le degré de tension ou de relâchement des consciences, et, par là, fixeraient leur place respective dans la série des êtres. » Henri Bergson[1]

Depuis l'avènement du film cinématographique à la toute fin du XIXe siècle, la photographie se trouve sommée de choisir entre une image statique et un continuum d'images inscrit dans le temps. Tout un mythe s'est développé autour du moment inerte de la photo-ablation, moment détaché du temps, comme antithétique au récit-cadre continu qu'offre le film.[2] On aurait pu croire que l'arrivée des bandes magnétiques puis des technologies digitales marquerait la fin de cette dichotomie. Ce n'est toutefois pas dans le « temps » qu'elle se dissout, mais dans la durée, laquelle échappe à toute définition établie. Il se trouve que l'hypothèse linéaire d'un temps universel ne sous-tend plus notre mode de réception de l'image photographique. Le temps tel que décrit par Bergson s'éprouve différemment selon les gens et les endroits, et selon l'âge de la vie chez une même personne. On peut parfaitement conceptualiser un passé linéaire ou diachronique : reste qu'il sera intériorisé de façon synchronique.

Intituler une exposition de photo et de vidéo « Mutations II », c'est aborder de front le processus ininterrompu du changement. Muter signifie subir ou causer une mutation, à savoir une transformation, un changement de nature, de forme ou de qualité. La mutation, ou le devenir (stade liminal), ne peut par définition se réduire à un temps linéaire, puisqu'il s'agit d'un processus ininterrompu de changement perpétuel. Ainsi le devenir existe-t-il comme « temps suspendu » dans un processus ininterrompu, temps qui ne saurait se comprendre que comme durée continue. Telle est peut-être la collision évoquée par T.S. Eliot : « le temps présent et le temps passé sont tous deux présents peut-être dans le temps futur, et le temps futur contenu dans le temps passé ».[3] C'est pourquoi le devenir demeure « perpétuelle possibilité » : cette conception de la durée, embrassée il y a bien longtemps par Bruce Nauman entre autres, explique pourquoi les nouveaux modes d'expression artistique à base de performance et de vidéo délient notre appréhension de ce qui fonde une image statique ou inscrite dans le temps. Deleuze, inspiré par Bergson, ne dit pas autre chose: « si bien que chaque fois qu'on se trouve devant une durée ou dans une durée, on pourra conclure à l'existence d'un tout qui change, et qui est ouvert quelque part. »[4] Ce qui n'exclut pas la causalité mais suggère l'existence de quelque chose de caché, de non immédiatement apparent. La mutation repose précisément sur ce principe, comme l'illustre bien sa forme la plus ordinaire: des amibes dans une boîte de Petri.[5] C'est cette addiction historique à un schisme dualiste entre image statique et image mouvante que questionnent systématiquement les praticiens de la photographie contemporaine et de la vidéo. Le mécanisme de la transformation demeure la réponse de la conscience humaine, une conscience qui n'est pas une fin en soi, mais plutôt le lieu d'un éveil continu tendu vers une direction unique aux aboutissements multiples.

Les praticiens de la nouvelle photographie digitale ainsi que des dernières technologies analogiques ont pu réaligner photographie et art vidéo hors du cadre déterministe d'une immuable linéarité temporelle. La nouvelle photographie s'est débarrassée de l'image-ablation telle que réduite au moment où l'on presse un bouton, de la même manière que la vidéo et le montage cinématographique se sont depuis longtemps émancipées d'hypothèses de continuité. Dans les deux cas les conditions sont devenues de plus en plus manipulables. Sachant cela, il nous faut accepter et embrasser les discontinuités croissantes sur lesquelles repose la vie moderne - Foucault déjà l'avait souligné.[6] Le mot « mutation » lui-même fournit une analogie et un corollaire intéressants : en linguistique, il désigne la modification phonétique d'un mot en fonction de son environnement morphologique ou syntaxique. Il n'est donc guère surprenant que mutation et mutualité aient le même préfixe latin : au sein d'un système actif discontinu, la relation est réciproque et marquée par une grande capacité d'adaptation. On a longtemps utilisé dans un contexte non biologique le mot mutation (relativement peu connoté) en opposition au mot évolution (relativement connoté). Le premier décrit le changement comme une adaptation discontinue ou aléatoire, tandis que le second traîne généralement dans son sillage la téléologie finalisante de la sélection naturelle : on se mue en, on évolue vers.

Ainsi photographie et vidéo ont-elles doublement gagné en pertinence ces trente

1 HENRI BERGSON, « DE LA DÉLIMITATION ET DE LA FIXATION DES IMAGES », MATIÈRE ET MÉMOIRE, PUF, PARIS, 1939, 7ÈME ÉDITION « QUADRIGE », 2004, P. 232.

2 ROLAND BARTHES ET SUSAN SONTAG ONT TOUS DEUX PARLÉ DE FATALITÉ OU DE MÉLANCOLIE AU REGARD DE LA PHOTOGRAPHIE, ÉTABLISSANT PAR LÀ UNE SORTE DE ROMANTISME STRUCTUREL QUI PIÈGE LA PHOTO ENTRE LE PUNCTUM (LE DÉTAIL POIGNANT) ET LE STUDIUM (BARTHES), OU DANS UNE « NARROWLY SELECTIVE TRANSPARENCY » [TRANSPARENCE ÉTROITEMENT SÉLECTIVE] (SONTAG). VOIR ROLAND BARTHES, LA CHAMBRE CLAIRE : NOTE SUR LA PHOTOGRAPHIE, GALLIMARD/SEUIL/CAHIERS DU CINÉMA, PARIS, 1980, PP. 48-49 ET SUSAN SONTAG, « DANS LA CAVERNE DE PLATON », SUR LA PHOTOGRAPHIE, CHRISTIAN BOURGOIS ÉDITEUR, 1973, P. 19 : « ÉTROITEMENT SÉLECTIVES LES UNES COMME LES AUTRES, UNE PEINTURE OU UNE DESCRIPTION NE PEUVENT JAMAIS ÊTRE AUTRE CHOSE QU'UNE INTERPRÉTATION, TANDIS QU'UNE PHOTOGRAPHIE PEUT ÊTRE TRAITÉ COMME UNE VERSION DE LA CHOSE ELLE-MÊME. »

3 T.S. ELIOT 'BURNT NORTON', IN QUATRE QUATUORS, SEUIL, 1950, TRADUCTION DE P. LEYRIS, P. 11. CE SONT LES TROIS PREMIERS VERS, QUI SE POURSUIVENT AINSI: « SI TOUT TEMPS EST PRÉSENT PENDANT L'ÉTERNITÉ, TOUT TEMPS EST IRRÉMISSIBLE ».

4 GILLES DELEUZE, L'IMAGE-MOUVEMENT, CINÉMA 1, THE MOVEMENT IMAGE, LES ÉDITIONS DE MINUIT (COLL. « CRITIQUE »), P. 20 ; DELEUZE SE RÉFÈRE ABONDAMMENT AUX OUVRAGES DE BERGSON MATIÈRE ET MÉMOIRE (OP. CIT) AND L'EVOLUTION CRÉATRICE (1907). POUR SON RAPPORT À BERGSON, SE RAPPORTER À : GILLES DELEUZE, LE BERGSONISM, PUF, PARIS, 1966.

5 LE MOT AMIBE VIENT DU GREC V'AMEIBΩ, « CHANGER ». IL A ÉTÉ EMPLOYÉ POUR LA PREMIÈRE FOIS PAR LE NATURALISTE FRANÇAIS JEAN-BAPTISTE BORY DE SAINT-VINCENT (1778-1846).

6 FOUCAULT PARLE D'UNE MULTIPLICATION INÉVITABLE DES DISCONTINUITÉS: « L'HISTOIRE APPARAIT ALORS NON COMME UNE LONGUE CONTINUITÉ SOUS UNE DISCONTINUITÉ APPARENTE, MAIS COMME UN ENCHEVÊTREMENT DE DISCONTINUITÉS. » [NDT: CITATION TRADUITE À PARTIR DE L'ÉDITION ANGLAISE] MICHEL FOUCAULT 'RETURN TO HISTORY', MICHEL FOUCAULT, ESSENTIAL WORKS OF FOUCAULT 1954-1984, VOL. 2, AESTHETICS, JAMES D. FAUBION (ED.), LONDON, HARMONDSWORTH (1998), 2000, (PP. 419-32) P. 429.

dernières années : d'une part on a vu s'effacer le vieux cliché du fossé entre image statique et image mouvante, de l'autre on assiste à un jeu d'interactions croissant au sein de chaque procédé issu du médium originel commun. C'est à cette intériorisation toujours plus grande des techniques de la photo et de la vidéo que se réfère mon sous-titre : « de l'espace et de la durée ». Dans la manière qu'a chaque artiste d'adapter les nouvelles technologies à sa propre pratique visuelle, on trouve, incorporée, telle une ombre singulière et idiosyncratique, une caractérisation ou conduite très personnelle de l'espace-temps. D'où le fait qu'aujourd'hui l'art photographique et vidéo ne s'occupe pas tant d'un sujet donné ou pré-défini que de ce à quoi ce sujet est sujet. Il travaille sur un état introspectif où les contenus temporels sont élastiques et forment souvent plis et replis. L'objet emblématique du temps n'est plus une montre mais une boucle, et cette boucle (ou ellipse) est la condition d'une circularité ou inflexion interne mesurée à l'aune d'un système auto-défini.[7]

Que ce soit comme outil critique d'une commercialisation et d'un consumérisme accrus liés à la télévision, ou dans le cadre de ce qui allait devenir l'Art vidéo, l'avènement de la vidéo comme expression artistique dans les années 1960 et 1970 portait en lui la remise en cause possible de la nature linéaire du temps – remise en cause inaccessible aux techniques antérieures.[8] Si le film, dans sa configuration d'images successives, permettait un système de montage par copié-collé, on était bien loin de l'immédiateté de la bande vidéo, avec ses possibilités de visionnage quasi immédiat, de superposition et de formes narratives potentiellement floues ou abstraites.[9] L'art vidéo a commencé par la critique des médias de masse, télévision et publicité, mais s'est rapidement attelé à déconstruire le principe même d'une cohérence narrative linéaire (contrairement au mouvement du « film structuraliste » qui opérait de l'intérieur du système filmique), permettant de confronter espace et temps d'une manière inédite.[10] Utilisé par Nauman, Acconci et bien d'autres dans leurs performances, pour en conserver une trace et interroger la nature même du performatif, il est rapidement devenu l'outil d'un questionnement de la nature des lieux de la représentation au travers de ce qui allait devenir l'installation vidéo.[11] Cette dernière, par le plein usage des projections multiples, a littéralement brouillé l'usage d'une temporalité différentielle. Un sentiment d'immédiateté relève par essence d'un « toujours présent » et l'équipement vidéo est de fait devenu une présence incontournable dans de nombreux ateliers d'artistes, au même titre que n'importe quel autre outil de travail. Ce qu'atteste d'ailleurs le rapport souvent intime qui s'est établi entre vidéo et peinture. Le moniteur vidéo, en tant qu'objet porteur d'image, s'est quant à lui fait sculpture, puis installation totale, permettant à la vidéo de devenir une réalité intersticielle, un point d'assemblage entre différent médiums. Tout en entrant pleinement en relation avec des choses fabriquées (conformes à la notion traditionnelle d'œuvre d'art), elle a interrogé leur statut d'œuvres d'art, leurs lieux de réception, et questionné l'historiographie des limites entre différents médiums. Comme l'espace entre les mots dans une pièce de Beckett, la vidéo à joué le rôle d'espace « en devenir » d'une durée temporelle incertaine.[12]

Elle a aussi obligé la pratique photographique à se repenser totalement - et ce bien avant l'entrée en lice des dernières technologies digitales - notamment parce que la possibilité d'extraire une image d'un film émoussait l'idée d'« instant décisif » de l'appareil photo.[13] La photo a tout d'abord été contrainte de reprendre en compte les dimensions temporelles de la fabrication des images. Si l'instantanéité a été l'impulsion initiale poussant la photographie de l'avant dans le sillage des innovation en matière d'appareil et de lentille, c'est de toute évidence le temps d'exposition, quel qu'il soit, qui a « cadré » les conditions d'extraction. On a désormais traité l'instant décisif, et l'époque existentielle à laquelle il appartenait, comme un moment de pure subjectivité. Par rapport aux premières vidéos qui offraient l'immédiateté du réel (en anglais « real »), un réel bien distinct de celui de la pellicule (en anglais « reel ») résultant d'un montage, la photo semblait avoir perdu le contact avec la « réalité objective » qui l'avait originellement établie.[14] Il en a résulté, à partir des années 80, un retour au sténopé et à la chambre noire. L'enjeu n'était pas la soit-disant plus grande objectivité de la réalité de la vidéo (malgré les revendications de ses débuts), mais la nouveauté et l'étendue du réseau de subjectivités plurielles ou pluri-temporelles qu'elle proposait. D'où la réintroduction de l'élasticité du temps dans la photographie, – évolution observable dans la réflexion autour

7 GILLES DELEUZE, « QU'EST-CE QU'UN ÉVÈNEMENT » LE PLI - LEIBNIZ ET LE BAROQUE, LES ÉDITIONS DE MINUIT (COLL. « CRITIQUE »), PARIS, 1988, « INSÉPARABLES DE CE PROCESSUS D'ACTUALISATION OU DE RÉALISATION DANS LESQUELS ILS ENTRENT, ILS N'ONT DE PERMANENCE QUE DANS LES LIMITES DES FLUX QUI LES RÉALISENT, OU DES PRÉHENSIONS QUI LES ACTUALISENT. » (P. 108).

8 LA VIDÉO EN TANT QU'EXPRESSION ARTISTIQUE EST D'ABORD APPARUE CHEZ DES ARTISTES COMME LES LEVINE ET FRANK GILLETTE, DONT L'APPROCHE ÉVOQUAIT LE DOCUMENTAIRE ACTIVISTE, AINSI QUE CHEZ NAM JUNE PAIK, DU MOUVEMENT FLUXUS, CONSIDÉRÉ COMME LE PÈRE DE L'ART VIDÉO. VOIR MICHAEL RUSH, NEW MEDIA IN THE LATE TWENTIETH CENTURY, LONDON, THAMES & HUDSON, 1999, PP. 80-81. POUR UNE ANALYSE FOUILLÉE DE L'ŒUVRE DE PAIK, VOIR THE WORLDS OF NAM JUNE PAIK, SOLOMON GUGGENHEIM MUSEUM, NEW YORK, 2000.

9 MICHAEL RUSH, VIDEO ART, LONDON THAMES & HUDSON, 2003, « LE PLUS STIMULANT DANS CETTE NOUVELLE TECHNOLOGIE, C'EST QU'ELLE CAPTURAIT INSTANTANÉMENT DES ÉVÈNEMENT RÉELS. EN UN SENS, LE TEMPS SE RETROUVAIT MANIPULÉ PAR L'INTERVENTION HUMAINE. » P. 15.

10 SEAN CUBITT, TIMESHIFT: ON VIDEO CULTURE, LONDON, ROULEDGE, 1991. VOIR AUSSI, DOUG HALL ET SALLY JO FIFER (EDS.), ILLUMINATING VIDEO: AN ESSENTIAL GUIDE TO VIDEO ART, NEW YORK, APERTURE, 1990, ET ÉDITIONS ULTÉRIEURES.

11 MICHAEL RUSH, "VIDEO INSTALLATION ART", IN NEW MEDIA....OP CIT, PP. 116-167.

12 IL N'EST GUÈRE SURPRENANT QUE NOMBRE DE VIDÉASTES AIENT CHERCHÉ LEUR INSPIRATION DU CÔTÉ BECKETT : CE FUT NOTAMMENT LE CAS DE NAUMAN ET DE JOHN JESURUN (QUI CONTINUE DE MENER UNE RECHERCHE MÊLANT THÉATRE ET MULTI-MÉDIA), AINSI QUE, DANS UNE CERTAINES MESURE, CELUI DE BILL VIOLA AU DÉBUT DE SA CARRIÈRE. VOIR ALAN RICKMAN (ET AL), BECKETT ON FILM, DVD, 2005, ET GIJS VAN TIJL, « HUMAN CONDITION/HUMAN BODY: BRUCE NAUMAN AND SAMUEL BECKETT », BRUCE NAUMAN, EX. CAT., HAYWARD GALLERY, LONDON, 1998, PP. 60-75.

13 NOTION INTRODUITE PAR HENRI CARTIER-BRESSON DANS SON PREMIER LIVRE, IMAGES À LA SAUVETTE, EDITIONS VERVE, PARIS, 1952, LONGTEMPS CONSIDÉRÉ COMME L'OUVRAGE DE RÉFÉRENCE SUR LA PHOTOGRAPHIE DU XXE SIÈCLE.

14 POUR UN APERÇU GÉNÉRAL DES ÉVOLUTIONS CULTURELLES DE LA PHOTOGRAPHIE DE SES DÉBUTS À NOS JOURS, VOIR MARY WARNER MARIEN, PHOTOGRAPHY: A CULTURAL HISTORY, LONDON, LAURENCE KING PUBLISHING, 2002.

de la reproduction (produits instantanés) comme de la production et de la modification des procédés.

L'avènement du numérique dans les années 1990s a marqué un certain déclin du rôle de la vidéo et du VHS dont l'utilisation récente tend à retourner vers le cinématique. Leur place a été prise par de nouvelles technologies de l'ère virtuelle et ils n'oseraient plus prétendre ni à l'instantanéité, ni à la représentation du réel. Exemples extrêmes, les excès mythico-poétiques de Matthew Barney reflètent les tendances actuelles de la vidéo et sa gravitation autour du cinéma.[15] Comme la reproductibilité n'est plus vraiment un problème, les médiums électroniques modernes et les technologies informatiques remplacent de plus en plus les anciennes fonctions de la bande magnétique.[16] En termes de temporalité, vidéo et photographie existent souvent côté à côte dans l'espace virtuel de l'ordinateur, ainsi que dans les possibilités de manipulation qu'offrent l'image extraite, sa modalité de production et sa présentation ultérieure. Ce qui implique une multiplicité croissante des contenus temporels, dont la nature exacte n'est pas établie, ou pas déterminable. En bref, photo et vidéo sont toutes les deux passées, en termes de contenus temporels, du certain à l'aléatoire. Or la forme aléatoire du temps, c'est la durée – cette durée, toujours virtuelle, et par là même insaisissable, dont la définition implique un « devenir » de possibilité simulée. Le virtuel ne s'oppose toutefois pas au réel : il existe en essence ou en incidence, à défaut d'exister dans les faits, ce qui revient à dire qu'il existe en pensée ou en imagination. Le monde virtuel n'est pas un monde alternatif – impossibilité épistémologique –, mais il propose une autre façon, imaginaire ou alternative, de se confronter à ce que l'on entend par le terme « réalité ». Et la réalité spéculative ainsi générée nous permet peut-être, selon la suggestion bergsonienne, d'« imaginer bien des rythmes différents » actifs dans notre conscience.

Les évolutions et changements d'orientations de la photo et de la vidéo ces trente dernières années touchent, directement ou indirectement, les artistes exposés dans « Mutations II ». Ce qui explique la grande diversité de leurs pratiques et de leurs approches en terme de procédés, tant en photo qu'en vidéo – revoici l'ombre singulière et idiosyncratique que j'évoquais plus haut. La temporalité et l'espace-temps se définissent en termes non seulement visuels mais encore auditifs. Or, si le son est ordinairement linéaire, c'est-à-dire dans un continuum à partir du moment où commence sa perception, il a lui aussi été mis au service de la fragmentation et du ré-assemblage temporel. Dans l'Opus 110a de Christoph Brech, on entend de la musique symphonique tandis que l'écran vidéo nous montre le dos d'une veste (sans doute une queue de pie), qu'on suppose être celle du chef d'orchestre – encore qu'il pourrait parfaitement s'agir là d'une simulation.[17] Se produit alors une collision entre le visuel et l'auditif à mesure que le rythme des mouvements et des motifs dessinés par la texture et les coutures de la veste nous hypnotise. On perd à un certain niveau la connexion son-image, mais on la rétablit à un autre. Cette expérience transitive est fréquente dans l'œuvre de Brech : elle exprime une action de sujet à objet mais nécessite un objet direct pour en compléter le sens. L'hypothèse étant que l'objet direct auquel s'adresse l'œuvre se trouve être le spectateur. On connait la relation qu'entretiennent depuis longtemps musique et vidéo, mais dans les vidéos pop, l'effet est généralement illustratif, tandis que chez Brech, le degré d'information est minimal (la vidéo se termine sur l'image de la partition) et c'est au spectateur de compléter l'œuvre. Spectateur et réception deviennent indispensables au sens même de l'œuvre.

C'est une stratégie caractéristique de nombreux artistes vidéo actuels, stratégie anti-illustrative et qui s'exprime en termes post-narratologiques.[18] C'est-à-dire qu'elle n'analyse pas la narration ou récit linéaire, au sens structurel de déterminer le résultat de la perception a priori, mais suscite les prolongations de la perception dont elle a besoin pour permettre d'achever l'œuvre. Le temps du spectateur et ses contenus temporels entrent ainsi en jeu en réponse à l'œuvre vidéo. Le travail d'Olga Chernysheva fonctionne inversement à celui de Brech : dans sa vidéo Windows, le spectateur joue le rôle du voyeur caché. Une série de prises de vue au travers de fenêtres, la nuit, constitue sous nos yeux une sorte de lexique de la vie quotidienne. Les fenêtres, banales, suggèrent des barres d'immeubles modernes et les intérieurs, opaques et mal éclairés, des appartements quelconques. Dans ces extraits présentés sur une série d'écrans vidéo, un homme regarde la télévision, trois personnes dansent en cercle, un homme seul joue de la guitare, une femme fait du repassage, un homme se tient dans sa salle de bain, etc. Il n'existe pas de lien direct entre les fenêtres, sinon le côté ordinaire des comportements invoqués par l'œuvre et une vague connexion typologique. L'a-temporalité ne suggère pas grand chose en terme de lieu et de situation géographique des évènements auxquels on assiste. Ont-ils été filmés au même moment, à des moments différents, dans des espaces urbains différents? Ce qui devient important, c'est qu'il s'agit de simples images vidéo, qui, parce qu'elles sont inscrites dans le temps, donnent au spectateur le rôle du voyeur. Si les images étaient fixes, ou s'il s'agissait de

15 NANCY SPECTOR, THYRZA GOODEVE ET NEVILLE WAKEFIELD, MATTHEW BARNES : THE CREMASTER CYCLE, NEW YORK, GUGGENHEIM MUSEUM PUBLICATIONS, 2002 ; ÉGALEMENT STEPHAN URBASCHEK ET BRANDON STOSUY, MATTHEW BARNEY, MUNICH, INGVILD GOETZ PUBLICATIONS, 2008.

16 TIMOTHY DRUCKREY (ED.), ARS ELECTRONICA: FACING THE FUTURE - A SURVEY OF TWO DECADES (ELECTRONIC CULTURE: HISTORY, THEORY AND PRACTICE), CAMBRIDGE MASS., MIT PRESS, 2001.

17 IL S'AGIT EN FAIT DE CHRISTOPH POPPEN DIRIGEANT L'ORCHESTRE DE CHAMBRE DE MUNICH DANS UNE INTERPRÉTATION DE L'OPUS 110A DE CHOSTAKOVITCH, ET DE CE QUE BRECH APPELLE UNE DÉMONSTRATION DE LA « DYNAMIQUE VISUELLE DE LA MUSIQUE ». NOTONS TOUTEFOIS QUE CE N'EST LÀ QU'UNE INFORMATION EXTRINSÈQUE SUR LAQUELLE NE REPOSE PAS LA COMPRÉHENSION DE L'ŒUVRE DE BRECH, MÊME SI CETTE COMPRÉHENSION PEUT SE TROUVER MODIFIÉE QUAND ON CONNAIT LE MORCEAU DE MUSIQUE EN QUESTION.

18 TRADITIONNELLEMENT, ON ASSOCIE LA « NARRATOLOGIE » STRUCTURELLE AU GROUPE DU FORMALISME RUSSE. TZVETAN TODOROV (NÉ EN 1939 À SOFIA, EN BULGARIE) A FORGÉ LE MOT ET SE RÉFÈRE À L'EXEMPLE DE VLADIMIR PROPP (1895-1970). VOIR MORPHOLOGIE DU CONTE (PUBLIÉ EN RUSSIE EN 1928), SEUIL, PARIS, 1970.

photographies, on n'obtiendrait pas cet effet de complicité du spectateur voyeur.

Le rôle interstitiel de la vidéo, ce qu'une collègue a appelé dans ce catalogue l'art de « cultiver l'entre-deux », demeure prévalent dans la production vidéo actuelle. Dans les œuvres de l'artiste israélien Ori Gersht intitulées Big Bang et Pomegranate, l'appropriation se fait à partir de la nature morte et de la peinture de fleurs. Big Bang commence par un écran noir ; un son aigu s'intensifie, puis apparaît progressivement une composition florale dans un vase de verre, inspirée de la tradition des natures mortes hollandaises du XVIIe siècle. Le rapport son-image et la stridence s'intensifient, faisant naître le sentiment qu'il va se passer quelque chose ; c'est alors que fleurs et vase explosent au ralenti. Les fragments tombent en une pluie lente et l'image s'efface progressivement jusqu'au retour de l'écran noir, avant que tout recommence en boucle. A bien y regarder, une dimension identitaire et biographique, tant personnelle que politique, marque tous les travaux de Gersht, et il n'est sans doute pas fortuit qu'il ait choisi de mettre en scène dans son autre vidéo une grenade, qui donne à l'œuvre son titre. Pomegranate (grenade, en anglais) nous montre, dans un cadre de tableau en perspective, une nature morte composée d'une part d'un chou et d'une grenade en suspens, de l'autre d'une citrouille et d'une courge posées sur ce qui, dans le tableau, serait la partie inférieure du cadre. La vidéo est silencieuse jusqu'à ce qu'une balle venue de la droite fasse exploser la grenade dont les graines tombent en cascade, là aussi au ralenti. Au registre personnel, on trouve non seulement une référence biblique précise et délibérée, la grenade étant l'un des sept fruits d'Israël, mais encore l'exploitation du double sens du mot, puisqu'en hébreu comme en français « grenade » désigne à la fois le fruit et l'arme.[19] Dans le travail de Gersht, il s'agit moins de brouiller le temps que d'en modifier l'expérience et de créer les conditions d'une attente, imprévue et violente - en d'autres termes, de mesurer « le degré de tension ou de relâchement des consciences. »

Si la peinture sert ici de référence à Gersht, le finlandais Tuomo Rainio semble pour sa part plutôt travailler sur la relation dessin/vidéo, entre-deux conjuré par un logiciel qu'il a lui-même créé. Dans le troublant Staircase (Crosswise) et City, une figure spectrale monte un escalier : expression picturale floue et indistincte, tonalité quelque peu gothique, surface de l'image rendue fantomatique par les multiples expositions – on pense bien sûr aux premières inspirations futuristes et au Nu descendant un escalier de Duchamp.[20] Pour facile qu'elle soit, cette référence nous rappelle que, depuis une vingtaine d'années, vidéo et photographie se sont remises à interroger et sonder leurs origines. A l'inverse, City est une image visuellement statique, mais, là encore, intensifiée en tant qu'image sonore par une bande son – vision urbaine gris noir d'un arrêt de tram ou de métro de plein air, évocation aux contours purement sonores : sifflements sinistres du vent, tintements de ferraille quand passent d'invisibles trains, occasionnels bruits de pas. L'image-temps fixe sert de référent à la répétition, en boucle, et cette répétition du temps, telle que suggérée, est d'une durée potentiellement infinie. L'image sonore City, en tant qu'œuvre, opère à l'interface de l'image fixe et de la vidéo, rassemblant dans un système hautement personnel et organisé l'espace entre les photos nées de longs temps d'expositions de quelqu'un comme Michael Wesley.[21]

Cette ré-interrogation des sources participe pleinement au travail d'Oliver Möst, dont l'utilisation vidéo du sténopé est un écho direct de la pré-histoire et des premières heures de la photographie. Dans une série d'œuvres qualifiées de Sténopés ou de Raccourcis, telles landescape, hide and seek ou kill your idols, il segmente ou superpose divers éléments temporels tout en revenant simultanément au principe de base de la combinaison temps, lumière, exposition.
La simple énumération de hide and seek comme les variations à peine perceptibles de landescape nous laissent empreints d'un sentiment d'infini, de torpeur. Si la vidéo s'est d'abord développée dans la sphère politico-culturelle comme outil de contestation des médias de masse, elle est entre temps devenu un médium des plus personnels. Une œuvre comme Dreamsequence de Gast Bouschet et Nadine Hilbert, tout en renvoyant à l'histoire du cinéma, est intentionnellement a-linéaire, et mêle l'évocation de postures politiques personnelles à des fragments de textes et de sons divers sans liens les uns avec les autres. Tel le bric-à-brac d'expériences sensorielles qu'on trouve dans les rêves, l'œuvre présente un mélange d'identification et d'expulsion du souvenir – une sorte de catharsis personnelle en somme. C'est au spectateur d'établir un lien possible entre les éléments. Une dimension politico-culturelle ne demeure qu'en ce qu'une vidéo artistique tend rarement à apaiser le spectateur : elle peut se vouloir indirectement spectacle, mais l'intention première reste d'interroger les limites de

19 ON TROUVE LA LISTE DES SEPT FRUITS (SHIVAT HAMINIM) D'ISRAËL DANS LE DEUTÉRONOME 8:7-8: « CAR L'ÉTERNEL, TON DIEU, VA TE FAIRE ENTRER DANS UN BON PAYS, PAYS DE COURS D'EAU, DE SOURCES ET DE LACS, QUI JAILLISSENT DANS LES VALLÉES ET DANS LES MONTAGNES; PAYS DE FROMENT, D'ORGE, DE VIGNES, DE FIGUIERS ET DE GRENADIERS; PAYS D'OLIVE ET DE MIEL. » GRENADE, EN HÉBREU, SE DIT RIMMÔN, QU'IL S'AGISSE DU FRUIT OU DE L'ARME.

20 L'ŒUVRE DES FUTURISTES COMME CELLE DE DUCHAMP DOIT BEAUCOUP AUX TRAVAUX D'EADWEARD MUYBRIDGE (1830-1904) ET D'ETIENNE-JULES MAREY (1830-1904), TOUS DEUX CHRONO-PHOTOGRAPHES TRÈS INTÉRESSÉS PAR LA DIMENSION ESPACE-TEMPS DU MOUVEMENT ET SA DÉCOMPOSITION. VOIR PHILLIP PRODGER, TIME STANDS STILL : MUYBRIDGE AND THE INSTANTANEOUS PHOTOGRAPHY MOVEMENT, LONDON, OXFORD UNIVERSITY PRESS, 2003, ET MARTA BRAUN, PICTURING TIME : WORK OF ETIENNE-JULES MAREY (1839-1904), CHICAGO AND LONDON, CHICAGO UNIVERSITY PRESS, 1994.

21 ON CONNAIT LE LONG TEMPS D'EXPOSITION - JUSQU'À TROIS OU QUATRE ANS – DES PHOTOGRAPHIES DE MICHAEL WESELY. D'UNE CERTAINE FAÇON, CE PROCÉDÉ TRAVAILLE À L'INVERSE DE LA VIDÉO EN PERMETTANT AU TEMPS LUI MÊME DE FAIRE SURGIR DES CONTENUS FANTOMATIQUES SUR DE TRÈS LONGUES PÉRIODES. VOIR MICHAEL WESELY OPEN SHUTTER, EX. CAT., THE MUSEUM OF MODERN ART NEW YORK, 2004, QUI COUVRE SANS INTERRUPTION LA PÉRIODE DE DÉMOLITION ET RECONSTRUCTION DU MOMA, ET POUR LA CONSTRUCTION DE LA PLACE DE LA POTSDAMER PLATZ, MICHAEL WESELY : DIE ERFINDUNG DES UNSICHTBAREN, EX. CAT., GUARDINI GALERIE BERLIN/FOTOHOF SALZBURG, 2005.

la représentation et de l'appréhension des images. Pour dire les choses simplement, la vidéo somme le spectateur de se demander ce que signifient les images. Que veut dire Ulrich Gebert quand il montre un rang de soldats en uniforme au repos face à un mur nu, l'image apparaissant/disparaissant dans un mitraillage stroboscopique sur fond de tac-tac-tac syncopé ? Certes, il y a là un hommage indirect à Gary Hill, entre autres précurseurs, et une évocation de la répétition, mais pour le reste, il revient à chacun de construire le champs des réceptions possibles.

Le développement le plus significatif réside dans le fait que photo et vidéo sont toutes deux entrées dans l'ère de la manipulation informatique et numérique. Loin de réduire les possibilités, la réalité virtuelle du monde de l'ordinateur a libéré la photographie de l'image statique, ou instant pétrifié, et libéré la vidéo de l'illusion de capter une réalité pour ainsi dire définitive. Elle a permis à un artiste comme Peter Aerschmann de devenir polyphonique dans sa capacité à assembler des éléments très divers allant du social au surréel. Paternoster et Union Square révèlent une diversité d'approche typique de nombreux artistes d'aujourd'hui. Dans Paternoster apparaît un décor théâtral d'ascenseurs ouverts où des personnages montent et descendent dans toute leur variété idiosyncratique. Ils représentent de petits univers auto-centrés, des comportements humains courants en situation décalée : femme jouant du violon, silhouette masculine en bleu de travail qui balaie, femme avec un vase, plante solitaire, etc. Aerschmann travaille souvent sur les archétypes – peut-être un écho de ses origines suisses (et, qui sait, d'une influence jungienne). Dans Union Square, le sol couvert de neige d'où sortent des troncs d'arbres nus forme un contraste étrange avec un fond rouge mat où passe un avion ; des bataillons de l'armée suisse sont massés dans la neige. L'image se déplace vers la droite et les souches stériles laissent la place à une forêt de conifères. Aerschmann remet directement en cause la dialectique image arrêtée / image en mouvement : son travail traite de l'espace et d'un passage indéterminé du temps. C'est pourquoi, d'une certaine façon, le virtuel permet à la photo et la vidéo d'opérer dans un contexte où temps et image peuvent être synthétisés bien plus que ne le permettaient les technologies antérieures. Dans la photo, cela se traduit notamment par la superposition en durée de moments multiples, tandis que dans la vidéo, ces temporalités sont comprimées, rallongées ou encore détournées et brouillées pour ouvrir de nouvelles et vertigineuses possibilités.

Où situer le concept de Temps dans tout cela ? Il demeure, comme l'a suggéré Bergson, dans divers types de conscience. Il n'y a rien d'étonnant à ce que le rapport que chacun entretient avec le temps soit éminemment personnel. Ce qu'impose le monde ne coïncide pas nécessairement avec ce que revendiquent l'esprit et l'imagination. Notre immersion toujours plus avant dans l'âge électronique doit se faire sans peur, dans l'ouverture au possible. « Mutation II » renvoie tout simplement aux nouvelles données de la pratique photographique et vidéo actuelles, aux possibilités qu'elle a su créer et qu'elle peut réaliser. Comment les employer, et à quelles fins – à nous de décider.

Mais notre propre nature, le rôle et la destination de notre personne, demeurent enveloppée d'un aussi grand mystère. Car d'où sortent, comment naissent, et à quoi doivent servir ces sensations élémentaires, inextensives, qui vont se développer dans l'espace ? Il faut les poser comme autant d'absolus, dont on ne voit ni l'origine, ni la fin.[22]

Mark Gisbourne

Mark Gisbourne a été professeur d'art contemporain à la Slade School of Fine Art, à l'Université de Londres et au Sotheby's Institute (dans le cadre du programme de maîtrise de l'Université de Manchester).
Ancien président de l'AICA (Grande-Bretagne) et ancien vice-president international de cette même association, il a publié de nombreux livres et catalogues et collaboré à la plupart des publications d'art en langue anglaise. Parmi ses expositions les plus récentes figure /Paul Klee : Adult Memories of Childhood/ (Centro Atlántico de Arte Moderno, Las Palmas). Il est actuellement commissaire en résidence au Rohkunstbau (www.rohkunstbau.de). Il vit et travaille à Berlin.

22 HENRI BERGSON « DE LA SÉLECTION DES IMAGES POUR LA REPRÉSENTATION », OP CIT, P. 65.

Peter Aerschmann

Né en 1969 à Fribourg/Suisse
Vit et travaille à Bern/Suisse
Diplômé de la Hochschule für Gestaltung
und Kunst, Bern
www.aerschmann.ch

Photographier l'espace tout en conservant une profondeur temporelle, produire des images au-delà de l'instantané et du figé afin d'en restituer le mouvement et le vivant : La figuration du temps dans l'espace constitue l'enjeu fondamental des œuvres de Peter Aerschmann.

« La vision est suspendue au mouvement » nous rappelle le philosophe et théoricien de l'art Maurice Merleau-Ponty dans« L'oeil et l'esprit » (1964), signifiant que si nous n'étions pas capable de nous mouvoir dans l'espace nous ne pourrions pas voir. Cependant le mouvement, celui du corps, n'est pas que le simple déplacement d'un objet d'un point vers un autre. Le mouvement effectivement perçu est d'un seul tenant et ne se confond pas avec l'espace parcouru ; C'est là que réside tout le paradoxe du mouvement : il se déroule dans l'espace mais paraît étranger à lui.

Dans les vidéos de Peter Aerschmann, l'aléatoire côtoie le prédéterminé, n'offrant au regardeur qu'une vision fragmentaire de la réalité du vivant. C'est ainsi qu'il parvient à nous faire perdre tout repères. D'où vient l'impression de vie alors que les éléments sont en nombres déterminés et que leurs mouvements décrivent des trajectoires prédéfinies ? Au lieu de nous donner à voir une image, Peter Aerschmann parvient à capter au travers de l'image le rythme des choses, leurs manières de s'inscrire dans la durée et dans la répétition. Il reconstitue un environnement qui garde de la réalité ses caractères formels : la mutabilité, la permanence, la durée et la présence d'objet. Ce n'est pas un hasard si les mini-séquences filmées sont presque toutes des fragments de mouvements dont la présentation répétitive et l'enchaînement préprogrammé créent une sorte d'humour mélancolique.

En mettant en scène des archétypes de la mémoire collective, les œuvres de Peter Aerschmann nous renvoient à notre propre réalité et deviennent des métaphores d'un monde dé-hiérarchisé dans lequel nous sommes tous, les uns pour les autres, des étrangers.

Alice Anderson

Née en 1976 à Londres
Vit et travaille à Londres
M.A Goldsmiths College, Londres (2002-2004)
1998-2001 Ecole Nationale Supérieure des
Beaux-Arts de Paris
www.alice-anderson.org

Construisant des récits puisés dans ses souvenirs et dans un imaginaire liés à l'enfance, l'artiste et réalisatrice française et anglaise Alice Anderson revisite la tradition des contes tout en réinventant leurs significations. Entre fiction et citation autobiographique, elle met en relief la dualité qui selon elle correspond à l'essence même du conte à la fois superficiel et profond, normatif et subversif pour plonger le spectateur dans un univers onirique intense d'où surgit une certaine noirceur, une atmosphère tour à tour violente ou effrayante. Si l'enfance et la notion de jeu revêtent une grande importance dans son travail, elles n'en restent pas moins intimement associées à une certaine gravité.

C'est en s'appuyant sur la force symbolique et poétique des objets du passé qu'elle convoque que se construit la trame de ses histoires. Aux antipodes d'une logique linéaire, le processus de narration qu'elle construit est plutôt circulaire, évoquant davantage les méandres d'un labyrinthe, l'univers fluctuant de Lewis Carroll ou les principes freudiens qui président à interprétation de l'inconscient. On peut alors voir dans chacune des histoires fantastiques que nous propose Alice Anderson une quête d'identité nous invitant à passer au delà du miroir, à la recherche de notre propre vécu, entre ravissement et effroi.

Gast Bouschet & Nadine Hilbert

Né en 1958 à Dudelange/Luxembourg / 1961 à Luxembourg, Luxembourg, vivent à Bruxelles et ailleurs
www.thetrustfiles.net

Nadine Hilbert et Gast Bouschet prennent – et montrent – leur photos et vidéos dans le monde entier depuis les années 80. Ils sont particulièrement fascinés par l'image enregistrée et sa capacité à reproduire et commenter la transformation de systèmes politiques et socio-économiques et leur symbolique particulièrment visibles dans la morphologie des tissus urbains et zones frontières.

Leur travail a été montré dans de nombreuses expositions, notamment au Center of Contemporary Arts (Glasgow), au Museum van Hedendaagse Kunst Muhka (Anvers), au Casino, Forum d'Art Contemporain (Luxembourg), à la Galerie Nei Liicht (Dudelange, Luxembourg), à la Busan Biennale of Contemporary Arts (Busan, Corée), au Camouflage, Centre africain d'Art contemporain (Bruxelles et Johannesbourg), au Domaine départemental de Chamarande (Paris) et dans le cadre de Krinzinger Projekte (Vienne) .

« Je est toujours l'autre. Si je dis nous, je désigne le moi coupable. Tout est clair désormais. Personne n'est plus la même personne. L'agression n'a rien changé, nous faisons corps avec nos ennemis, nous partageons l'esprit de nos adversaires. Il n'y a plus de limites, plus de barrières, nos identités se confondent. Mais la peur nous habite, l'angoisse ne nous lâche plus. La menace est quotidienne, elle nous détruit de l'intérieur. Le monde n'est plus le même, la lumière est différente. La nature est inconciliable, elle veut notre peau. Nous sommes des étrangers dans notre pays, nous parlons tous une langue inconnue qui nous effraie. Nos pires cauchemars sont dépourvus désormais de leurs délicieuses sueurs froides. Nos plus beaux rêves nous inquiètent par leur réconfort trompeur. Notre esprit produit et reproduit chaque jour son lent poison. Depuis longtemps, nous ne pouvons plus nous en passer. Nous avons sacrément besoin de ce pain quotidien. Nous avons mauvaise mine dans les champs où nous semons notre propre terreur. Ce sombre miroir de Nadine Hilbert et Gast Bouschet ». (François Olivieri)

Pirmin Blum

Né en 1969 à Pfaffnau/Suisse.
Vit et travaille à Vienne
Etudes à l'Ecole supérieure des Beaux-Arts à Genève (1997-99)
Etudes des médias numériques avec Peter Kogler à l'Académie des Beaux-Arts de Vienne (1999-2005)
www.pirminblum.com

Depuis quelques années, l'artiste suisse Pirmin Blum s'inspire d'Internet, fouillant dans les sites de ventes aux enchères, les moteurs de recherches et les forums. S'il s'intéresse à la Toile, c'est qu'elle est aujourd'hui accessible à tous. N'importe qui peut y mettre ses photos personnelles, ses vidéos, ses textes, et lire les documents intimes que d'autres y diffusent. De manière consciente (comme chez Blum) ou inconsciente, nous devenons des voyeurs et des consommateurs de la vie privée des autres. En plus de ce matériau trouvé, Blum se sert de films provenant de producteurs industriels et commerciaux, par exemple des vidéos de crash-tests réalisées par des constructeurs automobiles. Grâce à la sélection analytique et au montage de séquences spécifiques provenant de ces vidéos, des images initialement dénuées de valeur artistique revêtent des significations nouvelles. Des coupures rapides associées à des boucles stylisent des images d'un airbag qui éclate et se rétracte, formant une bulle étrange d'apparence organique (Airbag, 2000). Blum fait coïncider le moment de l'impact de l'airbag avec le rythme de la respiration humaine ; au bout de quelques boucles, le spectateur en vient à « respirer » en synchronie avec la vidéo.

On observe un effet analogue dans Spuk (2001) pour lequel Blum a choisi une vidéo-test qui montre un véhicule blindé dont on vérifie la résistance en soumettant le pare-brise à l'épreuve des balles. La séquence rapide, articulée autour de deux angles de caméra, alternant des vues de l'extérieur et de l'intérieur du pare-brise, génère une tension troublante et crée chez le spectateur le sentiment qu'il se trouve en plein milieu de l'action. On est tantôt à la place de celui qui tire, tantôt à celle de la victime assise dans la voiture, en train de subir l'assaut des balles. Le son est ici un facteur décisif : le martèlement sourd de basses profondes produites par des enceintes à raison de 130 battements par minute correspond à la fréquence utilisée par les DJs dans les raves afin d'obtenir une stimulation cardiaque optimale.

Christoph Brech

Né à Schweinfurt/Allemagne en1964
Vit et travaille à Munich
Etudes à l'Académie des Beaux-Arts de Munich (1989-1995)
www.christophbrech.com

« Les oeuvres vidéo de Christoph Brech transforment des événements banals en des instants chargés de sens ».

L'œuvre de Christoph Brech comporte des installations, de la photographie, de la vidéo et des interventions dans des lieux publics.

Les vidéos de Brech se caractérisent par la rigueur et la clarté de leur composition, la linéarité de leur réalisation et la simplicité des moyens mis en oeuvre. Parmi les éléments typiques du travail présenté ici figurent des phénomènes naturels, des objets et des impressions du quotidien auxquels répond le point de vue statique de la caméra.

Brech dévoile des situations qui révèlent leur dimension poétique à travers l'étirement du temps et l'impression de lenteur ainsi créée. Des événements banals se voient transformés en des instants chargés de sens.

Dans la vidéo intitulée Passage, il montre un verre d'eau sur une table dans la cabine d'un bateau de pêche, soumis aux vibrations et au tangage du navire. Break présente l'observation calme et d'abord silencieuse du fleuve Saint-Laurent, brumeux et gelé, et oppose au rythme lent de la nature la violence d'un brise-glace canadien qui se fraye un passage à travers la glace. Dans Opus 110a, Brech filme le chef d'orchestre Christoph Poppen de dos afin de restituer la dynamique de l'oeuvre de Dimitri Shostakovich dans le mouvement des plis de sa queue-de-pie. Christoph Brech sait capter à chaque fois dans ses images le « temps propre » d'un événement. Le spectateur est soumis à un rythme ralenti qui crée des ambiances quasi méditatives, comme en témoigne la vidéo Transito, réalisée à Rome en 2007, dans laquelle un lourd rideau à l'entrée d'une église balance au rythme du vent, produisant au sol une véritable danse de lumière et d'ombres. De tels moments de temporalité et de transition représentent l'essence même de l'oeuvre vidéo de Christoph Brech.

Elina Brotherus

Née en 1972 à Helsinki/Finlande
Vit à Helsink et à Avallon, France
MA 2000, University of Art and Design UIAH, Helsinki
www.sag.se/foto/elinabrotherus/elina.html

« Les photos de Le miroir, qui datent de 2000 ainsi que la vidéo Miroir (réalisée en 2001) n'ont pas pour thème « L'identité féminine » ou des sujets semblables comme le pensent certains. Je voulais simplement mettre photographiquement en évidence un phénomène physique somme toute banal comme la disparition de la buée sur un miroir. Si on veut pousser plus loin la réflexion, il est permis d'y voir une allégorie de la photographie. A ses origines, une photo était une plaque de cuivre argentée – donc un miroir – laquelle révélait un portrait lors du processus de développement. Sur un mode identique, on voit dans mon travail une image peu à peu se dessiner dans le miroir. Il est curieux de devoir constater à quel point les deux œuvres sont distinctes, même si la seule différence concerne la mise en parallèle, pour ce qui est de la photo, de deux états distincts alors que la vidéo révèle les moments intermédiaires qui s'inscrivent en continu dans une séquence chronologique. »

Dans Model Studies, il n'est pas question d'histoire personnelle ou de documentaire biographique. Les images sont construites pour des raisons visuelles. L'artiste s'attache à la lumière, aux couleurs, au rythme des masses, et à des thèmes et notions classiques. Le personnage tourne souvent le dos au spectateur. Ce geste invite à une contemplation paisible, non à une confrontation.[1]

Dans les vidéos du même titre, Elina Brotherus a utilisé des modèles des Beaux-Arts qui posent comme pour un séance de croquis. Au lieu de dessiner, elle les regarde à travers la caméra. Il s'agit de mettre en forme le regard particulier qu'un artiste porte sur un modèle : c'est un oeil distancié libéré de voyeurisme. « L'artiste qui dessine ou peint ne prétend pas connaître ou comprendre le modèle en tant que personne ; il ne s'agit pas de ça. On regarde attentivement, c'est tout : où sont les lumières et les ombres, comment se dessinent les lignes. Je veux faire sentir au public ce regard actif mais neutre de l'artiste, en quelque sorte le partager avec lui. C'est un privilège de pouvoir ainsi scruter la figure humaine.[2] »

Olga Chernysheva

Née en 1962 à Moscou où elle vit et travaille
Diplômée de l'Académie du Cinéma de Moscou (1986)
Diplômée de l'Académie des Beaux-Arts, Amsterdam (1995-96)
Participation à la 49e Biennale de Venise avec Second Life (Pavillon russe en 2001)
www.olgachernysheva.ru

Diplômée en cinématographie, Olga Chernysheva s'intéresse à la photographie, à la peinture, à la vidéo expérimentale et à l'installation vidéo. Son projet Fenêtres, créé en 2007, plonge le visiteur dans la vie quotidienne à l'époque Soviétique : à travers les fenêtres des immeubles « Khrouchtchev », on aperçoit des robes, de la vaisselle, des sous-vêtements, un verre de thé, un torse nu d'homme, un fer à repasser, une télé, du tulle à motif de fleurs, du linge qui sèche… Les gens vont et viennent : un vieillard s'étire, des jeunes s'amusent… Ici la fenêtre devient le cadre d'une scène, créant un espace éclairé comme celui d'un théâtre, où les personnages apparaissent et disparaissent dans l'arrière-scène sombre des appartements.

Les fenêtres de Chernysheva révèlent l'envers du décor de la vie quotidienne en Russie. En donnant à voir les routines quotidiennes et ordinaires, elles font appréhender le sens même de l'existence. De plus, tout est fait sans le moindre voyeurisme, sans la moindre curiosité déplacée, par le biais d'une approche distanciée, posée, calme.

Plusieurs clips vidéo qui tournent en même temps dans le cadre sombre de la nuit et sur l'écran du téléviseur évoquent un modèle idéal de vie en communauté (encadré par une musique de Chopin). Naissent ainsi une impression de forte présence et une chaleureuse nostalgie pour cette réalité soviétique qui n'a pas tout à fait disparu.

Ulrich Gebert

Né à Munich en 1976
Vit et travaille à Leipzig/Allemagne
Etudes de photographie à l'Académie des Arts visuels de Leipzig (1998-2005) et au Royal College of Art de Londres (2006)
www.klemms-berlin.com

L'oeuvre d'Ulrich Gebert s'articule souvent autour de concepts qui semblent d'emblée insaisissables, mais qui ont néanmoins un impact fondamental sur notre manière d'agir.

Elle met en relief avec beaucoup d'acuité les principes de l'ordre, de la pensée systémique, de la hiérarchisation et des mécanismes du pouvoir, les rendant palpables dans un contexte artistique. Selon les cas, il utilise divers modes de représentation : mise en scène, cinéma, documentaire, portrait , et intègre ceux-ci dans le processus de réalisation d'oeuvres pour la plupart photographiques, de façon à faire écho au support.

Pour son oeuvre vidéo Keine Dialoge (no dialogues) (2004), Ulrich Gebert utilise des images « trouvées » montrant des séances de formation d'un corps d'élite de gardes frontaliers appartenant à l'unité antiterroriste GSG 9 au sein de la police fédérale allemande. Il a monté à partir de ce matériau une boucle minimaliste qui montre cinq officiers en uniforme, alignés dans une salle sombre et fermée, en train de se soumettre à une épreuve de stress au moyen de flashs stroboscopiques. Au cours de l'épreuve, les officiers reçoivent des consignes qu'ils devront exécuter plus tard. Le bruit sec et continu du flash met le spectateur en contact direct avec cette expérimentation ; effet sonore auquel répond une suite ultrarapide d'images statiques consécutives qui semblent créer d'infimes mouvements chez les officiers. A l'instar de ces derniers, le spectateur, debout dans un espace de projection tout aussi restreint et sombre, se retrouve à son tour exposé à des flashs visuellement violents. La situation contraignante et tendue de l'épreuve à laquelle sont soumis les officiers du GSG 9 est ainsi vécue pleinement par le spectateur.

Ori Gersht

Né en 1967 à Tel-Aviv/Israël, vit et travaille à Londres
1988-1992 Licence en photographie, film et vidéo,
1993-95 maîtrise de photographie,
Royal College of Art, Londres,
Université de Westminster, Londres
www.mummeryschnelle.com

Dans son œuvre la plus récente, Ori Gersht interroge les relations entre film, photographie, technologie et perception optique. Ce travail survient à un moment clé de l'histoire de l'art où le numérique fait peser la menace d'une crise tout en promettant une véritable révolution. Dans ses deux films récents Pomegranate et Big Bang, Gersht recrée des natures mortes qui rappellent des tableaux de maître, retraçant l'évolution de la manière dont les artistes ont été fascinés par la représentation de la réalité depuis le 17e siècle. Contrairement à ces tableaux historiques qui s'appliquaient à figer des moments immobiles, les compositions de Gersht sont bouleversées par

1 DE « ELINA BROTHERUS EN CONVERSATION AVEC BIRGIT EUSTERSCHULTE ». EXPOSITION SELF-TIMER (SELBSTAUSLÖSER), KUNSTHALLE FRIDERICIANUM, KASSEL 2005.
2 EXTRAIT DU DOSSIER DE PRESSE POUR ELINA BROTHERUS : MODEL STUDIES, EXPOSITION À L' AGENCE GB,PARIS 2005.

des interventions rapides et violentes. Les références de Pomegranate sont d'une part une nature morte baroque de Juán Sanchez Cotán , et d'autre part les images stroboscopiques de Harold Edgerton. Une balle à haute vélocité traverse l'image au ralenti et anéantit une grenade suspendue, éclatant le fruit, le projetant dans l'air, évoquant une bouche écrasée et violée en train de cracher des graines rouge sang. Une image paisible se transforme en carnage, et un dialogue s'instaure entre calme et mouvement, paix et violence. De telles dichotomies sont aussi présentes dans Big Bang, un film qui semble à première vue être une nature morte flamande représentant des fleurs. Soudain l'illusion éclate en morceaux : les fleurs et le vase explosent sur fond de sirènes de guerre dont le son intense se transforme lentement en une voix mécanique aiguë. La scène se mue ensuite en une lente pluie cosmique de particules de fleurs multicolores et de poussière. Pomegranate et Big Bang se font ainsi l'écho des ondes de choc de l'histoire humaine.

Alors que beaucoup d'artistes cinéastes et vidéastes ayant une démarche politique produisent des œuvres proches du documentaire, Gersht explore la méditation provocatrice en maître incontesté du genre. (Andrew Mummery, Director Mummery + Schnelle Gallery, London, UK)

Terézia Golasová

Née à Bratislava/Slovaquie en1980
Vit et travaille à Bratislava
2002-2007 Études à l'Académie des Beaux-Arts de Bratislava,
2004 Faculté de Philosophie de l' Université Comenius, Bratislava
http://golasova.marencin.sk

Étudiante aux Beaux-Arts, Terézia Golasová correspond parfaitement aux critères qui définissent la « jeune artiste émergente ». Son œuvre, créée dans un atelier photographique, a pour unique thème l'emploi de différents moyens photographiques et vidéographiques pour rendre compte du concept de mutation. Aucune action ne se développe dans ses vidéos; elles ont pour sujet le mouvement et le flux temporel. Afin d'augmenter l'impact de ses œuvres, elle se sert d'une caméra vidéo fixe.

Dans la vidéo ...In One Bed..., une caméra tourne sur son axe à 360 degrés, créant l'impression d'une image panoramique.
Le fait que les personnages entrent dans une direction opposée au mouvement de la caméra a pour effet de séquencer l'action, à l'instar d'images fixes se succédant en série.

Quo vadis est un court document sur le flux temporel, selon l'artiste. Une caméra fixe filme un voyageur assis dans le métro et se déplaçant d'une station à l'autre. A travers la fenêtre du wagon, nous apercevons des objets qui défilent rapidement et qui contrastent avec la quasi immobilité des voyageurs ; les mouvements occasionnels de ces derniers ne font alors qu'intensifier l'impression que nous sommes face à une image fixe prise à l'intérieur de la rame. Afin de visualiser le flux temporel, une horloge en bas de l'image affiche l'heure exacte à la seconde près.

La dernière œuvre de Golasová To Be at a Loss peut être considérée comme la suite naturelle de ses recherches sur la notion de mutation. Elle utilise ici une caméra fixe pour saisir une personne immobile (l'artiste elle-même) devant son reflet dans un miroir. Les seuls facteurs de transformation sont assurés par la buée qui recouvre peu à peu l'image dans le miroir et par le flux sonore de l'eau qui coule. La vidéo se termine alors lorsque l'image du miroir a complètement disparu.

Laurent Goldring

Né en 1957 à Paris où il vit, fait de la peinture, sculpte, dessine et tourne des vidéos

« Le cinéma a le secret de la photo
La photographie s'était voulue ressemblance et Arago avait fait voter la loi qui l'authentifie comme telle. Or le cinéma encore chronophotographie a tout de suite su que cette fiction ne se fondait sur rien d'autre que sur son propre postulat incantatoire. C'est pour cette raison qu'il ne s'est jamais revendiqué comme vingt-quatre photos seconde, mais comme vingt-quatre images seconde.

Le cinéma prend des séries de photos en même temps. Il constate que deux clichés infiniment proches diffèrent entre eux d'une façon qui disqualifie l'idée de ressemblance. Et qui fait exploser symétriquement, l'idée d'une ressemblance du monde à lui-même. Dans le cas du portrait, c'est la fiction de l'individu qui saute. Dans le cas des paysages, la vérité de la perspective qui s'effondre. Une dissemblance fondamentale s'installe, celle-là même dont la photographie avait proclamé qu'elle n'existait pas.

Le cinéma a vu, aurait pu faire voir, a refusé de voir, a décrété qu'il n'avait rien vu, et s'est mis frénétiquement à s'interdire de voir.

Le cinéma est devenu d'emblée la dénégation massive, en pleine bonne (in)conscience, du secret de la photo : qu'elle ne ressemblait pas. Il s'est érigé en industrie de l'univoque et de la ressemblance, et d'abord de la ressemblance à soi-même, garante de toutes les autres industries. Hollywood a été la grande machine publicitaire de ce way of life où les objets et les humains, ont été sommés de se mettre à se ressembler imperturbablement.

Tout dans le cinéma s'explique par cette frénésie dénégatoire : casting, scénario, story-board, prise de vue, tout est destiné à nous faire croire qu'un individu existe, avec un visage et un corps, un caractère, un but et une idée... car on comprend aussi pourquoi une industrie qui n'existe que pour fonder une fiction ne peut concevoir d'image concevable que de fiction.

Le travail que je fais consiste à essayer de faire une image qui bouge en dehors du fictionnel, c'est-à-dire de la ressemblance. » (Laurent Goldring)

Laurent Grasso

Né en 1972 à Mulhouse/France
Vit et travaille à Paris
Études à la Cooper Union School de New York, à la Central Saint Martins School of Art de Londres ainsi qu'à l'École des Beaux-arts de Paris dont il est diplômé
www.galeriechezvalentin.com/fr/artistes/laurent_grasso/works/

Qu'il (re)travaille les formes plus ou moins identifiables de notre société de contrôle ou qu'il subvertisse les techniques et conventions cinématographiques qui façonnent l'imaginaire collectif, Laurent Grasso crée toujours des environnements dotés d'un fort potentiel narratif, mêlant peurs ataviques, preuves scientifiques et inquiétantes mythologies contemporaines. Dans sa vidéo Untitled, un énorme nuage menaçant avance dans les rues de Paris, s'approchant de nous tout en engloutissant les voitures et immeubles qui se trouvent sur son chemin.

Face à cet écran de poussière en mouvement, cette trace fictive d'une catastrophe inventée, nous sommes invités à nous engager dans un processus narratif, à projeter nos peurs ou à inventer notre propre scénario. En fonction de nos sensibilités individuelles et de nos référents historiques et culturels, ce nuage convoque des images de l'effondrement des Twin Towers, les scènes de violences urbaines ou bien encore les séquences spectaculaires de films d'action à effets spéciaux.

Les oeuvres de Grasso pourraient en quelque sorte ressusciter un goût pour les prophéties paranoïaques rétro-futuristes proférées par Charles Fourier il y a deux cents ans. Il incorpore régulièrement dans ses œuvres lumière, son et phénomènes naturels et météorologiques afin de créer des expériences sensorielles totalement inédites qui finissent par véhiculer des produits inachevés de l'imagination que le visiteur doit compléter.

En opérant une tension entre les œuvres présentées, leur environnement et les interprétations parfois dramatiques qui les accompagnent, Laurent Grasso crée des images mentales tenaces qui se dressent comme autant d'écrans devant ce que nous appelons communément le réel.

Tuomo Rainio

Né en 1983 à Espoo/Finlande
Vit et travaille actuellement à Helsinki
Bachelor of Arts du département photo de l' Université des Arts et du Design de Helsinki ;
Actuellement préparation d' un Master (2007-08)
Etudes à l'Université des Arts Musashino à Tokyo
Expositions en Finlande et au Japon
www.rainio.pp.fi

Presence of the Crowd

La mutation, le mouvement et la temporalité constituent les thèmes majeures des photos et vidéos de l'artiste finlandais Tuomo Rainio (né en 1983). La pensée visuelle qui caractérise ses œuvres puristes oscille entre l'esthétique de la photographie en noir et blanc et la tradition de l'art vidéo post-conceptuel. Si l'on devait qualifier le champ dans lequel ces éléments s'entremêlent, on pourrait dire que ce sont des « images en mouvement sans appartenance à un genre spécifique ». Que voyons-nous au juste lorsque nous regardons les œuvres de la série Tracescape ? On voit d'abord une image noire, comme un tableau noir, puis apparaissent lentement des paysages urbains mélancoliques et anonymes, des rues et des structures architecturales. Le seul élément de certitude est la ligne du mouvement. Les œuvres commencent comme des animations fantomatiques et soudain se transforment en univers reconnaissables sinon familiers. Il y a quelque chose de troublant dans l'atmosphère, peut-être la présence de la foule.

La réalité sociale se manifeste dans les traces des piétons qui empruntent leur parcours quotidien. Comme le souligne Raino, « Tracescape est une série d'œuvres vidéo qui interroge la structure sociale dans l'espace public. Dans l'espace urbain, le comportement de chacun est observé et contrôlé par les autres et par soi-même. »

Les œuvres City (2005) et Crosswise (2006) donnent à voir des carrefours, des chemins et le cycle de la vie urbaine qui se mue en un plan de ville aveugle. Ce sont comme des amoncellements d'images aux rayons X : on peut imaginer un corps vivant, mais son seul support est structurel. Les environnements sonores ancrent les images dans une expérience immersive du quotidien : feux de signalisation, voitures qui passent, tramways, bruits de pas qui résonnent. En même temps, des lignes de mouvement se chevauchent, forment des faisceaux, éclairent l'image. Enfin il ne s'agit plus d'un film avec sa pellicule photosensible, mais d'un algorithme généré par ordinateur qui calcule les images une à une et rend visible chaque mutation. En guise d'analogie, ces vidéos témoignent des changements rapides qui s'opèrent dans l'industrie de l'image numérique. La technique et le contenu sont inséparables. La grille des pixels atteint un nouveau plan de signification dans les images mémorables de Rainio, rendant ainsi visible la matrice de notre époque. (Leevi Haapala, Commissaire et chercheur au Kiasma,
Musée d'art contemporain d'Helsinki)

Jan Kuděj

Né à Prague en 1978
Vit et travaille à Prague
1997-1999 Faculté de Philosophie et des Arts, Université de Charles, Prague, avec une spécialisation en ethnologie
1999-2005 Académie des Arts, Architecture et Design, Prague – atelier du professeur Pavel Štecha
(2002-2003 Université des Arts, Berlin (bourse)

L'oeuvre de Jan Kuděj interroge la notion de temporalité. « Obtenir une trace absolue de la continuité temporelle est impossible », dit-il. Il a réalisé plusieurs « projections » qui mêlent la technique des images photographiques fixes à celle de la vidéo. Elles abordent la caméra vidéo à travers sa capacité à enregistrer 25 images par seconde ; contrainte conduisant nécessairement à la fragmentation du mouvement et du temps, quand bien même l'oeil humain les perçoit comme une continuité.

Dans sa « Projection » sur les escalators, il suit le mouvement cyclique des machines et enregistre un cycle entier au moyen d'une caméra vidéo fixe. La projection en boucle donne ensuite l'impression que l'escalator fonctionne de façon continue.

Avec une intention contraire, il a animé l'image d'un arbre pour que les mouvements de sa cime semblent séquentiellement interrompus pendant l'acte même de l'enregistrement.

La projection choisie pour cette exposition, qui montre des vagues qui viennent mourir sur une plage, relève du même principe que celle des escalators, autrement dit la perception de la continuité du temps qui passe.

« Cependant, d'un certain point de vue, toute projection est fermée sur elle-même : elle fige une action sous la forme d'images fixes. La temporalité n'est qu'une illusion ».

« Ma démarche consiste d'une part à enregistrer des images en continu au moyen d'une caméra vidéo, et d'autre part à interrompre délibérément des suites de prises de vue. Nous reconnaissons deux manières de percevoir le temps – un temps de l'instant et un temps de la durée. Cette sensation nous aide à vivre les contradictions simultanées d'une réalité qui se déroule. L'idée qu'on a de soi-même (et partant, du monde) n'est pas continue. Son caractère est infléchi par chaque nouveau processus mental. Or ces processus ne sont qu'une suite d'interruptions se répétant à l'infini. Nous percevons le déroulement du temps comme une suite d'instants ». (Jan Kuděj, 2005)

Ange Leccia

Né en 1952 à Minervu, Corse, vit et travaille à Paris
Études de cinéma et de philosophie à la Sorbonne
www.galeriealminerech.com

Invitation au voyage introspectif, œuvre métaphysique et contemplative, Orage est une installation vidéo particulièrement caractéristique du pouvoir onirique qui se dégage des œuvres d'Ange Leccia. Fasciné depuis l'enfance par le cinéma et l'image animée, cet artiste dont l'œuvre tout entière est traversée par une poétique de l'énergie, a nourri sa pratique d'une réflexion sur l'image et le matériau filmique qui lui permet d'approcher au plus près de l'indicible tout en insufflant à ses créations une forte densité émotionnelle.

Déployé dans un espace plongé dans l'obscurité, ce dispositif en diptyque qui se présente sous la forme d'une projection mise en boucle sur deux écrans en angle droit nous immerge dans un ciel nocturne tourmenté où les éclairs se déchaînent dans une temporalité qui semble suspendue. Filmé en plan fixe, ce flux d'énergie violente emplit l'image et l'espace sonore pour nous mettre face à la présence sensible et toute puissante des éléments, symbole d'une nature qui nous dépasse en dépit des efforts que nous faisons pour la maîtriser. Entre stase visuelle et étirement temporel, le rythme répétitif et l'effet de permanence qu'il contient opèrent un glissement vers l'abstraction pure tout en ouvrant la voie au transcendantal et au sublime tels que les définit Kant. Cet usage de la répétition, de la mise en boucle qui caractérise les images d'Ange Leccia donne ainsi le sentiment d'une régénérescence permanente qui doit être interprétée, selon le critique d'art Pascal Beausse, « dans une dimension organique de l'image, qui nous convie à un présent éternel ». Cette dilatation de la durée associée à l'immersion sensorielle que favorise la mise en espace des images nous offre ici la possibilité de convoquer celui de notre imaginaire le plus souterrain.

Oliver Möst

Né à Füssen, Allgäu/Allemagne en 1968
Vit et travaille à Berlin
Photographe et artiste vidéographe freelance
Premier projet vidéo en 1999 en collaboration avec un chorégraphe de danse
www.olivermoest.de

« Les images parfaitement nettes ont surmonté le flou ; mais elles passent à côté de ce qui peut être vécu lorsque la mise au point et la définition ne sont pas présentes. »[3]

L'oeuvre vidéo d'Oliver Möst, réalisée en 2007, s'inscrit dans la continuité de son travail photographique. Ce qui la caractérise à première vue est un manque évident de netteté, principe esthétique fondamental dans les photos et les vidéos de cet artiste. Le principe de la netteté permet d'appréhender le fondement de la conscience perceptive du créateur.

3 BRETTHAUER, BASTIAN, „SO EINE WELT OHNE ECKEN UND KANTEN"(UN MONDE OÙ TOUS LES ANGLES SONT ARRONDIS) IN K4 GALERIE, EDS., OLIVER MÖST, CLACKASTIGMAT 6.0 / K4 GALERIE (BERLIN, DORN, 2005).

Le processus de perception propre à Oliver Möst constitue un axe de recherche majeur dans l'ensemble de son travail. Il a une vue déficiente, et ses lunettes ont une correction de 2 dioptries à l'oeil gauche et 6 à l'oeil droit. Son oeuvre nous fait partager le regard subjectif du photographe ou du vidéaste, nous donnant à voir « ce qu'il a vu et perçu de cette façon ». Elle nous fait vivre en direct sa perception décalée et la façon dont il saisit l'espace qui l'entoure (between, hide & seek, brown eyes).

Une autre thématique importante dans l'oeuvre vidéographique de Möst est une réflexion sur la photographie et sur les spécificités liées à son support, réflexion qu'il mène en associant film et photographie. L'idée de combiner deux techniques photographiques l'a conduit à employer un sténopé (sans objectif), une camera obscura, l'appareil photo dans sa forme la plus élémentaire. Il a associé cette technique à celle de la vidéo numérique en enregistrant au moyen d'une caméra l'image projetée sur la plaque de l'appareil. De cette confrontation entre la « vieille » technologie du sténopé et celle de la vidéo moderne naît ce que Möst appelle la « vidéo-sténopé ». Elle témoigne de l'évolution de la photographie depuis le simple sténopé jusqu'aux dernières avancées de la vidéo numérique, faisant ainsi écho au développement des qualités spécifiques de la photographie au fil des ans.

Tim Parchikov

Né en 1983 à Moscou où il vit et travaille
2006 Diplômé de l'Institut russe de Cinéma, spécialisation cameraman

Le poète et photographe Tim Parchikov est un jeune Moscovite de moins de trente ans. Pour sa génération, le monde est devenu trop petit et, sur le plan géographique, parfois même trop visible et accessible. Fort heureusement, Tim Parchikov perçoit la vie en vrai poète, restituant pour le spectateur sa propre vision du monde ; vision qui a tant de force et qui est si pleine d'énergie et de jeunesse que le souci qu'elle puisse être prévisible ou de pure apparence peut être tranquillement écarté. Ses travaux sont dopés. Le sentiment de profonde mélancolie, une caractéristique de l'adolescence souvent, sa connaissance en profondeur de la photographie russe et internationale, n'atténuent en rien le sentiment électrisant de fraîcheur qui émane de son travail.

A l'individualité créative du jeune artiste répond un savoir-faire mûr et indépendant qui s'exprime dans de nombreux champs esthétiques de l'art. Son sens subtil de la couleur, sa forte affinité avec le nombre d'or et son goût pour la métaphore osée lui permettent de s'exprimer de façon audacieuse et originale. Il s'agit d'une nouvelle voix qui mérite d'être entendue.

La vidéo Gone to Sea est une miniature consacrée à la possibilité de disparaître en mer sans raison – autrement dit, nulle part. Gone to Sea rappelle « L'Avventura » de Michelangelo Antonioni, dont le personnage principal disparaît sans raison apparente. Mais ce qui intéresse chacun d'entre nous n'est pas tant le problème de la disparition que le fait de savoir si elle passera inaperçue…

Matteo Peterlini

Né en 1970 à Rovereto/Italie où il vit et travaille.
Diplômé en Informatique, il a suivi des cours de design graphique et de publicité organisés par la Province de Bolzano (1992)
Expositions à partir de 1997 notamment à Trento, Venise, Turin ainsi qu'au Musée d'art contemporain d'Istanbul
www.matteopeterlini.it

Utiliser les pixels comme unité de mesure représente dans l'oeuvre de Matteo Peterlini un véritable élément conceptuel et un choix programmatique. Eclatées et recomposées, les images de ses séries photographiques sont le résultat d' un processus qui tend vers l'infini, dans lequel le système employé pour recombiner les fragments est laissé au hasard puis appliqué grâce à une fonction algébrique. Peterlini porte son attention sur les mécanismes mêmes de la perception dans des logiciels spécialement conçus. Comment les images sont-elles générées dans notre esprit ? Choisis par l'imitation, l'apprentissage et le partage, les mécanismes habituellement employés pour comprendre le monde perdent leur efficacité face au flux généré par les processus électroniques. Le fait qu'il s'agit ici de genres picturaux traditionnels – portraits, nus, paysages – ne semble plus contradictoire. Grâce à l'aspect frontal des visages (ceux qui sont demandés pour une photo de passeport standard dans Meyouother), les silhouettes des corps (dans les six poses qu'adoptent les modèles dans V6), et le caractère fixe des paysages presque abstraits (Backscapes), il est possible d'apercevoir cette tendance inconsciente consistant à reconnaître ce qui est « déjà connu » (Gestalt, stéréotypes) et qui nous permet d'aborder la diversité des phénomènes. De plus, c'est précisément l'ambiguïté de cette technique qui révèle la nature analytique de son travail ; technique qui n'est artisanale qu'en apparence et que Peterlini emploie pour donner vie à ses séries photographiques. En effet, si l'on observe de près ces images (qui sont en réalité le résultat d'un flux créatif continu) elles fonctionnent comme un collage, alors que le processus mis en œuvre pour reconnaître l'image dans sa globalité est suspendu à la coexistence virtuelle de toutes les combinaisons possibles. (Cristina Natalicchio)

Peter Puklus & Melinda Sipos

Peter Puklus
Né à Koloszvár/Hongrie, en 1980
Diplômé en photographie en 2005 à l'Université des Arts Moholy-Nagy, Budapest
http://photolumen.hu/puklus
www.deuxprojects.blogspot.com

Melinda SIPOS
Née à Budapest/H en 1979. Vit et travaille à Budapest
Diplômé en design du verre en 2005 à l'Université des Arts Art Moholy-Nagy, Budapest ;
http://siposmelinda.blogspot.com
www.deuxprojects.blogspot.com

Si chacun travaille de façon individuelle et possède sa propre démarche artistique, Peter Puklus et Melinda Sipos ont néanmoins réalisé les deux projets ensemble, Imported Lights et Garden, dans le cadre d'un group appelé DEUX. Les titres des œuvres n'ont pas plus de sens que les données brutes qui les constituent. DEUX_00 Imported Lights est le « projet zéro » de ce collectif d'artistes. Faisant subir un traitement vidéographique à l'image fixe, l'idée est de capter le reflet de la lumière passant par une fenêtre et de le projeter dans une pièce aveugle.

Une logique analogue préside au projet DEUX_ 01 Garden. Il s'agit de l'enregistrement détaillé des formes successives que prend un jardin photographié pendant une longue période. Une photo par jour fut prise par la même fenêtre, une année durant. Il en résulte un ensemble d'infimes variations dans l'espace : des chaises déplacées, des saisons qui se succèdent… Comme un diaporama, cette œuvre crée l'impression que les mutations ont lieu dans le temps même de la projection.

A l'origine de ces travaux, on trouve des idées simples voire simplistes mises en œuvre de façon méticuleuse. Les choix techniques, comme par exemple le fait d'opter pour la photographie ou la vidéo et d'opérer des passages d'un médium à l'autre sont subordonnés aux choix artistiques à la différence de travaux d'autres artistes retenus dans cette sélection dont l'inspiration découle principalement du potentiel technique propre à un médium. Pour Puklus et Sipos, le dépassement de la photographie par la vidéo apportait la solution lumineuse aux considérations esthétiques qui étaient les leurs.

Jutta Strohmaier

Née à Tulln/Autriche en 1966, vit et travaille à Vienne
1996-1999 Etudes de peinture à L'Académie des Beaux-Arts de Vienne ; spécialisation dans la photographie et les nouveaux médias sous la direction de Eva Schlegel.
www.jutta-strohmaier.net

Quelles sont les relations entre les images et le réel ? Quel genre de réalité les images peuvent-elles créer ? Voici les questions auxquelles les vidéos, les photos et les installations de Jutta Strohmaier tentent de répondre.

Passenger (2004) est la compression d'un ensemble d'images représentant un intérieur vide avec deux grandes fenêtres, photographiées chaque minute pendant plusieurs jours, pour constituer une vidéo de moins de quinze minutes. Pendant la journée, les fenêtres laissent pénétrer dans la pièce une lumière si forte qu'il est difficile voire impossible de voir ce qui se trouve plus loin, mais à la tombée de la nuit l'extérieur et la façade de l'immeuble en face deviennent visibles peu à peu. Cette oeuvre joue sur la mutation graduelle de la perception d'une pièce, tout en interrogeant le concept de l'espace dans son rapport à des notions telles que l'inclusion et l'exclusion, le familier et l'étranger, l'ouverture et la fermeture[4].

Strohmaier revisite le principe des prises de vue consécutives présentées comme de la vidéo d'animation dans des oeuvres telle que Im Dickicht (2005) et Silent Stories (2006). Dans Im Dickicht, elle appuie sur le déclencheur à chaque pas en marchant dans les sous-bois d'une réserve forestière. Strohmaier comble les « trous » entre les clichés à l'aide du logiciel Photoshop; l'enchevêtrement des branches donne d'abord l'impression qu'elles sont rongées avant de repousser de plus belle dans une séquence ultérieure, pour enfin se dissoudre dans un ciel bleu.

Les photos satellites rassemblées dans la vidéo en boucle intitulée Journey (2005) offrent une vue de la Terre depuis l'espace – un point de vue qui nous est parfaitement familier grâce à la télévision et à Internet, mais que peu de gens ont pu personnellement expérimenter. Strohmaier fouille dans les archives d'images satellites qu'elle a rassemblées pendant des années. Mais au lieu de présenter une séquence linéaire de villes et de paysages, ces images se perforent et se pénètrent les unes les autres, s'érodant par couches successives, traversant et retraversant la planète Terre.

Wolfgang Thaler

Né en 1969 à Salzbourg/Autriche.

4 VOIR AUSSI LES COMMENTAIRES DE SARAH KOLB SUR L'EXPOSITION JUTTA STROHMAIER. DIESE WELT UND ANDERE, GALERIE HOHENLOHE, VIENNE, 2004.

Vit et travaille à Vienne
1989-1991 Etudes à l'Institut photographique de l'Etat de Bavière, Munich (aujourd'hui Université des Arts appliqués de Munich)
www.wolfgangthaler.at

L'œuvre de Wolfgang Thaler réunit photographie d'architecture (séries sur la gare Südbahnhof à Vienne et sur les ronds-points) et photographie documentaire (travail sur la chaîne de cafés traditionnels viennois Aida etc). Cette double inspiration témoigne de l'intérêt qu'il porte à la question de l'espace.

La série Matter of Selection (2007) nous invite à pénétrer dans l'appartement d'un collectionneur. D'abord Thaler utilise une pellicule noir et blanc haute résolution pour photographier ses meubles (un bahut, une bibliothèque) ; puis, tel un détective, il scanne le moindre détail des images sur un écran d'ordinateur. Des mutations se produisent alors à plusieurs niveaux. La capture photographique d'un seul instant se prolonge en un travelling sans fin; le fait que ce soit la photographie d'un objet qui est filmée plutôt que l'objet lui-même produit un glissement du réel. De plus, nous ne voyons que des détails isolés, jamais l'image dans son ensemble.

Bienvenue à Mep'Yuk – c'est par cette phrase que Thaler accueille les visiteurs de sa cité imaginaire qui porte le nom fictif de Mep'Yuk la Centrale, une ville sans habitants et composée de pièces vides. Die Zentrale (1999) est composée entièrement d'images d'espaces intérieurs. L'artiste prend d'abord des photos d'entrées d'immeubles de bureaux anonymes, d'espaces d'accueil, de bureaux et de salles d'attente dans diverses villes du monde. Malgré leur environnement culturel différent, ces lieux ont une chose en commun : ce sont des espaces (semi-)publics dont la fonction première est administrative, structurelle ou organisationnelle. Ensuite Thaler met en série les photos et les scanne petit à petit au moyen de travellings lents et horizontaux. Ici encore, Thaler interdit la vue d'ensemble de ces intérieurs au spectateur, ne donnant à voir que des détails. Nous avons rapidement l'impression d'observer ces lieux grâce à des caméras de vidéosurveillance et la question se pose : qu'y a t-il à observer si aucun être humain n'est de permanence à ce « poste de contrôle » ?

Mutations II. Moving Stills / L'avventura di un'immagine sotto tensione

Nell'ambito del Mese Europeo della Fotografia, avviato nel 2004 e di cui oggi fanno parte i Festival di Parigi, Berlino, Bratislava, Lussemburgo, Mosca, Roma e Vienna, si è reso lecito e necessario interrogarsi collettivamente sulle mutazioni del nostro mondo e, in particolar modo, su quella dell'immagine contemporanea. Questo è il dato di fatto sul quale si è aperta, nel 2006, la prima esposizione intitolata « Mutations I »: un evento che ha inteso concentrarsi sulle mutazioni tecnologiche e artistiche della fotografia.

La seconda edizione di questa manifestazione, intitolata « Mutations II », si propone di approfondire la riflessione intorno al medium del video, portando avanti l'esplorazione dei rapporti fecondi che legano l'immagine fissa e quella in movimento e cerando di delineare lo stato dell'arte della creazione contemporanea in Europa.

In un contesto caratterizzato dalla globalizzazione e dalla convergenza digitale di tutti i nostri supporti di comunicazione e di creazione, l'era del « post-medium » in cui ci addentriamo è « un'epoca caratterizzata dall'esplorazione dell'ibridazione delle tecnologie, in cui gli artisti combinano e ricombinano il video con un ampio ventaglio di materiali »[1] – fotografia, suono, video digitale, cinema, DVD, informatica, CD-Rom, grafica e animazione-. Per ogni arte diviene dunque possibile « coprire, in sé stessa, all'interno dei suoi limiti materiali, ma anche forzandoli un po', l'intero spettro della comunità che costituisce insieme alle altre arti »[2].

Nell'abbandonare il suo status di materiale atto a fissare la realtà registrata e facendo ricorso ad uno dei principali elementi dell'arte video, ossia la dimensione temporale, la fotografia si emancipa grazie ad infinite manipolazioni artistiche o ibridazioni tecniche, sia analogiche che digitali.

Pertanto, gli autori di « Mutations II » hanno scelto di mettere in luce gli artisti europei che, uniti dal gusto della sperimentazione di nuove forme di espressione - come Nancy Spector nel saggio « Art Photography after Photography »[3], si sono interrogati sui criteri specifici che fossero in grado di determinare la differenza tra un fotografo ed un artista che lavora con la fotografia.

Oggi, infatti, un numero sempre crescente di fotografi utilizza il video, facendo evolvere le particolarità che definiscono ognuna di queste due attività. Al di là della diversità delle considerazioni estetiche e delle tecniche visive utilizzate, i creatori presentati nell'ambito di « Mutations II » ci invitano a superare le logiche territoriali e le definizioni accademiche che limitano ognuno di questi campi artistici, al fine di esplorare le frontiere che li separano. In altri termini, « Mutations II » ci invita a scoprire nuovi territori dell'immagine fissa e dell'immagine in movimento, attraverso le tensioni che le animano. Tensione ontologica tra l'istantaneo e la durata; tensione estetica dovuta all'ibridazione dell'immagine argentea e di una immagine-flusso; tensione dialettica tra le modalità limitate di cui dispone l'immagine fotografica per catturare l'attenzione e « l'infinità di combinazioni percettive in cui si possono definire ed articolare le immagini elettroniche »[4] e, in particolare, la struttura del video.

Per Gilles Deleuze e Felix Guattari, « non ci sono territori senza vettore di uscita dal territorio stesso [...] senza sforzo per ri-territorializzarsi altrove »[5]. Se limitiamo questo interrogativo filosofico al mero campo artistico, possiamo sostenere che la dinamica che caratterizza qualsivoglia corrente artistica è una forza centrifuga che tende a prendere le distanze dalle convenzioni e dalle norme vigenti; si tratta di un

1 RUSH (MICHAEL). 2007. L'ART VIDÉO. LONDRES. THAMES & HUDSON.
2 BELLOUR (RAYMOND). 1999. L'ENTRE-IMAGES 2. P.O.L. PARIS.
3 MOVING PICTURES, CONTEMPORARY PHOTOGRAPHY AND VIDEO FROM THE GUGGENHEIM MUSEUM COLLECTIONS. 2003. NEW YORK. GUGGENHEIM MUSEUM PUBLICATIONS, P. 31-39.
4 VAILLANT (ALEXIS), PARFAIT (FRANÇOISE), JANKOVIC (NIKOLA). 2001. LES NOUVELLES IMAGES. TOME 1. CHRONIQUES DE L'AFAA. PARIS.
5 DELEUZE (GILLES). 2004. L'ABÉCÉDAIRE DE GILLES DELEUZE. PARIS. MONTPARNASSE, DVD.

ITALIAN

(Tutte le traduzioni a cura di Alessandra Rantucci, ad esclusione del testo di « Mutations II ». Moving stills / L'avventura di un'immagine sotto tensione tradotto da Francesca Ciotti.)

« vettore di uscita » la cui condizione necessaria per la sua esistenza è la novità dello sguardo che getta sul mondo.

Uno sguardo che, nei lavori di Peter Aerschmann, richiama la particolarità di scene che illustrano la sfida fondamentale raccolta dai suoi lavori: riuscire a fotografare uno spazio pur mantenendo la profondità temporale; produrre una fotografia che non sarebbe un mero scatto istantaneo e che, lungi dal fissare il movimento, possa essere in grado di darlo a vedere. Peter Aerschmann include dunque il tempo nella rappresentazione dello spazio. Egli sposta il principio della fissità dell'immagine per applicarlo al movimento che fissa nell'unità della sua realizzazione. In questo modo, Aerschmann fa « balbettare » il linguaggio videografico, mostrando personaggi che sembrano prigionieri delle azioni ripetitive che compiono ciclicamente.

Questa ricchezza semantica e stilistica inerente alla ripetizione ispira anche Gast Bouschet e Nadine Hilbert nella realizzazione di Dreamsequence, opera videografica creata nel 2006/07. Nel tornare sui luoghi in cui fu girato il film di Philipp Kauffman « Invasion of the bodysnatchers », realizzato negli anni '78, gli autori riattualizzano e ricontestualizzano l'idea della paranoia, attraverso l'uso di immagini ricorrenti e ossessive. Sacrificando appositamente il riflesso convenzionale di una narrazione lineare, questa sequenza onirica che è, nel contempo, poetica e politica, riposa su una rete relazionale costituita con frammenti di foto, video, suoni e testi, che interroga la nostra oggettività e mobilita tutta l'acuità della nostra percezione.

Anche Christoph Brech gioca con le nostre facoltà percettive, ma lo fa innanzitutto per catturare la nostra attenzione. Apparentemente immobili ma sempre in movimento, gli oggetti, i personaggi o i paesaggi che filma fanno scorrere lo sguardo da un livello di lettura all'altro: questo oscilla tra la volontà di decriptare l'immagine e la contemplazione che ispira immediatamente una scrittura videografica estremamente sobria. Break, opera ipnotica realizzata in un unico pianosequenza senza effetto camera, illustra perfettamente questa costruzione formale. Possiamo cogliere qui l'essenza stessa del movimento: la transitività, pur percependo in modo quasi viscerale la forza tettonica del tempo. Temporalità in corrispondenza con ciò che si dà a vedere: l'immensa distesa di un fiume gelato e lentamente spazzato da nubi di vapore acqueo che rispondono alla quasi impercettibile deriva dei ghiacci. Il rompighiaccio che attraversa questi elementi ostili prima di scomparire – lasciando dietro di sé soltanto una scia che il ghiaccio ostacola e assorbe immediatamente – offre un'allegoria che trae ispirazione dalla condizione umana.

Con Big Bang di Ori Gersht è la metafora politica dell'umanità gettata nel caos della guerra ad entrare in gioco. È proprio perché un conflitto e la violenza che vi si esprime costituiscono un punto di rottura, che gli interrogativi estetici e le ricerche plastiche di questo autore esplorano con tanta intensità il concetto di transizione. Si tratta di un percorso che, in questo caso, viene trasposto al passaggio dell'immagine fissa all'immagine in movimento. A prima vista, Big Bang assomiglia ad una natura morta barocca. Tuttavia, l'uso del suono a cui ricorre Ori Gersht, conferisce una dimensione temporale alla fissità del quadro e infonde una tensione drammatica che raggiunge il proprio apice con l'esplosione di una composizione floreale girata a rallentatore: una presa sostenuta del passaggio di un oggetto alla sua dislocazione. Questa transizione che va dalla figurazione all'astrazione pura, termina con una stasi ottica e rimanda all'immagine mentale che le sirene e le deflagrazioni del conflitto israelo-palestinese hanno lasciato nella memoria dell'infanzia dell'artista. Si tratta di un percorso artistico che, pur esplorando i rapporti tra fotografia, pittura e video, consiste sia in senso proprio che figurato, a « traversare » la forma per poi condurci al suo sacrificio.

L'opera del giovane artista finlandese Tuomo Rainio interroga il tempo e la mutazione, come avviene per il lavoro di Ori Gersht, ma il suo approccio è completamente diverso. Invece di considerare la natura estetica dell'immagine come punto di partenza, il percorso che intraprende si articola intorno alla natura del movimento. Grazie all'ausilio di un programma informatico di trattamento dell'immagine che egli stesso ha concepito, le immagini catturate mediante una semplice macchina fotografica ci mostrano degli ambienti urbani in cui l'attività dei cittadini è visibile soltanto sotto forma di tracce fantomatiche lasciate dal loro passaggio. Questo processo corrisponde ad un approccio che è, nel contempo, politico e concettuale: politico poiché rimanda ad uno spazio pubblico coperto da reti di telecamere di videosorveglianza; concettuale in quanto rappresenta la tensione dell'intermedio, ossia la permanenza della presenza e dell'assenza.

Anche Jutta Strohmaier sfrutta le potenzialità offerte dalle tecnologie digitali sia per far crescere l'immagine fissa dal punto centrale, sia per riconfigurarla con effetti di luce, con cut outs o scansioni elettroniche che la modificano continuamente.

In Journey o in Im Dickicht la sensazione di movimento emana dal fatto che l'immagine non appare mai completamente finita, ma sempre in transizione tra ciò che la precede e ciò che le succede. Di conseguenza, il presente non offre mai un'unità temporale ma piuttosto un'esplosione delle temporalità che destruttura l'immagine. Con Passenger, la compressione del tempo ottenuta mediante inquadrature realizzate ogni minuto per diversi giorni dall'interno di una stanza vuota, offre un approccio distanziato della quotidianità percepita attraverso il ritmo accelerato dei cicli diurni e notturni. Per Silent Stories le fotografie messe in scena sono sottoposte ad effetti di sovrapposizione, di fusione di trasparenza che ci propongono una rilettura cinematografica della realtà. Benché nelle sue composizioni di scenari Jutta Strohmaier utilizzi la fotografia come materia prima, la percezione del movimento, i processi di trasformazione e la decostruzione del tempo sono collocati al centro della sua opera: questo consente all'immagine di liberare la molteplicità di sensi che la compongono.

Per Olga Chernysheva, quello che prevale nella ricerca formale che dà origine alla composizione di Windows è la riflessione sullo spazio dell'immagine. Affascinata dalle vestigia dell'unità comunista ormai scomparsa, l'artista osserva la quotidianità dei Russi di oggi e la restituisce sotto forma di creazione in cui la messa in scena non ha nulla di casuale. Filmata di notte, con la telecamera in spalla, ogni finestra di un palazzo diventa la cornice di una scena in cui gli abitanti appaiono e scompaiono, come personaggi di teatro, nell'intimità delle quinte oscure dei loro appartamenti. La natura scenica di questi istanti di vita è messa in evidenza dal dispositivo multischermo che, pur distribuendo l'immagine nell'intero spazio espositivo consente di conferire all'aspetto intimo una maggior profondità, per aprire così il discorso tra l'opera e lo spettatore.

Questi artisti europei hanno quindi un punto in comune: quello di far subire alla fotografia o/e al video, a seconda delle rispettive necessità, un trattamento di deformazione. Essi esplorano così le fughe che si disegnano ai margini di questi territori ed instaurano un nuovo regime dell'immagine e della percezione. In questo modo, essi spingono il linguaggio fotografico e videografico verso i loro limiti, limiti che costituiscono la condizione di emergenza dell'inedito, dell'originalità e dello stile, secondo Deleuze.

La nostra scommessa è che queste nuove sperimentazioni che spingono la fotografia ed il video ai limiti o al di là del campo che sembrava essere stato loro assegnato, ci offrano un'occasione inedita per rinnovare il nostro sguardo sul mondo e ci stimolino a reinventare la nostra quotidianità, a « vederla secondo l'opera » per riprendere la formula utilizzata da Merleau-Ponty[6].

Jean-Luc Soret

con la collaborazione di Gunda Achleitner, Berthold Ecker, Paul Di Felice, Anna Gianesini, Kathrin Kohle, Ekaterina Kondranina, Zuzana Lapitkova, Emiliano Paoletti, Jean-Luc Monterosso, Pierre Stiwer, Olga Sviblova e Barbara Wolffer.

6 MERLEAU-PONTY (MAURICE). 1960. L'ŒIL ET L'ESPRIT. PARIS. FOLIO. ESSAIS.

Mutations II – Moving Stills

Coltivando l'in-between

La fotografia ed il video sono mezzi espressivi caratterizzati da una prossimità che è tanto grande quanto il divario che in origine li separa rispetto al loro rapporto con il tempo. Oggi, gli sviluppi in campo tecnologico incoraggiano gli artisti ad avvicinare i due mezzi: è possibile filmare con una macchina fotografica e scattare fotografie con una videocamera. Inoltre, entrambi passano attraverso fasi digitali, compresi i processi di sviluppo. Grazie al software, fermare l'immagine è semplice, e la funzione slideshow può essere avviata con un semplice clic. È pertanto possibile fermare il movimento oppure introdurre un continuum temporale: due gesti di grande semplicità tecnica, ma che determinano sovvertimenti considerevoli. Il punto non è tanto il divario tra i due mezzi (la video arte costituzionalmente esiste accanto ad altre pratiche artistiche) ma le opere d'arte che tale porosità genera. È questo territorio intermedio ad essere oggetto di esplorazione in « Mutations II ». Tutti gli artisti selezionati utilizzano il video per la tensione che lo lega all'immagine fotografica e ai suoi componenti: l'unità del fotogramma, il trascorrere del tempo ed il particolare modo di qualificare il trascorrere dell'istante. Alcuni di questi artisti portano avanti il loro progetti video insieme alla fotografia, passando costantemente dall'uno all'altra. Il risultato è un rapporto particolare con l'immagine che ci invita ad afferrarla sotto il profilo della sua instabilità, ma anche dal punto di vista delle questioni che solleva attraverso il mutare delle pratiche.

Lavorando con la profondità del tempo

Nel suo saggio « The Reflecting Pool de Bill Viola », Jean-Paul Fargier analizza i videotape di Viola, con i relativi processi di incrostazione, nel momento in cui l'artista si dedica completamente alla video arte, perché « l'immagine divisa può essere vista come l'essenza del video »[1]. Immagini create attraverso l'incrostazione, che contengono varie temporalità e storie multiple e parallele, pertanto costituirebbero caratteristiche forti della video arte. In ogni caso, ciò è quanto emerge con chiarezza in una serie di opere che presentano una forte correlazione con l'immagine fotografica e con il tempo sospeso, e che, come Bill Viola nel suo famoso videotape, funzionano in termini di disturbo, creando confusione nella percezione dell'immobilità e del movimento. Ad esempio, David Claerbout crea opere in cui fotografie di cui si è riappropriato vengono trasferite nel territorio del video grazie ad un intervento nella loro densità temporale nell'intento di trovare il tempo attuale dell'immagine. In Senza titolo (Sans titre (Carl et Julia)), 2000, l'immagine in bianco e nero mostra un uomo e sua figlia che fanno colazione. Quando entriamo nello spazio di proiezione, la ragazza rivolge il suo sguardo su di noi, fissandoci a sua volta tramite la capacità del video di riprodurre la vita e far rivivere nel presente ciò che è stato fissato nel passato. In una delle ultime opere di Claerbout, Coppia di ballerini (Dancing couple (after: Couples at square dance, McIntosh County, Oklahoma, 1939 or 1940)), 2008, il suo intervento è addirittura più radicale: una giovane coppia viene fotografata sulla pista da ballo, sorpresa dal flash che l'ha interrotta e strappata al presente. Claerbout ha recuperato questa immagine e l'ha proiettata, ricoprendo l'azione del flash con la luce emessa dal proiettore. La temporalità della proiezione pertanto afferma il suo carattere di presente necessario, contrastando l'immobilità del processo fotografico tramite il movimento della proiezione. L'artificiosità della costruzione viene affermata, e l'introduzione di una temporalità in movimento nel cuore dell'immagine fissa provoca una sensazione di vertigine e fastidio. L'in-between, questo essere a metà strada, in mezzo, è vicino al vuoto nel senso che viene prodotto nell'oscurità di installazioni accuratamente orchestrate ed in ambienti prevalentemente silenziosi in cui il suono spazializzato viene utilizzato con parsimonia.

Il processo di animazione è diventato piuttosto comune, soprattutto come estensione del disegno. Rende possibile una temporalità molto più radicale, e di combinare diversi supporti immagine come nel caso dell'inquietante animazione di disegni e fotografie di Hans op de Beeck. Gli spazi così rappresentati risultano strani perché vicini alla realtà pur non potendo mai essere confusi con essa. Jutta Strohmaier, giovane artista austriaca, produce immagini fisse che vengono animate lentamente in un secondo momento. Come nel caso di Claerbout, ci troviamo costantemente di fronte ad una situazione di indecisione rispetto allo stato dell'immagine, alla sua natura ed al suo rapporto con il tempo. L'accumulo di fotografie introduce l'impressione di movimento ma senza diventare sufficientemente rilevante da spezzare la stabilità fornita dall'immagine fissa. La luce svolge un ruolo fondamentale segnando il trascorrere del tempo nel cuore dello spazio fotografato, in cui per lo più non succede molto. In Passeggero (Passenger (2004) si verifica un cambiamento nell'atmosfera generata dalla luce grazie ad un'inquadratura fissa di una finestra, filmata dall'interno di una stanza vuota. Si va da uno stato colorato all'altro, mentre si passa dal blu, al rosa, e quindi al giallo, in una metamorfosi convulsa. I video di Strohmaier non cercano mai di dare vita all'illusione di continuità, ci fanno entrare in spazi intermedi (stanze vuote, un fitto sottobosco, spazi urbani congestionati dal traffico) attraverso uno sforzo considerevole che coinvolge distanza ed inquadratura, dal punto di vista di uno spettatore attento ma fuori fase. L'immagine viene inoltre fatta oggetto di una serie di operazioni artistiche, tra cui la sovrimpressione, la profilatura e la modifica dei colori, che sottolineano la dimensione inventata, costruita, dello sguardo rivolto sul mondo.

Il divario tra fotografia e video pertanto dà spazio a meditazioni su le nostre esperienze percettive. Anche l'artista svizzero Peter Aerschmann esplora gli abissi del

1 DA THE REFLECTING POOL DE BILL VIOLA, JEAN-PAUL FARGIER, EDIZIONI YELLOW NOW. CÔTÉ FILMS # 2, 2005, P.14.

tempo decostruendo il nostro rapporto con lo spazio-tempo. Le sue immagini sono il risultato di scatti diversi in cui gli elementi vengono messi fianco a fianco opponendo resistenza ad una percezione unitaria di un tutto. Ciascun personaggio e ciascun aspetto della scenografia ovviamente fa parte di una composizione globale, senza peraltro essere collegato da un'atmosfera condivisa. Come nelle opere di Paolo Uccello, le proporzioni sono rispettate, e la disposizione degli elementi visivi è coerente, ma ciò che viene affermata è una grande solitudine. La videocamera scivola di tre quarti attraverso questi allestimenti, scoprendo gradualmente i personaggi solitari, rinchiusi nella reiterazione di un gesto ed in paesaggi che mancano di unità. Nei video di Aerschmann, lo spazio-tempo è essenzialmente deregolamentato, ma il nostro sguardo continua comunque a viaggiare lentamente con la videocamera. Tra l'austera stasi degli elementi architettonici ed il movimento dei personaggi in un loop, tra fotografia, video e pittura, l'opera di Aerschmann si colloca al centro delle questioni affrontate da « Mutations II ».

L'inquadratura

L'inquadratura dell'immagine è un gesto di definizione, significa afferrare ma anche allontanare il visibile, ed implica l'assunzione di una posizione in relazione al mondo. Un approccio essenziale nella storia della video arte è stato l'atto di rivolgere la videocamera verso di sé. Vito Acconci, Peter Campus, Bruce Nauman, Joan Jonas e molti altri, hanno collocato il proprio corpo davanti allo specchio-videocamera in modi diversi. Ma al di là dell'immediatezza affascinante e voyeuristica di filmare se stessi, il rapporto con il riflesso rende possibile l'esplorazione della comparsa e scomparsa della propria immagine. Ecco perché negli anni '70 Jean Otth, altro artista svizzero, ha creato un dispositivo video e specchio tramite il quale giocava con la propria immagine definendola ed oscurandola e mettendo in discussione le emozioni che vengono proiettate nel momento in cui ci si trova davanti ad una simile manipolazione dell'immagine di sé. Il video gli consente di giocare con il riflesso prendendosi il tempo per interferire con esso, per metterlo in pericolo e pertanto per mostrare e far sentire il rapporto che instauriamo con la nostra immagine. Anche Specchio (Miroir) (2000), di Elina Brotherus, artista finlandese che lavora sia con la fotografia sia con il video, costituisce una messa in scena di sé che allontana il riflesso condizionando la sua comparsa nel trascorrere del tempo. Nella serie fotografica la Brotherus posa nuda di fronte allo specchio appannato del bagno. Inizialmente quindi non c'è alcun riflesso, il che impone quindi l'esperienza della dislocazione tra il corpo e la sua immagine. Tuttavia, il passaggio dal un'immagine all'altra consente allo specchio di rivelare gradualmente l'immagine che riflette. L'inquadratura è quasi la stessa in tutto il video, e richiama a prima vista la serie fotografia. Ma il movimento dell'immagine rende possibile la reintroduzione un elemento di vitalità nel processo garantendo una posizione essenziale al corpo sulla mutevole superficie dello specchio. Il respiro della Brotherus costituisce un elemento essenziale, agisce sull'atmosfera e partecipa del fenomeno di comparsa/scomparsa dell'immagine nello specchio, reintroducendo la dimensione organica in una situazione in cui il corpo è essenzialmente ciò che costituisce l'immagine.

Nella sua introduzione al saggio L'entre-images[2], Raymond Bellour spiega che « sembra che con il video e tutto ciò che comporta, stiamo entrando in una nuova era dell'immagine ». Anche quando il video viene composto utilizzando una tecnica fotografica, riprendendo il fotogramma, ciò che avviene in un lasso di tempo dà vita ad un altro rapporto con il tempo e lo spazio. Il giovane artista ceco Jan Kudĕj ha realizzato una serie di video che mettono in discussione l'esperienza del tempo. Ad esempio, egli mette insieme due proiezioni che mostrano due inquadrature fisse, una di un gruppo di quattro scale mobili e l'altra di un albero in un campo. Quello delle scale mobili è un breve loop scandito dai movimenti ascendenti e discendenti, mentre quello dell'albero è un montaggio di immagini fisse in cui il fogliame si sviluppa in modo discontinuo. L'associazione tra fluidità meccanica e discontinuità naturale allontana la percezione dinamica della realtà. In contrasto con una società nella quale il movimento è la regola, Kudĕj crea discontinuità e tagli nell'immagine, impedendoci di godere del senso di calma tipico di quando si guarda un albero le cui foglie stormiscono nel vento (filmato in modo magnifico da Claerbout in Boom, inquadratura fissa di un albero che assomiglia a quella di Kudĕj, ma che si crogiola nell'affascinante fluidità del movimento).

Analizzando il rapporto tra video e fotografia, la sua capacità di creare l'illusione della continuità viene messa in discussione. L'opera d'arte introduce disequilibrio ed instabilità nel nostro rapporto con il mondo attraverso la costruzione di situazioni di ritenzione del flusso.

La ricerca dello sguardo

Se il video è quindi messo in discussione dalla fotografia, costituisce però anche il luogo dello sviluppo di idee relative allo sguardo fotografico. È esattamente ciò che l'artista francese Laurent Goldring fa, lavorando nel solco della tradizione del ritratto fotografico. Egli mette in discussione le rappresentazioni fotografiche del corpo filmando frontalmente modelli in uno studio fotografico. La temporalità del video gli consente di investigare l'aspetto del « diventare un'immagine » dei corpi dei suoi modelli, che sono tutti ballerini (e la maggior parte di loro coreografi). Poiché il palco è stretto, e la videocamera è fissa, i ballerini possono muoversi appena, e quindi i loro movimenti sono concentrati sulla postura. Una volta assunta una posa, il corpo delicatamente scivola da un aspetto ad un altro, guidato da Laurent Goldring ed accentuato dall'illuminazione e dal gioco di luci ed ombre. Le immagini che emergono spesso hanno qualità mostruose, attirano lo sguardo e catturano l'immaginazione. Il movimento rende possibile il passaggio da uno stato del visibile all'altro,

2 DA RAYMOND BELLOUR, L'ENTRE-IMAGES, PHOTO, CINÉMA, VIDÉO, ÉDITIONS DE LA DIFFÉRENCE, 2002.

ma anche il coinvolgimento in un processo di distorsione simbolica, sebbene da ultimo i video si presentino come immagini fisse in successione. Lo sguardo viene catturato da ogni forma. Laurent Goldring quindi sviluppa le foto dal video. Ed ecco che si ritrova con un'immagine fissa attraverso uno spazio creativo che consente alle cose di diventare visibili al centro di un meccanismo estremamente costruito. L'instabilità del video allontana il riflesso di transustanziazione a cui siamo soggetti quando ci troviamo di fronte ad una fotografia. Le immagini/i corpi di Laurent Goldring affermano il proprio status simbolico, diffondendo i propri pixel quando vengono sviluppati su carta. Esemplificano la dislocazione della ricerca fotografica al centro del mezzo video.

Il passaggio da un mezzo all'altro è quindi ciò che consente il distanziamento di una prassi e la messa in discussione delle sue qualità, come nel caso del fotografo tedesco Oliver Möst. La sua opera deriva dal suo rapporto personale con la vista. I suoi problemi di vista lo hanno portato a costruire una visione fotografica dominata dall'appannamento e dalle sue qualità pittoriche. Tuttavia, il suo utilizzo del video non è una semplice estensione dei suoi esperimenti trasferiti nel campo del movimento. Corrisponde ad un'altra necessità, quella di mettere in scena il proprio rapporto con il visibile attraverso film su se stesso. Occhi castani, Nascondino e In mezzo (brown eyes, hide & seek e between) sono pertanto brevi scene filmate nel suo studio. Nella prima Möst gioca con i suoi occhi, biglie che egli tiene in mano e mette in bocca. Nel secondo, conta ad alta voce con gli occhi coperti da paraocchi rossi fino a che non viene abbagliato da un flash. Nel terzo lotta contro due pareti divisorie che chiude e separa. È sempre a torso nudo, fisicamente coinvolto in situazioni metaforiche relative al suo rapporto con lo sguardo: la critica dell'organo della vista che non funziona a dovere in brown eyes e la costruzione di un parallelo tra due stati di deficit visivo in hide & seek, uno causato dall'annientamento del momento della percezione (gli occhi coperti), l'altro causato da un eccesso di luce (il flash). In between, Möst esplora il modo giusto di percepire il mondo diversificando la costruzione dello spazio di presentazione. Naturalmente, tutte queste situazioni mettono anche in discussione l'attività fotografica, le sue condizioni ed i suoi pregiudizi. L'inquadratura dell'ultimo video, landescapes, assume la forma di una lente ottica ed è stata ottenuta dalla combinazione di uno stenoscopio ed una videocamera. Il suono proviene dall'esterno del campo visivo della videocamera, in contrasto quindi con l'immobilità del panorama, diviso un due riprese simmetriche ed il suono di un lanciapalle. Möst non è visibile nell'immagine, ma è presente attraverso le sue azioni. Questa volta, come lui, non vediamo nulla ad eccezione dell'immaginazione che egli provoca, i segni evidenti sulla superficie dell'acqua sono essenzialmente portatori di una visione.

Immagini sonore

La video arte ha beneficiato enormemente dalla sua complicità con la creazione musicale, dalla sua nascita con Fluxus e Nam June Paik. Il suono è spesso molto di più di una semplice colonna sonora che accompagna l'immagine, è intrinseca ad essa, al punto che a volte l'immagine viene trattata in modo sonoro. I video di Robert Cahen pertanto collocano la composizione musicale al centro della situazione oggetto della ripresa, e se il tempo riveste un'importanza particolare ciò avviene perché emerge dallo stretto rapporto tra suono ed immagine, esprimendo la percezione soggettiva della realtà. Il fotografo e video artista Gast Bouschet e la compositrice Nadine Hilbert lavorano insieme a partire da tale prospettiva. Nei loro video immagine e suono sono inscindibili, l'una contamina l'altro, e ne impregna la nascita. Ancora una volta l'immagine è molto spesso composta da inquadrature fisse in successione, senza transizione, ma secondo una modalità di accumulo. In « Sequenza onirica » (Dreamsequence), la videocamera ed il suono svelano parti degli universi attraversati (come foreste brumose, autostrade e centri cittadini), ma senza lasciarci fermare un momento o seguire lo sguardo. Passiamo da un punto di vista all'altro, come se ci trovassimo di fronte ad una serie fotografica, da una situazione sonora all'altra, con delle ripetizioni, ma senza il rassicurante riferimento della continuità. Il titolo colloca tale operazione in rapporto allo stato del sogno, in cui le distanze vengono continuamente attraversate, mentre si vaga tra vari spazi-tempi, con l'unica costante rappresentata dal punto di vista soggettivo di chi sogna, ed in questo caso dello spettatore. La video arte pertanto ci consente di trovare un ritmo che riecheggia l'esperienza della percezione, come in Opus 110a (2001) di Christoph Brech. Nel suo video, l'immagine è totalmente concentrata sulla schiena di un direttore d'orchestra durante un concerto. La presenza del suono è molto forte, e con l'immagine il ritmo musicale diventa un movimento monocromatico, vicino all'astrazione, pur essendo saturato dalla natura fisica dei gesti del direttore. Brech armonizza i movimenti della schiena, orchestra il tutto, rallentando, accelerando, e trattenendo oppure liberando il tempo per armonizzare suono ed immagine. La schiena diventa uno spazio di proiezione, ogni piega dell'abito un paesaggio, un punto di ancoraggio per il dispiegarsi dell'immaginazione.

Il suono può anche pilotare l'immagine, guidarla e riempirla di significato. Può inoltre dare vita ad un racconto, integrare il linguaggio nell'immagine o avviare un dialogo tra i due, come nell'opera di Gary Hill. Un testo parlato, letto o proclamato da un corpo è al centro dei suoi video, che mettono in discussione cosa crei un'immagine in termini verbali. La pratica del video è inoltre ispirata dal cinema, ma prende anche le distanze da quest'ultimo a causa di costrutti ambigui o contraddittori che fanno esplodere la narrazione e mettono in discussione i suoi codici. I video di Alice Anderson sono pertanto esteticamente molto vicini al cinema, ma anche molto diversi dal punto di vista dei mezzi narrativi. Il divario è particolarmente evidente in Diario (Journal), che presenta sequenze cinematografiche brevissime editate attraverso il suono. Il filo conduttore della narrazione viene mantenuto, e mentre le title card indicano un periodo di tempo (un mese, un giorno, un anno), la storia personale si ferma qui. Le immagini possono essere considerate indizi per entrare in un momento di un'esistenza, ma per lo più lasciano qualsiasi tentativo di interpretazione in sospeso. La durata è inoltre molto breve, e ciò non lascia molto tempo alle divagazioni. Journal lascia lo spettatore in balia di musica ed immagini evasive.

L'installazione dell'immagine

Il video è caratterizzato da una serie di requisiti di presentazione più vincolanti rispetto alla fotografia, e quindi deve essere installato in uno spazio adattato alla sua natura tecnica. Mentre le fotografie esposte danno essenzialmente vita ad un dialogo con lo spazio espositivo in cui le immagini si presentano tutte insieme allo sguardo, il video tende a richiedere isolamento e la negazione di uno spazio reale (come nelle « scatole nere » in cui l'immagine viene presentata nascosta nell'oscurità ed in buone condizioni sonore). Il video pertanto impone il proprio spazio-tempo, come nelle installazioni di Bill Viola. Tuttavia, alcuni artisti presentano video che dialogano con ciò che va al di là dell'immagine. Gli schermi/pareti di Claerbout costituiscono un esempio di questa « in-between-ness » poiché i video riecheggiano gli uni negli altri come in una mostra fotografica, essendo visibili attraverso le pareti bucate di tela sottile che fungono anche da supporti per le proiezioni. Anche l'installazione « In situ » è importante, in quanto luogo in cui il video prende possesso di uno spazio e lo abita echeggiando ciò che emana da sé. Ulrich Gebert ha concepito Keine Dialoge (2004) per uno spazio specifico, una struttura di cemento priva di finestre, divisa in strette stanze che accentuano l'aspetto oppressivo del lavoro. Le condizioni di presentazione sono state rese possibili dallo spazio espositivo, il Kunstbunker Tumulka di Monaco, senza dover quindi modificare nulla. Gli spettatori si sono potuti immergere in un freddo ambiente militare in cui hanno assistito ad un test psicologico somministrato ad una squadra di GSG 9 (un'unità speciale anti-terrorismo istituita successivamente alle vicende delle Olimpiadi di Monaco del 1972). Ulrich Gebert ci mostra questi uomini sottoposti alla luce emessa da un flash stroboscopico, prolungando l'esperienza per lo spettatore posto di fronte ad un video costituito da immagini fisse visivamente aggressive mostrate in successione convulsa. Il titolo attira l'attenzione sulla regressione inflitta a uomini giudicati per il loro autocontrollo. Il movimento è il luogo dell'aggressività in quanto è nella rimozione dell'immagine dalla sua fissità e nella creazione di una continuità sensoriale attraverso il video che le azioni stereoscopiche assumono significato e coinvolgono il corpo dello spettatore.

Il video presenta inoltre una dimensione scultorea quando, invece di cancellare la sua materialità attraverso proiezioni sconnesse dal tempo e dallo spazio della mostra, gli artisti si concentrano sul suo rapporto con la dipendenza da ciò da cui può emergere (e che deve esprimere nella sua presenza immateriale). La superficie/schermo può estendere l'immagine in volume, come gli occhi nell'opera di Tony Oursler, oppure l'artista può creare ambienti nei quali viene integrata l'immagine, come nelle installazioni di Thomas Hirschhorn. In linea con ciò, Pirmin Blum costruisce sculture di cartone con immagini fisse appese su di esse e monitor inseriti al loro interno. L'immagine video fa a meno della monumentalità della proiezione e dell'effetto della comparsa, ed afferma il proprio fondamento nella realtà. Una delle installazioni di Blum combina fotografie e due video realizzati in una fabbrica di automobili. Airbag è una inquadratura fissa in slow-motion dell'attivazione di un airbag. La tela si gonfia e si sgonfia in modo affascinante. Siamo spettatori del lieve dispiegamento di una forma in uno stato di permanente evoluzione. Il secondo video, Spuk, è un montaggio veloce dal punto di vista di due telecamere in occasione un test a cui viene sottoposto un parabrezza. Incorniciato nella calma ariosa e poetica di Airbag, Spuk è violento sotto il profilo visivo e sonoro. Insieme i due pezzi riuniscono in modo ironico ritmi molto diversi con un approccio fai-da-te che contrasta con la sofisticatezza industriale del luogo in cui le immagini sono state realizzate.

Alice Anderson ha selezionato una sequenza da Journal per creare l'installazione Insomnia (2006). Lo spettatore viene invitato a sdraiarsi su un letto a baldacchino di velluto viola e a guardare l'estratto video della durata di un minuto (presentato sotto forma di loop) su uno schermo sospeso. Si tratta di un'ambientazione in cui lo spettatore vede tali immagini come in uno stato di semi-coscienza, a metà tra la veglia ed il sonno, senza però avere il tempo sufficiente ad immergervisi completamente: quasi immediatamente dopo che lo spettatore si è sdraiato sul letto il video torna al punto di partenza scoraggiando quindi ogni ulteriore indugio. La video arte è generalmente difficile da guardare perché le opere sono spesso troppo lunghe e le condizioni di fruizione stancanti. Si tratta indubbiamente del suo principale vincolo, che ne rende difficile la presentazione e fruizione rispetto alla fotografia. È quindi forse necessario coltivare uno stato di insonnia, di in-betweenness, che predispone ad accogliere pratiche che si trovano a metà strada tra due mezzi espressivi, e ci fa muovere tra stati diversi dell'immagine.

Mathilde Roman

Mathilde Roman è dottore in arte e scienze dell'arte presso l'Università di Paris-Sorbonne, specializzata in video e autore del saggio «Art vidéo et mise en scène de soi», éd. L'Harmattan 2008.
Collabora come critica d'arte, membro dell'AICA, con diverse riviste come http://www.lacritique.org, Art press, Mouvement e insegna la storia dell'arte al Pavillon Bosio Ecole supérieure d'art et de scénographie di Monaco in Francia.

Il tempo diviso ed il tempo ritrovato (Sullo spazio e la durata nella fotografia e nella video arte)

« Nella realtà non esiste un unico ritmo di durata; è possibile immaginare molti ritmi diversi che, più lentamente o velocemente, misurano il grado di tensione o rilassamento delle diverse tipologie di coscienza, e pertanto fissano le rispettive posizioni nella scala dell'essere. » Henri Bergson[1]

Il dilemma della scelta « questo/quello », e cioè della scelta tra l'immagine statica e la sequenza ininterrotta di immagini basata sul tempo, perseguita la fotografia fin dall'avvento del cinema nell'ultima decade del diciannovesimo secolo. È nata una mistificazione intorno all'istante trascorso escisso dalla fotografia, un momento estratto dal tempo, come se fosse in opposizione con la narrativa continua basata sul fotogramma presentata dal cinema.[2] Con l'avvento della videocassetta a nastro magnetico, e più recentemente delle tecnologie digitali basate sui pixel si sarebbe potuto pensare che tale dicotomia fosse destinata a finire. Tuttavia, non finisce nel « tempo » ma nella durata, quest'ultima priva di definizione fissa o certa. Oggi la supposizione lineare di un tempo universale non costituisce più l'elemento che determina il modo in cui l'immagine fotografica viene vissuta. Il tempo, come sosteneva Bergson, viene vissuto in modo diverso da persone diverse, in luoghi diversi, e addirittura in modo diverso dalla stessa persona nelle diverse fasi della sua vita. Il passato lineare o diacronico può essere liberamente concettualizzato, tuttavia non costituisce il fondamento del modo in cui nella realtà il tempo viene sincronicamente interiorizzato.

Intitolare una mostra fotografica e di video arte « Mutations II » significa mettersi in rapporto diretto con il processo continuo del cambiamento. Mutare significa subire o causare una mutazione, che a sua volta viene definita un'alterazione o un cambiamento, come avviene in natura, nella forma o nella qualità. E la mutazione, o il divenire (il liminale), non può essere semplice come il tempo lineare; secondo la sua definizione letterale, si tratta di un processo continuo di cambiamento. Pertanto il divenire esiste come un « tempo sospeso » in un processo continuo che può essere compreso soltanto come tempo che è durata continua. È forse di questo impatto da collisione che Eliot ha detto: « Time present and time past/ Are both always present in time future,/ And time future contained in time past. »[3] (Il tempo presente ed il tempo passato/ sono sempre entrambi presenti nel tempo futuro,/ed il tempo futuro è contenuto nel tempo passato). Di conseguenza il « divenire » resta una « possibilità perpetua ». È questo un ponte durazionale attraversato molto tempo fa da Bruce Nauman ed altri, e rivela perché i nuovi media utilizzati nelle performance e nei video determinino una maggiore elasticità nella nostra comprensione di ciò che costituisce la base di un'immagine statica o basata sul tempo. Deleuze si esprime in modo chiaro a tale proposito (sicuramente prendendo spunto da Bergson) quando scrive: « cosicché ogni qualvolta ci troviamo di fronte alla durata, oppure in una durata, possiamo concludere che da qualche parte esista un tutto che cambia, e che da qualche parte è aperto ».[4] Ciò non nega la causalità, ma suggerisce che si tratti di qualcosa di nascosto, e di non immediatamente apparente. Per chiarire, la mutazione attinge da questo stesso principio, così come le più comuni forme di mutazione sono quelle delle amebe osservate in laboratorio in un piattino di coltura.[5] La dipendenza storica da uno scisma dualistico tra lo statico ed il movimento-immagine è ciò che oggi viene sistematicamente messo in discussione dagli operatori contemporanei della fotografia e del video. Il meccanismo di alterazione resta la risposta della coscienza umana, ma non della coscienza come un fine in sé, quanto nel processo di una « apertura continua » come obiettivo singolo che tuttavia presenta risultati multipli.

Nella nuova fotografia digitale, e anche nei moderni sviluppi che interessano tecnologie analoghe, gli operatori sono stati in grado di riallineare la fotografia e la video arte al di fuori della cornice del determinismo di una linearità temporale fissa. La nuova fotografia si è liberata dell'immagine escissa che può essere ridotta al momento in cui si preme un pulsante, così come la nozione di montaggio di un video o di un film da tempo non dipende più da presupposti di continuità. In entrambi i casi le condizioni sono diventate sempre più manipolabili. Su tale base, dobbiamo accettare ed accogliere le crescenti discontinuità che costituiscono il fondamento della vita moderna, un aspetto già sottolineato Foucault.[6] Esiste un'utile analogia ed un corollario che derivano dal termine mutazione stesso quando viene utilizzato in linguistica: designa un cambiamento determinatosi in un suono dalla sua assimilazione ad un altro suono vicino. Non deve sorprendere pertanto che mutation e mutuality (mutazione e reciprocità, in inglese, NdT) derivino dal medesimo tema latino. Il loro rapporto è reciproco e liberamente adattativo nell'ambito di un sistema discontinuo. L'utilizzo non biologico del termine mutazione (relativamente

1 HENRI BERGSON, "THE DELIMITING AND FIXING OF IMAGES", MATTER AND MEMORY, TRADUZIONE IN LINGUA INGLESE, N.M. PAUL AND W.S. PALMER, NEW YORK, ZONE BOOKS, 1991 (PP. 177-223) P. 207.

2 SIA ROLAND BARTHES SIA SUSAN SONTAG HANNO PARLATO DELLA FATALITÀ O DELLA MELANCONIA IN RELAZIONE ALLA FOTOGRAFIA, DANDO VITA A QUALCOSA DI SIMILE, IN TALE PROCESSO, AL ROMANTICISMO STRUTTURALE, E, DI CONSEGUENZA, LA FOTOGRAFIA IN QUALCHE MODO È RIMASTA IMPRIGIONATA TRA IL PUNCTUM, IL « L'INCIDENZA PUNTUALE » E LO STUDIUM (BARTHES), E LA « TRASPARENZA METICOLOSAMENTE SELETTIVA » (SONTAG). CFR. ROLAND BARTHES, CAMERA LUCIDA, TRADUZIONE IN LINGUA INGLESE. RICHARD HOWARD, LONDON (1982), 1984, PP. 26-27, E SUSAN SONTAG 'IN PLATO'S CAVE', ON PHOTOGRAPHY (1971), LONDON, HARMONDSWORTH, 1979, P. 6.

3 T.S. ELIOT "BURNT NORTON", IN FOUR QUARTETS, LONDON, FABER AND FABER (1944), 1979, P. 13; IL TESTO CONTINUA: "IF ALL TIME IS ETERNALLY PRESENT/ ALL TIME IS UNREDEEMABLE." (SE TUTTO IL TEMPO È ETERNAMENTE PRESENTE/TUTTO IL TEMPO È IRREDIMIBILE).

4 GILLES DELEUZE, CINEMA I, THE MOVEMENT IMAGE, LONDON, THE ATHLONE PRESS, 1992, PP. 9-10; DELEUZE IN EFFETTI FA AMPIAMENTE RIFERIMENTO A MATTER AND MEMORY (OP. CIT) DI BERGSON ED A CREATIVE EVOLUTION (1907). PER TALE RAPPORTO CON BERGSON, CFR. GILLES DELEUZE, BERGSONISM, NEW YORK, ZONE BOOKS, 1988A.

5 IL TERMINE AMIBE, DERIVATO DAL GRECO AMOIBÈ, CHE LETTERALMENTE SIGNIFICA « CAMBIAMENTO », È STATO UTILIZZATO PER LA PRIMA VOLTA DAL NATURALISTA FRANCESE JEAN-BAPTISTE BORY DE SAINT-VINCENT (1778-1846).

6 FOUCAULT PARLA DI UN'INEVITABILE MOLTIPLICAZIONE DELLE DISCONTINUITÀ: « LA STORIA APPARE QUINDI NON COME UNA GRANDE CONTINUITÀ CHE SOGGIACE AD UN'APPARENTE DISCONTINUITÀ, MA COME UN GROVIGLIO DI DISCONTINUITÀ SOVRAPPOSTE, » MICHEL FOUCAULT 'RETURN TO HISTORY', MICHEL FOUCAULT, ESSENTIAL WORKS OF FOUCAULT 1954-1984, VOL. 2, AESTHETICS, JAMES D. FAUBION (ED.), LONDON, HARMONDSWORTH (1998), 2000, (PP. 419-32) P.429.

privo di valore) per lungo tempo è stato contrapposto ad evoluzione (relativamente carico di valore). Il primo descrive il cambiamento molto semplicemente come uno stato discontinuo o casuale di adattamento, mentre il secondo in genere implica la teleologia finalizzata della selezione naturale – le cose mutano in qualcos'altro, o si evolvono verso qualcosa.

Pertanto, negli ultimi trenta anni circa, la crescente importanza per la fotografia ed il video non riguarda solo l'elusione di obsoleti cliché in relazione ai vecchi confini tra immagine statica ed in movimento, ma anche la possibilità di una maggiore interazione nei processi stessi tra le loro comuni origini strumentali. È la maggiore interiorizzazione dei processi integrati della fotografia e del video alla quale ho fatto riferimento nel mio sottotitolo sullo « spazio e la durata ». Emergono una caratterizzazione o accompagnamento personali dello spazio-tempo che vengono incorporati come un'ombra individuale definitoria nell'ambito dell'adattamento che ogni artista fa delle nuove tecnologie applicate alle proprie pratiche visive. Ecco perché la fotografia ed i video contemporanei hanno meno a che vedere con soggetti predefiniti o prestabiliti che con ciò a cui viene sottoposto il soggetto. Ma ciò a cui risponde è una condizione auto-riflessiva in cui tempo e contenuti sono elastici e spesso si ripiegano su ed in se stessi. Il tempo non è più l'orologio, ma un cerchio, ed il cerchio (o ellisse) è la condizione di una circolarità o inflessione interna misurata tramite un sistema auto-definente.[7]

Con l'avvento della video arte negli anni '60 e '70, sia in termini della sua applicazione come critica della crescente commercializzazione e consumismo determinati dalla televisione, o in ciò che successivamente è stata definita video arte, esisteva la possibilità di mettere in discussione la natura del tempo lineare, irrealizzabile con i mezzi fino ad allora disponibili.[8] Mentre la configurazione fotogramma per fotogramma del film prevedeva il sistema del montaggio « copia e incolla », non aveva nulla dell'immediatezza della videocassetta, con la sua capacità di un feedback istantaneo, sovrapposizione, e potenziale per narrazioni inconcludenti o astratte.[9] Ma se la video arte è iniziata come critica dei mass media televisivi e pubblicitari, ben presto (al contrario dei film strutturalisti, che operavano dall'interno del sistema cinematografico) ha cominciato a decostruire il principio stesso della coerenza lineare e narrativa.[10] Offriva approcci alternativi in base ai quali il tempo e lo spazio venivano uniti in modo nuovo. Non solo veniva utilizzata nelle performance e per registrare e mettere in discussione la natura stessa del performativo, come nel caso di Nauman ed Acconci, ma ben presto si è evoluta in una messa in discussione della natura dei siti della rappresentazione, attraverso ciò che successivamente è stata definita video installazione.[11] Quest'ultima, utilizzando elementi di canali multipli, ha in modo quasi letterale mescolato l'utilizzo di una temporalità differenziale. Un senso di immediatezza è, essenzialmente, il « sempre presente », e la videocassetta è diventata per estensione una presenza immediata in molti studi di artisti, da considerare in modo non diverso rispetto a qualsiasi altro strumento che un artista può trovare nel proprio atelier. Di fatto, il rapporto spesso presente tra video e pittura costituisce una chiara testimonianza del fenomeno. La capacità del monitor del video di agire come un oggetto che include l'immagine, e per estensione come una scultura, e di conseguenza come un'installazione ambientale completa, ha fatto sì che il video diventasse una realtà interstiziale, o punto di contatto tra mezzi diversi. Dava vita ad un rapporto con gli oggetti realizzati (nozioni tradizionali dell'opera d'arte), interrogava il loro status di opere d'arte, i siti di ricezione, e metteva in discussione la storiografia dei confini tra i diversi mezzi. Come lo spazio tra le parole in un'opera di Beckett, funzionava come lo spazio « in divenire » di una durata temporale incerta.[12]

In rapporto al video la pratica della fotografia stessa è stata costretta a ripensarsi. E ciò è avvenuto molto tempo prima che le ultimissime tecnologie digitali entrassero in campo, anche perché l'immagine fissa estratta da un video metteva in discussione la nozione del momento decisivo della macchina fotografica.[13] Il primo effetto è stato quello di costringere la fotografia riconsiderare i contenuti temporali della realizzazione delle immagini. Se l'istantaneità era stato l'impulso iniziale che aveva determinato l'evoluzione della fotografia sulla scia dei moderni sviluppi della macchina fotografica e degli obiettivi fotografici, era chiaro che il tempo di esposizione di qualsiasi durata fosse inquadrava (in entrambi in sensi) le condizioni dell'estrazione. Il momento decisivo, come il periodo esistenziale da cui proveniva, diventava un momento di pura soggettività. In rapporto ai primi video, che presentavano l'immediatezza del « reale », distinto dal rotolo montato di un film, si può affermare che la fotografia abbia perso contatto con la « realtà oggettiva » attraverso

7 GILLES DELEUZE, "WHAT IS AN EVENT?", THE FOLD: LEIBNIZ AND THE BAROQUE, TRADUZIONE IN LINGUA INGLESE, TOM CONLEY, LONDON, THE ATHLONE PRESS, 1993 "INSEPARABILI DAL PROCESSO DI ATTUALIZZAZIONE O REALIZZAZIONE NEL QUALE ENTRANO, DIVENTANO PERMANENTI SOLO NEI LIMITI DEL FLUSSO CHE LI CREA, O DELLA COMPRENSIONE CHE LI ATTUALIZZA (PP. 76-82) PP. 80-81.

8 IL VIDEO È EMERSO PER LA PRIMA VOLTA NEI TERMINI DEGLI APPROCCI AL DOCUMENTARIO POLITICO ATTIVISTA DI ARTISTI QUALI LES LEVINE E FRANK GILLETTE, O DEL VIDEO COME FORMA D'ARTE CON L'ARTISTA FLUXUS NAM JUNE PAIK. CFR. MICHAEL RUSH, NEW MEDIA IN THE LATE TWENTIETH CENTURY, LONDON, THAMES & HUDSON, 1999, PP. 80-81. PER UN'ANALISI ESTESA SU PAIK, CFR., THE WORLDS OF NAM JUNE PAIK, SOLOMON GUGGENHEIM MUSEUM, NEW YORK, 2000.

9 MICHAEL RUSH, VIDEO ART, LONDON THAMES & HUDSON, 2003, « CIÒ CHE ERA COSÌ ENTUSIASMANTE DI QUESTA NUOVA TECNOLOGIA È CHE CATTURAVA EVENTI REALI IN MODO ISTANTANEO. IN UN CERTO SENSO IL TEMPO VENIVA MANIPOLATO TRAMITE L'INTERVENTO UMANO. » P. 15.

10 SEAN CUBITT, TIMESHIFT: ON VIDEO CULTURE, LONDON, ROULEDGE, 1991. CFR. ANCHE, DOUG HALL E SALLY JO FIFER (EDS.), ILLUMINATING VIDEO: AN ESSENTIAL GUIDE TO VIDEO ART, NEW YORK, APERTURE, 1990, ED EDIZIONI SUCCESSIVE.

11 MICHAEL RUSH, "VIDEO INSTALLATION ART", IN NEW MEDIA....OP CIT, PP. 116-167.

12 NON SORPRENDE QUINDI CHE MOLTI DEI PRIMI VIDEO ARTISTI SI ISPIRASSERO A BECKETT, COME È INDUBBIAMENTE AVVENUTO NEL CASO DI NAUMAN E DELL'ONGOING MEDIA THEATRE DI JOHN JESURUN, MA ANCHE, IN UNA CERTA MISURA, NELLE PRIME OPERE DI BILL VIOLA. CFR. ALAN RICKMAN (ET AL), BECKETT ON FILM, DVD, 2005, E GIJS VAN TIJL, 'HUMAN CONDITION/ HUMAN BODY: BRUCE NAUMAN AND SAMUEL BECKETT', BRUCE NAUMAN, EX. CAT., HAYWARD GALLERY, LONDON, 1998, PP. 60-75.

13 HENRI CARTIER BRESSON, THE DECISIVE MOMENT, NEW YORK, SIMON AND SCHUSTER, 1952. QUEST'OPERA IN PASSATO ERA CONSIDERATA IL PRINCIPALE TESTO SULLA FOTOGRAFIA DEL VENTESIMO SECOLO.

la quale era stata formulata in origine.[14]
Di conseguenza dagli anni '80, c'è stato un ritorno alle tecnologie dello stenoscopio e della camera oscura. L'oggetto del contendere non era il fatto che la realtà del video fosse più oggettiva (sebbene ciò abbia fatto parte delle sue prime rivendicazioni), ma che mettesse in campo una nuova ed ampia serie di soggettività multi-temporali o pluralizzate. Da cui l'elasticità della fotografia riportata nel tempo, passaggio chiaramente discernibile dalle preoccupazioni relative a riproduzione (risultati istantanei), produzione ed all'intervento di sviluppo.

A seguito dell'avvento della digitalizzazione negli anni '90, il ruolo del video e del VHS ha iniziato a perdere in parte importanza, ed ultimamente si è registrato un suo ritorno al cinema. Molte delle nuove tecnologie cinematografiche virtuali hanno usurpato il suo ruolo originale, e la pretesa di essere istantaneo e di rappresentare la realtà non è più sostenibile. All'estremo, gli eccessi mitopoetici di Matthew Barney riflettono la crescente tendenza del video verso il cinema.[15] Poiché la riproducibilità non costituisce più un grande problema, i moderni mezzi elettronici e le tecnologie computerizzate sempre più spesso si sostituiscono alla vecchia funzione della videocassetta.[16] Dal punto di vista della temporalità il video e la fotografia esistono fianco a fianco molto spesso nello spazio virtuale del computer, e nelle possibilità manipolative tra l'immagine estratta, il suo processo di produzione e la sua successiva presentazione. Ciò implica una crescente molteplicità di contenuti temporali, la cui esatta natura non è fissa né determinabile. In breve, sia la fotografia, sia il video sono passati dallo specifico all'aspecifico per quanto riguarda i contenuti temporali. La generalità aspecifica del tempo è la durata. Tale durata, inoltre, è naturalmente sempre virtuale, e pertanto inafferrabile; di fatto, la definizione stessa del termine implica uno stato « in divenire » di possibilità simulata. Il virtuale, tuttavia, non si oppone al reale perché esiste ancora in essenza o effetto, ma non di fatto. Il che significa che esiste nella mente o nell'immaginazione. Il mondo virtuale non è un mondo alternativo, perché ciò sarebbe impossibile dal punto di vista epistemologico, pur offrendo, però, un aggancio immaginato o alternativo con ciò che si intende con il termine realtà. Una realtà ipotetica generata, e, forse, facendo seguito ai suggerimenti di Bergson, che noi siamo in grado di « immaginare con molti ritmi diversi » che operano a livello della nostra coscienza.

I fotografi ed i video artisti che espongono le proprie opere nell'ambito di « Mutations II » hanno subito gli effetti, direttamente o indirettamente, di tutti questi cambiamenti e tendenze su un arco temporale di trenta anni. Non sorprende che ciò determini una forte diversità in termini di pratiche ed approccio procedurale sia nel video sia nella fotografia, l'ombra individuale definitoria, a cui ho alluso nei paragrafi precedenti. La temporalità ed il tempo-spazio sono costituiti non solo in termini visivi, ma anche aurali. Ma laddove il suono è lineare, e cioè collocato nel continuum che si dipana dal primo momento in cui viene udito, anch'esso è stato messo al servizio della frammentazione e del riassemblamento temporale. In un'opera come quella di Christoph Brech, Opus 110a, mentre sentiamo la musica sinfonica ciò che vediamo riempire l'immagine inquadrata nel video è la parte posteriore della giacca (un frac, presumiamo) di colui che riteniamo essere il direttore d'orchestra – sebbene si possa tranquillamente trattare dell'equivalente simulato di un suonatore di « air guitar », cioè uno che finge di suonare una chitarra immaginaria.[17] L'effetto è quello di una collisione tra l'aspetto visivo di ciò che vediamo, e quello aurale di ciò che udiamo, man mano che veniamo ipnotizzati dai movimenti ritmici e dalle configurazioni assunte dalla stoffa e dalle cuciture della giacca. Nel corso di tale processo si perde il senso di connessione suono-immagine ad un livello, mentre tale riconnessione si produce ad un altro livello. L'esperienza è transitiva, ed è comune a molte delle opere di Brech, il che significa che esprime un'azione da un soggetto ad un oggetto, ma richiede un oggetto diretto per completare il proprio significato. Il presupposto è che lo spettatore sia l'oggetto diretto al quale è rivolto. Conosciamo sufficientemente bene il rapporto di lunga data esistente tra musica e video, ma nel caso dei video pop l'effetto è generalmente illustrativo. Ciò che fa Brech è fornire un livello minimo di informazione (il video termina con l'immagine dello spartito) e lasciare allo spettatore il compito di completare l'opera da sé. Di fatto lo spettatore e l'atto di recepire l'opera diventano una necessità per dare significato all'opera stessa.
Tale strategia è caratteristica di molti video artisti attivi oggi, il che significa che è anti-illustrativa, e spesso espressa in termini post-narratologici.[18] In altre parole, non analizza la narrativa o il racconto lineare in senso strutturale per determinare a priori i risultati della percezione, ma provoca e richiede percezioni espanse che contribuiscano al completamento dell'opera. Ciò fa entrare in gioco il tempo ed i contenuti temporali dello spettatore, in risposta all'opera video. L'opera di Olga Chernysheva è caratterizzata da modalità di funzionamento

14 PER UNA PANORAMICA SUI CAMBIAMENTI CULTURALI INTERVENUTI IN FOTOGRAFIA DALLA SUA NASCITA AI GIORNI NOSTRI, CFR. MARY WARNER MARIEN, PHOTOGRAPHY: A CULTURAL HISTORY, LONDON, LAURENCE KING PUBLISHING, 2002.

15 NANCY SPECTOR, THYRZA GOODEVE, E NEVILLE WAKEFIELD, MATTHEW BARNES: THE CREMASTER CYCLE, NEW YORK, GUGGENHEIM MUSEUM PUBLICATIONS, 2002; CFR. INOLTRE STEPHAN URBASCHEK E BRANDON STOSUY, MATTHEW BARNEY, MUNICH, INGVILD GOETZ PUBLICATIONS, 2008.

16 TIMOTHY DRUCKREY (ED.), ARS ELECTRONICA: FACING THE FUTURE - A SURVEY OF TWO DECADES (ELECTRONIC CULTURE: HISTORY, THEORY AND PRACTICE), CAMBRIDGE MASS., MIT PRESS, 2001.

17 SI TRATTA DI CHRISTOPH POPPEN CHE DIRIGE L'ORCHESTRA DA CAMERA DI MONACO NELLA SINFONIA DA CAMERA, OP. 110A DI SHOSTAKOVITCH, E CIÒ CHE BRECH DEFINISCE UN'ESERCITAZIONE NELLA « DINAMICA VISIVA DELLA MUSICA ». È TUTTAVIA IMPORTANTE COMPRENDERE COME SI TRATTI IN EFFETTI DI INFORMAZIONI NON PERTINENTI, E NON FONDAMENTALI PER LA COMPRENSIONE DELL'OPERA, SEBBENE TALE COMPRENSIONE POSSA DIFFERIRE QUALORA SI CONOSCA GIÀ L'OPERA MUSICALE.

18 TRADIZIONALMENTE, LA « NARRATOLOGIA » STRUTTURALE VIENE ASSOCIATA AL GRUPPO DEI COSIDDETTI FORMALISTI RUSSI. TZVETAN TODOROV (BULGARIA, NATO NEL 1939) HA CONIATO TALE TERMINE, E FA RIFERIMENTO ALL'ESEMPIO DI VLADIMIR PROPP (1895-1970). CFR. MORPHOLOGY OF THE FOLK TALE (RUSSIAN 1928), AUSTIN, UNIVERSITY OF TEXAS PRESS, 1968, ED EDIZIONI SUCCESSIVE.

contrarie rispetto a quelle di Brech. Nel suo video Windows, lo spettatore assume il ruolo di un voyeur nascosto, di un guardone. In una serie di brevi prese ritagliate attraverso delle finestre, di notte, ci viene presentata la cifra di un lessico della vita quotidiana. Le finestre sono banali e comuni, e suggeriscono un'edilizia popolare moderna, mentre gli interni opachi e scarsamente illuminati sono ordinari e simili gli uni agli altri. Nel suo video costituito da scatti multipli di scene di vita quotidiana, un uomo guarda la televisione, tre persone ballano in cerchio, un uomo suona la chitarra in solitudine, una donna stira, un uomo è in bagno, ecc. A parte il comportamento abituale che è deliberatamente invocato ed implicito nell'opera, non esiste alcun collegamento diretto tra le finestre, a parte quello vagamente tipologico. Tuttavia, l'atemporalità implica ben poco dal punto di vista di suggerire un posto o un luogo in relazione agli eventi presentati. Sono stati filmati nello stesso momento, in momenti diversi, o in spazi urbani diversi? Ciò che diventa importante è che si tratta di semplici immagini video, e che in quanto immagini basate sul tempo fanno sì che lo spettatore si trovi ad assumere il ruolo del voyeur nascosto o del guardone. Se si fosse trattato di fermi immagine o di fotografie non ne sarebbe conseguito questo senso di complicità da parte dello spettatore.

Il ruolo interstiziale del video, ciò che un collega nel presente catalogo ha definito un « coltivare l'in-between », predomina nella produzione video. Nelle opere dell'artista israeliano Ori Gersht, intitolate Big Bang e Pomegranate (Melograno), vi è un prestito dalle nature morte e dai dipinti floreali. In Big Bang compare uno schermo nero ed un suono acuto diventa sempre più intenso, e poi, gradualmente, compare una natura morta, un fiore in un vaso, tratto dalla tradizione pittorica olandese del XVII secolo. Il suono-immagine e la tonalità acuta si intensificano, e lentamente emerge una sensazione di aspettativa, fino all'esplosione di fiore e vaso. I frammenti piovono in avanti, e l'immagine gradualmente si dissolve nello schermo nero, per cominciare nuovamente in un loop. Se si analizzano le opere di Gersht ciò che emerge è un profondo senso di identità e biografia personale e politica, e non sembra una coincidenza che egli abbia scelto un melograno per il suo altro video. In Pomegranade vediamo un'immagine prospettica ed una natura morta di un cavolo cappuccio e di un melograno sospesi, mentre una zucca ed una zucchina giacciono su ciò che in un dipinto costituirebbe la parte inferiore del quadro the foreshortened lower frame. Il video è privo di sonoro fino a quando un proiettile attraversa l'inquadratura da destra a sinistra, facendo esplodere il melograno, i cui semi cadono a pioggia sempre al rallentatore. Da un punto di vista personale, non solo ci troviamo di fronte ad una connotazione biblica particolare e motivata, in quanto il melograno è uno dei sette frutti di Israele, ma occorre sottolineare che in ebraico si usa la stessa parola per melograno e granata.[19] Nell'opera di Gersht non ci troviamo tanto di fronte ad un rimescolamento del tempo, quanto ad un'alterazione dell'esperienza temporale ed alla creazione di una condizione di aspettativa imprevista ma violenta. In altre parole, si tratta di « misurare il grado di tensione o rilassamento delle diverse tipologie di coscienza ».

Se Gersht in queste sue opere in particolare fa riferimento alla pittura, l'in-betweenness del finlandese Tuomo Raino sembra evocare l'esistenza di un rapporto tra il disegno ed il video, creato attraverso il suo programma di elaborazione. Nelle sue opere Staircase (Crosswise) (Scala di traverso) e City, la prima crea un effetto sovrannaturale: una figura spettrale che sale una scala, con una qualità pittorica confusa ed indistinta. Il tono è in un certo senso gotico, la superficie dell'immagine è quella di un effetto spettrale con esposizioni multiple, e naturalmente richiama alla memoria le prime fonti futuristiche e il « Nudo che scende una scala » di Duchamp.[20] Sebbene un riferimento simile possa apparire scontato, ci ricorda il modo in cui il video e la fotografia abbiano fatto un passo indietro per mettere in discussione ed indagare le proprie origini da venti anni a questa parte. Per converso City è, dal punto di vista visivo, un'immagine fissa, ma anche in questo caso viene intensificata come suono-immagine grazie alla colonna sonora, una vista urbana nero-grigia di una ferrovia metropolitana o di una fermata del tram, in cui l'evocazione viene plasmata semplicemente dal suono di un vento spettrale, di treni invisibili che passano sferragliando, e ogni tanto un suono di passi. L'immagine fissa nel tempo agisce come il referente di una ripetizione, viene legata in un loop, e la ripetizione suggerita del tempo ha una durata potenzialmente infinita. City, opera costituita da suono e immagine, si colloca nell'interfaccia tra l'immagine fissa ed il video, unendo lo spazio tra le esposizioni a lungo termine ad esempio del fotografo Michael Wesely in un sistema altamente personale e programmato.[21]

L'effetto di un'indagine rinnovata ha un impatto diretto sull'opera di Oliver Möst, il cui uso dello stenoscopio per la realizzazione di video trova un'eco diretta nella preistoria e nei primi sviluppi della fotografia. In una serie di opere intitolate Pinhole (Stenoscopio) o Shortcuts (Scorciatoie), quali Landscape (Panorama), Hide and Seek (Nascondino) oppure Kill your idols (Uccidi

19 I SETTE FRUTTI (SHIVAT HAMINIM) DI ISRAELE SONO ELENCATI NEL DEUTERONOMIO 8:7-8, ED IL TERMINE IN EBRAICO SIA PER MELOGRANO SIA PER UNA GRANATA È RIMMÔN. « PERCHÉ IL SIGNORE TUO DIO STA PER FARTI ENTRARE IN UN PAESE FERTILE: PAESE DI TORRENTI, DI FONTI E DI ACQUE SOTTERRANEE CHE SCATURISCONO NELLA PIANURA E SULLA MONTAGNA; PAESE DI FRUMENTO, DI ORZO, DI VITI, DI FICHI E DI MELOGRANI; PAESE DI ULIVI, DI OLIO E DI MIELE; » IL TERMINE IN SPAGNOLO, FRANCESE ED INGLESE DERIVA DALLO STESSO TERMINE GRANATA (LE GRENADE) ED IL LIQUORE GRANATINA È FATTO CON IL MELOGRANO.

20 SIA I FUTURISTI SIA DUCHAMP SONO DEBITORI VERSO EADWEARD MUYBRIDGE (1830-1904) E ETIENNE-JULES MAREY (1830-1904), ENTRAMBI CRONO-FOTOGRAFI FORTEMENTE INTERESSATI ALLA LOCOMOZIONE SPAZIO-TEMPORALE ED ALLA SEQUENZIAZIONE DEL MOVIMENTO. CFR. PHILLIP PRODGER, TIME STANDS STILL: MUYBRIDGE AND THE INSTANTANEOUS PHOTOGRAPHY MOVEMENT, LONDON, OXFORD UNIVERSITY PRESS, 2003, E MARTA BRAUN, PICTURING TIME: WORK OF ETIENNE-JULES MAREY (1839-1904), CHICAGO AND LONDON, CHICAGO UNIVERSITY PRESS, 1994.

21 LE ESPOSIZIONI FOTOGRAFICHE CONTINUE A LUNGO TERMINE SU UN ARCO TEMPORALE DI TRE E QUATTRO ANNI DI MICHAEL WESELY SONO BEN NOTE, E SOTTO MOLTI ASPETTI OPERANO DAL VERSANTE OPPOSTO RISPETTO AL VIDEO, CONSENTENDO AL TEMPO STESSO DI GENERARE CONTENUTI SPETTRALI NELL'ARCO DI LUNGHI PERIODI. CFR. MICHAEL WESELY OPEN SHUTTER, EXH. CAT., THE MUSEUM OF MODERN ART NEW YORK, 2004, CHE COPRE IN MODO CONTINUO IL PERIODO DELLA DEMOLIZIONE E DELLA RICOSTRUZIONE DEL MOMA, ED IN RELAZIONE ALL'EDIFICIO UBICATO A POTSDAMER PLATZ, MICHAEL WESELY: DIE ERFINDUNG DES UNSICHTBAREN, EXH. CAT., GUARDINI GALERIE BERLIN/FOTOHOF SALZBURG, 2005.

i tuoi idoli) egli segmenta e sovrappone diversi elementi temporali, mentre torna alla premessa di base del tempo, della luce e dell'esposizione. Che si tratti del semplice conto di Hide and seek, o delle appena discernibili variazioni di Landscape, ci ritroviamo con uno strano senso di infinito e di intorpidimento. Se il video è nato nella sfera politica e culturale della contestazione, con il predominio dei mass media, si è poi evoluto nel periodo successivo diventando un mezzo altamente personale. Un'opera quale Dreamsequence (Sequenza onirica) di Gast Bouschet e Nadine Hilbert, se da un lato può fare riferimento alla storia del cinema, dall'altro è intenzionalmente non lineare, e fonde suggestioni politiche ed atteggiamenti personali con frammenti sconnessi di testo e suono provenienti da luoghi diversi. Come un miscuglio di esperienze sensoriali ricordate in un sogno, presenta un mix di identificazione e di revocazione della memoria – in breve una sorta di catarsi personale. Ogni collegamento è lasciato alla percezione dello spettatore per essere assimilato. Resta culturalmente politico solo nella misura in cui, in quanto video arte, non cerca in genere di calmare lo spettatore, e se da un lato può cercare di intrattenere, in modo indiretto, dall'altro il suo principale intento è quello di mettere in discussione i limiti della rappresentazione e della comprensione delle immagini. Quando viene posto in modo letterale, sfida lo spettatore a chiedersi quale sia il significato delle immagini. Che cosa intende Ulrich Gebert se colloca cinque individui, in uniforme da soldato in fila davanti ad un muro bianco, ripetendo il rat-ta-tat / luce accesa-luce spenta? A parte un omaggio indiretto a predecessori quali Gary Hill, e l'evocazione della ripetizione, sta a noi sviluppare il campo delle possibilità di ricezione.

Lo sviluppo più rivelatore è che sia il video sia la fotografia sono entrati nel mondo della manipolazione computerizzata e digitale. Invece di ridurre le possibilità, la realtà virtuale del mondo informatico ha liberato la fotografia dall'immagine statica, dal momento congelato nel tempo, ed ha affrancato il video dall'illusione di catturare una qualche forma di realtà ultima. Ha consentito ad un artista come Peter Aerschmann di diventare polifonico nella sua abilità di accostare elementi diversi, dal sociale al surreale. In opere quali Paternoster e Union Square egli rivela una diversità di approccio che caratterizza molti degli artisti di oggi. In Paternoster vediamo un fondale di ascensori aperti, con figure che salgono e scendono nella loro varietà idiosincratica. Rappresentano piccoli mondi di preoccupazioni sociali, comportamenti umani comuni in situazioni dislocate; una donna che suona un violino, una figura maschile in tuta che spazza, una donna con un vaso di fiori, una pianta in vaso solitaria, eccetera. Aerschmann spesso si concentra sugli archetipi, forse un influsso del suo background svizzero (forse junghiano). In Union Square troviamo il contrappunto surreale di un luogo coperto da candida neve e ceppi di albero, uno sfondo piatto di colore rosso opaco con un aereo che passa, e battaglioni dell'esercito svizzero sull'attenti nella neve, mentre l'immagine effettua una scansione da sinistra a destra, passando dai ceppi di alberi ad un bosco di conifere. Aerschmann contesta direttamente la dialettica dell'immagine congelata ed in movimento, e l'opera ha per oggetto lo spazio ed il trascorrere indefinito del tempo. Pertanto, in un certo senso, il virtuale, quando utilizzato nella fotografia e nel video, consente di realizzare una maggiore sintesi temporale e di immagini di quanto non sia mai stato possibile con le tecnologie preesistenti. Nella fotografia rende possibile la sovrapposizione di momenti temporali multipli unendoli in una durata, mentre nel video tali temporalità risultano compresse, estese, ribaltate e mescolate in possibilità nuove ed apparentemente infinite.

Ma dove si colloca il significato più ampio del tempo, in tutto ciò? Come suggerito da Bergson, risiede nelle diverse tipologie di coscienza. Non deve sorprendere che il rapporto che le persone hanno con il tempo sia profondamente personale. Ciò che il mondo impone non necessariamente coincide con ciò che la mente e l'immaginazione asseriscono. Man mano che ci immergiamo nell'era elettronica, dovremmo avere meno a che fare con la paura, e più con la possibilità. « Mutations II » molto semplicemente fa riferimento a tali cambiamenti nei parametri di possibilità generate da sé e realizzabili nell'ambito degli utilizzi attuali della fotografia e del video. Il modo in cui li utilizziamo, oppure l'uso che ne facciamo nel mondo resta una scelta del tutto individuale.

Tuttavia, la nostra natura, l'ufficio e la funzione della nostra personalità, restano avvolte nel medesimo mistero. Infatti, queste sensazioni elementari e puntuali che si sviluppano nello spazio da dove vengono, come nascono, a quale scopo servono? Dobbiamo presupporre che si tratti di altrettanti assoluti, di cui non vediamo né l'origine né la fine.[22]

Mark Gisbourne

Ex Lecturer e Senior Lecturer nel Corso di perfezionamento in Arte Contemporanea, Slade School of Fine Art, University of London e Sotheby's Institute (Master Programme della University of Manchester). Ex Presidente dell'AICA (Gran Bretagna), e Vice Presidente Internazionale AICA. Ha pubblicato vari volumi e cataloghi, e scritto per la maggior parte delle pubblicazioni in lingua inglese nel campo dell'arte. Le sue ultime mostre includono Paul Klee: Adult Memories of Childhood (Centro Atlántico de Arte Moderno, Las Palmas) e Rohkunstbau, di cui è curatore (www.rohkunstbau.de). Vive e lavora a Berlino.

22 HENRI BERGSON "OF THE SELECTION OF IMAGES", OP CIT, (PP. 17-76) P. 63.

Peter Aerschmann

Nato nel 1969 a Friburgo/CH
Vive e lavora a Berna in Svizzera
Hochschule f. Gestaltung und Kunst Bern
www.aerschmann.ch

Fotografare lo spazio preservando la profondità della temporalità, realizzando immagini che vanno oltre l'istante ed il fisso per rendere il movimento e la vita: la sfida fondamentale che caratterizza l'opera di Peter Aeschmann è come rappresentare il tempo nello spazio.

In « Occhio e mente » (« Eye and Mind ») (1964) il filosofo e teorico dell'arte Maurice Merleau-Ponty afferma che visione e movimento sono strettamente collegati, implicando che se non fossimo in grado di muoverci nello spazio, non saremmo in grado di vedere. In ogni caso, il movimento del corpo non è semplicemente lo spostamento di un oggetto da A a B. Il movimento effettivamente percepito è un tutto autonomo, e non può essere confuso con lo spazio che viene coperto quando si verifica il movimento stesso. Ecco in cosa risiede il paradosso del movimento: avviene nello spazio, ma sembra esservi estraneo.

Nei video di Peter Aerschmann, eventi casuali si verificano insieme ad eventi predeterminati, offrendo allo spettatore solo una visione frammentaria della realtà della vita. È questo il modo in cui l'artista riesce a disorientarci. È da ciò che proviene l'impressione della vita, anche se il numero di elementi è predeterminato ed i loro movimenti seguono traiettorie prestabilite? Invece di mostrare un'immagine, Peter Aerschmann riesce a catturare il ritmo delle cose attraverso l'immagine, ed il modo in cui si adattano al trascorrere del tempo ed alla ripetizione. Egli ricostruisce un ambiente che mantiene le caratteristiche formali della realtà: la capacità di cambiare, la permanenza, la durata e la presenza degli oggetti. Non è un caso che le mini-sequenze filmate siano quasi tutti frammenti di movimenti la cui presentazione ripetitiva ed il cui progresso predeterminato danno vita ad una sorta di umorismo malinconico.

Richiamando gli archetipi della memoria collettiva, l'opera di Peter Aerschmann ci riporta alla nostra stessa realtà, facendoci diventare metafore di un mondo privato delle sue gerarchie, nel quale siamo tutti estranei gli uni per gli altri.

Alice Anderson

Nata nel 1976 a Londra dove vive e lavora
1998-2001 Scuola Superiore delle Belle Arti di Parigi
2002-2004 M.A Goldsmiths College, Londra
www.alice-anderson.org

Unendo storie tratte dai suoi ricordi ad un mondo immaginario strettamente legato alla sua infanzia, l'artista e regista anglo-francese Alice Anderson torna alla tradizione del racconto popolare e ne reinventa il significato. La sua opera, che presenta elementi tipici della narrativa ma anche autobiografici, sottolinea la dualità che secondo l'artista corrisponde alla vera essenza della favola popolare, nel contempo superficiale e profonda, normativa e sovversiva, che sprofonda lo spettatore in un intenso mondo onirico dal quale spunta una forma di oscurità, creando un'atmosfera in alcuni momenti violenta e spaventosa. Sebbene l'infanzia e l'idea del gioco assumano un'importanza cruciale nella sua opera, implicano comunque un elemento di serietà.

L'artista costruisce le sue storie enfatizzando il potere simbolico e poetico degli oggetti provenienti dal passato, che utilizza. Lontano da una logica lineare, il processo narrativo che costruisce è in qualche modo circolare, e richiama gli involuti corridoi di un labirinto, il fluttuante mondo di Lewis Carroll, o i principi freudiani che determinano l'interpretazione dell'inconscio. Da ciascuna delle storie fantastiche di Alice Anderson emergono i temi della ricerca dell'identità, che ci invita ad attraversare lo specchio alla ricerca della nostra personale esperienza, a metà strada tra delizia e terrore.

Gast Bouschet & Nadine Hilbert

Nato nel 1958 a Dudelange/LUX / Nata nel 1961 a Lussemburgo
Vivono a Bruxelles ed altrove
www.thetrustfiles.net

Nadine Hilbert e Gast Bouschet hanno realizzato ed esposto le loro fotografie e video in tutto il mondo fin dagli anni '80. Sono affascinati soprattutto da immagine registrata e dalla sua capacità di riflettere e commentare la trasformazione dei sistemi politici e socio-economici, e dal loro simbolismo, particolarmente evidente nella morfologia delle strutture urbane e delle zone di confine.

La loro opera è stata esposta in numerose occasioni nelle seguenti sedi: Center of Contemporary Arts (Glasgow), Museum van Hedendaagse Kunst Muhka (Anversa), the Casino, Forum d'Art Contemporain (Lussemburgo), Nei Liicht Gallery (Dudelange, Lussemburgo), the Busan Biennale of Contemporary Arts (Busan, Korea), Camouflage, Centre of Africain Contemporary Art (Bruxellse e Johannesburg), Domaine départemental, Chamarande (Parigi) e nell'ambito del Krinzinger Projekte (Vienna).

« Io sono sempre l'altro. Se dico noi, designo la parte colpevole di me. D'ora in poi tutto è chiaro. Nessuno è più ciò che era prima. L'aggressione non ha cambiato nulla, siamo tutt'uno con i nostri nemici, condividiamo la forma mentis dei nostri avversari. Non ci sono più limiti né barriere, le nostre identità sono intrecciate. Tuttavia siamo consumati dalla paura, l'inquietudine non ci abbandona mai. La minaccia è quotidiana e ci distrugge dall'interno. Il mondo non è più lo stesso, la luce è diversa. La natura è irreconciliabile, ci vuole ghermire. Siamo stranieri nel nostro paese, parliamo tutti una lingua sconosciuta che ci spaventa. I nostri peggior incubi sono d'ora in poi spogliati di quel delizioso sudore freddo che li caratterizzava. I nostri sogni più belli ci preoccupano con la loro consolazione ingannevole. Ogni giorno, la nostra mente produce e riproduce il suo lento veleno. È un po' di tempo che non possiamo farne a meno. Abbiamo urgente bisogno di questo pane quotidiano. Abbiamo una brutta cera sui campi nei quali seminiamo il nostro terrore. L'oscuro specchio di Nadine Hilbert e Gast Bouschet »
(François Olivieri)

Pirmin Blum

Nato a Pfaffnau/CH 1969, vive a Vienna
1997-1999 Ecole supérieure des Beaux-Arts, Ginevra
1999-2005 Digital Media con Peter Kogler, Academy of Fine Arts, Vienna
www.pirminblum.com

Per diversi anni l'artista svizzero Pirmin Blum ha incentrato il proprio lavoro su Internet. Rovista nei siti delle aste on-line, nei motori di ricerca e nelle chat. Il suo interesse per la Rete deriva dal fatto che oggi chiunque può accedervi; chiunque può riempirla con le proprie fotografie, video, testi, ecc., e leggere materiale personale presentato da altri. Consciamente - come nel caso di Blum - o inconsciamente - diventiamo dei « voyeur » e consumatori delle vite private degli altri. Oltre che a tale materiale di repertorio, Blum ricorre al materiale girato da società industriali e commerciali, come ad esempio video sui test di sicurezza realizzati da varie aziende automobilistiche. Una selezione analitica di specifiche sequenze tratte da tali video ed il loro montaggio innalza immagini che sono state realizzate senza alcuna ambizione valoriale di tipo artistico a nuovi livelli di significato. Ad esempio tagli rapidi combinati con loop stilizzano le immagini di repertorio relative ad un airbag che esplode e si affloscia in una bolla di forma particolare ed apparentemente organica (Airbag, 2005). Blum adatta il momento dell'impatto dell'airbag al ritmo del respiro umano; dopo una serie di loop, lo spettatore « respira » in sincrono con il video.

Un simile effetto è stato ottenuto in Spuk (2001) per il quale Blum ha selezionato un video che mostra un veicolo blindato il cui parabrezza viene raggiunto da colpi di arma da fuoco. La rapida sequenza di due angoli di ripresa diversi - riprese del parabrezza dall'esterno del veicolo si alternano a riprese dall'interno - crea una tensione sovrannaturale, dando allo spettatore la sensazione di trovarsi nel bel mezzo all'azione. Lo spettatore si alterna tra la sensazione di essere colui che spara, e la vittima seduta nel veicolo, che vede i proiettili avvicinarsi. Un fattore decisivo è rappresentato dal suono; gravi note di basso rimbombano dalle casse che emettono musica Techno da rave a 130 battute al minuto, frequenza utilizzata dai DJ durante i rave per ottenere la massima stimolazione del cuore umano.

Christoph Brech

Christoph Brech è nato a Schweinfurt/GER e vive e lavora a Monaco
1989-1995 Accademia delle Belle Arti di Monaco
www.christophbrech.com

« I video di Christoph Brech trasformano eventi ordinari in momenti significativi ».

Le opere di Christoph Brech vanno dalle installazioni alla fotografia, ai video e all'arte in luoghi pubblici.

I suoi video sono concepiti in modo rigoroso e chiaro, lineari nell'esecuzione e semplici nei mezzi impiegati. I fenomeni naturali, gli oggetti e le impressioni della vita quotidiana, oltre all'occhio statico e silenziosamente osservatore della videocamera, costituiscono elementi tipici dell'opera presentata in occasione di questa mostra.

Brech mette a nudo situazioni che svelano la loro dimensione poetica attraverso la dilatazione del tempo ed il senso di lentezza che ciò determina - eventi ordinari trasformati in momenti significativi.

Nel video Passaggio (Passage) l'artista mostra un bicchiere d'acqua sul tavolo di una cabina in una nave container, soggetto ai flussi e riflussi causati dalle vibrazioni e dal beccheggio della nave. In Break Brech propone un'immagine calma ed inizialmente silenziosa del fiume St. Lawrence, ricoperto da nebbia e ghiacci, sottolineando il contrasto tra il ritmo lento della natura e la violenza del passaggio di una nave rompighiaccio canadese. In Opera 110a (Opus 110a) Brech riprende di spalle il direttore d'orchestra Christoph Poppen con l'intento di rendere visibile il dinamismo della musica di Dimitri Shostakovich attraverso il gioco delle pieghe del frac di Poppen, dimostrando tutta la sua abilità nel catturare il « tempo proprio » di un evento in un'immagine. Allo spettatore viene presentato un ritmo rallentato, che genera un'atmosfera quasi meditativa, come nel video Transito, realizzato a Roma nel 2007, nel quale un pesante tendaggio che ricopre l'ingresso di una chiesa viene agitato ritmicamente dal vento, dando vita ad una danza di luci ed ombre sul pavimento. Istanti di tempo e momenti di transizione come questi costituiscono l'essenza dei video di Christoph Brech.

Elina Brotherus

Nata nel 1972 ad Helsinki
Vive ad Helsinki e ad Avallon/F
Master, 2000, Università dell'Arte e del Design,UIAH, Helsinki

« Le fotografie Lo specchio (Le miroir), dal 2000, ed il video Specchio (Miroir), realizzato nel 2001, non riguardano affatto « l'identità femminile », come alcuni hanno suggerito. Volevo soltanto vedere che aspetto avrebbe avuto in fotografia il normale fenomeno fisico del vapore che svanisce. Ripensandoci, l'opera può essere vista come una piccola allegoria della fotografia. Agli inizi, una fotografia era una lastra di rame ricoperta d'argento - uno specchio, quindi - dal quale emergeva un ritratto durante il processo di sviluppo. Anche qui vediamo l'immagine che gradualmente appare dallo specchio. È curioso osservare quanto diverse siano le due opere, anche se l'unico elemento che le distingue in realtà è che le fotografie mostrano istanti separati, mentre il video unisce le pause tra le singole immagini in una linea temporale continua.

Studi di modelli (Model Studies) non riguarda vicende personali né si tratta di un documentario sulla vita di qualcuno. Le immagini sono state costruite per motivi visivi. L'artista è attratto dalla luce, dai colori, dal ritmo delle masse, e da contenuti che richiamano nozioni classiche. La figura spesso gira le spalle allo spettatore. Tale gesto invita ad una tranquilla contemplazione, piuttosto che allo scontro»[1].

Nei suoi video con lo stesso titolo, Elina Brotherus ha utilizzato modelli professionisti che posano come in una lezione di disegno dal vivo. Invece di disegnare, li guarda attraverso la videocamera. La questione è quella dello sguardo speciale di un artista che guarda un modello: uno sguardo distaccato privo di voyeurismo.

« Un artista che disegna o dipinge non pretende di conoscere o comprendere la personalità del modello: non è questo il punto. Si tratta di guardare con attenzione, ecco tutto: dove sono le luci e le ombre, dove vanno le linee. Desidero mostrare al pubblico lo sguardo attivo ma neutrale di un artista, per condividerlo. È un privilegio poter osservare una figura umana in tale modo[2]».

Olga Chernysheva

1962 nata a Mosca, vive e lavora a Mosca
1986 Laureata all'Accademia di Cinema di Mosca
1995-96 laureata all'Accademia Reale di Belle Arti, Amsterdam

Olga Chernysheva è laureata in cinematografia. I suoi interessi spaziano dalla fotografia, alla pittura ai video sperimentali ed alle video installazioni. Il suo progetto Finestre (Windows), realizzato nel 2007, riporta lo spettatore alla vita di tutti i giorni nell'era sovietica: nelle finestre degli appartamenti « Khrushhev » a Mosca si vedono vestiti, stoviglie, biancheria intima, un bicchiere di tè, un torso maschile nudo, un ferro da stiro, un apparecchio televisivo, del tulle con un motivo floreale, biancheria stesa, il vetro rotto di una finestra incollato con la carta... Persone che vanno e vengono: un uomo beve da un bollitore, un vecchio si stiracchia, giovani che si divertono... La finestra stessa in questo caso diventa il perimetro di un palcoscenico, una cornice, che crea uno spazio illuminato simile a quello teatrale, in cui i personaggi/inquilini compaiono e spariscono nelle quinte oscure degli appartamenti.

Le finestre di Chernysheva rivelano la vita di tutti i giorni in Russia, ribaltandola e consentendoci di contemplare la routine quotidiana, lentamente ma con costanza, trasmettendo il significato dell'esistenza. Tutto ciò viene realizzato senza il minimo senso di voyeurismo, di furtività o curiosità – tutto resta molto distante, calmo e concentrato.

Vari videoclip che scorrono simultaneamente nella cornice scura della notte e sul televisore creano un modello di vita comune ideale (accompagnata dalla musica di Chopin), producendo un effetto di presenza e dando vita ad un forte sentimento di nostalgia nei confronti di una realtà sovietica che non è ancora completamente scomparsa.

Ulrich Gebert

Nato a Monaco nel 1976, vive e lavora a Lipsia/GER
1998-2005 Fotografia presso l'Accademia delle Arti Visive di Lipsia ed al Royal College of Art di Londra, 2006
www.klemms-berlin.com

La fotografia di Ulrich Gebert spesso affronta tematiche che ad un primo impatto possono risultare astratte ed inaccessibili, ma che in realtà hanno un'influenza decisiva sul modo in cui ci comportiamo in contesti sociali.

Gebert sottopone ad analisi serrata i principi di ordine, pensiero sistemico, gerarchizzazione ed i meccanismi del potere, rendendoli tangibili nei rispettivi contesti artistici. A seconda del contesto, quindi, utilizza modalità di rappresentazione preparate, cinematografiche, documentarie o ritrattistiche utilizzandole per creare le sue opere, per lo più fotografiche, in modo da operare una riflessione sui media stessi.

Per il suo video Nessun dialogo (no dialogues) del 2004, Ulrich Gebert ha utilizzato immagini di repertorio relative all'addestramento di un corpo speciale di polizia di frontiera appartenente all'unità antiterrorismo GSG 9 della polizia federale tedesca. A partire dal materiale raccolto l'artista ha assemblato un loop minimalista che mostra cinque agenti in uniforme in fila in una stanza buia e chiusa a chiave, mentre vengono sottoposti a stress test tramite l'utilizzo di un flash stroboscopico. Nel corso del test, agli agenti vengono fornite istruzioni che dovranno successivamente eseguire. La luce intermittente del flash pone direttamente di fronte allo spettatore la proiezione e l'ambiente circostante, attraverso una sequenza rapida, scandita dal flash, di singole immagini statiche che, susseguendosi in rapida successione, sembrano dare vita a movimenti sia pure infinitesimali da parte degli agenti. Come questi ultimi, lo spettatore viene esposto all'impatto visivo violento del flash, mentre si trova in uno spazio ristretto e buio molto simile, in cui viene presentato il video. Lo spettatore quindi si trova a sperimentare direttamente la situazione di oppressione e di tensione tipica dello stress test a cui sono sottoposti gli agenti del GSG 9.

Ori Gersht

Nato nel 1967 a Tel-Aviv vive e lavora a Londra.
1989-92 BA in Fotografia, Film e Video, University of Westminster, Londra
1993-95 MA in Fotografia, Royal College of Art, Londra
www.mummeryschnelle.com

Nella sua opera più recente Ori Gersht indaga sul rapporto tra video, fotografia, tecnologia e percezione ottica in un momento emblematico nella storia dell'arte in cui la tecnologia digitale minaccia una crisi e promette sviluppi importanti.

Nei suoi due ultimi lavori Melograno (Pomegranate) e Big Bang, Gersht ha ricreato delle composizioni di natura morta nello stile dei grandi classici della pittura, percorrendo in questo modo l'evoluzione della fascinazione dell'artista per le varie modalità di rappresentazione della realtà dal diciassettesimo secolo ai nostri giorni. Laddove, nella loro forma originale, dipinti di questo tipo intendevano fermare nel tempo un momento, le composizioni di Gersht sono sconvolte da interventi rapidi e violenti. In

7 DA « CONVERSAZIONE TRA ELINA BROTHERUS CON BIRGIT EUSTERSCHULTE ». MOSTRA SELF-TIMER (SELBSTA USLÖSER), KUNSTHALE FRIDERICIANUM, KASEL 2005.
8 DALLA RASSEGNA STAMPA DI ELINA BROTHERUS: MODEL STUDIES, MOSTRA TENUTA PRESSO LA GB AGENCY, PARIGI 2005.

Melograno (Pomegranate), un film che fa riferimento sia ad una natura morta barocca di Juán Sanchez Cotán , sia alla fotografia stroboscopica di Harold Edgerton, un proiettile attraversa l'immagine e colpisce violentemente un melograno sospeso che si spacca e in slow motion rilascia microscopici frammenti in aria come una bocca violata e trafitta che getta fuori semi rosso sangue. Un'immagine dall'apparenza pacifica si trasforma in un massacro e si stabilisce un dialogo tra l'immobilità e il movimento, la pace e la violenza. Dicotomie di questo tipo sono presenti anche in Big Bang, un video che a prima vista sembra rappresentare dei fiori in una natura morta tipicamente olandese. L'illusione si infrange improvvisamente nel momento in cui i fiori e il vaso esplodono al suono di intense sirene di guerra, che si trasformano lentamente in una isterica voce meccanica. La scena si trasforma poi in una lenta pioggia di particelle floreali e polvere. Entrambi i lavori, Melograno (Pomegranate) e Big Bang, comunicano le ondate di cambiamento violento della storia dell'umanità.

In un tempo in cui molti artisti di film e video che si occupano di politica producono lavori che sono più vicini al mezzo classico del documentario, il lavoro di Gersht esplora un genere in cui è all'avanguardia, quello della meditazione provocativa. (Andrew Mummery, Direttore Galleria Mummery + Schnelle, Londra)

Terézia Golasová

Nata nel 1980 a Bratislava, dove vive e lavora
2002-2007 Accademia delle Belle Arti a Bratislava, con specializzazione in Fotografia e Nuovi Media
2004 Facoltà of Filosofia dell'Università di Comenius a Bratislava
http://golasova.marencin.sk

Terézia Golasová é una studentessa dell'Accademia delle Belle Arti, rappresenta appieno l'idea di giovane artista emergente. La sua opera, creata in uno studio fotografico, affronta esclusivamente la questione dell'utilizzo di mezzi diversi, fotografia e video, per rappresentare il concetto del cambiamento. Nei suoi video non si sviluppa alcuna azione. Sono il movimento ed il trascorrere del tempo ad essere i protagonisti. Per sottolinearne l'impatto, utilizza una videocamera fissa.

Nel video ...In un letto... (...In One Bed...) la videocamera fissata in un punto compie un giro di 360 gradi. Crea l'impressione di una ripresa panoramica, di una stanza in cui entrano persone che si muovono in direzione opposta rispetto al movimento della videocamera. Ciò sottolinea l'illusione della sequenzialità dell'azione, come avviene nelle immagini fisse.

« Quo Vadis è un breve documento sul trascorrere del tempo » dice l'autrice. Una videocamera fissa cattura l'immagine di un passeggero seduto in un punto mentre si muove - viaggia da una fermata all'altra della metropolitana. Attraverso il finestrino è possibile vedere oggetti che scorrono velocemente, suggerendo quindi la reale velocità del veicolo, in forte contrasto con la quasi totale immobilità dei passeggeri. I loro movimenti occasionali non fanno altro che acuire l'impressione di guardare, di fatto, un'immagine fissa realizzata all'interno della carrozza. Per visualizzare il trascorrere del tempo, un orologio mostra l'ora esatta, fino ai secondi.

L'ultima opera della Golasová, Perplessità (To be at a Loss), può essere considerata lo sviluppo naturale dei suoi studi sul cambiamento e sui mezzi di rappresentazione. Anche in questo caso l'artista utilizza una videocamera fissa. Questa volta l'illusione di trovarsi di fronte ad un'immagine fissa viene rafforzata ritraendo deliberatamente una persona immobile (l'autrice stessa) ed il suo riflesso nello specchio. L'unico elemento di cambiamento è rappresentato dal vapore che lentamente copre l'immagine riflessa nello specchio ed il rumore dell'acqua che scorre. Il video termina quando l'immagine nello specchio scompare completamente. L'idea può non essere così originale in una produzione a cavallo tra il video e la fotografia, ma costituisce sicuramente uno sviluppo logico nell'opera della Golasová.

Laurent Goldring

Nato a Parigi nel 1957 dove vive e lavora come scultore, pittore, designatore ed autore di video. Suo lavoro artistico ha contributo a svilupare la danza contemporanea; ha participato a diverse mostre un piu dappertutto

Il cinema conosce il segreto della fotografia. La fotografia riguardava la somiglianza, ed Arago fece approvare la legge che l'avrebbe autenticata in quanto tale. Dal canto suo, il cinema, che era ancora cronofotografia, aveva immediatamente compreso che tale finzione si basava soltanto sul suo stesso postulato incantatorio. Ecco perché non ha mai preteso di mostrare ventiquattro foto al secondo, ma ventiquattro immagini al secondo.

Il cinema scatta una serie di fotografie nello stesso momento. Ha a che fare soltanto con due scatti ravvicinati che differiscono in modo tale da smentire l'idea di somiglianza. Ciò fa esplodere in modo simmetrico l'idea della somiglianza tra il mondo e se stesso. Nel caso del ritratto, è la finzione dell'individuo ad essere fatta esplodere. Nel caso del paesaggio, la verità della prospettiva crolla. Prende piede una differenza fondamentale che la fotografia aveva dichiarato inesistente.

Il cinema ha visto, avrebbe potuto far vedere, ha rifiutato di vedere, ha decretato di non aver visto nulla, e ha freneticamente proibito a se stesso di vedere.

Il cinema è improvvisamente diventato la negazione massiccia e pienamente (in)consapevole del segreto della fotografia: che non era una somiglianza. Si è dedicata all'affare dell'inequivocabile ed alla somiglianza, ed in primo luogo alla somiglianza con se stesso, il garante di tutti gli altri affari. Hollywood era la grande macchina pubblicitaria di questo modo di vita in cui ad oggetti ed esseri umani era invariabilmente imposto di somigliare a se stessi.

Nel cinema tutto viene spiegato attraverso questa frenesia del diniego: casting, sceneggiatura, storyboard, riprese. Tutto è destinato a farci credere che esista un individuo, con un volto ed un corpo, una personalità, un obiettivo ed un'idea perché noi comprendiamo anche perché un'industria che esiste esclusivamente per creare finzione possa solamente concepire un'immagine concepibile come una finzione.

Il mio lavoro consiste nel cercare di realizzare un'immagine in movimento al di fuori della finzione, in altre parole al di fuori della somiglianza. (Laurent Goldring)

Laurent Grasso

Nato nel 1972 in Mulhouse/F, vive e lavora a Parigi
Cooper Union School, New York, Central Saint Martins School of Art, Londra ; Scuola delle Belle Arti di Parigi
www.galeriechezvalentin.com/fr/artistes/laurent_grasso/works/

Che (ri)plasmi le forme più o meno identificabili della nostra società ossessionata dal controllo o che stia sovvertendo le tecniche e le convenzioni cinematografiche che plasmano la nostra immaginazione collettiva, Laurent Grasso crea ambienti caratterizzati da un forte potenziale narrativo, combinando timori atavici, prove scientifiche ed inquietanti miti contemporanei. Nel suo video Untitled, una nuvola, enorme e minacciosa, si muove attraverso le strade di Parigi, in direzione dello spettatore ingoiando automobili ed edifici mentre procede. Di fronte a questo muro di polvere in movimento, a questa immaginaria traccia di una catastrofe inventata, siamo spinti ad entrare in un processo narrativo, a proiettare le nostre paure, ad inventare la nostra sceneggiatura. A seconda delle nostre sensibilità individuali e riferimenti culturali e storici, ci ricorda immagini del crollo delle Torri gemelle, scene di violenza urbana, o forse momenti spettacolari da film di azione con effetti speciali.

La sua opera in un certo senso può richiamare alla mente quel gusto per le profezie paranoiche retro-futuristiche annunciate da Charles Fourier duecento anni fa. Di fatto, i fenomeni luminosi, sonori, naturali, paranormali e meteorologici vengono regolarmente inclusi nella sua opera per dare vita ad un'esperienza sensoriale totalmente nuova, che diventa veicolo di prodotti parzialmente finiti dell'immaginazione, che dovranno essere completati dallo spettatore.

Generando una tensione tra le opere in mostra, il loro ambiente e le relative e a volte drammatiche interpretazioni che generano, Laurent Grasso crea immagini mentali fastidiose che tendono ad oscurare la nostra visione di ciò che comunemente definiamo « realtà ».

Tuomo Rainio

Nato ad Espoo/FI, nel 1983. Vive e lavora ad Helsinki. Si è laureato all'Università dell'Arte e del Design di Helsinki in Fotografia, e sta conseguendo un Master presso la stessa università. Nel 2007-2008 ha frequentato la Musashino Art University di Tokio. Dal 2002 espone le proprie opere in Finlandia e Giappone
www.rainio.pp.fi

La presenza della folla

Cambiamento, movimento e tempo sono i temi centrali delle fotografie e dei video dell'artista finlandese Tuomo Rainio. Nelle sue opere puriste il pensiero visivo è sintonizzato a metà strada tra l'estetica delle fotografie in bianco e nero e la tradizione della video arte post concettuale. Forse, immagine in movimento priva di specificità di genere è il modo migliore per descrive il campo nel quale tali interessi si incontrano. Che cosa vediamo realmente quando ci poniamo di fronte alle opere di Rainio che appartengono alla serie Paesaggio di tracce (Tracescape)? Innanzi tutto un'immagine nera, come una lavagna, poi gradualmente compaiono paesaggi urbani anonimi e malinconici, prospettive di strade e strutture architettoniche. Di fatto, l'unica cosa certa è la linea di movimento. Le opere iniziano come animazioni fantasma, ed improvvisamente si trasformano in ambienti familiari, o quanto meno riconoscibili. C'è qualcosa di sovrannaturale nell'atmosfera – forse la presenza della folla.

La realtà sociale è presente sotto forma di tracce di passanti che seguono i propri percorsi quotidiani. Come sottolineato da Raino, « Tracescape costituisce una serie di video sulla struttura sociale in luoghi pubblici. Nello spazio urbano, il comportamento di ogni individuo viene osservato e controllato dagli altri e da se stesso ».

Le opere « Città » (City) (2005) e « In croce » (Crosswise) (2006) presentano incroci visibili, percorsi e cicli di vita cittadina che trasformano la carta topografica cieca della città. Sono simili a strati di immagini a raggi x: è possibile immaginare il corpo vivo, ma di fatto si vede soltanto il sostegno strutturale. I paesaggi sonori dei video riportano le immagini sul piano dell'esperienza quotidiana dell'immersione. Sentiamo il rumore dei semafori, delle automobili che passano, dei tram e l'eco dei passi. Nel contempo, diverse linee di movimento si intersecano, sovrapponendosi ed illuminando l'immagine. In ultima analisi, non si tratta della pellicola e della sua membrana sensibile alla luce, ma di un algoritmo programmato da un computer che calcola le immagini fotogramma per fotogramma e rende visibili i cambiamenti. Per analogia, i video costituiscono testimonianze del rapido cambiamento che si sta verificando nel settore dell'immagine digitalizzata. Tecnica e contenuti non possono essere separati. La griglia dei pixel ha trovato un altro livello di significato nelle memorabili immagini in movimento di Rainio; essa rende visibile la matrice del nostro tempo.
Leevi Haapala (Curatore e Ricercatore, Kiasma, Museo di Arte Contemporanea, Helsinki)

Jan Kuděj

Nato nel 1978 a Praga, dove vive e lavora.
1997-1999 Etnologia alle Facoltà di Filosogia e di Arte presso la Charles University di Praga
Ha studiato 1999-2005 Architettura e Design all'Accademia d'Arte a Pragua
2002-2003 Università d'Arte a Berlino.

Nella sua opera egli esplora in modo sistematico il tema del tempo. « Non è possibile documentare in modo assoluto la continuità del tempo », egli afferma. L'artista ha realizzato una serie di « Proiezioni » (Projections) che combinano due tecniche: quella dell'immagine fotografica fissa e quella delle immagini video in movimento. Tutte affrontano il tema della capacità della videocamera di registrare 25 immagini al secondo. Si tratta di un vincolo che necessariamente porta alla frammentazione del movimento e del tempo, sebbene l'occhio umano li percepisca come continui.

Nella sua proiezione di scale mobili, egli segue il movimento ciclico delle macchine. Con una videocamera fissata in un punto ha registrato un intero ciclo. In una proiezione loop pertanto la scala mobile sembra non fermarsi mai.

Con intento opposto, l'artista ha animato l'immagine di un albero, per cui i movimenti della sua chioma vengono interrotti in sequenza dall'atto di registrazione stesso. La proiezione relativa al movimento delle onde che si infrangono sulla costa, selezionata per la presente mostra, deriva dallo stesso principio adottato nel caso delle scale mobili: la percezione della continuità del tempo che passa. « Tuttavia, da un certo punto di vista, tutte le proiezioni sono chiuse, e fissano un'azione sotto forma di un immagine fissa. Il tempo è una mera illusione ». « Per quanto mi riguarda, l'approccio che adotto consiste nella registrazione continua tramite una videocamera, e in un'intenzionale registrazione interrotta di riprese. Riconosciamo due percezioni alla volta – un tempo basato sull'istante, ed un tempo basato sulla durata. Tale sensazione ci aiuta a sperimentare le contraddizioni simultanee della realtà nel momento in cui questa si dispiega. Il concetto che ciascuno di noi ha di se stesso (oppure del mondo) non è continuo. Cambia carattere ogni volta che viene avviato un nuovo processo mentale. Tale processo in sé costituisce un'interruzione che si ripete costantemente. Percepiamo il tempo come qualcosa che si dispiega in instanti ». (dalla tesi di laurea di Kuděj, 2005).

Ange Leccia

Nato nel 1952 a Minervu, in Corsica/F, vive e lavora a Parigi
Ha studiato Cinema e Filosogia alla Sorbonna di Parigi
www.galeriealminerech.com

La video installazione Orage è un opera metafisica e contemplativa che ci invita ad un viaggio introspettivo, ed è fortemente caratteristica della potenza onirica di tutta l'opera di Ange Leccia. Fin da bambino l'artista è rimasto affascinato dal cinema e dalle immagini in movimento, e tutta la sua opera è caratterizzata dalla poetica dell'energia e nutrita da un'indagine nell'immagine e nel film; ciò lo ha portato il più vicino possibile all'inesprimibile, ma anche ad imprimere una forte densità emotiva ai suoi pezzi.

Ambientato in uno spazio buio, questo dittico sotto forma di un loop su due schermi perpendicolari ci getta in un torbido cielo notturno nel quale cadono fulmini in un tempo apparentemente sospeso. Filmato con un'inquadratura fissa, questo flusso di energia violenta riempie sia l'immagine sia la colonna sonora, collocandoci faccia a faccia con la presenza palpabile e onnipotente degli elementi, e simboleggiando il fatto che la Natura ci supera sempre, malgrado i nostri tentativi di soggiogarla. Situato a metà tra la stasi visiva ed il trascorrere del tempo, il suo ritmo ripetitivo e la sua permanenza apparente scivolano verso la pura astrazione, pur aprendo la strada al trascendentale ed al sublime. Il ricorso alla ripetizione ed al loop che caratterizza le immagini di Ange Leccia si porta dietro un sentimento di rigenerazione permanente che deve essere interpretato, secondo il critico d'arte Pascal Beasse « rispetto ad una dimensione organica dell'immagine, che ci invita in un presente eterno ». Questa dilatazione del tempo, associata ad un'immersione sensoriale resa possibile dal modo in cui le immagini vengono presentate, ci mette nelle condizioni di poter fare appello alle forze più nascoste della nostra immaginazione.

Oliver Möst

Nato a Füssen, Allgäu/GER, nel 1968, vive e lavora a Berlino
Fotografo freelance e video artista. Il suo primo progetto video è stato realizzato nel 1999 in collaborazione con un coreografo
www.olivermoest.de

« Le immagini caratterizzate da una messa a fuoco nitida hanno superato l'assenza di messa a fuoco. Ignorano ciò che può essere vissuto nell'assenza di messa a fuoco e di definizione. »[3]

L'opera video di Oliver Möst's, prodotta nel 2007, costituisce il seguito dei suoi lavori fotografici. A prima vista è caratterizzata da un'evidente mancanza di definizione, che rappresenta il principio estetico guida dell'artista sia nelle sue fotografie, sia nei suoi video. Il principio della nitidezza esplicita il nucleo della consapevolezza percettiva dell'artista.

Il personale processo percettivo di Oliver Möst costituisce la chiave di volta di tutta la sua opera. È affetto da deficit visivo, e gli occhiali che utilizza devono compensare 2.0 diottrie nell'occhio sinistro e 6.0 nel destro. La sua opera fotografica e cinematografica ci consente di sperimentare lo sguardo soggettivo del fotografo secondo la modalità « ecco-ciò-che-ha-visto-e-percepito-lì-in-questo-modo », di condividere la sua percezione idiosincratica ed il modo in cui egli vive lo spazio circostante [nel mezzo (between), nascondino (hide & seek), occhi castani (brown eyes)].

Un'altra tematica importante dei video di Möst è costituita dalla riflessione sulla fotografia e sulle sue qualità immanenti ai media tramite un raffronto tra film e fotografia. L'idea di combinare due tecniche fotografiche ha portato l'artista ad utilizzare uno stenoscopio (privo di lente), una camera oscura, la forma base della macchina fotografica. Möst ha unito tale tecnica alla tecnologia video digitale filmando e registrando con una videocamera l'immagine proiettata sulla lastra dello stenoscopio. In tale confronto tra la « vecchia » tecnologia dello stenoscopio da un lato e la tecnologia video digitale moderna dall'altro, l'artista crea ciò che definisce una serie di « pinhole videos », video stenoscopici (in inglese lo stenoscopio è denominato pinhole camera). Tali opere riflettono lo sviluppo tecnico che ha caratterizzato la fotografia, dal semplice stenoscopio alla videocamera digitale, altamente sofisticata sotto il profilo tecnico, e quindi anche le qualità implicite nel medium fotografico con riferimento al modo in cui sono state ulteriormente sviluppate nel corso degli anni.

3 BASTIAN BRETTHAUER, „SO EINE WELT OHNE ECKEN UND KANTEN" IN K4 GALERIE, EDS., OLIVER MÖST, CLACKASTIGMAT 6.0 / K4 GALERIE (BERLIN, DORN, 2005).

Tim Parchikov

Tim Parchikov (nato nel 1983 a Mosca) si laurea nel dipartimento di regia dell'Istituto russo di Cinematografia (2006). Vincitore del premio annuale per il miglior documentario su Mosca con « Silver Camera » (2005). Tra le varie personali a Mosca, ha partecipato recentemente ad un progetto di gruppo di Fotografia e Video contemporanei in Russia al Festival Internazionale di 'Europalia in Belgio (2005), e al Festival Internazionale di Fotografia di Pingyao (2008). Vive e lavora a Mosca.

Tim Parchikov, poeta e fotografo, è un ventenne moscovita. Per la sua generazione il mondo è diventato davvero troppo piccolo, ed in termini geografici a volte addirittura troppo visibile ed accessibile. Fortunatamente, la percezione della vita di Tim Parchikov è autenticamente poetica, ed egli ricostruisce per lo spettatore il suo modello di mondo, un modello carico di tale energia e di una vitale sensazione di giovinezza da consentirci di dimenticare i problemi che derivano dalla prevedibilità e dall'ovvietà. La sua opera è ricca di ozono. Il sentimento di dolore universale, che spesso caratterizza i giovani, ed una profonda conoscenza della fotografia russa e mondiale non soffocano in alcun modo l'elettrica sensazione di vitalità che la sua opera emana.

L'individualità creativa del giovane artista e l'ampiezza della sua personalità indicano in modo chiaro un talento vero, maturo ed indipendente in riferimento a varie tipologie di arte classica. Un sottile senso del colore, un forte intuito nei confronti della sezione aurea ed un audace pensiero metaforico consentono a Tim Parchikov di esprimersi in modo ardito ed originale. È una nuova voce a cui vale la pena di dare ascolto.

Il video Per mare (Gone to Sea) è una miniatura dedicata alla possibilità di scomparire senza nessun motivo in particolare in mare, ovvero, da nessuna parte. Gone to Sea riporta alla mente « L'Avventura » di Michelangelo Antonioni, in cui l'eroina improvvisamente scompare senza ragione apparente. Ciò che ci interessa in particolare, tuttavia, non è solo il problema della scomparsa, ma se passerà o meno inosservata...

Matteo Peterlini

Nato nel 1970 a Rovereto, vive e lavora a Trento, 1970. Diplomato in Informatica, frequenta nel 1992 il corso di « Comunicazione grafica e pubblicitaria » organizzato dalla provincia di Bolzano.
Ha iniziato ad esporre le sue opere nel 1997 e da allora ha esposto a Trento, Venezia, Torino, Istanbul Contemporary Art museum. Ed inoltre, File 2007, San Paolo, Brasile; Bellavita, New Chinatown Barbershop Gallery, Los Angeles, USA; www.matteopeterlini.it

Usare i pixel come unità di misura: nel lavoro fotografico di Matteo Peterlini rappresenta un vero elemento concettuale, una scelta programmatica.

Così scomposte e ricomposte, le immagini che appartengono alle sue serie fotografiche risultano da un processo di calcolo che tende all'infinito, dove le modalità di combinazione dei frammenti sono affidate al caso, amministrato da una funzione algebrica.

Nella messa a punto di software specifici, Peterlini azzarda il peccato originale e punta la lente di ingrandimento sui meccanismi stessi della percezione. Come si generano le immagini nella nostra mente? Gli schemi, scelti per imitazione, apprendimento e condivisione, che utilizziamo abitualmente per la nostra comprensione del mondo, di fronte al flusso associativo generato dal processo elettronico perdono la loro efficacia. Da qui, non risulti contradditorio che ci si trovi all'interno dei generi pittorici tradizionali: il ritratto, il nudo, il paesaggio. Infatti, grazie alla frontalità dei volti (quella richiesta dallo standard della fototessera in Meyouother), le silhouette dei corpi (quelle delineate dalle sei pose commissionate alle modelle in V6), la fissità di paesaggi al limite dell'astratto (Backscapes), è possibile prendere atto di quella tendenza inconsapevole al riconoscimento del « già noto » (la Gestalt, lo stereotipo) che ci permette di solito di fronteggiare la diversità dei fenomeni.

E inoltre, è proprio nella beffa di una tecnica solo apparentemente « artigianale », con cui Peterlini dà vita alle sue serie fotografiche, che si rivela la natura analitica del suo lavoro. Se osservate da vicino, infatti, le immagini (in realtà frame di un flusso in continuo divenire) funzionano come collage, ma al contrario: dove il processo di riconoscimento dell'insieme è sospeso in una coesistenza virtuale di tutte le combinazioni possibili. (Cristina Natalicchio)

Peter Puklus & Melinda Sipos

Peter Puklus (vedi Sipos)
Nato nel 1980 a Koloszvár/H, vive e lavora a Budapest. Laureato in Fotografia nel 2005 all'Università di Arte Moholy-Nagy, a Budapest, in Ungheria.
http://photolumen.hu/puklus
www.deuxprojects.blogspot.com

Melinda Sipos
Nata nel 1979 a Budapest, in Ungheria dove vive e lavora. Laureata in Design del Vetro nel 2005 all'Università di Arte Moholy-Nagy, a Budapest, in Ungheria.
http://siposmelinda.blogspot.com
www.deuxprojects.blogspot.com

Peter Puklus & Melinda Sipos entrambi lavorano individualmente; ciascuno ha il proprio e personale approccio artistico. Tuttavia, hanno realizzato insieme i due progetti Luci importate (Imported Lights) e Giardino (Garden), in un gruppo denominato DEUX. I titoli delle opere non hanno un significato ulteriore se non quello che riguarda i dati grezzi.

DEUX_00 Imported Lights è ciò che il gruppo definisce come il proprio « progetto zero ». L'idea è piuttosto concettuale: catturare il riflesso della luce che entra da una finestra e proiettarlo in una stanza cieca. Dal punto di vista di « Mutations II » ciò che si ottiene è un immagine fissa proiettata come un video.

Una logica simile è stata applicata a DEUX_01 Garden, il primo progetto comune avviato da Peter Puklus e Melinda Sipos, come chiaramente indicato dal titolo. Si tratta della registrazione dettagliata di un giardino nell'arco di un lungo periodo. Ogni giorno è stata scattata una fotografia, dalla stessa finestra, e per la durata di un anno. Il risultato è un portfolio di piccoli cambiamenti intervenuti nello spazio; sedie spostate, il susseguirsi delle stagioni... La sequenza di immagini crea l'impressione che i cambiamenti si verifichino durante il tempo della proiezione stessa.

Entrambe le opere si basano su idee semplici ma ben realizzate. Gli aspetti tecnici, come la scelta dei mezzi, fotografia e video, e la conversione di uno nell'altro, sono di importanza relativamente secondaria, e sono determinati dalla loro concezione artistica; diversamente da altri autori presentati in questa selezione, le cui creazioni sono state ispirate da opportunità tecniche. Per Pukus e Sipos, l'approccio della transizione dalla fotografia al video si è imposto come una soluzione logica per realizzare il loro intento artistico.

Jutta Strohmaier

Nata a Tulln/A nel 1966, vive a Vienna
Pittura, specializzazione in fotografia e new media con Eva Schlegel, Academy of Fine Arts, Vienna, 1996-99
www.jutta-strohmaier.net

Come si correlano immagini e realtà? Quale tipo di realtà possono creare le immagini? Sono queste le domande alle quali i video, le fotografie e le installazioni di Jutta Strohmaier cercano di dare risposta.

Passeggero (Passenger) (2004) comprime immagini di un interno vuoto, con due grandi finestre riprese minuto per minuto nell'arco di giorni, in un video di durata inferiore ai 15 minuti. Mentre nell'arco della giornata le finestre rendono la stanza talmente luminosa che risulta difficile se non impossibile vedere alcunché al di fuori di esse, man mano che cala la sera emergono gradualmente l'esterno e la facciata dell'edificio antistante. L'opera gioca con la percezione di una stanza nella sua graduale evoluzione, esaminando il concetto di spazio rispetto a categorie quali inclusione/esclusione, interno/estraneo, apertura/chiusura (cfr. anche il commento di Sarah Kolb sulla mostra « Jutta Strohmaier. diese Welt und andere, » Galerie Hohenlohe, Vienna, 2004).

Strohmaier torna al principio degli scatti fotografici consecutivi presentato sotto forma di video animato in opere quali Im Dickicht (2005) e Storie mute (Silent Stories) (2006). Nel primo, rilascia l'otturatore ad ogni passo attraverso il sottobosco di una riserva naturale. Strohmaier edita i « vuoti » tra i singoli fotogrammi utilizzando Photoshop; il groviglio di rami inizialmente sembra essere « corroso » prima di ricrescere con densità ancora maggiore in una sequenza successiva, per poi dissolversi in un cielo azzurro.

Le fotografie satellitari assemblate per realizzare il loop Viaggio (Journey) (2005) presentano una visione della terra dallo spazio – un punto di vista che tutti conosciamo, grazie alla televisione e ad Internet, ma che pochi sono stati in grado di adottare direttamente. Strohmaier scava nel proprio archivio di immagini satellitari che ha raccolto nel corso degli anni. Tuttavia, invece di presentare una sequenza lineare delle città e dei paesaggi naturali, queste immagini si perforano e si penetrano reciprocamente, vengono abrase strato dopo strato, attraverso il pianeta terra, per poi tornare indietro.

Wolfgang Thaler

Nato a Salisburgo/A, 1969, vive a Vienna.
Istituto Fotografico di Stato bavarese, Monaco (oggi: Università delle Scienze Applicate di Monaco), 1989-91
www.wolfgangthaler.at

L'opera di Wolfgang Thaler comprende fotografia architettonica (la serie sulla stazione ferroviaria viennese Südbahnhof, o quella sulle rotatorie) e fotografia documentaria (sulla catena di caffetterie tradizionali viennesi Aida, ecc.) manifestando il suo interesse – a volte altamente analitico – nello spazio.

La serie Questione di selezione (Matter of Selection) (2007) ci consente di visitare l'appartamento di un collezionista. Utilizzando materiale di repertorio in bianco e nero ad alta risoluzione, Thaler prima fotografa i mobili (un cassettone, una libreria), quindi, come un detective, effettua una scansione di ogni singolo dettaglio della relativa fotografia tramite uno schermo di computer. Ciò produce una trasmutazione ad una serie di livelli; la cattura fotografica di un singolo momento viene espansa in un piano sequenza infinito; la realtà viene dislocata nel momento in cui la fotografia di un oggetto viene filmata in luogo dell'oggetto stesso; e di tale fotografia vediamo soltanto dei dettagli, e mai l'immagine completa. Benvenuti a Mep'Yuk (Welcome to Mep'Yuk)- così Thaler accoglie i visitatori nella sua città abbandonata immaginaria Mep'Yuk. Die Zentrale (1999), che consiste esclusivamente in spazi interni. L'artista scatta fotografie di comuni atri di edifici aziendali, di lobby, spazi uffici e sale d'attesa in varie città in tutto il mondo; nonostante la diversità nel retroterra culturale e nelle ambientazioni, tali luoghi hanno un elemento in comune: sono spazi (semi) pubblici la cui principale funzione è amministrativa, strutturale o organizzativa. L'artista ha messo in serie le varie fotografie ed effettuato una scansione, passo dopo passo, in lenti piani sequenza orizzontali. Ancora una volta Thaler nega allo spettatore una prospettiva totalizzante, offrendo solo dettagli degli interni. Ben presto emerge l'impressione che stiamo osservando tali siti attraverso telecamere di sorveglianza, e con essa la domanda: che cosa c'è da osservare se nessun essere umano presidia questo « centro di comando »?

Mutácie II / o obraze v napätí

Pre Európsky mesiac fotografie, ktorého história siaha do roku 2004 a ktorý v súčasnosti združujuje festivaly v Paríži, Berlíne, Bratislave, Luxemburgu, Moskve, Ríme a Viedni, je nevyhnutné, aby sa na zásadné zmeny tohto sveta, predovšetkým v oblasti súčasného obrazu, pozeralo kolektívnym pohľadom. Toto bol zámer výstavy v roku 2006, nazvanej Mutácie I, ktorá sledovala technickú a umeleckú zmenu v oblasti fotografie.

Nasledujúca výstava Mutácie II aplikuje túto myšlienkovú líniu na predmet videa. Tentoraz skúma plodné vzťahy, ktoré vznikli medzi statickými a pohyblivými obrazmi. Odhaľuje tak, kde sa súčasné umenie v Európe nachádza dnes.

V prostredí, kde sú všetky komunikačné prostriedky a umelecké médiá ovplyvnené globalizáciou a digitalizáciou, vstupujeme do obdobia „post-média", pre ktoré je typický záujem o hybridnú techniku. Umelci nachádzajú rôzne kombinácie videa s množstvom iných médií[1] – napríklad fotografiou, zvukom, digitálnym videom, filmom, DVD, počítačom, CD-Romom, grafikou a animáciou.

Každá umelecká forma teraz viac ako kedykoľvek predtým reprezentuje samú seba v rámci „hraníc vlastných materiálnych možností (...), zároveň však tieto hranice posúva, aby vyplnila celé spektrum spojení, ktoré vytvára s inými umeleckými formami."[2]

Fotografia opúšťa svoju pozíciu média založeného na konzervovaní zaznamenávanej skutočnosti a z videoumenia si prepožičiava jednu z jeho základných vlastnosti, a to časovú dimenziu. Tak sa fotografia, analógová aj digitálna, emancipuje prostredníctvom rozličných umeleckých manipulácií a vytvárania technických hybridov.

Organizátori „Mutations II" sa preto rozhodli vystaviť diela tých európskych umelcov, ktorí spoločne zdieľajú záujem o experimentovanie s novými formami výrazu. Tak ako Nancy Spector vo svojej eseji „Art Photography after Photography" (Umelecká fotografia po fotografii)[3] aj oni úspešne spochybňujú špecifické kritériá, ktoré kedysi pomáhali rozlišovať fotografa od umelca pracujúceho s fotografiou.

Stále viac fotografov pracuje s videom, čím sa menia špecifické kritériá, ktoré charakterizujú oba postupy. Okrem rôznorodosti estetických prístupov a vizuálnych techník nám umelci výstavy Mutácie II ponúkajú prienik mimo územných vymedzení a akademických definícií, ktoré skôr stavajú ohradu okolo jednotlivých oblastí umenia. Títo umelci nás vedú k skúmaniu deliacich hraníc. Inými slovami, Mutácie II nás inšpirujú, aby sme objavovali nové teritóriá statických a pohyblivých obrazov skúmaním napätí, ktoré ich podnecujú. Sem patrí napätie z ontologického hľadiska, napätie medzi okamihom a trvaním. Napätie z estetického hľadiska vzniká prelínaním tradičného fotografického obrazu a pohybujúceho sa obrazu. Napätie z dialektického hľadiska vzniká medzi obmedzeným množstvom možnosti vystavenia fotografie a nekonečnosťou kombinácií procesu vnímania, prostredníctvom ktorých nadobúdajú elektronické obrazy jasnú podobu[4], predovšetkým v prípade videoinštalácie.

Ako tvrdia Gilles Deleuze a Felix Guattari, neexistuje žiadne územie bez vektora smerujúceho von z tohto územia (...), bez úsilia o premiestnie sa niekde inde."[5] Ak túto filozofickú otázku vymedzíme na oblasť umenia, môžeme skonštatovať, že dynamika vlastná akémukoľvek umeleckému trendu je odstredivou silou, ktorá nás vynáša smerom od bežných konvencií a noriem, je vektorom

1 RUSH (MICHAEL). 2007. L'ART VIDÉO. LONDÝN. THAMES & HUDSON.
2 BELLOUR (RAYMOND). 1999. L'ENTRE-IMAGES 2. P.O.L. PARÍŽ.
3 MOVING PICTURES, CONTEMPORARY PHOTOGRAPHY AND VIDEO FROM THE GUGGENHEIM MUSEUM COLLECTIONS. 2003. NEW YORK. GUGGENHEIM MUSEUM PUBLICATIONS.
4 VAILLANT (ALEXIS), PARFAIT (FRANÇOISE), JANKOVIC (NIKOLA). 2001. LES NOUVELLES IMAGES. DIEL 1. CHRONIQUES DE L'AFAA. PARÍŽ.
5 DELEUZE (GILLES). 2004. L'ABÉCÉDAIRE DE GILLES DELEUZE. PARÍŽ. MONTPARNASSE. DVD.

opustenia územia, ktorého existencia je predurčená inovatívnosťou pohľadu na svet.

Pohľad Petra Aerschmanna, ktorý dodáva nádych zvláštnosti drobným scénkam v jeho prácach, ilustruje podstatu celého jeho diela: hľadanie prostriedkov fotografovania daného priestoru bez straty časovej hĺbky, prostriedkov vytvorenia fotografie, ktorá nie je záznamom okamihu a ktorá na miesto znehybnenia pohyb pridáva. Peter Aerschmann tak do reprezentácie priestoru vnáša čas. Vnáša princíp pevnej uzavretosti obrazu do princípu pohybu tým, že ho konzervuje v jednote počas toho, ako sa realizuje. Týmto spôsobom vytvára Aerschmann „koktanie" v jazyku videa. Jeho ľudské postavy pôsobia ako väzni opakovaných pohybov v nekonečnej slučke.

Sémantická a štylistická bohatosť obsiahnutá v opakovaní inšpirovala aj Gasta Bouscheta a Nadine Hilbertovú pri diele Dream Sequence (Snová sekvencia), videu z roku 2005. Umelci sa vrátili na miesto vzniku filmu Philippa Kauffmana Invasion of the Bodysnatchers (Invázia zlodejov tiel) z roku 1978, zaktualizovali a rekontextualizovali jeho predstavu paranoje spodobenej prostredníctvom obsesívneho opakovania obrazov. Zámerne porušili konvenčnú formu lineárneho príbehu. Táto poetická a politická snová sekvencia spočíva na sieti vzťahov medzi fragmentami fotografií, videí, zvukov a textov, ktoré útočia na našu schopnosť objektivity a maximálne mobilizujú naše vnímanie.

Ak sa aj Christoph Brech pohráva s našimi schopnosťami vnímania, ide mu predovšetkým o to, aby zaujal našu pozornosť. Objekty, postavy a krajiny, ktoré sníma, zdanlivo nehybné, v skutočnosti však v neustálom pohybe, vedú naše oko od jednej roviny interpretácie k druhej. Oko váha medzi túžbou dešifrovať obraz a túžbou rozjímať nad podobou videa krajne jednoduchého charakteru. Break (Prielom), hypnotická práca zosnímaná ako jedna neprerušená sekvencia bez akýchkoľvek kamerových efektov, je výborným príkladom tejto formálnej čistoty. Pochopíme, že základ pohybu je v prechodnosti, a akýmsi vnútorným vnemom cítime tektonickú silu času. Časový rozmer sa tu spája s tým, čo je možné vidieť: po nekonečnej mase zamrznutej rieky sa pomaly kĺžu oblaky vodnej pary, ktoré uvádza do pohybu temer nepostrehnuteľný posun ľadu. Ľadoborec, ktorý prechádza týmto nehostinným prostredím, až kým nezmizne, zachováva za sebou len brázdu, ktorú narušuje a vzápätí pohlcuje ľad. Tým nám ponúka alegóriu inšpirovanú osudom človeka.

Big Bang Oriho Gershta je politickou metaforou ľudstva hodeného do chaosu vojny. Konflikt a násilie, ktoré sa v ňom prejavuje, vedú k bodu zlomu, a ten je dôvodom, prečo Gersht realizuje svoje estetické a umelecké skúmanie premeny s takou intenzitou. Proces premeny vyjadruje statický obraz meniaci sa na obraz v pohybe. Na prvý pohľad pripomína Big Bang barokové zátišie. Avšak zvuk, ktorým Ori Gersht zasahuje do výjavu, vnáša do nehybného obrazu časový rozmer a vdychuje mu dramatické napätie, ktoré vrcholí výbuchom kompozície kvetov v spomalenom pohybe. Je to záznam, ktorý chce zobraziť smerovanie objektu k svojmu rozkladu. Táto premena od figuratívneho k čistej abstrakcii vyúsťuje do optickej nehybnosti. Oživuje obrazy, ktoré zanechali sirény a výbuchy izraelsko-palestínskeho konfliktu v pamäti umelca ako dieťaťa. Umelecký postup, ktorý sa sústreďuje na skúmanie vzťahov medzi fotografiou, maľbou a videom, spočíva doslova aj obrazne v premene formy až k jej obetovaniu.

Dielo mladého fínskeho umelca Tuoma Rainia sa síce zaoberá časom a mutáciou tak, ako práce Oriho Gershta, ale jeho prístup je úplne iný. Východiskom mu nie je estetická stránka obrazu, ale podstata pohybu. Prostredníctvom vlastného počítačového programu, ktorý upravuje obraz, nám snímky jednoduchým aparátom sprostredkúvajú pohľady z mestského prostredia, kde je aktivita obyvateľov prítomná len vo forme priezračných stôp, ktoré zanechali, keď tadiaľto prechádzali. Takýto prístup je politický a zároveň konceptuálny. Politický v tom, že sa zaoberá verejným priestranstvom kontrolovaným kamerami. Konceptuálny v tom, že zachytáva napätie medzi dvoma stavmi, trvalosťou prítomnosti a neprítomnosťou.

Jutta Strohmaierová tiež využíva možnosti digitálnej technológie, a to buď na to, aby nechala obraz vyrastať zo seba samého, alebo aby ho prestavala prostredníctvom svetla, prúdu kvapiek pixelov alebo prúdov elektronov, ktoré ho neustále modifikujú. V dielach Journey (Cestovanie) a Im Dickicht (V húštine) spočíva dojem pohybu v tom, že obraz sa vlastne nikdy nejaví ako dokončený. Akoby bol v neustálom procese premeny medzi tým, čo predchádzalo, a tým, čo nasleduje. Potom prítomnosť nikdy neposkytuje časovú jednotu, ale roztrieštenosť časových foriem, ktoré rozkladajú obraz. V práci Passenger (Prechod) vytvárajú zábery z prázdnej miestnosti, odfotografované každú minútu počas viacerých dní, charakter stlačenosti času. Tým vzniká odstup od denného života pozorovaného prostredníctvom zrýchleného rytmu striedania dňa a noci. Vrstvením, rozostrovaním a prelínaním fotografií v diele Silent Stories (Tiché príbehy) sa nám otvára možnosť fiktívnej reinterpretácie reality. Hoci Jutta Strohmaierová pracuje s fotografiou ako so surovým materiálom, z ktorého vytvára kompozície svojích scenárov, vnímanie pohybu, proces transformácie a dekonštrukcie času tu predstavujú ústredné miesto. Obraz tak zároveň môže poskytnúť množstvo významov, ktoré sú všetky v ňom obsiahnuté.

Inštalácia Windows (Okná) Oľgy Černyševovej vychádza predovšetkým z formálneho výskumu priestoru obrazu. Umelkyňa, fascinovaná stopami komunizmu, pozoruje súčasný každodenný život Rusov a rekonštruuje ho v podobe inštalácie, kde nič nie je ponechané náhode. Každé okno budovy, snímané v noci kamerou držanou v ruke, sa stáva rámom scény, kde sa obyvatelia zjavujú a miznú ako postavy v divadle. Strácajú sa v intimite kulís pozadia svojho bytu. Divadelný charakter týchto okamihov života zdôrazňuje forma premietania na viacerých obrazovkách. Obraz tak získava dominantné postavenie v priestore projekcie a intímnu nekonečného množstva podôb (mise en abîme), ktorá nabáda k dialógu medzi dielom a divákom.

Všetkých týchto európskych umelcov spája zámer vystaviť fotografiu alebo/a video rôznym formám narušenia. Každý to realizuje podľa svojich potrieb. Takto skúmajú línie úniku, ktoré sa formujú na hraniciach teritórií týchto médií a stanovujú nový princíp obrazu a vnímania. Zároveň posúvajú výjadrovacie prostriedky fotografie a videa až na hranice ich možností. Tie podľa Deleuza formujú podmienky pre vznik originality a štýlu.

Tieto nové experimenty, ktoré majú posúvať fotografiu a video za ich bežné hranice, nám ponújakú jedinečnú možnosť pozrieť sa na svet novým pohľadom a inšpirujú nás zmeniť náš každodenný život „v súlade s umením", jako to povedal Merleau-Ponty[6].

Jean-Luc Soret

6 MERLEAU-PONTY (MAURICE). 1960. L'ŒIL ET L'ESPRIT. PARÍŽ. FOLIO. ESSAIS.

Tvorba v medzipriestore

Fotografia a video sú si v mnohom také blízke, ako sú si zároveň odpočiatku vzdialené svojim vzťahom k času. Technický rozvoj inšpiruje umelcov, aby obe médiá navzájom zbližovali: dnes je možné filmovať fotoaparátom a fotografovať videokamerou. Naviac obe techniky prechádzajú digitalizáciou vrátane emulzných procesov. Vďaka softvéru je veľmi jednoduché zastaviť bežiaci obraz a funkciu slideshow možno spustiť jediným kliknutím. Inými slovami, je možné prerušiť pohyb alebo spustiť časové plynutie: dva technicky nenáročné úkony, ktoré však vedú k výrazne rozdielnym výsledkom. Samotná hranica medzi oboma médiami však nie je natoľko podstatná (videoumenie vždy existovalo v blízkosti iného druhu umenia) ako diela, ktoré z tejto priepustnosti vznikajú. Výstava Mutácie II skúma práve tento medzipriestor. Všetci vybraní autori využívajú video, aby zachytili napätie, ktoré ho spája s fotografickým obrazom a jeho komponentmi: rovnaké vymedzenie obrazu, plynutie času a zvlášť faktor plynutia momentu. Niektorí z týchto umelcov skúmajú médium videa popri svojej fotografickej tvorbe, pričom neustále prechádzajú od jedného k druhému. Výsledkom je osobitý vzťah k obrazu, ktorý nás vďaka svojej nestálosti a svojmu pôvodu v mutácii láka, aby sme sa ho snažili uchopiť.

Práca s dočasnou hĺbkou

Vo svojej eseji The Reflecting Pool de Bill Viola (Bazén zrkadliaci obraz od Billa Violu) analyzuje Jean-Paul Fargier Violovu videopásku a procesy vrstvenia materiálu ako umelcov spôsob, ktorým preniká do umenia videa, pretože „obraz rozdelený na časti možno vnímať ako podstatu videa"[1]. Z tohto pohľadu obrazy, ktoré vznikli vrstvením a obsahujú prvky dočasnosti a tiež viaceré paralelné príbehy, zásadne charakterizujú videoumenie. V každom prípade práve toto nachádzame v mnohých ďalších prácach, ktoré sú úzko späté s fotografickým obrazom a využívajú prvok zastavenia času. Tak ako B. Viola vo svojej slávnej videopáske,

1 THE REFLECTING POOL DE BILL VIOLA, JEAN-PAUL FARGIER, VYD. YELLOW NOW CÔTÉ FILMS 2, 2005, S. 14.

aj tieto diela pracujú s princípom prerušovania, takže v nás vyvolávajú neistotu pri vnímaní pokoja a pohybu. Napríklad David Claerbout vytvára diela prenášaním upravených fotografií do sféry videa tak, že vstupuje do jeho povahy časovej hustoty, aby objavil podobu obrazu fotografie v prítomnosti. Vo videu Sans titre (Carl et Julia), [(Bez názvu (Carl a Julia)], 2000 vidíme najprv čierno-bielu fotografiu muža a jeho dcéry pri raňajkách. Keď sa dostaneme do priestoru deja, dievča otočí pohľad k nám, čím sa prostredníctvom videa meníme na statický element my a oživí sa v prítomnosti to, čo znehybnelo v minulosti. V jednej z Claerboutovych posledných prác Dancing couple (after: Couple at square dance, McIntosh County, Oklahoma, 1939 or 1940) (Tancujúci pár (podľa: Pár tancujúci štvorylku, okres McIntosh, Oklahoma, 1939 alebo 1940), 2008 je autorov zásah ešte radikálnejší: mladý pár niekto fotografoval na tanečnom parkete. Zábleskom ich prekvapil, takže pár zastal, a tým vystúpil z daného momentu. Claerbout tento obraz použil a premietol ho, pričom prepojil okamih záblesku so svetlom premietačky. Dočasnosť aktu premietania tak zdôrazňuje nevyhnutnosť jeho existencie v prítomnosti, čím zároveň stojí v protiklade s nehybnosťou fotografického procesu počas premietania. Umelá povaha konštrukcie je priznaná a takéto prenesenie pohybujúcej sa dočasnosti do jadra statického obrazu vyvoláva pocit závrate a znepokojenia. „Medzipriestor" je podobný prázdnote v tom zmysle, že vzniká v nejasných miestach starostlivo zostavených inštalácií a v prevažne tichom prostredí, kde sa priestorový zvuk používa len zriedka.

V súčasnosti sa veľmi často používa animácia, ktorá predovšetkým nadväzuje na kresbu. Umožňuje dosiahnuť oveľa radikálnejší charakter plynutia v čase a kombinovať rozličné formy obrazu, ako je to v znepokojujúcej animácii Hansa op de Beecka, ktorá sa skladá z kresieb a fotografií. Takto zobrazené priestory pôsobia zvláštne, pretože stoja veľmi blízko skutočnosti, ale nikdy sa s ňou nedajú stotožniť. Aj Jutta Strohmaierová, mladá rakúska fotografka, vytvára nehybné zábery, ktoré sa pomaly menia v animácii. Tak ako pri Claerboutovi aj tu sme neustále konfrontovaní so stavom nejasnosti obrazu, jeho povahy a vzťahu k času. Vrstvenie fotografií vyvoláva dojem pohybu, ktorý ale nie je dostatočne výrazný, aby narušil stabilitu obsiahnutú v zábere. Významnú úlohu hrá svetlo, tým že definuje chod času vo fotografovanom priestore, kde sa väčšinou veľa neudeje. V diele Passenger (Premena, 10', 2004) ide o premenu svetelnej atmosféry v statickom zábere okna zvnútra prázdnej miestnosti. Prechádzame od jednej farebnosti k druhej. V trhanej metamorfóze sa biela mení na modrú, ružovú a potom na žltú. Strohmaierovej videá sa nesnažia vyvolať ilúziu kontinuity. Výraznými prostriedkami, ako je vzdialenosť a vymedzenie obrazu, nás vedú do medzipriestorov (prázdne miestnosti, hustý podrast, oblasti mestských komunikácií) videných očami diváka, ktorý je síce pozorný, ale stojí mimo diania. Obraz samotný podlieha mnohým umeleckým postupom, ako sú viacnásobná tlač, zvýraznenie obrysov a modifikácia farieb, čím vystupuje do popredia vymyslená, vykonštruovaná dimenzia pohľadu na svet.

Rozhranie medzi fotografiou a videom nám teda ponúka priestor na meditáciu o našich prežitkoch vnímania. Švajčiarsky umelec Peter Aershmann tiež skúma hĺbku času tým, že rozkladá náš vzťah k časopriestoru. Jeho obrazy sú výsledkom spájania rôznych záberov, v ktorých sú jednotlivé prvky priradené k sebe tak, že neumožňujú jednotný pohľad na celok. Každý aktér a každý aspekt scenérie je samozrejme súčasťou celkovej kompozície, ale nezjednocuje ich navzájom žiadna spoločná atmosféra. Tak ako v Uccellovych maľbách, aj tu sú proporcie zachované a vizuálna skladba navzájom súvisí, avšak výsledný dojem vyjadruje jednu veľkú osamotenosť. Kamera sa doslova kĺže popred tieto zoskupenia a neustále nachádza osamelé postavy, ktoré uviazli v opakovanom pohybe a v prostredí bez jednoty. V Aerschamnnovych videách je časopriestor zásadne neusporiadaný, ale náš pohľad napriek tomu pomaly nasleduje kameru. Medzi prísnou rovnováhou architektonických prvkov a pohybom postáv v slučke, medzi fotografiu, videom a maľbou sa Aerschmannove práce dotýkajú priamo podstaty zámeru výstavy „Mutations II".

Vymedzenie obrazu

Vymedzenie obrazu je aktom definovania, uchopenia, ale aj vytvorenia si odstupu od viditeľného. A vyžaduje si vlastný postoj k svetu. Významným počinom v histórii videoumenia bolo otočenie kamery na seba. Vito Acconci, Peter Campus, Bruce Nauman, Joan Jonas (a mnohí ďalší) sa rozličnými spôsobmi postavili pred video-zrkadlo. Ale popri fascinujúcej, voyeuristickej bezprostrednosti filmovania samého seba, umožňuje vzťah k odrazu skúmať zjavovanie sa a miznutie vlastného obrazu. V 70. rokoch skonštruoval iný švajčiarsky umelec, Jean Otth, zariadenie zo zrkadla a videa a pohrával sa so zaostrovaním a znejasňovaním svojej podoby, skúmal emócie prítomné pri manipulácii s ňou. Video mu umožnilo zasahovať do vlastného odrazu, pomaly ho rušiť, ohrozovať jeho existenciu, a tým ukázať a nechať počuť, aký vzťah si udržujeme s obrazom seba. Miroir (Zrkadlo, 2000) od Eliny Brotherusovej, fínskej umelkyne, ktorá pracuje s fotografiou aj videom, je tiež formou vystavenia samého seba, pričom viditeľnosť odrazu a jeho dostupnosť divákovi je podmienená plynutím času. Vo svojom fotografickom cykle pózuje Brotherusová nahá pred zapareným zrkadlom v kúpeľni. Preto najskôr nevidno žiadny odraz, takže zažívame moment dislokácie medzi ním a telom. Ale postupne záber za záberom sa obraz v zrkadle odhaľuje. Vo videu je výjav temer rovnaký. Na prvý pohľad tak opakuje fotografický cyklus. Avšak pohyb umožňuje vniesť do procesu život, čím telo získava dominantné miesto na meniacom sa povrchu zrkadla. Brotherusovej dýchanie je ústredným prvkom, dotvára atmosféru a podieľa sa na zjavovaní a miznutí odrazu v zrkadle. Dodáva organický rozmer situácii, v ktorej je telo nadôležitejším obsahom obrazu.

V úvode eseje L'entre-images (Medziobrazy) vysvetľuje Raymond Bellour[2], že „sa zdá, že s videom a všetkým, čo s ním súvisí,

2 RAYMOND BELLOUR, L'ENTRE-IMAGES, PHOTO, CINÉMA, VIDÉO, VYD. ÉDITION DE LA DIFFÉRENCE, 2002.

vstupujeme do iného obrazového času". Aj v prípade, že je video vytvorené fotografickým spôsobom a staticky sníma jeden pohľad, to, čo sa deje v priebehu času, vytvára rozdielny vzťah k času a priestoru. Mladý český umelec Jan Kuděj je autorom niekoľkých videí, ktoré skúmajú prežitok času. Vytvoril napríklad dvojicu projekcií, z ktorých jedna zachytáva štyri bežiace schody a druhá strom v poli. Schody predstavujú krátke video v slučke v skutočnej rýchlosti ich vzostupného a zostupného pohybu. Na druhej strane strom je montážou statických záberov, takže jeho koruna sa hýbe trhane. Dojem mechanickej plynulosti a prerušovanosti pohybu v prírode nás vzďaľuje od dynamického vnímania skutočnosti. V protiklade k spoločnosti, kde je všetko riadené pohybom, vytvára Kuděj medzery a strihy v obraze, ktoré nám zabraňujú vychutnať si pokojný pohľad na strom povievajúci vo vánku (podobne ako Clearboutov skvelý záznam pre Boom, statický obraz stromu, pripomínajúci ten Kudějov, ale oddávajúci sa fascinujúcej plynulosti pohybu). Postavením videa do vzťahu s fotografiou je spochybnená jeho schopnosť vytvoriť ilúziu kontinuity. Nahromadením stavov plynutia vyvolávajú umelecké diela nerovnováhu a nestabilitu v našom vzťahu k svetu.

Pátranie po pohľade

Ak teda prostredníctvom fotografie vyvstali pochybnosti o videu, objavuje sa tu zároveň priestor pre rozvíjanie prístupov využívajúcich fotografický pohľad. Presne tomu sa venuje francúzsky umelec Laurent Goldring zaoberajúci sa tradíciou fotografického portrétu. Spochybňuje fotografickú reprezentáciu tela tým, že frontálne filmuje modely vo fotoštúdiu. Časový rozmer videozáznamu mu dáva priestor skúmať aspekt „vzniku obrazu" z tiel modelov, ktorí sú všetci tanečníkmi (a väčšina z nich aj choreografmi). Keďže pódium je úzke a kamera sa nehýbe, tanečníci sa môžu sotva pohybovať, takže skôr vytvárajú pózy. Zaujmúc jednu polohu, telo podľa Goldringovych inštrukcií ľahko mení podoby z jednej do druhej, čo je zvýrazňované svetlom a hrou tieňa. Výsledné obrazy pôsobia často monštrózne. Zachycujú pohľad a vyjadrujú predstavivosť. Pohyb nám síce umožňuje prechádzať od jednej podoby k druhej a tiež zapojiť sa do procesu symbolického narušenia, ale v konečnom dôsledku videá vyznievajú ako sled statických obrazov. Každý tvar zachytáva istý pohľad. Laurent Goldring potom z videa vyvoláva fotografie. Takže nakoniec dospieva k statickému záberu získanému prostredníctvom tvorivého priestoru, ktorý napomáha zviditeľniť veci uprostred extrémne vykonštruovaného mechanizmu. Nestabilita videa nás vzďaluje od odrazu premeny, ktorej sme vystavení pri fotografii. Obrazy/telá Laurenta Goldringa priznávajú svoju symbolickú povahu, rozkladajú sa vo forme pixelov na papiery. Sú príkladom prenosu fotografického záujmu do videa.

Prechod od jedného média k druhému dáva možnosť odvrátiť sa od ich postupov a od skúmania ich charakteru, ako to robí nemecký fotograf Oliver Möst. Jeho dielo vychádza z jeho osobného vzťahu k videniu. Problémy so zrakom ho doviedli priamo ku konštruovaniu fotografického pohľadu založeného na rozostrení a na obrazových kvalitách, ktoré z toho vyplývajú. Napriek tomu práca s videom nie je len rozšírením jeho experimentov prenesených do oblasti pohybu. Súvisí s inou potrebou, s potrebou predstaviť svoj vzťah k viditeľnému prostredníctvom filmov o sebe samom. Brown Eyes (Hnedé oči), Hide & Seek (Schovávačka) a Between (Medzi) sú krátkymi scénami zrealizovanými v jeho štúdiu. V prvom z nich sa Möst hrá so svojimi „očami", guľôčkami, ktoré drží medzi prstami a vloží si ich do úst. V druhom nahlas odpočítava s červenými klapkami na očiach, kým ho neoslepí blesk. V treťom zápasí s dvoma prepážkami steny, ktoré zatvára a otvára. Vždy je obnažený do polpása, fyzicky zúčastnený na metaforických situáciách zobrazujúcich jeho vzťah k videniu: kritika nedostatočného orgánu zraku v Hnedých očiach a konštruovanie paralely medzi dvoma stavmi zhoršenia videnia v Schovávačke, jedno spôsobené znemožnením vnímania (zakrytím očí), druhé vystavením svetlu (zábleskú). Vo videu Medzi hľadá Möst spôsob, ako správne pristupovať k svetu tým, že obmieňa konštrukciu priestoru prezentácie. Všetky tieto situácie samozrejme zároveň skúmajú proces fotografovania, jeho podmienky a tendencie. Obraz posledného videa Landscapes (Krajiny) má tvar optickej šošovky a vznikol kombináciou camery obscury a videokamery. Zvuk hádzania lopty prichádza spoza záberu kamery, čím kontrastuje s nehybnosťou krajiny, ktorá je citlivo rozdelená na dva symetrické zábery. Mösta nie je na obraze vidno, ale je prítomný prostredníctvom efektu svojej činnosti. Tentoraz tak, ako Möst, nevidíme nič, je to len naša predstavivosť, ktorú autor provokuje. Obrazy viditeľné na povrchu vody sú vo veľkej miere všetko, čo sa dá zahliadnuť.

Zvukové obrazy

Videoumenie značne ťaží zo spriaznenosti s hudobnou tvorbou, ako aj z faktu, že vzniklo z podstaty Fluxusu a nemenej ho ovplyvnil Nam June Paik. Zvuk v ňom často hrá oveľa významnejšiu úlohu ako len soundtrack, ktorý doprevádza obraz. Je súčasťou videa do takej miery, že samotný obraz občas podlieha hubobným princípom. Robert Cahen vo svojich videách podriaďuje filmovanie hudobnej kompozícii. Ak tu hrá čas dôležitú úlohu, tak je to preto, že Cahen vždy vychádza z úzkeho vzťahu medzi zvukom a obrazom, a vyjadruje subjektívnu povahu vnímania reality. Toto je východiskom aj pre spoločnú tvorbu fotografa a videoumelca Gasta Bouscheta a hudobnú skladateľku Nadine Hilbertovú. V ich videách sú obraz a zvuk neodlúčiteľné, jeden splýva s druhým a napĺňa jeho existenciu. Obraz opäť tvoria väčšinou statické zábery, ktoré neprechádzajú jeden do druhého, ale vrstvia sa na seba. V diele Dream Sequence (Snová sekvencia) nám kamera a zvuk prinášajú fragmenty rôznych prostredí (zahmlený les, cesta, centrá miest), ktoré sa navzájom prelínajú, ale nedovoľujú nám zastaviť sa a sledovať jeden záber. Prechádzame od jedného pohľadu k druhému, akoby sme si prezerali fotografický cyklus, od jednej hudobnej nálady k druhej, plnej opakovaní, ale bez akéhokoľvek náznaku kontinuity. Názov stavia tento princíp do vzťahu k stavu snívania, kde sú v rôznych časopriestoroch neustále prekonávané vzdialenosti a jedinou konštantou je tu subjektívne videnie snívajúceho, či v tomto prípade diváka. Takto nám videoumenie umožňuje nájsť priestor, ktorý odzrkadľuje prežitok vnímania, ako je to v diele Christopha Brecha Opus 110 (24', 2001). Video sa sústreďuje na dirigentov chrbát počas koncertu. Zvuk je v ňom výrazne prítomný a spolu s obrazom sa hudobný rytmus stáva monochrómnym pohybom blízkym abstrakcii, hoci vychádza z fyzikálnej podstaty dirigentových gest. Brech harmonizuje pohyby chrbta, kontroluje celok, spomaľuje, zrýchľuje, zadržiava alebo nechráva voľne plynúť čas, aby dosiahol harmóniu medzi zvukom a obrazom. Chrbát sa stáva miestom projekcie, každý záhyb na saku predstavuje krajinu, východisko pre rozvinutie fantázie.

Zvuk môže tiež určovať obraz, viesť ho a naplniť ho významom. Môže vytvoriť príbeh, zapojiť do obrazu reč a vytvoriť medzi nimi dialóg, tak ako je to v diele Garyho Hilla. Ústredným prvkom jeho videotvorby je text, rozprávaný, čítaný alebo vyjadrený telom, ktorý spochybňuje, čím je obraz vytvorený z verbálneho hľadiska. Médium videa je inšpirované aj filmom. Zároveň je však od neho vzdialené dvojakosťou alebo protichodnosťou konštrukcií, ktoré spochybňujú dej, a jeho kódy. Videá Alice Andersonovej sú sice esteticky veľmi blízke filmom, ale z hľadiska prostriedkov deja sú veľmi odlišné. Najvýraznejšie sa tento rozdiel javí v diele Journal (Denník), ktorý pozostáva z veľmi krátkych filmových sekvencií prepojených zvukom. Dejová línia je zachovaná, a hoci nadpisy naznačujú plynutie času (mesiac, deň, rok), intímny príbeh sa nehýbe ďalej. Obrazy môžeme vnímať ako kľúč k preniknutiu v istom momente života. Ale väčšinou nechávajú akýkoľvek pokus o interpretáciu bez pevného základu. Denník uväzňuje diváka v zovretí záludnej hudby a obrazov.

Inštalovanie obrazu

Video kladie oveľa špecifickejšie nároky na inštaláciu ako fotografia. Potrebuje priestor zodpovedajúci jeho technickému charakteru. Vystavená fotografia je predovšetkým dialógom s priestorom a obrazy sú každý rovnako prístupné pohľadu. Video si skôr vyžaduje izoláciu a negovanie skutočného prostredia (ako v čiernych skrinkách, kde je obraz skrytý v temnote s výbornými zvukovými podmienkami). Video tak pracuje s vlastným časopriestorom, príkladom je inštalácia Billa Violu. Ale niektorí umelci vytvárajú videá, ktoré vedú dialóg s tým, čo je mimo obrazu. Clearboutove plátna/steny stelesňujú túto ideu na rozhraní. Videá sú vo vzájomnom vzťahu ako na fotografickej výstave, vidno ich cez priezory tenkých plátien, ktoré zároveň slúžia ako podstavec premietačky. Inštalácia „in situ" je tiež dôležitá. Video ovládne priestor a naplní ho jemu vlastným obsahom. Ulrich Gebert vytvoril Keine Dialoge (Žiadne rozhovory, 2004) pre nejaký interiér, betónovú stavbu bez okien, rozdelenú na úzke miestnosti, ktoré ešte zvýrazňujú atmosféru stiesnenosti. Takéto podmienky prezentácie mu bez potreby akejkoľvek úpravy poskytol Umelecký bunker Tumulka v Mníchove. Diváci sa vnorili do studeného vojenského prostredia, kde sa zúčastnili psychologického testu tímu GSG 9 (elitnej antiteroristickej jednotky založenej po udalostiach na Mníchovskej olympiáde 1972). Ulrich Gebert nám týchto mužov ukazuje vystavených zábleskom stroboskopického svetla, a zároveň sprostredkúva tento prežitok aj divákovi tým, že ho konfrontuje s videom pozostávajúcim s vizuálne agresívnych záberov premietaných v prerušovanom slede. Názov upozorňuje na agresívny nátlak pôsobiaci na vojakov, ktorí podstupujú skúšku sebakontroly. Pohyb je podstatou agresivity, pretože stereoskopický postup získava svoj význam práve odoberaním statickosti obrazu a vytváraním zmyslovej kontinuity videom, a tým zároveň vťahuje diváka do diela.

Video má aj sochársky rozmer, keď sa umelec namiesto potláčania jeho materiality projekciou mimo času a priestoru vystavenia sústreďuje na závislosť výsledného videodiela od zdroja, z ktorého môže vzniknúť (a ktorého nehmatateľnú prítomnosť musí vyjadriť). Obrazovka splývajúca s povrchom diela dokáže rozšíriť rozmer obrazu, ako oči v práci Tonyho Ourselera. Rovnako vytvárajú umelci priestory, do ktorých obraz zapoja, napríklad inštalácie Thomasa Hirschhorna. S rovnkým prístupom zostavuje Pirmin Blum sochy z kartónu, na ktoré pripína fotografické snímky a do ktorých vkladá monitory. Obrazu videa chýba akákoľvek monumentalita projekcie a efekt prezentácie, priznáva svoj základ v realite. Jedna z inštalácií Pirmina Bluma kombinuje fotografie s dvoma videami testov bezpečnosti v automobilovom závode. Airbag je spomaleným záznamom aktivovania sa airbagu nafilmovaným statickou kamerou. Zariadenie sa nafúkne a vyfúkne fascinujúcim spôsobom. Druhé video Spuk je rýchlou montážou pohľadov dvoch kamier počas testovania predného skla auta. Popri vzdušnom a poeticky pokojnom videu Airbag, je Spuk vizuálne aj zvukovo agresívny. Tieto dve diela tak spolu ironicky spájajú veľmy rozdielny rytmus s prístupom „urob si sám", kontrastujúcim s priemyselnou sofistikovanosťou miesta, v ktorom vznikli obrazy.

Alice Andersonová vybrala jednu sekvenciu z videa Denník a vytvorila inštaláciu Insomnia (Nespavosť, 2006). Divák si môže ľahnúť na fialovú zamatovú posteľ s baldachýnom a sledovať minútové video v slučke na obrazovke zavesenej zhora. Takéto prostredie vedie diváka, aby tieto obrazy vnímal ako výtvory vedomia medzi spánkom a bdelosťou, do ktorých sa nikdy úplne neponorí: akonáhle si divák ľahne, projekcia sa začne, takže nedáva priestor na žiadne prevaľovanie sa. Umelecké video je vo všeobecnosti divácky veľmi náročné. Diela sú často príliš dlhé a podmienky sledovania unavujúce. To je nepochybne jeho najväčší nedostatok a jeho vystavovanie a prezeranie je tým oproti fotografii náročnejšie. Preto je asi potrebné zaoberať sa stavom nespavosti, priestorom na rozhraní, ktorý nás vedie k postupom na polceste medzi dvoma médiami a núti nás prechádzať rozličnými podobami obrazu.

Mathilde Roman

Teoretička umenia na Univerzité de Paris- Sorbonne, Mathilde Roman, má doktorát z umenia a špecializuje sa na video umenie. Je autorkou eseje „Art vidéo et mise en scène de soi" (Videoart a inscenovanie seba)", vyd. L'Harmattan, 2008. Ako kritička umenia je členkou AICA a spolupracuje namnohých revue fotografie ako www.lacritique.org, Art press, Mouvement. Mathilde Roman vyučuje dejiny umenia na vysokej škole umení a scénografie mesta Monako, Le Pavillon Bosio.

Čas rozdelený a čas znovu získaný (O priestore a trvaní vo fotografii a videoumení)

„Vskutočnosti neexistuje jeden rytmus trvania. Dokážeme si predstaviť mnoho rôznych rytmov, ktoré pomalšie či rýchlejšie merajú stupeň napätia alebo uvoľnenia rozličných druhov vedomia, a tým si stanovujú patričné miesto v škále bytia." Henri Bergson[1]

Výstraha buď/alebo, teda buď statický obraz, alebo časová kontinuita obrazu, prenasledovala fotografiu od zrodu kinematografického filmu v posledom desaťročí 19. storočia. Okolo mŕtveho momentu „vyňatej" fotografie, momentu extrahovaného z času, sa vytvorila fikcia, akoby jej princíp stál v protiklade k plynúcemu príbehu vo filme.[2] S nástupom magnetickej videopásky a po nej digitálnych technológií založených na pixeloch sa dalo predpokladať, že prišiel koniec tejto dichotómie. Nejde však o koniec z hľadiska „času", ale trvania, faktoru bez ustálenej alebo presnej definície. Dnes už lineárna predstava univerzálneho času neurčuje vnímanie fotografického obrazu. Ako tvrdil Bergson, rozliční ľudia na rôznych miestach vnímajú čas rozdielne. A dokonca aj tomu istému človeku pripadá inak v rôznych obdobiach svojho života. Lineárnu alebo diachronickú minulosť môžeme voľne konceptualizovať, to však nezodpovedá tomu, ako ju skutočne vnímame, keď sa uskutočňuje.

Názov Mutácie II pre výstavu fotografie a videa presne vystihuje procesy tejto neustálej premeny. Mutovať znamená spôsobiť mutáciou alebo prejsť mutáciou, teda obmenou alebo zmenou charakteru, formy alebo kvality. Mutácia alebo nadobúdanie stavu/stávanie sa niečím (liminal) sa neodvíja ako jednoduchý lineárny čas. Vo svojej doslovnej definícii je to nepretržitý proces plynulej zmeny. Preto nadobúdanie nejakého stavu existuje ako „čas zastavený" v nepretržitom procese, čo možno chápať len ako čas, ktorý kontinuálne trvá. Toto je zrejme ten moment rozporuplnosti, ktorého princíp spočíva podľa Eliota v tom, že „ čas prítomnosti a čas minulosti sa vždy nachádza v čase budúcnosti, a zároveň čas minulosti vždy obsahuje čas budúcnosti".[3] V dôsledku toho zostáva „nadobúdanie stavu/stávanie sa niečím" ako „vždy prítomná možnosť"'. Toto bol most trvania, ktorý už dávno prekročil Bruce Nauman a iní a ktorý odhaľuje, prečo nás nové médiá zaoberajúce sa performensom a videom vedú k väčšej elasticite chápania toho, čo predstavuje základ statického alebo plynúceho obrazu. Deleuze ponúka vysvetlenie (bez akéhokoľvek spochybnenia Bergsona) svojím výrokom, že „každý raz, keď sa stretávame s trvaním, alebo sme mu vystavení, môžeme dospieť k názoru, že kdesi existuje diera, ktorá prechádza zmenou a ktorá je niekde otvorená."[4] To nie je v rozpore s náhodnosťou, len naznačuje, že náhodnosť je niekedy skrytá a na prvý pohľad neviditeľná. Na vysvetlenie, ako do tohto princípu zapadá mutácia, treba dodať, že najbežnejšie formy mutácie majú charakter meňavky pozorovanej v laboratórnej Petriho miske.[5] Historickú závislosť na dualistickej schizme medzi statickým a pohybujúcim sa obrazom dnes systematicky napádajú súčasní tvorcovia fotografie a videa. Mechanizmus rozporu zostáva odpoveďou ľudského vedomia. Ale nejde o vedomie, ktoré je konečným bodom sebe samému. Skôr jestvuje v procese

1 HENRI BERGSON, 'THE DELIMITING AND FIXING OF IMAGES', MATTER AND MEMORY,, NEW YORK: N.M. PAUL AND W.S. PALMER ZONE BOOKS, 1991, S. 207

2 ROLAND BARTHES AKO AJ SUSAN SONTAGOVÁ HOVORILI V SÚVISLOSTI S FOTOGRAFIOU BUĎ O FATALITE, ALEBO O MELANCHÓLII, ČÍM JU DÁVALI DO VZŤAHU K ŠTRUKTURÁLNEMU ROMANTIZMU. TÝM UVÄZNILI FOTOGRAFIU MEDZI PUNCTUM, „ZVIERAVÝ MOMENT", A STUDIUM (BARTHES) ALEBO „ÚZKO SELEKTÍVNU TRANSPARENTNOSŤ" (SONTAGOVÁ). POZRI ROLAND BARTHES, CAMERA LUCIDA. LONDÝN: RICHARD HOWARD, (1982), 1984, S. 26-27, A SUSAN SONTAG ‚IN PLATO'S CAVE', ON PHOTOGRAPHY (1971). LONDÝN: HARMONDSWORTH, 1979, S. 6

3 T.S. ELIOT 'BURNT NORTON', IN FOUR QUARTETS. LONDÝN: FABER AND FABER (1944), 1979, S. 13; ĎALEJ POKRAČUJE „...AK JE PRÍTOMNÝ CELÝ ČAS, POTOM JE CELÝ ČAS NEZREKONŠTRUOVATEĽNÝ."

4 GILLES DELEUZE, CINEMA I, THE MOVEMENT IMAGE, LONDÝN, THE ATHLONE PRESS, 1992, S. 9-10; DELEUZE VLASTNE DO VEĽKEJ MIERY ŤAŽÍ Y BERGSONOVYCH DIEL MATTER AND MEMORY (VYŠŠIE CIT) A CREATIVE EVOLUTION (1907). O JEHO VZŤAHU K BERGSONOVI, POZRI GILLES DELEUZE, BERGSONISM. NEW YORK, ZONE BOOKS, 1988

5 SLOVO POCHÁDZA Z GRÉCKEHO AMOIBÈ, KTORÉ DOSLOVA ZNAMENÁ 'ZMENA'. PRVÝKRÁT BOLO POUŽITÉ FRANCÚZSKYM NATURALISTOM JEANOM-BAPTISTOM BORYM DE SAINT-VINCENT (1778-1846)

kontinuálneho „otvárania sa", ktoré predstavuje jediný cieľ, ale s mnohými výsledkami.

V novej digitálnej fotografii a dokonca aj s modernými analógovými technikami dokázali tvorcovia opäť spojiť fotografiu a videoumenie mimo pevnej časovej linearity. Nová fotografia sa oslobodila od obrazu vyňatého z času, ktorý je možné zúžiť na okamih stlačenia spúšte. Práve tak sa chápanie tvorby videa alebo filmu odpútalo od predpokladu kontinuity. V oboch prípadoch sa podmienky stávajú čím ďalej, tým viac manipulovateľné. Potom musíme tiež prijať a počítať s narastajúcimi diskontinuitami, ktoré tvoria základ nášho moderného života, fakt, na ktorý Foucault poukázal už dávno.[6] Zo samotného slova mutácia vychádza jedna užitočná analógia a dôsledok.V latinčine má slovo mutácia rovnakú predponu koreňa ako slovo vzájomný, mutuus. Medzi nimi teda existuje vzájemný vzťah, ktorý je voľne prispôsobiteľný platnému diskontinuitnému systému. Používanie slova mutácia v inom ako biologickom význame stálo (viac menej bez hodnotiaceho významu) dlho v protiklade k evolúcii (väčšinou zaťažené hodnotiacim významom). Prvý pojem označuje zmenu ako diskontinuitný alebo náhodný stav adaptácie, kým ten druhý obyčajne znamená zámernú teleológiu prírodného výberu – veci mutujú na niečo iné, veci sa k niečomu vyvíjajú.

Rovnako ani narastajúci význam fotografie a videa za posledných asi tridsať rokov nevedie len k prekonávaniu starých klišé napríklad o pôvodných hraniciach medzi statickým a pohyblivým obrazom, ale umožňuje aj rozsiahlejšie prelínanie sa procesov vychádzajúcich zo spoločného pôvodu týchto médií. Vo svojom podtitule O priestore a trvaní som narážal na skutočnosť, že integrované procesy fotografie a videa sa stále výraznejšie obracajú do vnútra. Pri každej adaptácii nových technológií nachádza umelec osobnú charakteristiku alebo sprievodné znaky časopriestoru a využíva ich ako definíciu vlastného tieňa, aby vyjadril svoje vizuálne procesy. Súčasná fotografia a video teda nepracuje ani tak s preddefinovaným alebo stanoveným námetom. Skôr sa obe zaoberajú otázkou, akému námetu sa podriaďujú. Rozhodne však reagujú na sebareflexívne podmienky, kde je čas ako obsah elastický a spravidla sa jednotlivé časy ukladajú na a do seba. Čas už nie sú hodinky, ale slučka, a slučka (alebo elipsa) je podmienkou tvaru vnútorného kruhu alebo ohnutia meraného vlastným sebadefinujúcim systémom.[7]

S nástupom videoartu v 60. a 70. rokoch sa naskytla aj možnosť, nerealizovateľná staršími médiami, spochybniť povahu lineárneho času, a to prostredníctvom kritiky narastajúceho komercionalizmu a konzumu, prinášaného televíziou, alebo postupmi, ktoré boli neskôr pomenované ako umelecké video.[8] Hoci radenie obrazu za obrazom vo filme dávalo možnosť vystrihovania a dolepovania, nevyrovnalo sa bezprostrednosti videopásky s jej dostupnosťou okamžitej spätnej väzby, možnosťou vrstvenia a nejednoznačného alebo abstraktného deja.[9] Ak sa videoumenie aj začalo ako kritika televízie a reklamy, čoskoro sa sústredilo na rozkladanie podstaty princípu lineárnej a dejovej konzistencie (na rozdiel od štrukturalistického filmu, ktorý vychádzal z podstaty filmového systému).[10] Ponúklo alternatívne prístupy, ktorými sa čas a priestor spájali novým spôsobom. Video sa využívalo nielen v performense a na zaznamenávanie a analyzovanie samotnej povahy performatívneho, ako to robili Nauman, Acconci a mnohí ďalší. Rýchlo sa vyvinulo do média spochybňujúceho podoby reprezentácie, ktoré sa neskôr začalo nazývať umenie videoinštalácie.[11] Práve toto priam doslova zamiešalo používanie rozličného času prostredníctvom viacerých kanálov. Bezprostrednosť je vo svojej podstate chápaná ako to, „čo je vždy prítomné". A videopáska sa v širšom zmysle bezprostrednej prítomnosti dostala do mnohých umeleckých ateliérov ako nástroj rovnakej povahy ako všetky ostatné, ktoré umelec v svojom štúdiu môže nájsť. Často spomínaný vzťah medzi videom a maľbou je jasným dôkazom tohto javu. Vlastnosť videomonitora vystupovať ako objekt, ktorého súčasťou je obraz, alebo dokonca ako socha či ako celá environmentálna inštalácia znamenalo, že video sa stalo realitou v medzere medzi rozličnými médiami alebo spojnicou medzi. Obsiahlo vzťahy s vytvorenými vecami (tradičná predstava umeleckého diela), skúmalo ich postavenie ako umeleckých diel, aspekty ich vnímania a spochybňovalo historickú hranicu medzi rozličnými médiami. Ako medzery medzi slovami v Beckettovej hre, video fungovalo ako priestor „nadobúdania stavu/stávania sa niečím" v neistom trvaní času.[12]

Vo vzťahu s videom bola fotografia nútená prehodnotiť svoj charakter. Stalo sa tak dávno predtým, než vstúpili do hry najnovšie digitálne technológie. Jednou z príčin bola skutočnosť, že statický obraz získaný z videa spochybnil predstavy o rozhodujúcom momente fotoaparátu.[13] V prvom rade sa fotografia začala opäť zaoberať časom ako obsahom pri vzniku obrazu. Ak hľadisko

6 FOUCAULT HOVORÍ O NEVYHNUTNOM ZMNOŽOVANÍ DISKONTINUÍT, „DEJINY SA POTOM NEJAVIA AKO JEDNA VEĽKÁ KONTINUITA V POZADÍ ZA VÝSTUPUJÚCOU DISKONTINUITOU, ALE AKO ZHLUK NA SEBA UKLADANÝCH DISKONTINUÍT." MICHEL FOUCAULT, ‚RETURN TO HISTORY', IN MICHEL FOUCAULT, ESSENTIAL WORKS OF FOUCAULT 1954-1984, DIEL 2, AESTHETICS, LONDÝN: JAMES D. FAUBION (VYD.), HARMONDSWORTH (1998), 2000, S.429

7 GILLES DELEUZE, 'WHAT IS AN EVENT?', IN THE FOLD: LEIBNITZ AND THE BAROQUE, LONDÝN: TOM CONLEY, THE ATHLONE PRESS, 1993 „SÚ NEODDELITEĽNÉ OD PROCESU AKTUALIZÁCIE ALEBO REALIZÁCIE. SVOJU KVALITU TRVALOSTI ZÍSKAVAJÚ IBA V MEDZIACH FLUXUSU, Z KTORÉHO VZNIKAJÚ, ALEBO POCHOPENIA, KTORÉ ICH AKTUALIZUJE.", S. 80-81

8 VIDEO NAJPRV VYUŽÍVALI V RÁMCI SVOJICH DOKUMENTÁRNYCH PRÍSTUPOV POLITICKÉHO AKTIVIZMU UMELCI, AKO LES LEVINE A FRANK GILLETTE, ALEBO VIDEO AKO UMENIE V TVORBE UMELCA FLUXUSU NAMA JUNA PAIKA; POZRI MICHAEL RUSH, NEW MEDIA IN THE LATE TWENTIETH CENTURY. LONDÝN: THAMES & HUDSON, 1999, S. 80-81. PRE PODROBNEJŠIU ANALÝZU PAIKA POZRI THE WORLDS OF NAM JUNE PAIK. NEW YORK: SOLOMON GUGGENHEIM MUSEUM, 2000.

9 MICHAEL RUSH, VIDEO ART. LONDÝN: THAMES & HUDSON, 2003, „NA TEJTO TECHNIKE BOLO VZRUŠUJÚCE TO, ŽE DOKÁZALA BEZPROSTREDNE ZAZNAMENÁVAŤ SKUTOČNÉ UDALOSTI. V ISTOM ZMYSLE BOL ČAS MANIPULOVANÝ ĽUDSKÝM ZÁSAHOM (S. 15)."

10 SEAN CUBITT, TIMESHIFT: ON VIDEO CULTURE. LONDÝN: ROULEDGE, 1991. POZRI TIEŽ DOUG HALL AND SALLY JO FIFER (VYD.), ILLUMINATING VIDEO: AN ESSENTIAL GUIDE TO VIDEO ART. NEW YORK: APERTURE, 1990.

11 MICHAEL RUSH, 'VIDEO INSTALLATION ART'. IN NEW MEDIA....VYŠŠIE CIT, S. 116-167.

12 VÔBEC NIE JE PREKVAPUJÚCE, ŽE MNOHO PRIEKOPNÍKOV VIDEOUMENIA SA INŠPIROVALO BECKETTOM. BOLO TO TAK AJ V PRÍPADE NAUMANA, V PRÍPADE DIVADLA NEPRETRŽITÉHO MÉDIA AJ JOHNA JESURUNA A ČIASTOČNE V PRÍPADE RANÝCH DIEL BILLA VIOLU. POZRI ALAN RICKMAN (A KOL.), BECKETT ON FILM. DVD, 2005; GIJS VAN TIJL, ‚HUMAN CONDITION/ HUMAN BODY: BRUCE NAUMAN AND SAMUEL BECKETT'. BRUCE NAUMAN. KATALÓG VÝSTAVY, LONDÝN: HAYWARD GALLERY, 1998, S. 60-75

13 HENRI CARTIER BRESSON, THE DECISIVE MOMENT. NEW YORK: SIMON AND SCHUSTER, 1952. V ISTOM OBDOBÍ BOLA TÁTO KNIHA POVAŽOVANÁ ZA NAJDÔLEŽITEJŠIU KNIHU O FOTOGRAFII 20. STOROČIA.

bezprostrednosti postrčilo fotografiu v stopách vývoja modernej techniky aparátu a šošovky, potom čas expozície akejkoľvek dĺžky jednoznačne vymedzil podmienky vynímania obrazu z reality. Ako v existencializme, odkiaľ táto myšlienka pochádza, rozhodujúcim prvkom sa stal prvok výlučnej subjektivity. Na rozdiel od raného videa, ktoré podávalo bezprostrednosť „skutočného" v protiklade k upravovanému filmu, fotografia stratila kontakt s „objektívnou realitou", ktorá bola pôvodne jej základom.[14] To v 80. rokoch privodilo návrat ku camere obscure a s ňou spojeným technikám. Nešlo tu však o to, že by realita videa bola objektívnejšia (hoci to mohlo byť jedno z jeho pôvodných tvrdení). Objavil sa však nový a rozsiahlejší súbor viacčasových alebo zmnožených subjektivít. Tak sa pružnosť času znovu stala súčasťou fotografie, to bol výrazný posun od reprodukcie (bezprostredných výsledkov) k produkcii a zásahu do tvorivého procesu.

S nástupom digitalizácie v 90. rokoch začal význam videa čiastočne upadať. A v súčasnosti našlo opäť využitie v oblasti filmu. Mnohé nové technológie virtuálneho filmu si uzurpovali pôvodné miesto videa. To si už nemohlo nárokovať, že je bezprostredné a schopné prezentovať skutočnosť. Mytologicko-poetické excesy Matthewa Barneyho vo svojej najkrajnejšej forme odrážajú novú tendenciu videa priblížiť sa filmu.[15] Keďže reprodukovateľnosť už nie je vážnym problémom, moderné elektronické média a počítačové technológie stále vo väčšej miere nahrádzajú pôvodnú funkciu videopásky.[16] Z hľadiska času stoja video a fotografia vedľa seba často vo virtuálnom svete počítača a vo forme mnohorakých možností, ktoré existujú medzi obrazom vyňatým z reality a procesmi jeho vzniku či následnouprezentáciou.

14 PREHĽAD KULTÚRNYCH PREMIEN VO FOTOGRAFII OD JEJ POČIATKOV AŽ PO DNES PONÚKA KNIHA MARY WARNER MARIEN, PHOTOGRAPHY: A CULTURAL HISTORY. LONDÝN: LAURENCE KING PUBLISHING, 2002.

15 NANCY SPECTOR, THYRZA GOODEVE A NEVILLE WAKEFIELD, MATTHEW BARNES : THE CREMASTER CYCLE. NEW YORK: GUGGENHEIM MUSEUM PUBLICATIONS, 2002; TIEŽ STEPHAN URBASCHEK AND BRANDON STOSUY, MATTHEW BARNEY. MUNICH: INGVILD GOETZ PUBLICATIONS, 2008.

16 TIMOTHY DRUCKREY (VYD.), ARS ELECTRONICA: FACING THE FUTURE - A SURVEY OF TWO DECADES (ELECTRONIC CULTURE: HISTORY, THEORY AND PRACTICE): CAMBRIDGE (MASS.): MIT PRESS, 2001.

To vedie k stále väčšiemu počtu v diele obsiahnutých časov, ktorých povaha nie je nemenná, ani presne stanoviteľná. Stručne povedané, fotografia aj video prešli v súvislosti s časovým obsahom od určitého k neurčitému. Neurčitým zovšeobecnením času je trvanie. Pričom trvanie je samozrejme vždy virtuálne, a preto neuchopiteľné. Presná definícia tohto slova samozrejme naznačuje proces „stávania sa niečím/nadobúdania stavu"ako simulovanej možnosti. Virtuálne však nie je v protiklade ku skutočnému, pretože existuje len v princípe alebo jeho dôsledkoch, ale nie v skutkovej podstate. Inými slovami, existuje v našom vedomí alebo predstave. Virtuálny svet nie je alternatívnym svetom, to by bolo nemožné z epistemologického hľadiska. Ponúka však alternatívny alebo v našej predstavivosti vytvorený vzťah k tomu, čo chápeme pod pojmom realita. Špekulatívna realita je základom toho, že, ako naznačil Bergson, naše vedomie je schopné „si predstaviť veľa rôznych realizujúcich sa rytmov".

Fotografi a videoumelci vystavujúci na „Mutations II" sú priamo či nepriamo ovplyvnené všetkými zmenami a trendmi, ktoré sa odohrali za posledných tridsať rokov. Rozhodne nie je prekvapujúce, že to vedie k značnej rôznorodosti v tvorbe aj v prístupe vo videu aj fotografii. Je to ten tieň určujúci individualitu, o ktorom som hovoril vyššie. Časovosť a časopriestor nevznikajú len vizuálnymi, ale aj zvukovými prostriedkami. A hoci je zvuk väčšinou lineárny, teda plynule sa odvíja od prvého momentu počutia, tiež slúži fragmentácii a dočasnému znovuspojeniu. V diele Opus 110a od Christopha Brecha počujeme sice symfonickú hudbu, ale všetko, čo vidíme, je zadná časť saka (možno smoking), ktorá vypĺňa celý obraz a pod ktorou si predstavujeme dirigenta – hoci to celkom dobre môže byť napodobenie niekoho, kto predstiera, že hrá na symfonickej gitare.[17] Výsledkom je rozpor medzi tým, čo vidíme, rytmické momenty a skladby látky a záhybov saka, a tým, čo počujeme. Pritom strácame spojitosť medzi zvukom a obrazom na jednej úrovni, ale opäť ju nadobúdame na inej. Tento prežitok, prítomný vo väčšine Brechovych diel, je prenosný, čo znamená, že diela vyjadrujú pôsobenie od subjektu k objektu, pričom si ale vyžadujú priamy objekt, aby bol ich význam úplný. Predpokladá sa, že priamym objektom, ktorému je dielo adresované, je divák. Dlhá história vzťahu medzi hudbou a videom je nám dobre známa, ale v prípade populárnych videí je efekt zväčša ilustratívny. Brechovým princípom je poskytnúť minimálne množstvo informácií (video sa končí pohľadom na notový záznam) a ponechať diváka, aby sám dokončil dielo. Divák a jeho vnímanie sa vlastne stávajú nevyhnutnosťou, ktorá dáva dielu význam.

17 VSKUTOČNOSTI VIDÍME CHRISTOPHA POPPENA AKO DIRIGUJE MNÍCHOVSKÝ KOMORNÝ ORCHESTER PRI ŠOSTAKOVIČOVEJ KOMORNEJ SYMFÓNII, OPUS 110A. BRECH TENTO VÝJAV NAZÝVA „VIZUÁLNA DYNAMIKA HUDBY". TREBA SI VŠAK UVEDOMIŤ, ŽE TOTO JE PRI POCHOPENÍ DIELA LEN VEDĽAJŠIA A NEPODSTATNÁ INFORMÁCIA. HOCI NA DRUHEJ STRANE VAŠE CHÁPANIE MÔŽE BYŤ INÉ, AK TOTO HUDOBNÉ DIELO POZNÁTE

Táto stratégia, antiilustratívna a často spomínaná v súvislosti s post-naratologickým princípom, je charakteristická pre mnohých súčasných videoumelcov.[18] V jej rámci sa neanalyzuje naratívne alebo lineárne podanie príbehu v štrukturálnom zmysle charakterizovania výsledkov vnímania a priori, ale sa podnecuje a vyžaduje si rozšírené vnímanie, ktoré vedie k dokončeniu diela. To zapája čas a časové obsahy, ktoré si vytvoril divák, do hry v reakcii na video. Dielo Oľgy Černyševovej je založené na opačnom princípe ako Brechovo. Vo videu Windows (Okná) sa divák ocitá v úlohe nevideného voyeura alebo nakúkajúceho zvedavca. Prostredníctvom série drobných vytrhnutých pohľadov do okien v noci sa nám predstavuje priam lexikón každodenného života. Okná sú všedné a banálne, zodpovedajú typu moderného masového bývania. A temné, slabo osvetlené interiéry pôsobia bežne a všetky rovnako. Na videozáberoch každodenného života bežiacich na viacerých obrazovkách pozerá nejaký muž televízor, traja ľudia tancujú v kruhu, iný muž hrá osamote na gitare, žena žehlí, ďalší muž je v kúpeľni... Okrem zaužívaného správania, ktoré je zámerom diela, neexistuje

18 UŽ TRADIČNE SA ŠTRUKTURÁLNA „NARATOLÓGIA" SPÁJA SO SKUPINOU RUSKÝCH FORMALISTOV. CVETAN TODOROV VYMYSLEL TOTO SLOVO A NARÁŽA TÝM NA PRÍKLAD VLADIMÍRA PROPPA (1895-1970). POZRI MORPHOLOGY OF A FOLKTALE (V RUŠTINE 1928). AUSTIN: UNIVERSITY OF TEXAS PRESS, 1968.

žiadna priama spojitosť medzi oknami, iba to, že navzájom voľne typologicky súvisia. Avšak fakt, že sú vyňaté z časového kontextu, neumožňuje skoro žiadne závery o mieste alebo prostredí odohrávajúcich sa dejov. Boli nafilmované všetky súčasne, alebo každý inokedy a v rôznych častiach mesta? Dôležité je, že sú to jednoducho viedeozábery a ako obrazy prebiehajúce v čase stavajú diváka do úlohy nevideného voyeura alebo nazízajúceho zvedavca. V prípade statických záberov alebo fotografií by z diela takýto význam v súvislosti s divákovou spoluúčasťou nevyplynul.

Úloha videa vypĺňať medzery, to, čo moja kolegyňa v tomto katalógu nazvala „tvorba v medzipriestore", stále prevláda vo videoprodukcii. V dielach izraelského umelca Oriho Gershta Big Bang a Pomegranate (Granátové jablko) videá pôsobia ako zátišie a obraz kvetov. V práci Big Bang sa najprv objaví čierna obrazovka a počuť vysoký silnejúci piskot. Potom sa postupne vynára kvetinové zátišie v sklenej váze v duchu holandského maliarstva 17. storočia. Obraz aj zvuk sa stávajú stále výraznejšími, čo pomaly vyvoláva očakávanie niečoho neurčitého, až kým nakoniec kvety a váza nevybuchnú. Roztrhané kusy pršia dolu a obraz postupne prechádza do čiernej, aby sa opäť začal, stále dokola v slučke. Keď sa na Gershtove dielo pozrieme zblízka, zistíme, že jeho význam tkvie hlboko v osobnej a politickej identite a životnej skúsenosti autora. Preto sa výber granátového jablka pre ďalšie video vôbec nejaví ako náhoda. Kompozícia Granátového jablka pozostáva z trojrozmerného rámu obrazu, visiacej kapusty a granátového jablka, kým tekvica a dyňa ležia na niečom, čo by v skutočnej maľbe predstavovalo zbiehajúci sa nižší rám. Video beží ticho, až kým sprava nevyletí strela, ktorá rozdrví jablko a jeho semienka sa rozprsknú; všetko v spomalenom tempe. Z hľadiska osobných súvislostí s autorom si treba uvedomiť, že ide o konkrétnu biblickú citáciu, námetom je jedno zo siedmich ovocí Izraela. Rovnako je dôležité, že v hebrejčine označuje rovnaké slovo granátové jablko aj granát.[19] V Gershtovom diele nejde ani tak o miešanie sa časov, ako o obmieňanie prežitkov času a vytváranie podmienok nepredvídateľného, ale intenzívneho očakávania. Inými slovami, ide o „meranie stupňa napätia a uvoľnenia rôznych druhov uvedomovania si."

Ak sa Gershtove diela odvolávajú na maľbu, potom u Fína Tuoma Rainia sa zdá, že medzipriestor spája kresbu a video. Vytvoril si na to vlastný program. V práci Staircase (Crosswise) (Schodište (Naprieč) nejasná osoba vystupuje hore schodmi, čím vzniká dojem prízračnosti a tajuplnosti a obrazová kompozícia je rozmazaná a nejasná. Celá nálada je akosi gotická, povrch obrazu tvoria viacnásobné expozície strašidelného výrazu, čo samozrejme hneď pripomína prvé futuristické diela a Duchampov Akt schádzajúci po schodoch.[20] Táto odvolávka nám má pripomenúť, ako sa za posledných dvadsať rokov video aj fotografia vrátili ku skúmaniu a spochybňovaniu svojho pôvodu. Naopak, video City (Mesto) pôsobí ako statický záber, ale jeho zvuk z neho robí zvukový obraz. Predstavuje čierno-šedý pohľad na časť mesta s mestskou železnicou alebo zastávku električky. Celý dojem je založený len na zvuku záhadných závanov vetra, neviditeľných rachotiacich vlakov a občasných krokov. Statický obraz,v ktorom plynie čas, naznačuje dojem opakovania a beží dokola v slučke. Takto naznačené opakovanie času môže v princípe trvať nekonečne dlho. Zvukovo-obrazové dielo Mesto je založené na prelínaní sa statického obrazu a videa, pričom usporadúva priestor medzi dlhými momentmi expozície, ako je to napríklad u Michaela Weselyho, do výsostne osobného a naprogramovaného systému.[21]

Účinok obnoveného pátrania sa priamo dotýka diela Olivera Mösta, ktorého tvorba založená na práci s videom vytvoreným z camery obscury nachádza bezprostrednú podobnosť v postupoch prehistórie a ranného vývoja fotografie. V cykle prác, ktoré súhrnne nazýva Camera Obscura alebo Skratka a kam patria Landescape (Krajina), Hide and Seek (Schovávačka) alebo Kill Your Idols (Zabi svoje idoly), delí a vrství rozličné časové úseky a zároveň sa vracia k základnému predpokladu času, svetla a expozície. Či už je to v jednoduchom odpočítavaní v Schovávačke alebo v sotva rozoznateľných zmenách Krajiny, vždy na nás vyžaruje zvláštny pocit nekonečna a ľahostajnosti. Ak sa video najprv používalo v politickej a kultúrnej sfére na súboj s prevládajúcimi masmédiami, medzičasom sa vyvinulo na výlučne osobné médium. Dielo ako Dreamsequence (Snová sekvencia) od Gasta Bouscheta a Nadine Hilbertovej je zámerne alineárne, mieša náznaky osobného postoja a prístupov s navzájom nesúvisiacimi fragmentmi textu a zvuku rôzneho pôvodu. Ako zmes zmyslových prežitkov opakujúcich sa v sne, video predstavuje kombináciu identifikácie a spomienok pamäti – teda druh osobnej katarzie. Akákoľvek spojitosť je ponechaná na divákovo vnímanie. Dielo však zostáva kultúrne politické už len preto, že sa ako umelecké video nesnaží diváka zamedziť v aktivite a, hoci nepriamo má aj pobaviť, jeho hlavným zámerom je skúmať hranice reprezentácie a pochopenia obrazu. Doslova vyzýva diváka, aby si kládol otázku, čo tieto obrazy znamenajú. A čo má na mysli Ulrich Gebert, keď päť ľudí vo vojenských uniformách a s pohľadom upretým na prázdnu stenu jednoducho postaví do radu, pričom

19 SEDEM OVOCÍ (SHIVAT HAMINIM) IZRAELA SA NACHÁDZA V MOJŽIŠOVEJ KNIHE DEUTERONOMIUM 8:7-8. HEBREJSKÉ SLOVO OZNAČUJÚCE AJ GRANÁTOVÉ JABLKO AJ BALISTICKÝ GRANÁT JE RIMMÔN.

20 FUTURISTI, AKO AJ DUCHAMP, V MNOHOM ŤAŽILI Z EADWEARDDA MUYBRIDGEA (1830-1904) A ETIENNA-JULESA MAREYA (1830-1904). OBAJA BOLI CHRONOFOTOGRAFMI, VENOVALI SA ČASOVO-PRIESTOROVÉMU PREMIESTŇOVANIU A DELENIU POHYBU NA SEKVENCIE. POZRI PHILLIP PRODGER, TIME STANDS STILL: MUYBRIDGE AND THE INSTANTANEOUS PHOTOGRAPHY MOVEMENT. LONDÝN: OXFORD UNIVERSITY PRESS, 2003 A MARTA BRAUN, PICTURING TIME: WORK OF ETIENNE-JULES MAREY (1839-1904). CHICAGO A LONDÝN: CHICAGO UNIVERSITY PRESS, 1994

21 PRÁCE MICHAELA WESELYHO S NÁMETOM PLYNULÉHO POHYBU STROMU A FOTOGRAFIE SNÍMANEJ POČAS ŠTYROCH ROKOV SÚ DOBRE ZNÁME. V ISTOM ZMYSLE PRACUJÚ S OBRÁTENOU STRÁNKOU VIDEA, TÝM ŽE DOVOĽUJÚ ČASU, ABY POČAS VEĽMI DLHÉHO OBDOBIA VYTVORIL PRÍZRAČNÉ OBSAHY. POZRI MICHAEL WESELY OPEN SHUTTER, KATALÓG VÝSTAVY, THE MUSEUM OF MODERN ART NEW YORK, 2004, KTORÝ ZACHYTÁVA CELÉ OBDOBIE ZBÚRANIA A PRESTAVBY MÚZEA MODERNÉHO UMENIA MOMA A VÝSTAVBU NÁMESTIA POTSDAMMER PLATZ. MICHAEL WESELY: DIE ERFINDUNG DES UNSICHTBAREN, KATALÓG VÝSTAVY, GUARDINI GALERIE BERLIN/FOTOHOF SALZBURG, 2005.

sa so zvukom rat-ta-tat zažína a zhasína svetlo. Okrem nepriamej pocty predchodcom ako Gary Hill a náznaku opakovania, všetky ostatné možnosti vnímania musíme rozvíjať sami.

Najvýraznejším pokrokom je, že video aj fotografiu môžeme digitálne manipulovať. Virtuálna realita počítačového sveta oslobodila fotografiu od statického obrazu, zmrazeného momentu a video od sebklamu, že zaznamenáva akúsi definitívnu realitu. To umožnilo umelcovi ako Peter Aerschmann tvoriť polyfonicky, priraďovať k sebe rôzne prvky zo sociálneho prostredia do surreálneho. V prácach Paternoster a Union Square (Námestie jednoty) odhaľuje rôznorodosť prístupu, ktorý je charakteristický pre mnohých súčasných umelcov. Pozadie scény v diele Paternoster predstavujú otvorené výťahy, v ktorých sa hore-dole vezú ľudia vo všetkých svojich idiosynkratických podobách. Reprezentujú drobné svety sociálneho sebauvedomenia, spoločné ľudské správania vytrhnuté z kontextu. Žena hrá na husliach, mužská postava v monterkách zametá, žena s vázou kvetov, kvet v kvetináči a tak ďalej. Aerschmann sa často sústreďuje na archetypy, čo môže byť vplyv švajčiarskeho prostredia (možno Carla Gustava Junga). Námestie jednoty predstavuje surrealistický protiklad predošlého diela. Vidíme tu biely priestor plný snehu a kmene stromov, ploché, matne červené pozadie, popred ktoré prelieta lietadlo, a oddiel švajčiarskej armády v štyroch zásupoch v snežnej krajine. Obraz prechádza zľava do prava od suchých kmeňov k ihličnatému lesu. Aerschmann priamo útočí na dialektiku medzi zmrazeným a pohyblivým obrazom. Celá práca je o priestore a nedefinovanom plynutí času. Takže v istom zmysle umožňuje virtuálno pri fotografii a videu väčšiu časovú a obrazovú syntézu, ako bolo kedy možné so staršími technikami. Vo fotografii sa dajú vrstviť viaceré časové momenty do efektu plynutia, kým vo videu sú časové úseky stlačené, predĺžené alebo obrátené a zlúčené do nových a zdanlivo nekonečných možností.

Kde je v tom všetkom všeobecnejší význam času? Tak, ako to vyjadril Bergson, spočíva v rôznych druhoch uvedomovania si. Prečo by malo byť prekvapujúce, že vzťah ľudí k času je hlboko osobný? To, čo stanovuje svet, nemusí byť nevyhnutne to, čo tvrdí vedomie a predstavivosť. V čase, keď nas čím ďalej tým viac zasahuje elektronická doba, by sme sa mali menej poddávať strachu a viac veriť možnostiam sveta. Výstava Mutácie II sa dotýka zmien týchto veličín v možnostiach, ktoré sa objavili a sú realizovateľné v súčasnej fotografii a videu. Ako ich použijeme, alebo na aký účel, to stále zostáva len na nás samých.

Ale povaha, jadro a pôsobenie našej osobnosti je zahalené rovnakou záhadou. Ako vznikajú a čomu slúžia tieto základné vnemy, ktoré sa rozvíjajú v priestore, z ktorého pochádzajú? Musíme ich prijať ako veľa iných absolút, ktorých začiatok ani koniec nevidíme.[22]

Mark Gisbourne

Mark Gisbourne prednášal na univerzite University of London, Slade School of Fine Art vrámci postgraduálneho štúdia moderného umenia a na inštitúte Sotheby's Institute (magisterský program univerzity University of Manchaster). Je bývalým prezidentom medzinárodného združenia kritikov umenia AICA (Veľká Británia) a v súčasnosti pôsobí ako medzinárodný vice prezident združenia. Je autorom mnohých kníh a katalógov. Písal temer pre všetky najvýznamnejšie umelecké publikácie v anglickom jazyku. K jeho najposlednejším výstavám patrí Paul Klee: Adult Memories of Childhood (Centro Atlántico de Arte Moderno, Las Palmas). Tiež je posledným kurátorom projektu Rohkunstbau (pozri: www.rohkunstbau.de). Žije a pracuje v Berlíne.

22 HENRI BERGSON, OF THE SELECTION OF IMAGES, VYŠŠIE CIT, S. 6

Peter Aerschmann

Narodený v roku 1969 vo Fribourgu vo Švajčiarsku,
žije a pracuje v Berne vo Švajčiarsku,
vysoká škola Hochschule f. Gestaltung und Kunst,
Bern
www.aerschmann.ch

Fotografovanie priestoru pričom hĺbka dočasnosti zostáva zachovaná, tvorba obrazov, ktoré presahujú okamih a statickosť, aby zachytili pohyb a život, základným motívom tvorby Petra Aerschmanna je hľadanie spôsobu, ako sprítomniť čas v priestore.

Vo svojej knihe "Oko a duch" (1964) vyslovil filozof a teoretik umenia Maurice Merleau-Ponty názor, že zrak a pohyb sú prepojené. Teda keby sme sa nedokázali pohybovať v priestore, neboli by sme schopní ani vidieť. V každom prípade nie je pohyb tela iba obyčajným premiestnením predmetu z bodu A do B. Pohyb, ktorý vnímame, je autonómnym celkom a nesmieme ho zamieňať s priestorom, ktorý zaberie, keď sa uskutočňuje. V tom tkvie paradox pohybu: odohráva sa v priestore, napriek tomu sa v ňom javí ako cudzorodý.

Vo videách Petra Aerschmanna sa objavuje náhodné spolu s tým, čo je vopred dané, čím sa divákovi dostáva len neúplný obraz reality života. Takto nás privedie k tomu, že strácame orientáciu. Je v tomto podstata dojmu života, i keď mnohé časti sú naplánované a ich pohyby sledujú predurčenú trajektóriu? Peter Aerschmann nám neukazuje obraz. Prostredníctvom obrazu zaznamenáva rytmus vecí a spôsob, akým zapadajú do plynúceho času a opakovania. Rekonštruuje prostredie, ktoré nesie formálne znaky reality: schopnosť meniť sa, trvalosť a prítomnosť objektov. To, že temer všetky nafilmované minisekvencie sú fragmentami pohybov, pričom ich opakovanie a vopred naplánovaný vývoj vyznieva akosi melancholicky humorne, nie je žiadna náhoda.

Pripomienkami archetypov kolektívnej pamäte nás diela Petra Aerschmanna privádza k našej vlastnej realite. Stávajú sa metaforami sveta oprosteného od hierarchií, kde sme si navzájom cudzí.

Alice Andersonová

Narodená v roku 1976 v Londýne, žije a pracuje
v Londýne,
2002-2004 magisterské štúdium na Goldsmiths
College, Londýn,
1998-2001 Vysoká škola výtvarných umení v Paríži.
www.alice-anderson.org

Anglo-francúzska umelkyňa a filmárka Alice Andersonová spája príbehy vlastných spomienok a svet predstáv úzko spätý s jej vlastným detstvom, a tak sa vracia k tradícii ľudových rozprávok a znovu objavuje ich významy. Jej práce, plné fikcie aj autobiografických citácií, zdôrazňujú dualitu, ktorá je podľa nej podstatou ľudových rozprávok. Sú povrchné, ale aj hlboko pravdivé, normatívne, ale aj deštrukčné. Vťahujú diváka do hlboko snového sveta, z ktorého vyviera forma tmy a tá vytvára atmosféru drsnú a desivú zároveň. Detstvo a predstava hry sú v autorkinej práci veľmi dôležité, avšak nesú prvok vážnosti.

Keď Andersonová vytvára príbeh, zdôrazňuje symbolickú a poetickú silu predmetov z minulosti, s ktorými pracuje. Jej naratívny proces má ďaleko od lineárneho princípu. Je to skôr kruh pripomínajúci cestičky bludiska, premenlivý svet Lewisa Carrolla alebo freudovské princípy, ktorými je daná interpretácia podvedomia. V každom fantastickom príbehu Alice Andersonovej môžeme vypozorovať hľadanie identity, ktoré nás nabáda prejsť zrkadlom za vlastnou skúsenosťou, niekam medzi potešenie a hrôzu.

Gast Bouschet & Nadine Hilbertová

G. Bouchet, narodený v roku 1958 v Dudelange,
Luxembursko,
N. Hilbertová, narodená v roku 1961v Luxemburgu,
žijú okrem iného aj v Bruseli.
www.thetrustfiles.net

Dreamsequence (They are us) (Snová sekvencia /Oni sú my/)
Videoinštalácia, Nadine Hilbertová a Gast Bouschet, hudobný motív: „The Bomarr Monk and Telephone Jim Jesus"

Od 80. rokov tvorili a vystavovali Nadine Hilbertová a Gast Bouschet svoje fotografie a videá po celom svete. V prvom rade ich fascinuje zosnímaný obraz a jeho schopnosť odzrkadľovať a komentovať transformáciu politických a socio-ekonomických systémov a ich symbolizmus. Toto je obzvlášť dobre viditeľné v morfológii mestských štruktúr a ich hraničných zón.

Svoje práce prezentovali na mnohých výstavách, predovšetkým v Center of Contemorary Art (Glasgow), Museum van Hedendaagse Kunst Muhka (Antverpy), Casino, Forum d'Art Contemporain (Luxemburg), Neil Liicht Galllery (Dudelange, Luxembursko), Busan Biennale of Contemporary Arts (Busan, Korea), Camouflage, Centre of African Contemporary Art (Brusel a Johanesburg), Domaine départemental v Chamarande (Paríž) a v rámci projektu Krinzinger Projekte (Viedeň).

„Vždy som ten druhý. Ak hovorím my, tak označujem seba ako vinníka. Tým je všetko jasné. Nikto už nie je tým, čím bol. Agresia nič nezmenila, tvoríme jeden celok s našimi nepriateľmi, zdieľame rovnaké myslenie s našimi protovníkmi. Už neexistujú žiadne hranice alebo prekážky, naše identity sú prepojené. Ale zožiera nás strach, úzkosť v nás stále zostáva. Každý deň je tu prítomná táto hrozba, rozkladá nás zvnútra. Svet sa zmenil, svetlo je iné. Príroda je nezmieriteľná, chce nás dostať. Sme cudzincami vo vlastnej krajine, všetci hovoríme neznámym jazykom, ktorý nás ľaká. Odteraz sú naše najstrašnejšie nočné mory pozbavené svojho lahodného studeného potu. Naše najkrajšie sny nás znepokojujú svojím klamlivým uspokojením. Každý deň naša myseľ vytvára a obnovuje svoj pomalý jed. Už nejaký čas nie sme schopní žiť bez neho. Ženie nás naliehavá núdza po tomto každodennom chlebe. Odvraciame sa od farby na poliach, kde sme sadili vlastnú hrôzu. Chmúrne zrkadlo Nadine Hilbertovej a Gasta Bouscheta." (François Olivieri)

Pirmin Blum

Narodený v roku 1969 v Pfaffnau (Švajčiarsko),
žije vo Viedni,
1997-99 – Vysoká škola výtvarných umení, Ženeva,
1999-2005 – štúdium digitálnych médií u Petra
Koglera, Akadémia výtvarných umení, Viedeň.
www.pirminblum.com

Už niekoľko rokov sa dielo švajčiarskeho umelca Pirmina Bluma sústreďuje na internet. Prehliada stránky internetových aukcií, vyhľadávače a četovacie fóra. Jeho záujem o web vychádza zo skutočnosti, že dnes má k nemu prístup každý. Hocikto doň môže vložiť osobné fotografie, videá, alebo texty, alebo si prečítať informácie od niekoho iného. Vedome či nevedome – v Blumovom prípade platí to prvé – sa stávame „vojermi" a konzumentami súkromných životov iných. Popri tomto nájdenom materiáli pracuje Blum aj s filmami priemyselných a komerčných producentov, ako sú záznamy testov bezpečnosti rôznych automobilových výrobcov. Analytický výber určitých sekvencií z týchto videí a ich montáž posúva obrazy, ktoré vznikli bez akejkoľvek umeleckej ambície, do novej významovej roviny. Napríklad rýchle strihy skombinované s uzavretím videa do slučky štylizujú airbag, ktorý praská a spľasúva, na zvláštnu a zdanlivo organickú bublinu (Airbag, 2000). Blum prispôsobil moment nárazu airbagu rytmu ľudského dychu. Po niekoľkých prehratiach filmu „dýcha" divák synchrónne s videom.

Podobný efekt dosiahol Blum aj v diele Spuk (2001), kde použil video z testovania obrneného vozu, ktorého ochranné sklo je vystavené streľbe. Rýchle striedanie pohľadov dvoch kamier – strely v ochrannom skle z vonkajšej strany vozidla a z jeho vnútornej strany – vytvára zvláštne napätie, dojem, že divák sa nachádza uprostred diania. Raz je strieľajúcim páchateľom a potom zase obeťou sediacou v aute, sledujúcou, ako sa k nej blížia strely. Dôležitým prvkom je tu zvuk. Z reproduktorov, aké sa používajú pre techno-rave, búšia nízke basové tóny rýchlosťou 130 úderov za sekundu, čo je frekvencia, s ktorou často pracujú disdžokeji pri rave party, aby dosiahli optimálnu stimuláciu ľudského srdca.

Christoph Brech

Christoph Brech, narodený v roku 1964 v Schweinfurte, žije a pracuje v Mníchove. Študoval na Vysokej škole výtvarných umení v Mníchove (1989-1995).
www.christophbrech.com

„Videá Christopha Brecha pretvárajú bežné udalosti na dôležité momenty."

Dielo Christopha Brecha zahŕňa práce od inštalácií v interiéri po fotografie, video a umenie na verejných miestach.

Brechove videá sa vyznačujú strohosťou a jasnosťou koncepcie, lineárnosťou prevedenia a jednoduchosťou použitých prostriedkov. Prirodzené javy, predmety a dojmy každodenného života, statická a ticho pozorujúca kamera, to sú typické znaky prác tejto výstavy.

Brech odhaľuje situácie, ktoré odkrývajú svoj poetický rozmer prostredníctvom predĺženia času a pomalosťou, ktorá tak vzniká – bežné udalosti pretvorené na dôležité momenty.

Vo videu Passage (Preplavenie) nám ukazuje pohár s vodou na stole kajuty nákladnej lode vystavený silnejúcim a slabnúcim otrasom a kymácaniu. V diele Break (Prielom) pozoruje pokojnú a sprvu tichú rieku Sv. Vavrinca, zamrznutú a zahalenú hmlou. Kladie tu do protikladu pozvoľné tempo prírody a drsnosť, s ako prechádza kanadský ľadoborec. Vo videu Opus 110a sníma chrbát dirigenta Christopha Poppena, akoby chcel reprodukovať dynamiku hudby Dimitrija Šostakoviča do hry záhybov na fraku – Christoph Brech dokáže zachytiť vlastný čas udalosti do obrazov. Pred divákom sa odvíja spomalený rytmus, ktorý vytvára temer meditatívnu náladu. Tak je to aj vo videu Transito (Priechod), ktoré vzniklo v Ríme v roku 2007, kde vo vetre rytmicky povieva ťažký záves na dverách kostola, čím vzniká tanec svetla a tieňa na podlahe. Momenty času a prechodu, ako sú tieto, predstavujú podstatu videí Christopha Brecha.

Elina Brotherusová

Narodená v roku 1972 v Helsinkách (Fínsko), žije v Helsinkách (Fínsko) a v Avallone (Francúzsko); štúdium: titul magister v roku 2000, Vysoká škola umenia a dizajnu UIAH, Helsinki
www.sag.se/foto/elinabrotherus/elina.html

„Fotografie Le miroir (Zrkadlo, 2000) a video Miroir (Zrkadlo, 2001) nie sú o ženskej identite alebo niečom podobnom, ako to niektorí podávali. Prosto som chcela vidieť, ako bude vyzerať ten každodenný jav miznúcej pary, keď sa odfotografuje. Pri hlbšom zamyslení možno v tejto práci vidieť drobnú alegóriu fotografie. Zo začiatku bola fotografia medenou doskou potiahnutou striebornou vrstvou – teda zrkadlom. Pri vyvolávaní sa v nej objavil portrét. Tu sa tiež postupne vynára obraz v zrkadle. Je zaujímavé sledovať, ako sú obe práce rozdielne. Hoci jedinou skutočnou odlišnosťou medzi nimi je, že fotografie podávajú oddelené okamihy, kým video sceľuje medzery medzi jednotlivými obrazmi do plynulej časovej línie.

„Dielo Model Studies (Štúdium modelu) nelíči osobný príbeh a nie je ani dokumentom o niečom živote. Obrazy vznikli z vizuálnych dôvodov. Autorku zaujíma svetlo, farby, rytmus hmôt a námet v klasickom ponímaní. Postava sa často obracia k divákovi chrbtom. Toto gesto nabáda skôr k pokojnej kontemplácii než ku konfrontácii."[1]

Vo svojich videách s rovnakým názvom využíva Elina Brotherusová profesionálnych modelov a modelky, ktorí akoby pózovali na hodine kreslenia. Miesto kreslenia sa však fotografka na nich díva cez svoju kameru. Ide tu o osobitosť pohľadu umelca sledujúceho model: oko sledujúce s odstupom, oslobodené od vojerizmu. „Umelec, ktorý kreslí alebo maľuje, nepredstiera, že pozná alebo chápe osobnosť modelu. V tom to nie je. Ide o to, dívať sa pozorne, to je všetko: kde sú svetlá a tiene, ako idú línie. Chcem tento aktívy, ale neutrálny pohľad umelca ukázať ľuďom, chcem sa s nimi oň podeliť. Je to výsada byť schopný dívať sa na ľudskú postavu týmto spôsobom."[2]

Oľga Černyševová

Narodená v roku 1962 v Moskve, Ruská federácia, žije a pracuje v Moskve,
1996 - ukončila Moskovskú filmovú akadémiu,
1995-96 – ukončila Kráľovskú akadémiu výtvarných umení v Amsterdame.

Oľga Černyševová vyštudovala kinematografiu. Pracuje s fotografiou, maľbou, experimentálnym videom a videoinštaláciami. Jej projekt Windows (Okná) z roku 2007 prenáša diváka späť do každodenného života sovietskej éry. V oknách moskovských

„chruščovovských" panelákov ste mohli vidieť oblečenie, riad, spodné prádlo, pohár čaju, nahé mužské telo, žehličku, televízor, drapériu s kvetinovým vzorom, sušiaca sa bielizeň, okennú tabuľu zalepenú papierom... Ľudia prichádzajú a odchádzajú: muž pije z kanvice, starec sa naťahuje, mladí ľudia sa zabávajú... Tu sa samotné okno stáva ohraničením javiska, rámom, ktorý vytvára osvetlený priestor podobný tomu divadelnému, kde sa postavy/obyvatelia zjavujú a miznú v tme zákulisia bytu.

Černyševovej okná odhaľujú každodenný ruský život. Vyvracajú ho zvnútra von, a tak nám umožňujú pozorovať bežnú dennú rutinu, ktorá v nás pomaly, ale nepretržite vyvoláva pocit, ktorý vnímame ako existenciu. A to všetko sa deje bez náznaku vojerizmu, nazízania alebo zvedavosti – všetko je to veľmi vzdialené, pokojné a sústredené.

Niekoľko videoklipov, ktoré bežia súčasne v čiernej atmosfére noci a na televíznej obrazovke, vytvára model ideálneho spoločného života (za doprovodu Chopinovej hudby), vyvoláva dojem prítomnosti a vzbudzuje teplý pocit nostalgie za sovietskou realitou, ktorá ešte celkom nevymizla.

Názov Černyševovej videa je Windows (Okná), 2007, video, 1 min., slučka, niekoľko obrazoviek.

Ulrich Gebert

Narodený v roku 1976 v Mníchove, žije a pracuje v Lipsku,
v rokoch 1998-2005 študoval fotografiu na Vysokej škole výtvarných umení v Lipsku, 2006 štúdium na vysokej škole výtvarných umení Royal College of Art v Londýne.
www.klemms-berlin.com

Fotografie Ulricha Geberta sa často dotýkajú konceptov, ktoré sa sprvu javia abstraktnými a neuchopiteľnými, napriek tomu však majú určujúci vplyv na naše konanie v spoločenskom prostredí. Gebert sa zameriava na princípy poriadku, systematického myslenia, hierarchizácie a mechanizmov moci a odhaľuje ich v ich umeleckom kontexte. V závislosti od daných súvislostí si vyberá svoje spôsoby inscenovania, filmu, dokumetu alebo portrétu a zapája ich do procesu tvorby svojich prevažne fotografických diel, pričom zohľadňuje charakter samotných médií.

Pre svoje video no dialogues (Žiadne rozhovory) z roku 2004 použil Ulrich Gebert nájdený film o tréningu elitných pohraničných stráží GSG 9, antiteroristickej jednotky nemeckej federálnej polície. Z tohto materiálu zostavil minimalistické video – slučku, kde sa v zatemnenej uzamknutej miestnosti päť dôstojníkov v rade podrobuje testu stresu založenom na ostrých zábleskoch svetla. Počas testu sú dôstojníci poverení príkazmi, ktoré musia neskôr splniť. Neustále klikanie blesku stavia diváka do priamej konfrontácie s projekciou a okolitým priestorom prostredníctvom rýchleho sledu zábleskov jednotlivých statických obrazov. Tie vytvárajú dojem, že sa striedajú v rýchlej následnosti, čím vzniká dojem minimálneho pohybu dôstojníkov. Divák je tak ako dôstojník GSG 9 vystavený nepríjemným zábleskom v malom, tmavom priestore, kde sa video premieta. Stiesňujúca a napätá situácia testu stresu, v ktorej sa ocitajú dôstojníci, sa tak úplne otvára aj divákovým vnemom.

Ori Gersht

Narodený v roku 1967 v Tel-Avive, v Izraeli.
Žije a pracuje v Londýne.
1993-95 magister, odbor fotografia, vysoká škola výtvarných umení Royal College of Art, Londýn, UK.
Bakalár v odbore fotografia, film a video, University of Westminister, Londýn, UK.
www.mummeryschnelle.com

Vo svojich najposlednejších dielach skúma Ori Gersht vzťah medzi filmom, fotografiou, technikou a optickým vnemom. Robí to v takom rozhodujúcom momente dejín umenia, kedy preň digitálna technológia predstavuje na jednej strane hrozbu krízy a na druhej prísľub prelomu. Vo svojich dvoch najnovších filmoch Pomegranate (Granátové jablko) a Big Bang vytvoril Gersht kompozície zátiší v štýle malieb starých majstrov, čím sleduje evolúciu fascinácie umelca reprezentáciou reality počnúc sedemnástym storočím až dodnes. Kým v pôvodnej podobe sa takáto maľba snažila zachytiť moment nehybnosti zamrznutý v čase, Gershtove kompozície vždy rozbije nejaká rýchla a násilná intervencia. Vo filme Granátové jablko, ktorý odkazuje jednak na barokové zátišie Juana Sancheza Cotana a tiež na stroboskopickú fotografiu Harolda Edgertona, preletí v spomalenom pohybe rýchla strela rámom a roztrhá visiace granátové jablko, pričom ho nesie vzduchom ako rozbité ústa rozsýpajúce krvavočervené semienka. Pokojný obraz sa zmenil na krvipreliatie a vzniká tu dialóg medzi nehybnosťou a pohybom, mierom a násilím. Podobné dichotómie sú prítomné aj vo filme Big Bang, ktorý na prvý pohľad pôsobí ako holandské zátišie kvetov. Táto ilúzia pominie vo chvíli, keď kvety a váza vybuchnú za prenikavého zvuku sirén signalizujúcich nebezpečenstvo vojny, ktoré sa pomaly menia na vysoký mechanický hlas. Potom scéna prejde do tichého a pomalého kozmického dažďa farebných kúskov kvetov a prachu. Obe diela, Granátové jablko aj Big Bang, odrážajú šokujúce záchvevy ľudskej histórie.

V dobe, keď veľa umelcov, ktorí sa zaoberajú politikou vo filme alebo videu, vytvára diela blízke skôr dokumentu, Gershtove práce skúmajú žáner provokujúcej meditácie. Samotný žáner stojí na prvom mieste v jeho tvorbe. (Andrew Mummery, Riaditeľ galérie Mummery + Schnelle Gallery, Londýn)

Terézia Golasová

Narodená v roku 1980 v Bratislave, Slovenská republika, žije v Bratislave,
2002-2007, Vysoká škola výtvarných umení, Bratislava, odbor fotografia a nové médiá, ateliér prof. Miloty Havránkovej,
od roku 2004 – Filozofická fakulta, Univerzita Komenského, odbor čínština a interkultúrna komunikácia.
http://golasova.marencin.sk

Terézia Golasová, ktorá stále ešte študuje výtvarné umenie, síňa kritérium mladého nádejného umelca do bodky. Jej práce, ktoré vznikli v ateliéri fotografie, sa zaoberajú výlučne problémom, ako zachytiť princíp zmeny rozdielnymi prostriedkami fotografie a videa. V jej videách sa dej nevyvíja. Ich predmetom je plynutie času a pohyb. Aby zvýraznila svoj zámer, používa statickú videokameru, snímajúcu obraz z jedného bodu.

Vo videu „...v jednej posteli..." sa kamera na statíve otáča o 360 stupňov. To vyvoláva dojem panoramatického obrazu izby, do ktorej ľudia vchádzajú proti smeru pohybu kamery. Tým vzniká ešte silnejšia ilúzia členenia deja na sekvencie, ako pri fotografických záberoch.

„ ‚Quo vadis...' je krátkym dokumentom o plynutí času." Statická videokamera zaznamenáva cestujúceho, ktorý sedí na jednom mieste, hoci sa pri tom hýbe – cestuje metrom z jednej zastávky na inú. Cez okno môžeme vidieť rýchlo sa mihajúce prostredie vonku, čo naznačuje skutočnú rýchlosť metra. To je však vo výraznom protiklade k cestujúcim, ktori sú väčšinu času temer nehybní. Ich občasné pohyby len umocňujú dojem statického záberu v dopravnom prostriedku. Aby bola skutočnosť plynutia času ešte zjavnejšia, na obraze dolu sa odpočítava čas záznamu s presnosťou na sekundy.

Zatiaľ posledná práca Golasovej „Kam z konopí" odzrkadľuje prirodzený posun v jej experimentovaní so zmenou a médiom. Opäť pracuje so statickou videokamerou. V tomto prípade má dojem fotografického záberu vyvolávať obraz osoby, ktorá sa zámerne nehýbe, a jej odraz v zrkadle. Jediným prvkom zmeny je para, postupne prekrývajúca zrkadlo, a zvuk tečúcej vody. Video sa konči, keď obraz v zrkadle úplne zmizne. Tento nápad možno nie je ojedinelým v tvorbe na pomedzí videa a fotografie, ale určite predstavuje logický vývoj v tvorbe Terézie Golasovej.

Laurent Goldring

Narodený v roku 1957 v Paríži, kde stále žije, pracuje, maľuje, kreslí, tvorí sochý a videá.
Jeho dielo významne prispelo k evolúcii súčasného tanca. Mal mnoho výstav po celom svete.

Kino pozná tajomstvo fotografie.
Fotografia bola o podobnosti a Arago presadil zákon, ktorý ju ako takú prijal. Film, ktorý bol stále chronofotografiou, hneď pochopil, že táto predstava je založená na zbožnom želaní. A preto sa o filme nikdy netvrdilo, že ukazuje 24 fotografií za sekundu, ale skôr 24 obrazov za sekundu.

Film zaznamenáva niekoľko fotografií súčasne. Pracuje s dvoma veľmi podobnými zábermi, ktoré sú natoľko odlišné, že vylučujú možnosť podobnosti. Film symetricky vyvracia myšlienku podobnosti so svetom. V prípade portrétu popiera klamlivú predstavu o jednotlivcovi. Pri krajine rúca pravdu o perspektíve. Základný rozdiel tkvie v tom, že fotografia vyhlásila niečo, čo nejestvuje.

Film uvidel, bol by schopný zviditeľniť, odmietol vidieť, rozhodol, že nič nevidel, a šialene si zakázal vidieť. Film sa okamžite stal vehementným a úplným (ne)vedomým popretím tajomstva fotografie: že nejde o podobnosť. Zasiahol do záležitostí jednoznačnosti a podobnosti, v prvom rade podobnosti sebe samému, záruke všektých ostatných záležitostí. Hollywood bol veľkou reklamnou mašinériou tej stránky života, kde sú predmety a ľudia neustále vedení k tomu, aby napodobňovali sami seba.

Všetko vo filme možno vysvetliť týmto popierajúcim šialenstvom: kasting, scenár, schéma príbehu, filmovanie. Všetko nás má presvedčiť, že táto osoba existuje, s touto tvárou a telom, s týmto charakterom, cieľmi a predstavami... Zároveň chápeme, prečo si priemysel, ktorý existuje len preto, aby vytvoril fikciu, dokáže predstaviť iba obraz prijateľný ako fikcia.

V dielach, ktoré tvorím, sa snažím vytvoriť pohyblivý obraz, ktorý nemá nič spoločné s fikciou, respektíve s podobnosťou.
(Laurent Goldring)

Laurent Grasso

Narodený v roku 1972 v Mulhouse, Francúzsko, žije a pracuje v Paríži,
študoval na Cooper Union School, New York,
Central Saint Martins School of Art, London a Vysokej škole výtvarných umení, Paríž.
www.galeriechezvalentin.com/fr/artistes/laurent_grasso/works/

Či už vy/pretvára viac menej identifikovateľné formy našej spoločnosti plnej kontroly, alebo rozkladá filmové techniky a konvencie, ktoré formujú našu kolektívnu predstavivosť, Laurent Grasso tvorí prostredia so silným naratívnym potenciálom. Spája atavistický strach, vedecký dôkaz a zlovestnú súčasnú mytológiu. Vo videu Bez názvu sa obrovský hrozivý mrak valí ulicami Paríža smerom k divákovi. Ako postupuje, pohlcuje autá a budovy. Keď sa dívame na túto pohybujúcu sa obrazovku prachu, stopu vymyslenej katastrofy, chtiac nechtiac musíme vstúpiť do procesu tvorby príbehu. Vnášame doňho vlastný strach alebo vymýšľame svoj scenár. V závislosti od našej individuálnej citlivosti a kultúrno-historickému zázemiu, video v nás vyvoláva obrazy pádu Dvojičiek, scény mestského násilia, či spektakulárne momenty špeciálnych efektov z filmov.

Jeho práce by do istej miery mohli znovu oživiť obdiv k paranoidným retro-futuristickým proroctvám Charlesa Fouriera spred dvoch storočí. Svetlo, zvuk, prirodzené, paranormálne a meteorologické javy sa pravidelne objavujú v jeho dielach. Prinášajú úplne nové zmyslové zážitky, ktoré poháňajú diváka, aby dotvoril neúplné výplody predstavivosti.

Tým, že vyvoláva napätie medzi premietanými dielami, ich prostredím a občas dramatickou interpretáciou, ku ktorej inšpirujú, konštruuje Laurent Grasso dotieravé mentálne obrazy, ktoré znejasňujú náš pohľad na to, čo bežne nazývame „realitou".

Tuomo Rainio

Narodený v roku 1983 v Espoo vo Fínsku, žije a pracuje v Helsinkách,
Získal titul bakalár v odbore fotografie na Univerzite umenia a dizajnu v Helsinkách a pokračuje v magisterskom štúdiu na tej istej unverzite,
2007-08 – študoval na vysokej škole Musashino Art University v Tokiu.
www.rainio.pp.fi

Prítomnosť davu.
Zmena, pohyb a čas sú ústrednými námetmi fotografií a videí fínskeho umelca Tuoma Rainia. Vizuálne myslenie jeho puristických diel stojí na pomedzí estetiky čierno-bielych fotografií a tradície postkonceptuálneho videoumenia. Asi najvhodnejšou charakteristikou oblasti, kde sa tieto záujmy prelínajú, je označenie pohyblivý obraz bez žánrovej

špecifikácie. Čo to vlastne vidíme, keď sa dívame na Rainiove práce z cyklu Tracescape (Scenéria stôp)? Najprv je to len obraz čierny ako tabuľa. Potom sa postupne objavujú melancholické anonymné scenérie mesta, ulice a architektonické štruktúry. Jediná vec, ktorou si môžeme byť skutočne istí, je stopa pohybu. Jeho diela pôsobia najprv ako prízračne anonymné a odrazu sa menia na známe alebo aspoň rozoznateľné prostredie. V ich atmosfére je niečo tajomné, snáď prítomnosť davu. Sociálna realita je tu prítomná vo forme stôp chodcov sledujúcich svoju každodennú rutinu. Ako zdôrazňuje sám Rainio: „Scenéria stôp je cyklom videoprác o sociálnej štruktúre vo verejnom priestore. V prostredí mesta pozorujú a kontrolujú správanie ľudí iní jedinci, ale aj oni sami."

Práce City (Mesto, 2005) a Crosswise (Naprieč, 2006) predstavujú viditeľné križovatky, cesty a cyklus mestského života, ktorý vyznieva ako slepá mapa mesta. Ich obrazy sú ako hromady roentgenových snímkov. Dokážete si predstaviť živý organizmus, ale vždy vidíte len stavebnú oporu. Zvuk videí vracia výjavy späť na úroveň každodennej skúsenosti bytia v tomto svete. Počujeme dopravné svetlá, prechádzajúce autá, električky a ozývajúce sa kroky. Zároveň sa rôzne línie pohybu spájajú, prelínajú a zosvetľujú obraz. Nakoniec už nejde o film a jeho membránu citlivú na svetlo, ale o algoritmus naprogramovaný v počítači, ktorý vypočítava obrazy zaradom a zviditeľňuje zmeny. Analogicky aj video ako médium zaznamenáva rýchlu zmenu v digitalizovanom obrazovom priemysle. Technika a obsah sú prepojené. Sieť pixelov našla ďalšiu významovú rovinu v pozoruhodných pohyblivých obrazoch Tuoma Rainia. Zviditeľňuje model našej doby. (Leevi Haapala, kurátor a vedec, Kiasma, Múzeum súčasného umenia, Helsinki)

Jan Kuděj

Narodený v roku 1978 v Prahe, Česká republika, žije v Prahe, 1997-1999 Filozofická fakulta, Karlova Univerzita, Praha – etnológia, 1999-2005 Akadémia výtvarných umení, architektúry a dizajnu, Praha – ateliér prof. Pavla Štechu, 2002-2003 Universität der Kunsten (Vysoká škola výtvarných umení), Berlín (štipendium)

vo svojich dielach systematicky skúma otázku času. „Absolútny záznam kontinuity času nie je možný", hovorí. Vytvoril niekoľko „Projekcií", ktoré v sebe spájajú dva princípy, princíp statického fotografického obrazu a videozáznam pohybu. Každá z nich iným spôsobom zohľadňuje skutočnosť, že kamera je schopná zaznamenať 25 obrazov za sekundu. Je to obmedzený počet, čo nevyhnutne vedie k fragmentácii pohybu a času, hoci ľudské oko ich vníma ako plynulé.

V projekcii pohyblivých schodov Kuděj sleduje okruh, ktorý zariadenie urobí. Statickou videokamerou zosnímal z jedného bodu celý cyklus, až kým sa schody nevrátili presne do východzej polohy. Pri premietaní v slučke tak eskalátor beží plynule v kruhu. Ako protikladné riešenie si vzal za základ fotografiu stromu, ktorého korunu animoval prerušovanými záznamami jej pohybu. Projekcia vody nepretržite sa vlniacej k brehu, ktorá bola vybratá pre túto výstavu, predstavuje rovnaký princíp vnímania kontinuity plynutia času ako pohyblivé schody.

„Rovnako sú však ... projekcie z určitého pohľadu uzavreté a dejovo nemenné. Čas je len ilúziou."

„Pre mňa je v prístupe podstatný kontinuálny záznam spustenej kamery a vedome prerušovaný záznam záberov. Môžeme rozlíšiť prežitok dvoch časov – času okamihu a čas trvania. Tento pocit nám umožňuje prežívať súčasne protiklady odvíjania skutočnosti. Myšlienka seba (sveta) nie je kontinuálna. Predstava mení svoje vyznenie pri každom novom myslení. Samotný proces myslenia je neustále sa vracajúcou pretržitosťou. Čas sa pre nás odvíja v okamihoch. (z diplomovej práce Kuděja, 2005)

Ange Leccia

Narodený v roku 1952 v Minerviu, Korzika, žije a pracuje v Paríži, film a filozofia, Sorbona, Paríž, Francúzsko. www.galeriealminerech.com

Videoinštalácia Búrka je metafyzickým a kontemplatívnym dielom, ktoré nás inšpiruje k sebaskúmaniu. Vyznačuje sa snovou silou príznačnou pre celú tvorbu Angea Lecciu. Od detstva ho fascinoval film a animované obrazy a všetky jeho práce sú plné poetiky energie a skúmania obrazu a filmu. Týmto sa dostáva tak nablízko, jako je to len možné, k nevyjadriteľnému, a to mu tiež umožňuje vkladať do jeho diel výraznú emocionalitu.

Tento diptych vo forme dvoch projekcií v slučke, premietaných na dvoch kolmých plochách v priestore ponorenom do tmy, nás prenáša do burácajúcej nočnej oblohy, kde blesk udiera v zdanlivo pozastavenom okamihu. Tento prúd divej energie, nasnímaný ako statický záber, vypĺňa tak obraz, ako aj zvuk. Konfrontuje nás s priam hmatateľnou a všemocnou prítomnosťou prírodných živlov a symbolizuje skutočnosť, že príroda nás vždy premôže, akokoľvek sa budeme snažiť ju ovládnuť. Opakujúci sa rytmus a zjavná nekonečnosť videa, ktoré stojí niekde medzi vizuálnou vyrovnanosťou a rozpínaním sa času, ho posúva k čistej abstrakcii, čím sa otvára priestor pre transcendentálne a vznešené. Opakovanie a uzatváranie videa do slučky, oboje typické pre obrazy Angea Lecciu, prináša so sebou pocit neustálej regenerácie. Podľa kritika umenia Pascala Beaussa treba túto kvalitu interpretovať „s ohľadom na organické dimenzie obrazu, ktorý nás vťahuje do večnej prítomnosti". Toto rozpínanie sa času spojené s pohrúžením sa zmyslov, ktoré autor docielil formou prezentácie obrazov, nás vedie k tomu, aby sme siahli po tých najhlbších silách našej predstavivosti.

Oliver Möst

Oliver Möst, narodený v roku 1968 vo Füssene v Allgäu, žije a pracuje v Berlíne. Tvorí ako slobodný umelec vo fotografii a videu. Jeho prvý videoprojekt vznikol v spolupráci s tanečným choreografom v roku 1999. www.olivermoest.de

„Dokonale zaostrené obrazy vyvažujú nedostatok pozornosti. Prehliadajú to, čo možno vnímať pri neostrosti."[4]

1 BASTIAN BRETTHAUER, SO EINE WELT OHNE ECKEN UND KANTEN (TAK TEDA SVET BEZ KÚTOV A STRÁN) V GALÉRII K4 GALERIE, VYD., OLIVER MÖST, CLACKASTIGMAT 6.0 / K4 GALERIE (BERLÍN, DORN, 2005)

Videá Olivera Mösta, ktoré vznikli v roku 2007, nadväzujú na jeho fotografické práce. Už na prvý pohľad je pre ne charakteristická nápadná neostrosť, čo je umelcovým určujúcim estetickým princípom tak vo fotografii, ako aj vo videu. Tento prístup k ostrosti nám odhaľuje podstatu vnímania samotného umelca.

Möstov vlastný proces zmyslového vnímania je témou všetkých jeho prác. Má veľmi slabý zrak, takže musí nosiť okuliare s 2.0 dioptriami na ľavom oku a s 6.0 na pravom. Umelcove fotografie a filmy nám umožňujú stotožniť sa s jeho subjektívnym pohľadom formou „to-čo-tam-takto-videl-a-vnímal". Naviac nám dovoľujú vnímať viacmenej jeho idiosynkratické preciťovanie a spôsob, ako si osvojuje priestor okolo seba [between (Medzi), hide & seek (Schovávačka), brown eyes (Hnedé oči).

Fotografia ako médium a jej vlastnosti sú ďalším dôležitým námetom Möstovych video prác, ktorý realizuje ako konfrontáciu filmu a fotografie. Myšlienka spájania dvoch fotografických techník ho priviedla k tomu, že začal používať cameru obscuru, prvotnú formu snímacieho aparátu, (bez šošovky). K nej pridal efekt digitálneho videa tým, že videokamerou nasnímal obraz odrazený na platni camery obscury. Touto konfrontáciou medzi „starou" technikou camery obscury na jednej strane a modernou technikou digitálneho videa na druhej strane vytvára Möst „videá camery obscury" („pinhole videos", ako ich nazýva). Odzrkadľujú vývoj fotografie od jednoduchej camery obscury k digitálnej a technicky vyspelej videokamere. Rovnako vyzdvihujú kvality média fotografie, ktoré sa v priebehu rokov neustále rozvíjali.

Tim Paršikov

Narodený v roku 1983 v Moskve, Ruská federácia, žije a pracuje v Moskve,
2006 - ukončil štúdium odboru kameraman na Ruskom inštitúte kinematografie,
2005 - ocenennie Strieborná kamera za najlepšiu reportáž o Moskve.

Tim Paršikov, básnik a fotograf okolo dvadsiatky, žije v Moskve. Pre túto generáciu sa svet skutočne stal príliš malý a z hľadiska geografie často dokonca príliš zjavný a dosiahnuteľný. Našťastie Tim Paršikov vníma život ako pravý básnik a divákovi rekonštruuje svoj vlastný model sveta, model plný energie a sviežeho nádychu mladosti, takže ľahko zabudnete, že čosi môže byť aj predvídateľné alebo zjavné. Jeho dielo je plné ozónu. Pocit všeobecného smútku, ktorý je taký charakteristický pre mladých ľudí, a hlboké znalosti ruskej a svetovej fotografie v žiadnom prípade nezmenšujú ten vzrušujúci pocit sviežosti, ktorý vyžaruje z jeho prác.

Tvorivá individualita mladého umelca a rozmer jeho osobnosti jasne určujú skutočný, zrelý a nezávislý talent v niekoľkých druhoch klasického umeniach. Jemný zmysel pre farbu, silný zmysel pre zlatý rez a odvážne metaforické myslenie dovoľujú Timovi Paršikovovi vyjadriť sa trúfalým a originálnym spôsobom. Je novým hlasom, ktorému sa oplatí načúvať.

Video Gone to Sea (Stratený v mori) je miniatúrou, ktorá sa zaoberá možnosťou bezdôvodného zmiznutia v mori – teda nikde. Stratený v mori nám pripomína film Michelangela Antonioniho „L' Aventura" (Dobrodružstvo), kde hlavná hrdinka odrazu bez akéhokoľvek dôvodu zmizne. Ale viac než problém zmiznutia nás všetkých zaujíma predovšetkým, či si to vôbec niekto všimne...

Matteo Peterlini

Narodený v roku 1970 v Roverete v Trente (Taliansko), žije a pracuje v Roverete, v Trente (Taliansko),
vyštudoval informatiku,
1992 navštevoval kurz grafického dizajnu a reklamy organizovaný provinciou Bolzano, 1999 – workshop „Zuppa digital 2" usporiadaný mestskou radou Benátok, 2000 – workshop v inštitúcii Fabrica.
www.matteopeterlini.it

Narábanie s pixelom ako s jednotkou miery, to je prístup, ktorý predstavuje veľmi reálny konceptuálny element, pragmatickú voľbu Mattea Peterliniho v jeho fotografických prácach. Takto rozložené a opäť poskladané obrazy v jeho cykloch sú výsledkom procesu výpočtov smerujúcemu až k nekonečnu, pričom systém, ktorým sa fragmenty spájajú, je ponechaný na náhodu a používa sa ako algebraická funkcia.

Peterlini sa dokonca neboji pôvodný hriech priznať a sústreďuje sa na samotný mechanizmus vnímania prostredníctvom špeciálne vytvoreného typu softvéru. Ako sa v našej mysli tvoria obrazy? Imitácia, poznávanie a vymena informácií, mechanizmy, ktoré bežne využívame, aby sme pochopili svet, strácajú svoju účinnosť v konfrontácii s prúdom zlučujúcim fragmenty, vygenerovaným elektronickým procesom. V rozpore s tým nie je ani fakt, že ide o žánre maľby, ako je portrét, akt, krajinomaľba. Práve vďaka frontálnosti tvárí (aké sa požadujú na štandardnej pasovej fotografii) v cykle Meyouother (Jatyiný), siluetám tela (odzrkadľujúcim šesť póz, ktoré zaujali modely na požiadanie v projekte V6), nemennosti krajín, ktoré sú temer abstraktné (Backscapes (Scenérie pozadia) je možné oceniť tú podvedomú tendenciu rozoznávať to, čo už poznáme (Gestalt – podoba, stereotypy). To nám umožňuje venovať pozornosť rôznorodosti javov.

Naviac analytická povaha jeho diela je práve v technickom klame, ktorý jediný nesie kvalitu zručnosti a ktorý Peterlini využíva, aby oživil svoje fotografické cykly. Ak sa na tieto obrazy (ktoré sú výsledkom neustáleho kreatívneho prúdu) pozrieme zblízka, budú na nás pôsobiť ako koláž. Kým proces, ktorým ich rozozávame ako celok, sa naopak nachádza niekde vo virtuálnej koexistencii všetkých možných kombinácií. (Cristina Natalicchio)

Peter Puklus & Melinda Siposová

Péter Puklus
Narodený v roku 1980 v Kolozsvári, Maďarsko, žije v Budapešti, Maďarsko,
vzdelanie: v roku 2005 ukončil štúdium fotografie na Vysokej škole výtvarných umení Moholya-Nagya v Budapešti.
http://photolumen.hu/puklus
www.deuxprojects.blogspot.com/

Melinda Siposová
Narodená v roku 1979 v Budapešti, Maďarsko, žije v Budapešti, Maďarsko,
v roku 2005 ukončila štúdum dizajnu skla na Vysokej škola výtvarných umení Moholya-Nagya,

Budapešť, Maďarsko.
http://siposmelinda.blogspot.com
www.deuxprojects.blogspot.com

tvoria samostatne a obaja majú svoj individuálny umelecký prístup. Ale dva projekty Imported Lights (Importované svetlá) a Garden (Záhrada) vytvorili spolu ako umelecká skupina DEUX. Názvy týchto diel neznamenajú nič iné ako presné údaje. DEUX_00 Imported Lights je „nultým projektom" skupiny, ako ho sami nazývajú. Jeho myšlienka je konceptuálna. Odfotografovali odraz svetla prichádzajúceho cez okno a premietli ho ako video v miestnosti bez prirodzeného svetla. Z pohľadu nášho prístupu v projekte Mutácie II ide o statický obraz premietnutý ako video.

Podobný princíp je uplatnený aj v práci „DEUX _01 Garden", ktorý je podľa názvu prvým spoločným projektom Petra Puklusa a Melindy Siposovej. Je to detailný záznam jednej záhrady v priebehu dlhšieho časového úseku. Počas jedného roka urobili každý deň jednu fotografiu záhrady z toho istého okna. Výsledkom je portfólio drobných zmien v tomto priestore, premiestnené stoličky, striedanie ročných odbobí... Vo forme slide show vzniká dojem, že proces premeny sa deje priamo počas premietania.

Obe práce sú založené na jednoduchej ale veľmi dobre prepracovanej myšlienke. Narozdiel od niektorých indých autorov v tomto výbere, ktorých tvorbu inšpirovali technické možnosti, pre Pukusa a Siposovú bola otázka výberu média, fotografie a videa a transformácie jedného do druhého skôr druhoradou. Vyplynula až z umeleckej koncepcie. Pre týchto umelcov je prístup prekonávania hraníc medzi videom a fotografiou logickým riešením ich umeleckého záměru.

Jutta Strohmaierová

Narodená v roku 1966 v Tullne (Rakúsko), žije vo Viedni, v rokoch 1996-99 štúdovala maľbu. Sústreďuje sa na štúdium fotografie a nových médií u Evy Schlegelovej na Vysokej škole výtvarných umení vo Vedeni.
www.jutta-strohmaier.net

V akom vzťahu sú obrazy a skutočnosť? Čo za skutočnosť vytvára obraz? Tieto otázky nastolujú videá, fotografie a inštalácie Jutty Strohmaierovej. Dielo Passenger (Prechod, 2004) zhusťuje do ani nie 15-minútového videa zábery, ktoré boli odfotografované každú minútu počas jedného dňa v prázdnom interiéri s dvoma veľkými oknami. Kým cez deň okná osvetľujú miestnosť tak intenzívne, že je takmer nemožné cez ne vidieť, so stmievaním sa postupne objavuje priečelie budovy oproti cez ulicu. Dielo sa pohráva s vnímaním miestnosti v procese jej premeny. Zaoberá sa predstavou priestoru v súvislosti s kategóriami ako včlenenie/vylúčenie, súkromné/cudzie, otvorenosť/uzavretosť (pozri tiež poznámky Sarah Kolbovej k výstave Jutta Strohmaierová. Diese Welt und andere (Tento svet a iné), Galéria Hohenlohe, Viedeň, 2004).

Strohmaierová sa vracia k princípu plynúcich fotografických záberov v podobe animovaného videa v prácach ako Im Dickicht (V húštine, 2005) a Silent Stories (Tiché príbehy, 2006). V tom prvom stláča spúšť pri každom kroku cez nízky porast územia mokraďového lesa. Strohmaierová prepája medzery medzi jednotlivými zábermi vo Photoshope. Spleť konárov sa najprv akoby stráca, potom v nasledujúcej sekvencii zhustne a nakoniec sa rozplynie v modrej oblohe.

Satelitné fotografie zozbierané pre video Journey (Cestovanie, 2005) nám podávajú obraz Zeme z výšky – výhľad, ktorý nám je dobre známy vďaka televízii a internetu, ale ktorý prijalo len pár ľudí. Strohmaierová sa prehŕňa snímkami satelitu, ktoré zbierala roky. Avšak miesto toho, aby prezentovala lineárny sled miest a krajín, obrazy prenikajú jeden do druhého, navzájom sa prestupujú, strácajú vrstvu po vrstve priamo naprieč planétou Zem a späť.

Wolfgang Thaler

Narodený v roku 1969 v Salzburgu (Rakúsko), žije vo Viedni, v rokoch 1989-91 študoval na Bavorskom štátnom inštitúte fotografie v Mníchove (dnes: Mníchovská univerzita pomocných vied).
www.wolfgangthaler.at

Dielo Wolfganga Thalera zahŕňa fotografiu architektúry (cyklus o viedenskej železničnej stanici Südbahnhof alebo o kruhových objazdoch) a dokumentárnu fotografiu (o viedenskej tradičnej sieti kaviarní Aida atď.), čo dokladá jeho - väčšinou výrazne analytický - záujem o priestor.

Cyklus Matter of Selection (Záležitosť výberu, 2007) nás vťahuje do bytu zberateľa. Thaler najprv fotografuje jeho nábytok (skriňu so šatami, policu s knihami) na čierno-biely film s vysokým rozlíšením. Potom ako detektív skenuje každý detail výsledných fotografií na obrazovku počítača. To vedie k premene na mnohých úrovniach. Fotografický záber jediného momentu sa rozrastie na nekonečný záznam procesu pozorovania. Skutočnosť sa odhaľuje prostredníctvom filmovania fotografie objektu, nie objektu samotného. A čo sa týka fotografie, vždy vidíme len jej detaily, nikdy nie celok.

Welcome to Mep'Yuk (Vítajte v Mep'Yuk-u takto víta Thaler víta návštevníkov vo svojom vymyslenom opustenom meste Mep'Yuk. Die Zentrale (Centrála, 1999) ktorá pozostáva výluène z priestorov interiérov.pozostáva výlučne z priestorov interiérov. Umelec fotografuje prozaické vstupné haly spoločností, verejné priestory inštitúcií, kancelárie a čakárne pre hostí v rozličných mestách sveta. Napriek odlišnému kultúrnemu prostrediu majú tieto miesta jednu vec spoločnú. Sú to (polo-) verejné priestory a ich najdôležitejšou funkciou je administratíva, štrukturalizácia alebo organizácia. Thaler zoskupuje fotografie do sérií a skenuje ich po častiach v pomalom horizontálne bežiacom zázname. Opäť tu odopiera divákovi celistvú perspektívu, keďže odhaľuje iba detaily interiérov. Čoskoro nadobúdame dojem, že tieto priestory sledujeme kamerou. Pritom sa natíska otázka: čo sa tu dá pozorovať, ak žiadne ľudské bytosti nevládnu tomuto „centru riadenia"?